The Economics of News Media

The Economics of News Media

Sangwoo Yang
Graduate School of Economics
Yonsei University
Seoul, South Korea

ELSEVIER
AMSTERDAM • BOSTON • HEIDELBERG • LONDON • NEW YORK • OXFORD
PARIS • SAN DIEGO • SAN FRANCISCO • SINGAPORE • SYDNEY • TOKYO
Academic Press is an imprint of Elsevier

Academic Press is an imprint of Elsevier
125 London Wall, London EC2Y 5AS, United Kingdom
525 B Street, Suite 1650, San Diego, CA 92101, United States
50 Hampshire Street, 5th Floor, Cambridge, MA 02139, United States

ISBN: 978-0-443-45044-0

For Information on all Academic Press publications
visit our website at https://www.elsevier.com/books-and-journals

Publisher: Peter Linsley
Acquisitions Editor: Peter Linsley
Editorial Project Manager: Bhaviya Koul
Project Manager: Ashok Ravi
Cover Designer: Greg Harris

Typeset by MPS Limited, Chennai, India

Last digit is the print number: 9 8 7 6 5 4 3 2 1

Contents

More to Explore

Preface

WHY THE ECONOMICS OF NEWS MEDIA?

To see the truth, hold no opinion.

— *Zen Proverb*

The press is a strange mixture of good and evil.

— *Alexis de Tocqueville*[a]

The economics of news media is a relative latecomer among economic disciplines and remains unfamiliar to many journalism and media scholars, media experts (including journalists), and even economists. This is unfortunate, considering the significant academic contributions economists have made to understanding the nature and realities of the press. These studies provide rational explanations for aspects of the news media that are difficult to grasp through traditional journalistic approaches. They also challenge many long-held misconceptions about the media and journalism. Yet, most readers as well as many scholars and researchers have remained distant from these insights.

This book, *The Economics of News Media*, seeks to bridge this gap by presenting a collection of perspectives and academic achievements by economists on the news media and its dynamics. It is the first of its kind to make this knowledge accessible to both general readers and expert researchers, thereby narrowing the existing divide.

For a long time, most people have understood the press primarily through frameworks and methods provided by journalism and media studies. Much of journalism, whether as a professional practice or an academic discipline, is shaped by both normative ideals—such as what the media ought to be—and empirical approaches that examine how the media actually functions. Rooted in such ideals, journalism often engages with questions of values, such as defining good journalism or ethical practices.

In contrast, the economics of news media focuses on the realities of how the news market operates. It examines the behavior of news providers and consumers, paying particular attention to their self-interested motives rather than idealized notions of altruistic journalists or truth-seeking audiences. By analyzing the interactions between these suppliers and consumers, it seeks to uncover the underlying principles that drive the news market. Just as economics aims to improve the efficiency of markets and maximize welfare, the economics of news media aims to enhance the

[a]This epigraph is not a direct quotation. It is a paraphrased adaptation inspired by Alexis de Tocqueville's discussion of the press in *Democracy in America*.

informational welfare of news consumers by understanding and addressing the challenges of the news market.

While journalism and media studies keep their gaze fixed on the light of ideals—like a lighthouse guiding the way through a dark sea—economics turns its attention to the wind, waves, currents, and hidden reefs that shape the reality of the journey.

Some readers may readily accept the idea of understanding the media through political science but find the notion of understanding it through economics less intuitive. After all, economics traditionally deals with questions like what to purchase, how much to consume or save, what goods and services to produce, and how to determine prices. At its heart, however, economics is the study of decision-making—of choices. If human choice is the ultimate subject of economics, then understanding the media through economics is not strange at all.

Journalists and news organizations choose which stories to report, while news consumers decide which newspapers to read or which broadcasts to watch. Furthermore, news consumers make choices based on the information they acquire—what products or services to buy, which candidates or political parties to support in elections. Understanding the media through economics means analyzing the choices made by all actors involved in the production, distribution, and consumption of news, as well as the consequences of those choices.

This economic perspective enriches our objective understanding of both human behavior and the news media in several ways:

First, an economic perspective can help overcome the entrenched structural and ideological divides among the various actors involved in the phenomenon of the news media. The norms and ideologies held by these actors often prevent them from understanding, let alone accepting, opposing viewpoints about the media and its workings. For instance, progressives expect the news media to serve the cause of "social progress," while conservatives see it as a defender of "conservative values." Between these opposing ideals, there is no room for compromise.

This divide extends beyond ideology. A deep and wide gulf also separates news consumers and journalists. News consumers believe that journalists should deliver the truth without bias, while journalists assume that news consumers seek the truth without bias. Yet both sides remain entrenched in their everyday biases and rely on those biases to judge what they consider to be the truth. These conflicting expectations—shaped by ideology and the roles they occupy in the media landscape—hinder an objective understanding of the press.

In this regard, a relatively value-neutral, nonnormative economic perspective provides answers to questions that both progressives and conservatives tend to overlook in their interpretations and judgments of the news. It also offers insights into the dynamics between news consumers and journalists, who often hold and project differing expectations of one another.

Second, an economic perspective proves even more valuable in the face of the growing industrialization and commercialization of the news media. For public broadcasters, who operate outside market competition, journalism scholars play an important role in maintaining focus on the media's normative mission. However, for private media outlets competing in fiercely contested markets, understanding market realities and exploring alternatives becomes a greater priority—one where the role of economists is particularly significant.

Moreover, the revolutionary advances in information and communication technology have caused seismic shifts in the material foundations of the news media. In such a rapidly changing environment, economic analysis is more critical than ever for understanding these transformations and their implications.

While journalism has traditionally overlooked economic dynamics, economics itself has yet to fully explore the complexities of the news media market. Trust in the media is embarrassingly low worldwide, and the "crisis of journalism" has become a universal lament, yet our understanding of this crisis remains narrow. Journalists, media executives, and news consumers each hold different understandings, norms, and expectations about the press, resulting in divergent evaluations and proposed solutions to the crisis.

However, the crisis affecting most countries cannot be attributed to any single stakeholder in the media. In democratic countries, the crisis of journalism is not solely a result of journalists' reporting practices; rather, it is driven—and exacerbated—by profound changes in the economic foundations of the news market. This highlights the essential role of economics in understanding the crisis.

There is a saying that to see things clearly, one must first discard their preconceived notions. The same applies when seeking the "objective truth" about the news media. To truly understand the media, one must look beyond the norms and values rooted in progressivism, conservatism, traditional media, or new media. Instead, it requires considering the circumstances and positions of all actors involved—news consumers, journalists, and news media firms' owners alike.

In this regard, economics proves to be particularly effective. I hope that readers of this book will come to appreciate the value of economics, with its relatively value-neutral and nonnormative perspective, as an effective lens for understanding the news market and journalism—particularly when compared to the more normative approaches of journalism studies.

Of course, economic research on the news media explains only certain aspects, not the whole picture. Journalism and media studies remain essential for addressing normative and ethical questions, and together with economics, they provide a more comprehensive understanding of the complexities of news media.

In addition, news markets vary greatly across countries due to differences in history, economic conditions, institutions, and cultural practices. Therefore, readers should exercise caution when interpreting and applying foreign cases discussed in this book to their own contexts. Despite these limitations, I firmly believe that an economic approach to the news media offers valuable insights into both its present realities and future prospects.

I have strived to write this book in a way that anyone with interest and willingness can read, even without prior knowledge of economics. To that end, I have minimized the use of mathematical arguments and technical jargon employed by economists, keeping mathematical content to a minimum.

Nevertheless, much of the economic research introduced in this book is fundamentally grounded in mathematical reasoning. Modern economics places great emphasis on advanced logical reasoning and inference, with mathematics serving as a powerful and effective tool to support them. For those with a deep understanding of mathematics—such as economists—mathematically expressed logic prevents the loss or distortion of meaning caused by linguistic differences and facilitates precise, objective communication. As economist Paul Samuelson (1915–2009, Nobel Laureate in Economics, 1970) famously said, "Mathematics is a language" (Samuelson, 1952: 56)[b].

Thus, for students using this book as a textbook, or for researchers treating it as a reference, I strongly recommend reading the footnotes and the supplementary sections labeled More to Explore, as they provide additional sources and insights that enrich the main discussion.

In writing this book, I kept in mind the countless citizens disillusioned with the news media, journalists worried about its future, media executives striving for sustainable paths, and members of digital platforms emerging as new players in the information market. I earnestly hope this book inspires broader public discourse and thoughtful deliberation to help revive the media in crisis.

This book aims to analyze the news media through the lens of economics, offering a contrast to the idealistic and normative perspectives traditionally associated with journalism studies. By applying economic theories and tools, it seeks to decode the complex dynamics of news production, distribution, and consumption in modern society. The book is structured as follows:

Chapter 1, ***Distant but Close Neighbors: Economics and Media***, examines the intersections between economics and journalism, introducing economic tools that help us better understand the news media's structure and behavior.

Chapter 2, ***The News Market and Its Key Players***, outlines the structure of the news market, focusing on the key players involved and the forces that shape both the production and consumption of news.

Chapter 3, ***The Development of the News Market and the Transformation of Journalism***, traces the historical evolution of journalism, highlighting the impact of technological advancements and shifting economic conditions on the news market.

Chapter 4, ***The Role of News Media for Democracy***, explores the role of news media in supporting democracy, while also addressing the complexities of their influence on political accountability and public discourse.

Chapter 5, ***Theories of Media Bias: The Inescapable Shackles***, analyzes media bias as a systemic and inevitable feature of journalism, offering explanations rooted in economic theories.

Chapter 6, ***News Quality: Double Standards and Objective Criteria***, investigates how subjective perceptions of news quality are formed and proposes economic approaches to establish objective standards.

[b]Samuelson, P. A. (1952). "Economic Theory and Mathematics – An Appraisal." The American Economic Review, 42(2), 56–66.

Chapter 7, ***The Virtues and Vices of Competition in News Markets***, examines the dual nature of competition in news markets, discussing its potential to uncover truth, its role in spreading misinformation, and the need for thoughtful policy interventions.

Chapter 8, ***The Myth of Unbiased Reporting: Empirical Evidence***, presents empirical evidence of media bias, highlighting its implications for democracy and consumer understanding.

Chapter 9, ***Media Capture and Media Power***, delves into the concepts of media capture and media power, analyzing their theoretical foundations and offering insights through an economic lens.

Chapter 10, ***Case Studies of Media Capture Around the Globe***, provides a range of case studies from across the world, illustrating patterns of political and economic influence on media.

Chapter 11, ***The Digital Age and News Media***, addresses the challenges and opportunities faced by news media in the digital era, including the rise of social media, evolving consumer biases, and the transformative impact of AI and algorithms.

In addition, ***References*** are provided at the end of each chapter, totaling over 300 works cited throughout the book, including those in the footnotes. These citations form a robust foundation for the book's exploration.

Finally, I hope this journey through the economics of news media offers both insight and reflection. In doing so, may it serve as a small yet meaningful step toward understanding—and perhaps healing—the broken trust in our media today.

Acknowledgments

Many people have contributed to the completion of this book. I would like to express my deep gratitude to colleagues from journalism, academia, civil society, and the business community who generously read through the disorganized early drafts and offered invaluable feedback and suggestions. Their insights have significantly improved the quality of the final manuscript. I am especially indebted to Professor Hakbae Lee and Professor Taeyoon Sung of Yonsei University's College of Commerce and Economics; the former's strong encouragement to publish this book provided the initial motivation for writing it. I thank Dr. Kyung Woong Koh, the first and most devoted reader of my work, for his careful comments on early drafts—even down to the smallest punctuation.

I also owe much to my years of experience in journalism and news media management. My time as both a journalist and, later, CEO at *The Hankyoreh*—an independent newspaper that emerged under historically exceptional circumstances in Korea—and my subsequent role as Board Chairman and Director of Journalism Responsibility at YTN, Korea's leading 24-hour news channel, allowed me to engage deeply with the realities of the press. These experiences laid the foundation for adopting the perspectives of economists as an alternative lens through which to understand the media, and eventually led me to pursue the path of an academic.

However, this book would never have come into being without the unwavering support and encouragement of Heejin Kim, who stood by me as I embarked on this scholarly journey later in life. I am deeply grateful to my two sons, Jeonghwan and Jeongjae, my daughters-in-law, Dayoon and Hyeji, and my grandson Seulchan, whose presence brought me joy throughout the writing process. I also give thanks to God, who sent all of them into my life.

Sangwoo Yang
October 2025

NOTE

Journalism and media studies have long had a field called the *political economy of the media* (or *political economy of communication*). However, this differs significantly from the content addressed in this book. In those disciplines, the political economy of the media is primarily concerned with the relationship between societal power groups and the media, and how this relationship influences media reporting and program production. These topics overlap only partially with areas that economists study, such as media capture and media power.

Despite its name, the political economy of the media in journalism and media studies rarely employs the concepts and methods of economics, making it difficult to classify as a subfield of economics. To distinguish this book's focus from their political economy of the media, I refer to the economic study of the news media as "news media economics" or "the economics of news media." Unless otherwise specified, the term *media* in this book is used interchangeably with *news media* or the *press*.

CHAPTER

1 Distant but Close Neighbors: Economics and Media

Chapter Outline

The peculiar evil of silencing the expression of opinion
lies in robbing humanity—not only the current generation but also posterity.
If the opinion is correct, society is deprived of the opportunity
to exchange error for truth.
If it is wrong, society loses the clearer perception and
livelier impression of truth that emerges from its collision with error.
—John Stuart Mill, On Liberty (1859[2006])

John Stuart Mill (1806–1873) is among the most influential philosophers and intellectuals, whose ideas have profoundly shaped modern philosophy, sociology, and the foundations of media studies. Those who have encountered his assertion that "no one should have the right to silence their opponents" might recall the stirring inspiration it brought.

The Economics of News Media. DOI: http://dx.doi.org/10.1016/B978-0-443-45044-0.00006-4

John Stuart Mill (c.1870)

Public domain via Wikimedia Commons.

Mill's *On Liberty* (Mill, 1859), which contains this iconic assertion, is a masterpiece that marked a watershed in intellectual history. Through it, liberalism became firmly established as one of the most influential ideologies in modern politics, economics, and society. Mill argued that no opinion, even one deemed "wrong" or "false," should be suppressed. He argued that unrestricted freedom of expression is essential for societal progress.[1] Few, if any, journalists or media scholars could be unfamiliar with Mill's enduring legacy.

Economists, too, are well-acquainted with Mill. Mill was one of the pivotal figures in the birth of economics as a discipline. Eleven years before *On Liberty*, Mill authored *Principles of Political Economy* (1848), a seminal work in classical economics (Mill, 2004). This book served as a foundational text for British economists, functioning almost as a scripture until Alfred Marshall's *Principles of Economics* (1890) (Marshall, 2013) was published.

Ironically, despite being both a distinguished economist and a key figure in shaping the intellectual foundations of media and communication, Mill never systematically applied an economic perspective to understanding the press. The reasons for this remain unclear. However, considering how long it took even after Mill for anyone to imagine the intersection of economics and journalism, it is perhaps unsurprising that Mill regarded the two fields as separate domains.

Today, more than 150 years after Mill's passing, the landscape has changed significantly. Many scholars, following in Mill's footsteps as economists, now delve into the nature and role of media through the lens of economics. Using advanced mathematical models and rigorous empirical methods far beyond Mill's time, they investigate topics such as the role and influence of media in representative democracy, media bias, media capture by the powerful and wealthy, and the transformation of news media in the digital age.

Why, then, has the economic study of journalism emerged in stark contrast to Mill's time? To answer this question, we must first explore the background that gave rise to and nurtured the growth of the political economy of news media. At the heart

[1] Mill believed that freedom of expression was essential for societal progress, but he did not argue that such freedom should be entirely without limits. For instance, he proposed the harm principle, which holds that individual liberty should only be allowed insofar as it does not cause harm to others.

of this development lies the fact that core economic concepts and perspectives—such as markets, incentives, persuasion,[2] and human decision-making—offer powerful analytical tools for understanding journalism and media phenomena.

1.1 ECONOMICS: THE STUDY OF HUMAN AND SOCIETAL CHOICES

Economics often gives the impression of being "difficult" to the average person. This perception likely stems from the heavy reliance on mathematics and logic—subjects that many found challenging in school—and from the frequent use of unfamiliar terms, like "elasticity" and "equilibrium." Despite this, economics remains one of the most accessible academic disciplines. People cannot ignore economic issues in their daily lives, which is why most individuals, while finding economics difficult, recognize it as an essential field of knowledge. This dual perception is reflected in the constant publication of popular economics books. Economics is, in this sense, both distant and yet ever-present.

Beyond this perception of "difficulty," there are other common misconceptions about economics. One major misunderstanding is the belief that economics is solely concerned with prices, goods, inflation, or income—issues confined strictly to economic life. Modern economics, however, extends far beyond the study of money, production, and consumption. It delves into much broader areas than most people realize. It encompasses human decision-making, such as choosing a career, deciding whether to have children, or balancing work and leisure. It also examines choices like which newspapers or broadcasts to follow and which news to report. Even a voter's decision to support or oppose a political party or candidate after encountering news falls within the domain of economics. These choices made by individuals and societies all serve as subjects for economic inquiry.

The early economists did not limit their studies to purely economic phenomena. The original name of the discipline, political economy, reflects this broader scope, as it did not separate politics from economics. In the early 20th century, economics emerged as a discipline distinct from politics, with the "political" aspect removed.[3]

[2] In the context of news media economics, incentives and persuasion play distinct but complementary roles. Incentives refer to mechanisms—such as monetary rewards, structural constraints, or strategic payoffs—that influence behavior by altering the structure of choices. In contrast, persuasion concerns the alteration of beliefs or attitudes through information framing, emotional appeal, or cognitive bias. While the former is central to analyzing strategic decisions made by news producers and consumers, the latter is crucial for understanding how media content can shape public opinion. These distinctions parallel differences in economic subfields: incentives are often explored in contract theory, organizational economics, and game theory, whereas persuasion aligns more closely with research in information economics, behavioral economics, and political psychology.

[3] The term economics began to replace political economy with the publication of Alfred Marshall's Principles of Economics in 1890, marking a shift toward a more distinct and mathematically grounded discipline.

Economists during this period focused on purely economic phenomena, but this focus did not last long. Within less than half a century, economists began expanding their scope again, revisiting political and other social science domains to broaden the field of economics.

This renewed expansion of economics differed from early political economy in one crucial way: the incorporation of advanced mathematical reasoning. Mathematics became a new and powerful tool for economic analysis, enabling economists to strengthen their arguments and broaden the field's academic influence. Armed with mathematics as a universal language,[4] economists from the mid-20th century onward ventured into adjacent social sciences like political science and sociology. Among these new areas of study was the exploration of media and journalism.

The expansion of economics into media—specifically the news market and news media—was made possible by the foundational work of scholars such as Kenneth Joseph Arrow (1921–2017, Nobel Laureate in Economics, 1972), Anthony Downs (1930–2021), and Gary Becker (1930–2014, Nobel Laureate in Economics, 1992). Their theories not only shaped modern economics but also had a profound impact on political science, sociology, and other social sciences. During this period, the academic foundation for analyzing media phenomena through an economic lens was established.

1.1.1 THE ECONOMIC THEORIES OF DEMOCRACY

The press and democracy are deeply interconnected, with their mutual reliance shaping both institutions. Within this context, economic theories on democracy have acted as a bridge, leading economists to explore the press—including modern news media shaped by advances in Information and Communication Technology. These ideas have significantly influenced subsequent studies on the economics of media. Let us briefly examine two foundational theories, both pivotal to understanding modern politics. If democracy can be analyzed through the framework of economics, there is no reason why the press cannot be similarly examined. Moreover, if economic theories on democracy have demonstrated their importance to society, there is little doubt that applying economic principles to the news media can offer equally meaningful insights.

In 1951, during the onset of the Cold War following World War II and the Korean War, Kenneth Joseph Arrow, at just 30 years old, introduced the world to his famous Impossibility Theorem. This theorem proves that democratic and rational social choice is inherently impossible. In essence, it suggested that rational decision-making can only be achieved by a dictator, not through democratic means.[5] Arrow's

[4] Paul Samuelson (1915–2009, Nobel Laureate in Economics, 1970) famously stated that "mathematics is language" (Samuelson, 1952: 56). He argued that while profound ideas expressed in ordinary words and writing often lead to differences in interpretation, the language of mathematics eliminates such discrepancies.

[5] The Impossibility Theorem assumes a society in which accurate information is perfectly shared (Arrow, 2012).

Kenneth J. Arrow

Impossibility Theorem caused a significant stir in Western academia and intellectual circles. It shook the very foundations of the legitimacy and superiority of the liberal democratic systems championed by the West in their ideological conflict with the Soviet Union and the communist bloc. Yet, the genius of Arrow's mathematical logic[6] in proving his theorem left no room for dispute.[7]

While Arrow's "Impossibility Theorem" dealt with the ideals and realities of social choice, Anthony Downs focused on the mechanisms of representative democracy and electoral politics in his economic theory of democracy. In his 1957 book, *An Economic Theory of Democracy*, Downs (1957) explained various features and concepts of political choice in democratic societies using economic concepts and theories. His work exerted significant influence even in political science.

Downs analyzed the behavior of voters, who make political choices, and politicians (or political parties), who seek to win their votes, through the lens of economic theory. He interpreted elections as a form of transaction occurring in the political market, where voters and politicians interact. In this market, voters' casting ballots were akin to consumers purchasing policies, while politicians (or parties) behaved like suppliers offering policies (or promises) in exchange for votes. This perspective can similarly apply to the news market, substituting political parties and voters with news media and news consumers, respectively.

---

[6] Unlike general logic that uses language, it is a type of logic that employs symbols. It is also referred to as "symbolic logic." By avoiding the errors that can arise from using language, it enables the effective handling of propositions. For instance, the proposition "A is either B or C" can be expressed in mathematical logic as $A \rightarrow (B \vee C)$.

[7] In his book Social Choice and Individual Values, which introduced the Impossibility Theorem, Arrow expressed his gratitude to more than ten scholars who assisted with the writing. Among them were Tjalling Koopmans, Franco Modigliani, Theodore Schultz, Herbert Simon, and Milton Friedman—all of whom later received the Nobel Prize in Economics. Arrow himself was awarded the Nobel Prize in Economics at the young age of 51 for his contributions to advancing economics through mathematical reasoning, including the Impossibility Theorem.

Based on these economic concepts and theories, Downs proposed several influential theories explaining various political phenomena. Among these, the most well-known is the Median Voter Theorem,[8] which asserts that the key to elections lies in the preferences of the median voter. He also introduced other principles that have become foundational in both political science and economics, such as the Downs Dilemma and Rational Ignorance. The Downs Dilemma suggests that as two parties compete for the median voter, their policies converge, resulting in minimal differentiation. Rational Ignorance posits that in large electorates, when individual voters recognize their minimal impact on the outcome, they tend to find it more rational to remain uninformed and may therefore abstain from voting.

[More to Explore] Social Choice Theory, Public Choice Theory, Political Economy, and the Economics of News Media

Kenneth Arrow and Anthony Downs, as introduced earlier, are pioneering figures in two key branches of economic theory: Social Choice Theory and Public Choice Theory. Both theories are closely tied to the economics of news media and merit a brief elaboration.

Social Choice Theory investigates how individual preferences can be aggregated into collective decisions, offering the theoretical and normative underpinnings of group choice. Among its foremost contributors is Amartya Sen, recipient of the 1998 Nobel Prize in Economics. Sen (1970) expanded the scope of this theory by incorporating ethical dimensions such as justice, freedom, and capability into social choice frameworks. Notably, he emphasized the freedom to access information as a critical condition for collective decision-making, arguing that the structure and functioning of the media fundamentally influence the quality of these decisions (Sen, 1999).

Public Choice Theory, by contrast, applies economic methodology to the analysis of political behavior. It models politicians, bureaucrats, and voters as rational agents driven by self-interest, and seeks to explain political institutions and policy outcomes as products of their interactions. For example, Buchanan and Tullock (1962) examined institutional design under the assumption that political actors pursue personal gain, while Niskanen (1971) argued that bureaucrats seek to maximize their agency budgets, leading to inefficiencies in the public sector.

---

[8] The Median Voter Theorem, which suggests that parties appeal to moderate voters to win elections, is based on the assumption that voter preferences follow a single-peaked symmetric distribution (1). However, if voter preferences exhibit a double-peaked symmetric distribution (2), party platforms do not converge at the median. This is because, as party platforms move closer to the median, they distance themselves from voters at their respective bases, resulting in a loss of support from these core voters that outweighs the gains from moderate voters at the center. This reflects one of the most common patterns in real-world politics.

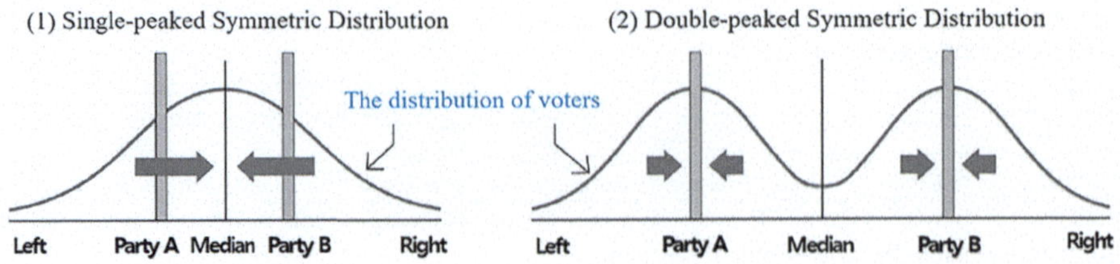

Political Economy, in the modern sense, emerges as a broader analytical framework that synthesizes these two traditions. It investigates the interplay between politics and economics by combining theoretical insights from social choice theory with the actor-centered models of public choice. It explores democracy, institutional design, policy formation, and the media through both empirical and theoretical analysis. Within this framework, the news media and information markets are viewed as critical intermediaries for shaping voter awareness and enabling collective choice.

In sum, Social Choice Theory underscores the essential role of the media in informing group decision-making, while Public Choice Theory interprets media actors as strategic agents embedded in interest-driven environments. Together, these traditions converge in Political Economy, which offers a comprehensive toolkit for analyzing the functions and limitations of journalism—and serves as a foundational pillar of the economics of news media.

1.1.2 THE ECONOMIC THEORIES ON HUMAN CHOICE

Gary Becker began to expand the scope of economics beyond political phenomena to encompass broader social phenomena within a decade of Arrow and Downs presenting their theories. Becker employed the rational choice theory, which posits that all individuals act to maximize their benefits while minimizing costs through rational calculations. Using this framework, he applied economic principles to explain diverse social phenomena previously considered unrelated to economics, such as marriage, childbirth, parenting, racial discrimination, drug addiction, and crime.

Gary Becker

Public domain (Mike80, 2008), via Wikimedia Commons.

For example, Becker argued that marriage occurs because men and women can achieve significantly higher productivity (of the household) through complementary division of labor, and that marriage is essentially a transaction conducted in the marriage market based on a cost-benefit analysis. Conversely, rising divorce rates reflect an increase in the perceived benefits of divorce and a reduction in its associated costs.

Similarly, Becker viewed childbirth as akin to purchasing a durable good, such as a refrigerator, with decisions based on costs and utility. The costs include money and time spent on raising children, as well as opportunity costs like giving up a job to focus on parenting. The utility comes from the joy of raising children and the prospect of support from grown children in old age. Declining birthrates, he argued, stem from the perception that having children is no longer a profitable endeavor. Thus, Becker advocated for reducing the overall long-term costs of parenting, including childcare expenses, to increase birthrates (Becker, 1991[1981]).[9]

Becker also suggested that criminals commit crimes because they perceive the benefits of criminal activity to outweigh its costs—such as the probability of being caught multiplied by the severity of the punishment. To reduce crime, he argued, society must increase the costs of criminal activity through higher arrest and conviction rates and stricter penalties (Becker, 1968).

Becker's theories and perspectives were not without criticism. One prominent critic was Friedrich Hayek (1899–1992, Nobel Laureate in Economics, 1974), who argued that Becker overestimated human rationality, making his theories unsuitable for understanding humans, markets, and society. Nevertheless, Becker's work profoundly influenced fields including sociology, psychology, education, criminology, and social policy[10], earning him the Nobel Prize in Economics in 1992.[11]

John Nash
Public domain via Wikimedia Commons.

John von Neumann
Public domain via Wikimedia Commons.

[9] Among Becker's various views, his perspective on family dynamics faced significant criticism, particularly for downplaying the importance of familial bonds and moral considerations.

[10] The term "economics imperialism" emerged after the work of Gary Becker. It is often used critically to describe the academic tendency to apply economic methods and reasoning to traditionally non-economic domains such as crime, law, family, prejudice, preferences, politics, society, sports, culture, religion, and science. A seminal articulation of this idea is found in Edward P. Lazear's (2000) article.

[11] Becker also pioneered the concept of "human capital": recognizing knowledge, health, and other human attributes as forms of capital. He argued that human capital is even more important than physical capital, such as land. In particular, he emphasized the significance of education and training in developing human capital—a view that continues to have a profound impact on governments, businesses, and various sectors of society (Becker, 2009[1964]).

No discussion of economic theories on human choice would be complete without mentioning game theory. Unlike rational choice theory, which has a distinctly academic tone, game theory is relatively well-known even among the general public. As is widely recognized, game theory examines optimal decision-making in situations where outcomes depend on interactions between individuals.

The foundation of game theory was laid by John von Neumann (1903–1957) and Oskar Morgenstern (1902–1977), with further development by John Nash (1928–2015, Nobel Laureate in Economics, 1994), famously portrayed by Russell Crowe in the film *A Beautiful Mind*.

There are many examples of games in real life. People navigating busy streets engage in a form of game with others walking in various directions. Similarly, haggling between buyers and sellers in a store is a type of game. Other classic examples include wage negotiations between labor unions and management, or diplomatic negotiations between countries. In political economy, or the economics of news media, interactions between politicians and voters, news media and consumers, competing media outlets, and those offering incentives to suppress unfavorable coverage and the media outlets themselves, can all be viewed as games. Game theory provides a mathematical framework for analyzing optimal decision-making in such scenarios, where one individual's choices influence those of others.

The idealized decision-making framework of game theory has been applied to a wide range of fields—not only politics and diplomacy but also military strategy, public administration, evolutionary biology, and philosophy. However, game theory assumes that decision-makers are akin to emotionless computers, making decisions purely based on reason.

Behavioral Nobelists: Herbert Simon, Daniel Kahneman, Richard Thaler (left to right)

(A) Public domain images via Wikimedia Commons

(B) CC BY-SA 2.0 photograph via Wikimedia Commons

(C) Public domain images via Wikimedia Commons

While mainstream economists have traditionally explored human choice under the grand assumption that humans are self-interested and rational, behavioral economics, which emerged in the latter half of the 20th century, focuses on humans' irrational choices.

Pioneering behavioral economists like Herbert Simon (1916–2001, Nobel Laureate in Economics, 1978), Daniel Kahneman (1934–2024, Nobel Laureate in Economics, 2002), and Richard H. Thaler (Nobel Laureate in Economics, 2017) expanded economics to encompass the irrational and imperfect nature of human thinking and behavior. They emphasized that humans are often driven by various everyday biases, are emotional, and have cognitive limitations. Behavioral economists revealed the principles behind these "irrational choices," significantly broadening the public's engagement with economics.

Herbert Simon laid the groundwork with his concept of bounded rationality, which posits that individuals act rationally only within the constraints of limited information, inherent cognitive limitations, and time constraints (Simon, 1972). Building on Simon's work, Daniel Kahneman and Amos Tversky developed the dual system theory, which explains that human thought operates through two systems: "intuition" and "rational reasoning." This theory elaborated on bounded rationality and identified diverse mechanisms behind irrational decision-making (Kahneman, 2002).

In summary, economics has expanded its scope beyond purely economic phenomena to encompass human and social choices. When individuals make decisions, the most critical foundation is the information they acquire beforehand. It is therefore natural that modern economics, as a discipline focused on decision-making, turned its attention to the exchange of information[12] and the news market. Moreover, given the prominence of the media in shaping industries and markets since the 20th century, it is only logical that economists have devoted themselves to studying the media.

1.2 THE DIFFERENCE BETWEEN ECONOMICS AND MEDIA STUDIES

Before formally introducing the political economy of news media, we briefly examined its academic roots and background. To summarize:

First, economics has long expanded its scope beyond purely economic phenomena to encompass a wide range of social phenomena. As a result, the field of economics has continually diversified. It is therefore unsurprising that economists study phenomena such as "biased reporting" in the news media or the "capture" of news media by political and financial forces.

[12] A representative study on the exchange of information is Crawford and Sobel (1982), which is considered a must-read for economics students interested in this field. This seminal paper introduced the "cheap talk" model, analyzing strategic communication between informed senders and less-informed receivers whose preferences are not perfectly aligned. It shows that the extent of information transmission depends on the degree of preference divergence: the greater the conflict of interest, the less precise the transmitted message. The model has since become a foundational tool in information economics, with applications in political communication, regulation, organizational behavior, and beyond.

Second, the primary purpose of the press lies in enabling the functioning of democratic systems. Economic theories on the functioning of democracy have provided fertile ground for the development of news media economics. One of the central branches of political economy is *social choice theory*,[13] which examines how individual preferences are aggregated into collective social choices through the lens of economics. A classic work in this field is Anthony Downs' *An Economic Theory of Democracy*. As we will see, economic theories on democratic political phenomena closely resemble the political economy of news media. Research on the interaction between "news media" and "news consumers" has evolved and grown from studies of the interaction between political parties (or politicians) and voters.

Third, the political economy of news media continues the tradition of economics as a discipline of choice. The news market is a series of choices from start to finish. Journalists or information gatherers choose among countless facts available in the world. They then decide which facts and contexts to include in their news. They also choose the methods, quantity, and format in which they present the news to consumers. Throughout this process, whether consciously or unconsciously, the ideological or political biases of news providers often play a role. Once producers and providers release the news, it is the news consumers who choose which news to consume. Their individual preferences and biases also shape these choices. Ultimately, the choices of news consumers collectively influence the choices made within a society. Thus, the concepts and tools of economics, which have evolved as a discipline of choice, are highly useful for understanding and studying the news market and its participants.

This raises the question: what differentiates the political economy of news media from media studies? Scholars of economics, including luminaries such as Kenneth Arrow, Anthony Downs, Gary Becker, Herbert Simon, and Daniel Kahneman, generally avoid normative thinking, such as *justice will prevail* or *journalists must report the truth*. Instead, economists tend to focus on understanding the realities of self-interested human behavior. From the perspective of mainstream economics, the fundamental premise of the field is simply that humans are self-interested and rational. Economists address the absence of value judgments by relying on value-neutral reasoning and inference. Economic studies of news and the news market have also developed and grown within this unique academic tradition of economics.

In contrast, scholars of media studies and working journalists often exhibit a strong tendency toward normative thinking—asking what *ought to be*. They strive to identify *right and proper* practices through repeated value judgments, aiming to understand both news media and news consumers from a normative perspective. This characteristic keeps media scholars perpetually focused on the ideal vision of journalism as envisioned by contemporary society.

However, normative approaches in media studies face significant challenges when judgments and expectations about the media differ among people. For instance, supporters of the ruling party might criticize the media for opposition bias, while

[13] The term social choice theory is also referred to as public choice theory. When distinguished, the former encompasses various forms of social collectives, while the latter is limited to the political process. For a deeper understanding, refer to List (2022).

opposition supporters might worry about incumbency bias. Such disagreements also occur among media scholars and journalists themselves, who, despite frequently invoking concepts like *objectivity* and *balance*, find it difficult to achieve these ideals in reality. It is natural for people with differing values, such as progressives and conservatives, to interpret the same issue differently.

For this reason, the value-neutral approach of economics can be highly effective in understanding the realities of news media, journalism, and news consumers without preconceived notions. By minimizing value judgments and focusing on understanding the realities of human selfishness and limitations, economics, with its aim of maximizing informational welfare, can significantly advance our understanding of humanity and the media. Furthermore, as the commercialization and industrialization of the media continue to advance, an economic understanding of news media becomes increasingly essential.

Critics of economics often argue that the field prioritizes money and quantifiable metrics over human aspects and relies excessively on simplistic and extreme hypotheses and theories. While there is some merit to this criticism, the fact that economics is the only social science recognized among the six Nobel Prize categories[14] highlights its practical significance. Moreover, economists have been studying news media, audiences, and the news market for over 30 years—an area of research that remains relatively unfamiliar not only to the general public, but also in many academic fields, including even economics and communication studies. Since the turn of the 21st century, the field has achieved remarkable theoretical and empirical advancements. It is not implausible that a future Nobel laureate in economics could emerge from the political economy of news media. What follows may well persuade even the skeptical: the political economy of news media is no longer a marginal pursuit—it is an increasingly vital part of economics.

1.3 THE RISE OF POLITICAL ECONOMY OF NEWS MEDIA

The John Bates Clark Medal is awarded every two years by the American Economic Association (AEA) to an economist under the age of 40 who has made significant contributions to the field. Often referred to as an indicator for a future Nobel laureate in economics, its prestige is evident from the fact that, as of 2024, 15 of the 46 medal recipients went on to win the Nobel Prize in Economics. In 2014, the award was presented to Matthew Gentzkow, then a Professor at the University of Chicago. According to the AEA's Honors and Awards Committee, he was recognized for his "fundamental contributions to our understanding of the economic forces driving the

[14] The Nobel Prize categories include Peace, Physics, Literature, Chemistry, and Physiology or Medicine. The Sveriges Riksbank Prize in Economic Sciences in Memory of Alfred Nobel is awarded alongside these categories.

creation of media products, the changing nature and role of media in the digital environment, and the effect of media on education and civic engagement."

The awarding of the Clark Medal to Gentzkow reflects the increasing scholarly attention to the economics of news, particularly the supply of news by media outlets and the consumption behavior of individual news users. His recognition stands as compelling evidence of the field's growing academic momentum.

Gentzkow received the John Bates Clark Medal for his groundbreaking contributions to understanding the news media and news markets—namely, the press—through the lens of economics. He has made significant advances in both the theoretical and empirical dimensions of the political economy of news media. To illustrate the scope and nature of this emerging field, we briefly review five of Gentzkow's studies cited by the Clark Medal selection committee. These and other works will be discussed in greater detail in later chapters of this book.

(1) *Major US daily newspapers exhibit political bias in their coverage of the Republican and Democratic parties. An empirical analysis found that the political bias of newspapers is determined more by their "readers" than by their "owners"* (Gentzkow and Shapiro, 2010).

(2) *An analysis of the US newspaper industry spanning 132 years (1872–2004) revealed that "news reporting has been biased." The primary cause of this bias was newspapers' efforts to cater to reader demand, making "unbiased reporting by news media" more of a "myth" than a "reality." Additionally, competition among newspapers was identified as a fundamental driver of ideological diversity in the news market* (Gentzkow, Shapiro and Sinkinson, 2014).

(3) *News media report the bias their audiences desire because consumers trust news that aligns with their own beliefs. However, excessive bias can damage the media's reputation for reporting quality in the long run, leading news media to moderate their bias* (Gentzkow and Shapiro, 2006).

(4) *The "echo chamber effect," in which individuals with similar views share only the news they want to hear, is no stronger online than in offline settings. A comparison of ideological homogeneity among users of the same internet platform and residents of the same geographic area revealed that the latter exhibited greater homogeneity* (Gentzkow and Shapiro, 2011).

(5) *The future of print newspapers looks grim. The growing demand for online news reduces demand for print newspapers, as online and offline news media are substitutes. As digital news consumption increases, the use of print newspapers inevitably declines. Gentzkow was among the first to predict this outcome theoretically and empirically* (Gentzkow, 2007).

While Gentzkow's findings are not without limitations and have sparked disagreements among scholars, his work has provided a valuable foundation for numerous subsequent studies in economics. Andrei Shleifer, a Professor of economics at Harvard University and Gentzkow's mentor, succinctly summarized Gentzkow's contributions and the current state of the economics of news media in an article celebrating the Clark Medal award:

> *"Ten years ago, we knew almost nothing about how newspapers actually report news. There were questions, but no answers—just media hype. Today, we actually have answers to many of the questions that were raised initially. We know that media reporting is systematically slanted, that slant is largely driven by demand, and that competition allows more of the viewpoints to get out. We also know that media influence their audiences for sure in getting them to participate in politics and sometimes in how they vote as well. At the same time, we have many new questions about the media: How exactly do they persuade? How do readers decide how many sources to attend to? How will the rise of new digital platforms and revenue models affect media content and political discourse? That media economics is now a full-fledged field is significantly a consequence of the contributions made by Matthew Gentzkow."*
>
> **(Shleifer and Gentzkow, 2015, p. 191)**

This perspective is especially important in light of a common misconception that persists outside the field. A media studies Professor who translated a media economics textbook was once asked in an interview, "Can economics explain the media?" He replied, "Economics explains the media industry, not the media itself." However, this response reflects a misunderstanding of modern economics. It is akin to claiming that economics can explain the "political industry" but not "political decision-making." As discussed earlier in this chapter, economics investigates not only institutions but also the principles and consequences of political and media behavior. Likewise, the economics of news media seeks to analyze and explain the fundamental nature of news and its societal function.

As visualized—albeit in simplified form—in Fig. 1.1, News Media Economics resides at the intersection of Media Economics and Political Economy, reflecting its interdisciplinary nature within economics.

FIGURE 1.1

The position of news media economics within the broader field of economics.

References

Arrow, K.J., 2012. Social Choice and Individual Values, Vol. 12. Yale University Press.

Becker, G.S., 1991. [1981]. A Treatise on the Family. Harvard University Press.

Becker, G.S., 2009. [1964]. Human Capital: A Theoretical and Empirical Analysis, with Special Reference to Education. University of Chicago Press.

Becker, Gary S., 1968. Crime and punishment: an economic approach. Journal of Political Economy 76 (2), 169–217. https://doi.org/10.1086/259394.

Buchanan, J. M., Tullock, G., 1962. The Calculus of Consent: Logical Foundations of Constitutional Democracy. Ann Arbor: University of Michigan Press.

Crawford, V.P., Sobel, J., 1982. Strategic information transmission. Econometrica 50 (6), 1431–1451.

Downs, A., 1957. An Economic Theory of Democracy. Harper and Row.

Gentzkow, M., Shapiro, J.M., 2011. Ideological segregation online and offline. Quarterly Journal of Economics 126 (4), 1799–1839. https://doi.org/10.1093/qje/qjr044.

Gentzkow, M., Shapiro, J.M., 2006. Media bias and reputation. Journal of Political Economy 114 (2), 280–316. https://doi.org/10.1086/499414.

Gentzkow, M., Shapiro, J.M., 2010. What drives media slant? Evidence from U.S. daily newspapers. Econometrica 78 (1), 35–71. https://doi.org/10.3982/ECTA7195.

Gentzkow, M., Shapiro, J.M., Sinkinson, M., 2014. Competition and ideological diversity: historical evidence from US newspapers. American Economic Association, United States American Economic Review 104 (10), 3073–3114. Available from: http://pubs.aeaweb.org/doi/pdfplus/10.1257/aer.104.10.3073. https://doi.org/10.1257/aer.104.10.3073.

Gentzkow, Matthew, 2007. Valuing new goods in a model with complementarity: online newspapers. American Economic Review 97 (3), 713–744. https://doi.org/10.1257/aer.97.3.713.

Kahneman, D., 2002. Maps of bounded rationality: a perspective on intuitive judgment and choice. Nobel Prize Lecture 8 (1), 351–401.

Lazear, E.P., 2000. Economic imperialism. The Quarterly Journal of Economics 115 (1), 99–146. https://doi.org/10.1162/003355300554683.

List, C., 2022. "Social choice theory.". In: Zalta, E.N., Nodelman, U. (Eds.), The Stanford Encyclopedia of Philosophy, Fall 2022 Edition. Retrieved from: https://plato.stanford.edu/archives/fall2022/entries/social-choice/.

Marshall, A., 2013. Principles of Economics, 8th ed. Palgrave Macmillan., (Original work published 1890).

Mill, J.S. [1859] 2006. *On Liberty*. London: Parker and Son, West Strand. [Reprinted in *Ideas of the First Amendment*, V. Blasi (Ed.), Saint Paul, MN: Thomson/West, 318–366].

Mill, J.S., 2004. In: Ashley, A. (Ed.), Principles of Political Economy: With Some of Their Applications to Social Philosophy. Oxford University Press. (Original work published 1848).

Niskanen, W.A., 1971. Bureaucracy and representative government.

Samuelson, P., 1952. Economic theory and mathematics—an appraisal. American Economic Review 42, 56–66.

Sen, A., 1970. Collective choice and social welfare.

Sen, A., 1999. Development as freedom. New York: Alfred A. Knopf.

Shleifer, Andrei, Gentzkow, Matthew, 2015. Winner of the 2014 Clark medal. Journal of Economic Perspectives 29 (1), 181–192. 0895–3309. https://doi.org/10.1257/jep.29.1.181.

Simon, H.A., 1972. Theories of bounded rationality. In: McGuire, C.B., Radner, R. (Eds.), Decision and Organization. North-Holland, Amsterdam, pp. 161–176.

CHAPTER

2 The News Market and Its Key Players

Chapter Outline

All men by nature desire to know.
—Aristotle, Metaphysics (4th century BCE)

Time is the mother of truth. Yet time is a luxury that those who deal in news have never been able to afford.[1]
—A 17th-century European journalist

[1] Quoted in Stephens (2010), A History of News (3rd ed., 2007).

The Economics of News Media. DOI: http://dx.doi.org/10.1016/B978-0-443-45044-0.00001-5

Let us now embark on a full-fledged journey across the vast and shifting sea of the news market, aboard the vessel of the economics of news media. This chapter marks the beginning of that voyage by introducing the core components, structure, and functions of the vessel we will use to navigate this complex domain. Specifically, we examine news as an economic good, the two principal actors in the news market—news consumers and news providers—and the structural dynamics and key phenomena that emerge from their interactions.

As noted in the previous chapter, the economics of news media is rooted in the broader tradition of political economy. Yet, compared to other branches—such as those examining "political markets" through social choice theory—it is more closely aligned with mainstream economics. This is because the news market is not a metaphorical construct like the political market, but a real and observable marketplace.

Accordingly, just as in any other market for goods or services, the news market is shaped by the interaction between its consumers and providers. The decisions they make collectively determine the content and form of the product—news itself.

2.1 THE DRIVING FORCE OF NEWS: CONSUMERS

News consumers take many forms—readers of newspapers, viewers of television broadcasts, and users of online news platforms. Broadly defined, a news consumer is someone who seeks to learn "new information" through the medium of communication. But what exactly is this "medium," and who is this person seeking new information? And why did the news market emerge in the first place? To answer these questions is to deepen our understanding of the news consumer.

2.1.1 THE PRIMAL ROOTS OF THE NEWS MARKET: HUMAN INSTINCT AND SOCIAL LIVING

Language is the foundation from which all forms of media have emerged. There are many competing theories about its origin, aside from the creationist view that posits it was a gift from the divine. Among the more widely accepted evolutionary perspectives, several notable thinkers have offered intriguing explanations. Jean-Jacques Rousseau (1998) (1712–1778) suggested that language emerged from the needs of the weak to seek help from the strong in moments of hardship. Friedrich Engels (1940) (1820–1895) believed it was born from the necessities of cooperation during joint labor. Meanwhile, Japanese thinker Seigow Matsuoka (2000) traced its origin to courtship—specifically, to communication driven by the instinct for reproduction after humans lost visible signs of sexual readiness.[2]

[2] Research into the origin of language remains active among evolutionary anthropologists. In a 2001 Nature paper, Lai et al. (2001) reported that a mutation in a gene found in mammals—FOXP2—enabled humans to develop speech, garnering global attention. The study was conducted by the Max Planck Institute for Evolutionary Anthropology in Germany and the University of Oxford in the United Kingdom. However, while such genetic mutations may explain the innate capacity for language, they do not fully explain why humans began to speak in the first place.

Though differing in detail, all three perspectives share two critical insights. First, language arose from a basic survival instinct. Second, it presupposes the existence of a group of others with whom communication is necessary. The former aligns closely with the foundational assumption in mainstream economics: that humans are driven by self-interest. The latter suggests the essential condition of any market—a community or what we might call society.

Viewed from this lens, the group that communicates through language to seek and share information constitutes the foundation of the news market. So who, then, is the news consumer in this context? A traditional Korean proverb says, "A word without legs can travel a thousand miles." If we substitute "word" with "news," then the ones receiving that message across great distances are the news consumers. Simply put, if no one is interested in a piece of news, it will not travel—news cannot exist without its audience. The news consumer therefore is the most fundamental condition for the existence of both the news market and its providers.

In practice, the central concern of journalists and news organizations is to understand what their audience wants to know. This is the essence of what is commonly referred to as news value. News value reflects the characteristics of a story that align with the audience's desire to know.[3] The greater the interest of news consumers in a particular story, the higher its news value, and the more important it becomes to news providers. In short, the audience defines what is newsworthy.

2.1.2 MULTIFACETED NEWS CONSUMERS

Humans do not seek only rational and utilitarian news for survival. They also desire sensational and curiosity-driven news that stimulates instinct and peripheral emotion. These two opposing forms of news demand exist in everyone, and it is difficult to establish a clear priority between them.

Moreover, most news consumers claim they want truthful, honest, and unbiased news. In practice, however, all news consumers possess a confirmation bias—a tendency to accept information that aligns with their existing thoughts, values, or beliefs while ignoring or rejecting information that contradicts them. Consumers evaluate whether news is truthful or biased based on this confirmation bias. That is, an ordinary news consumer tends to regard news that reflects their own bias as honest and truthful (Gentzkow and Shapiro, 2006).[4] Without a strong external trigger, people rarely reflect on their own biases. In this way, when choosing among news products, consumers apply not only universal instincts but also their own specific biases and experiences as criteria for evaluation and selection.[5]

---

[3] Journalism scholars have identified several criteria that define news value, including timeliness, proximity, unexpectedness, conflict, consequence, prominence, emotional appeal, and human interest.

[4] The psychological tendency of consumers to prefer news that confirms their preexisting beliefs is also empirically supported by economists (Gentzkow & Shapiro, 2010; Gentzkow & Shapiro, 2008b).

[5] News is an experience good—a product whose value is difficult to assess before it is consumed.

Yet, news consumption behavior based on such bias and experience varies widely. Some individuals prefer news that matches their confirmation bias, while others intentionally seek out news with opposing views or neutral perspectives. In fact, such preferences differ by country. According to 2020 data, in South Korea, 44% of news consumers preferred news that aligned with their own views, while only 4% sought out opposing perspectives. In contrast, in Finland, only 11% preferred like-minded news, while 12% preferred opposing views (Reuters Institute for the Study of Journalism, 2020).[6]

In any case, news providers want as many people as possible to consume the news that they produce. For this reason, understanding what news consumers prefer is critically important to providers. News providers consciously respond to consumers' biases and instinctive desires in shaping the tone, topic, and format of the news.[7]

In this sense, the standard by which news is produced is the consumer. However, it is difficult to reduce human beings—as consumers—to a single trait or form. Therefore scholars in the economics of news media—just like in other fields of economics—make diverse assumptions about the nature of news consumers. The most common assumption is that of the rational consumer. This category includes both the perfectly rational, truth-seeking consumer and those who may prefer news that aligns with their prior beliefs and expectations but still update those beliefs rationally when new information becomes available. Some scholars instead assume irrational consumers, who show a strong preference for news that merely confirms their biases. Still others posit consumers with bounded rationality, emphasizing that their reasoning is constrained by cognitive limitations and shaped by various psychological biases.

These differing assumptions suggest that no single definition of the news consumer suffices. Rather, by considering all of these assumptions together, we may better approach the true nature of both media and the people who engage with it. In the following section, we will examine the major assumptions about news consumers that appear frequently in the economics of news media and the key concepts associated with them.

2.1.2.1 Rational consumers

One of the most common assumptions economists make about news consumers is that they rationally prefer information—or news—that aligns with their existing biases. In this context, rationally means that although consumers have inherent biases, they update their beliefs and make choices about news and media outlets through logical inference whenever they encounter new information.

For example, suppose a consumer trusts a particular news outlet with 80% confidence. If the consumer is rational, they would lower that trust to under 80% when

[6] See Fig. 5.2 and Fig. 5.3 for cross-country variations in news bias (Section 5.3.1).

[7] Even when news providers attempt to influence consumer judgment by embedding their own intentions in news reports, the consumer remains the ultimate reference point for production. News that no one reads renders such intentions meaningless.

new evidence contradicts the outlet's reporting and raise it to over 80% when the evidence supports it.

In economics, consumers who update their prior beliefs based on new information in this way are referred to as Bayesian consumers. The term originates from the work of the 18th-century British statistician Thomas Bayes (1701–61), who formalized a method of reasoning—Bayesian inference—for updating initial probabilities as new data become available. This form of reasoning allows individuals to refine their probability estimates by combining new evidence with prior beliefs, rather than treating each data point in isolation.[8]

In general, news consumers tend to regard reporting as accurate when the media's bias matches their own confirmation bias. However, if they are Bayesian, they continually revise their level of trust in news outlets in response to new evidence. That is, they increase their trust in outlets whose reporting proves consistent with the facts and decrease their trust in those that deviate from them. Over time, this process allows them to selectively consume news from more reliable sources.

2.1.2.2 Persuasion in shaping judgments

Economics, as a discipline that studies human decision-making and choice, has also examined why people change their initial decisions—or how they are led to change them. Economists have identified two primary mechanisms that can influence people's thinking without resorting to coercion or force. One is incentives, such as money or recognition. The other is persuasion—that is, the strategic provision of information. While the role of incentives in economics is widely known, the study of persuasion has received relatively less public attention.

The economics of persuasion has been a prominent area of research since the early 1960s. A key starting point is Stigler's (1961) seminal paper, which interpreted advertising as a form of persuasion (i.e., information provision) targeted at potential buyers. In the following year, Nerlove and Arrow (1962) developed a model of optimal advertising, showing how firms could continuously persuade consumers to maintain their purchase intentions. Since then, economists have continued to explore the mechanisms and effects of persuasion.

In economics, persuasion refers to the act of changing the beliefs or behavior of rational individuals by providing information or by shaping the way that information is presented. In the context of news media economics, persuasion refers to how the reporting of news can influence consumers' beliefs, including their confirmation biases, and ultimately affect which media outlets they choose to consume.

In addition to these early studies, notable research in the 1980s by Sanford Grossman and Oliver Hart and by Paul Milgrom and John Roberts revealed a counterintuitive finding. If the persuader holds private information that the persuadee (i.e., the recipient of persuasion) does not possess and cannot lie about it, then the

[8] Bayesian inference is a method of statistical reasoning based on Bayes' theorem. It updates the probability of a hypothesis by integrating new evidence with existing beliefs (prior probabilities), enabling more precise judgments than interpreting new data independently.

persuader must disclose all relevant information—not just selected parts—for persuasion to succeed. When only partial information is revealed, the persuadee may suspect that the persuader is hiding the worst possible truth. In such cases, selective omission leads the persuadee to assume that what is hidden must be worse than what is shown (Grossman and Hart, 1980; Milgrom and Roberts, 1986).

These findings contradict the common intuition that persuaders can simply present favorable facts and withhold the rest. According to these economists, even "ugly truths" are better than omission. The most effective way to persuade, then, is to disclose everything.

More recently, in the 2010s, Kamenica and Gentzkow (2011) demonstrated that even small pieces of information can effectively persuade, provided that both the persuader and the persuadee are rational agents who engage in Bayesian inference.[9]

These lines of research suggest that it is possible to change people's thoughts and behavior not through tangible rewards such as money or recognition, but simply by providing information. At least within the framework of economics, which assumes rational individuals, this is entirely plausible. Applied to the news media, the implication is that the most effective way for a media outlet to enhance the persuasive power of its reporting is to avoid omitting specific information. Even minor details can influence the beliefs of news consumers.

2.1.2.3 The careless and biased humans—bounded rationality

The previous discussions assumed that people exchange and evaluate information rationally. But in reality, people are not fully rational. Acts of persuasion in everyday life often appeal to emotion or even rely on information that later turns out to be false or fake. This is because human decision-making is influenced not only by reason but also by emotion, instinct, and intuition.

As discussed earlier in Section 1.1.2 on economic theories of human choice, behavioral economists have emphasized that humans are often guided by persistent biases, emotions, and cognitive limitations. According to their view, people do not think in purely rational terms. Rather, they frequently rely on intuitive shortcuts—heuristics—and are only boundedly rational in their decision-making.

Daniel Kahneman and Amos Tversky, pioneers of behavioral economics, argued that human thinking operates through two distinct cognitive systems: intuition and reason. People do engage in rational thinking, but their judgments are frequently flawed because they evaluate information and make decisions using these two systems independently (Kahneman, 2002). The same applies to how people consume news and information. Although people often claim to evaluate news rationally,

[9] Kamenica and Gentzkow (2011) present an intriguing example in which a prosecutor, by presenting seemingly minor information to a judge who initially estimates the defendant's guilt at 30%, raises the judge's belief above 50%. This scenario is particularly engaging for mathematically inclined legal scholars.

in reality, both laypeople and experts frequently make inaccurate judgments. All humans, to some degree, are careless and biased.

In practice, people process information using both intuitive and rational faculties. While they derive utility from information that is objectively valid and logical, they may also experience psychological satisfaction from information that resonates with their emotions or instincts—even if it is irrational. Kahneman and Tversky distinguished these two systems of thought based on the level of cognitive effort required. Intuitive or instinctive judgments require little effort, whereas rational evaluations demand deliberate and effortful processing.

[More to Explore] Heuristics: Intuitive and Experience-Based Judgments

A heuristic is a core concept in behavioral economics. The term derives from the Greek word for "to discover" and was first applied to bounded rationality by Herbert Simon. Heuristics refer to mental shortcuts or intuitive rules of thumb that people use to solve problems quickly. Rather than relying on systematic reasoning, individuals often make simple, rapid judgments based on intuition and past experience. This cognitive strategy is considered an evolved human trait, dating back to prehistoric times when quick decision-making was essential for survival.

People routinely depend on various heuristics in everyday life, making judgments without engaging in deep or deliberate reasoning. These "imperfect yet efficient" heuristics underlie many of the irrational decisions observed in both the production and consumption of news. Several common types of heuristics are introduced below:

Representativeness heuristic: This is the tendency to judge based on perceived similarity or stereotypes—what might be called the "if you've seen one, you've seen them all" approach.[10] A classic example is forming judgments about individuals based on race or place of origin. The gambler's fallacy—believing that if a coin has landed heads several times, it is "due" to land tails next—is also a manifestation of this heuristic.

Availability heuristic: When estimating how likely an event is, people often rely on examples that are vivid or memorable rather than on objective data. For instance, because news reports of airplane crashes are especially striking, many individuals perceive flying as more dangerous than driving, even though the statistical risk is lower.

Affect heuristic: This refers to the tendency to make rapid judgments based on emotional reactions such as fear or pleasure. Although a survival rate of 80% and a death rate of 20% convey the same information, people tend to feel more reassured by the former. Similarly, people are more alarmed by the statement "200 out of 1000 people experience side effects" than by "a 20% chance of side effects," even though the two are equivalent. This reflects the fact that people respond with stronger emotion to frequencies than to abstract probabilities.

[10] Tversky and Kahneman (1983) presented participants with a fictional profile of a woman named Linda: a 31-year-old single philosophy major who was active in antinuclear and antidiscrimination movements. Participants were then asked to assess which was more probable: (a) Linda is a bank teller, or (b) Linda is a bank teller, and a feminist. Most people chose (b), even though logically (a) must always be more probable than (b). This error occurred because participants judged that "feminist" fit the stereotype they had formed about Linda—a classic example of the representativeness heuristic.

2.2 THE DESTINY AND LIMITS OF NEWS PROVIDERS

Let us now examine news providers. Long before the emergence of the modern news market, figures akin to today's journalists—heralds, messengers, and chroniclers—fulfilled enduring roles across eras. Examples include the Greek messenger Pheidippides—who, according to legend, delivered news of victory in the battle against Persia on the plains of Marathon—and those who beat drums or lit beacons to transmit news to distant places. Those who trained homing pigeons for communication were also part of this lineage. Since the dawn of humanity, news providers, whether ancient messengers or modern journalists, have embodied enduring traits that transcend time and context.

2.2.1 "FASTER, FURTHER, MORE ACCURATELY"—THE INESCAPABLE FATE: COMPETITION

As societies evolved from early forms into tribal communities and structured power systems, leaders—such as chiefs, nobles, and kings—needed ways to communicate their will to the people and to gather information on the state of affairs, both of which were essential for maintaining and expanding their power. Those assigned to deliver these messages—whether on behalf of leaders or to inform the public—had to be fast runners, skilled horse riders, or proficient in using available modes of transportation and communication to ensure accurate delivery.

Even in the modern news market, the timeless mission of news providers is to outpace competitors by delivering news faster, further, and more accurately. This enables them to reach a larger audience and broaden their market. However, no matter how quickly news is delivered, "inaccurate" or "false" news can significantly erode a news provider's credibility. Therefore unless there is a compelling reason to deceive news consumers, providers strive to deliver more accurate news than their competitors. Yet, the persistent trade-off remains: prioritizing speed often compromises accuracy while ensuring precision inevitably slows down delivery. This dilemma is one that all news providers face.

News providers have always employed every possible means to outcompete their rivals. In the past, some shot down their competitors' homing pigeons with arrows. Later, they kidnapped trains carrying rival newspapers or bribed stagecoach drivers to overtake competitors' deliveries. Early newspaper publishers invested in stagecoaches, homing pigeons, hot air balloons, trains, and fast ships to obtain news faster than competitors (Gentzkow and Shapiro, 2008a, p. 142). They also attacked the weaknesses in their competitors' reports and, even if no flaws were found, criticized them from different frames. Such attempts to undermine competitors' news reports have persisted to this day.

Thus, whether in the past or present, the primary mission for news providers has always been to deliver news "faster, further, and more accurately." In this process, competition among news providers is an unavoidable fate.

2.2.2 NEWS PROVIDERS YIELDING TO POWER AND WEALTH

Until the emergence of modern democratic societies, news providers were thoroughly subservient to political and economic elites. Early messengers took the form of court scribes, town criers, envoys, or informants, all of whom served the information needs of kings, nobles, or wealthy merchants under their patronage or employment. These individuals did not merely transmit information; they often selected, omitted, or framed content according to the employer's intent.

Some news, such as royal decrees or battlefield victories, reached the public, but most information was transmitted in a restricted and asymmetric manner. The general populace had limited access to news, which was often used as a tool for administration or political propaganda. The social role of news providers was deeply entwined with the dominant governance systems of their time. In feudal China, for example, the central government used administrative systems such as the "baojia system"[11] to disseminate orders and information. In medieval Europe, public criers were appointed by local rulers to operate under their authority. Similarly, in the early Islamic caliphates, khabar (news) was disseminated under state control, often reinforcing religious conformity and obedience.

These messengers were not independent actors but extensions of ruling power—functioning at times as slaves or salaried couriers. Their loyalty was not to truth or the public, but to their employers.

Did things truly change with the advent of modern democracy and the rise of the free press? On the surface, yes. The institutionalization of free press systems in the 18th and 19th centuries and the emergence of competitive news markets led to the rise of independent journalists and private news organizations. However, the subservience of news providers merely changed its form rather than disappearing altogether.

While direct political coercion diminished, it was replaced by more subtle influences: economic dependence on advertisers, alliances with political parties, the logic of large media corporations, editorial routines, and bureaucratic controls. Even in democratic systems, media organizations are often subject to influence from advertisers, governments, and wealthy owners or stakeholders (Herman and Chomsky, 1988; Curran and Seaton, 2018). Media scholars such as Gans (1979) and McManus (1994) have argued that editorial decisions are influenced not only by political ideologies but also by commercial imperatives, organizational structures, and institutional routines that constrain journalistic autonomy.

Even today, in democratic societies, news providers remain vulnerable to the pressures of political and financial power. The withdrawal of advertisers, government funding cuts, and algorithmic suppression on digital platforms continue to be used to shape agendas, frame narratives, and silence inconvenient truths.

[11] Baojia system: A community-based administrative and policing system developed in imperial China, especially during the Song and Ming dynasties. Households were grouped into units of 10 or a hundred, with mutual responsibility for maintaining order and reporting to the state.

In the end, although physical coercion has diminished, the structural capture of news by power and wealth remains unresolved. The tension between journalistic autonomy and external power has never been an exception—it has been a persistent reality throughout human history.

2.2.3 THE HUMAN LIMITS OF NEWS PROVIDERS

Journalists who see their work as a calling strive to report the truth based on impartiality and accuracy. However, they cannot entirely transcend human limitations. It is common for news providers to carry their own confirmation biases and be bound by their personal experiences, political beliefs, or economic interests. Like any human being, they are prone to emotional sway, carelessness, and self-serving desires. News providers also face relentless time constraints. Unlike scholars or other professionals who may not experience such constraints, time pressure is an everyday reality for news providers. Much like a test-taking student who rushes to make uncertain choices due to time constraints, news providers often find themselves in similar situations. Time pressure highlights their human limitations. Yet, few news consumers are sympathetic to the time constraints faced by news providers. Although time is crucial for gathering facts and pursuing the truth, news providers rarely have enough of it. This inherent limitation is part of their professional reality.

Furthermore, when reporting news or truths that contradict conventional wisdom, news providers must overcome the barrier of consumers' "common beliefs." A shared confirmation bias among news consumers leads them to reject information that challenges their views. Competing news providers also exploit these biases to criticize reports that deviate from convention. Therefore news providers seeking to break through conventional beliefs and convey new truths must present more evidence than usual to validate their reports. However, this requires more time and effort, but the time given is always insufficient.

Thus the social inertia and the opposition from competing news media that stand in the way of discovering new truths continually test the human limitations of news providers. Furthermore, journalists trained to uphold fair and objective journalism are also human. So, it is not easy for them to completely overcome these human limitations. In addition, when major news media are captured by political, social, or economic powers that seek to suppress the truth, it becomes even harder for the truth to come to light.

In short, tasked with delivering the news faster, further, and more accurately, news providers—like consumers—are emotional beings. They cannot fully escape their confirmation biases or self-interest. Moreover, they operate under constant time pressure and often find themselves entangled in the webs of wealth and power. This has been the case not just for decades but for centuries and even millennia.

2.3 THE STRUCTURE AND MAJOR PHENOMENA OF THE NEWS MARKET

The political economy of news media focuses on the "news market." In the modern news market, news media as suppliers provide news content to consumers, and consumers provide "monetary compensation" or "page views" in return. (Page views are the source of advertising revenue from advertisers.)[12] Through this exchange, news media as suppliers aim to maximize profits, while readers or viewers, as consumers, seek to maximize their utility by consuming news.

In this way, the basic structure of the news market is no different from that of any other market. However, the news market, unlike typical markets, is heavily influenced by external entities such as governments, political parties, politicians, corporations, and interest groups. For instance, political powers or large corporations provide tangible and intangible incentives to news media to prevent unfavorable reporting or to encourage favorable coverage. As a result, the news market is frequently subject to interference and disruption by external entities attempting to shape news consumption. This distinguishes the news market from other markets.

In comparison, in the fruit market, it is uncommon for governments or corporations to intervene to make consumers buy specific types of fruit. However, in the news market, it is common for governments or corporations to intervene—whether to serve political or commercial interests—to prevent or promote the supply of particular news.

Moreover, the information provided to consumers in the news market inevitably influences the political and social decision-making processes within society. In a market where apples are bought and sold, the process is simply about producing, supplying, and consuming apples. However, in the news market, consumption of news does not end with consumption; it directly influences individual thoughts and actions, which ultimately lead to political and economic choices in society.

2.3.1 PHENOMENA ADDRESSED BY THE POLITICAL ECONOMY OF NEWS MEDIA

The political economy of news media studies the news market by analyzing the actions and influences exchanged among internal and external actors in the market, covering the following areas through both theoretical and empirical approaches:

First, it investigates the role of the news media in promoting the *political accountability of politicians* under representative democracy. This field studies how news

[12] In the news market, consumers include not only primary audiences who engage with news content but also advertisers who purchase space and airtime offered by media outlets. Advertising revenue is generally tied to the size of the news audience, making advertisers secondary consumers in the news media market.

media reports affect government policies, politicians' decisions and actions, and the political choices of the public. The focus is on the conditions in the news market and government policies that ensure news media provide useful information for the political choices of news consumers.

Second, it deals with *media capture*, where political powers, capital (corporations), and interest groups manipulate the news media to ensure favorable coverage for themselves. This field studies how political forces, governments, or corporations capture news media for their benefit and what the outcomes of such capture are.

Third, it explores *media power*, examining how news media or their personnel seek to maximize their influence through the media for their own purposes and how such actions should be regulated.

In general, when news consumers and news media are weak, and political or corporate power is strong, "media capture" is more likely to occur. Conversely, when the power of news media is strong, "media power" phenomena are more prevalent. Both cases diminish truthful reporting and distort the news market. Thus reducing these two phenomena in relation to the news media is a key topic of discussion in the political economy of news.

Lastly, the study of *media bias* investigates why and how bias arises in news reports. Since every phenomenon in the news market is related to bias, this is a central field in the political economy of news media. On a broader level, both *media capture* and *media power* result in biased news. On a more specific level, it examines media bias arising from news suppliers, news consumers, and the interactions between them. Fig. 2.1 illustrates the basic structure of the news market and the key phenomena of the political economy of news media: (1) media capture, (2) media power, and (3) media bias.

So far, we have briefly examined the basic characteristics and functions of the news market, as well as how the consumers and suppliers in this market differ from those in other typical markets. A more detailed explanation will follow in later chapters. In this chapter, we will conclude by discussing another characteristic of the news market: the two-sided market.

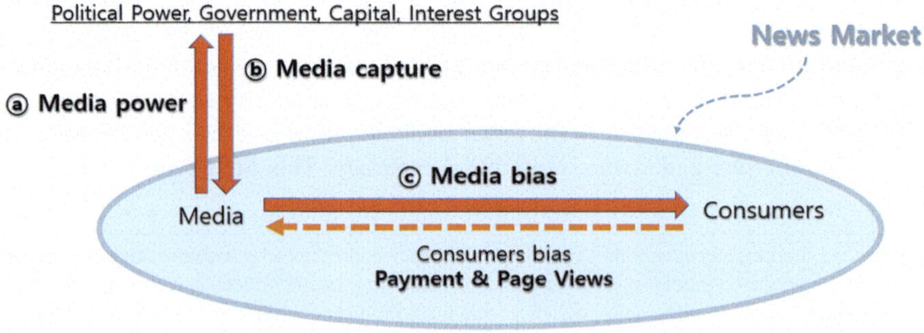

FIGURE 2.1

The structure and phenomena of the news market.

2.3.2 THE NEWS MARKET AS A TWO-SIDED MARKET

"If you are not paying for the product, you are the product."

—*Netflix documentary, The Social Dilemma (2020)*

We live in a world where, when people use a product for free, it is often said that they themselves become the product. In the digital age, many people access web portals like Google and social media platforms such as Facebook without paying any fees. However, as the saying goes, "everything comes at a cost." Every moment users engage with web portals or social media, they become the commodity sold to advertisers by those platforms.

This is a classic example of a "two-sided market." French economist Jean Tirole (Nobel Prize in Economics, 2014) and Jean-Charles Rochet theorized that a two-sided market is one where different user groups interact through a platform. Representative examples of such platforms include web portals, social media platforms, and online shopping sites like Amazon, eBay, or Alibaba. A two-sided platform typically involves two distinct user groups, such as buyers and sellers on an online shopping site. When more than two user groups are involved, the platform is sometimes called a "multisided platform."

The digital news market, which is now the primary platform for news consumption, is a two-sided or multisided market. Traditional news markets also exhibit these two-sided market characteristics (Anderson and Gabszewicz, 2006; Armstrong, 2006). In the early days of newspapers, before advertising was common, the only participants in the news market were news consumers who purchased the content. However, with the introduction of advertisements, two distinct groups—readers (or viewers) and advertisers—formed the customer base of newspapers and broadcasting outlets.[13]

In this sense, mass news media act as a platform between news consumers and advertisers, providing content to the former and access to the latter. Fig. 2.2 shows the relative proportions of advertising and circulation as the two main revenue sources for newspapers, illustrating how their balance has shifted over time.

This two-sided nature of the news market means that news media are not entirely independent of advertisers. News media revenue depends on both news consumers and advertisers. As a result, news media may slant their reports to suit the preferences of advertisers.

Among the two groups—news consumers and advertisers—news consumers are more fundamental to news media. Advertising revenue depends on the quantity and quality of news consumers. If the preferences of news consumers and advertisers diverge, news media focusing exclusively on advertisers risk losing their news

[13] The turning point when the news market became a two-sided market was in the 1830s, with the advent of inexpensive mass-circulation newspapers known as the "Penny Papers" or "Penny Press." Thanks to advances in mass printing, these newspapers were able to significantly lower their prices while starting to run advertisements extensively.

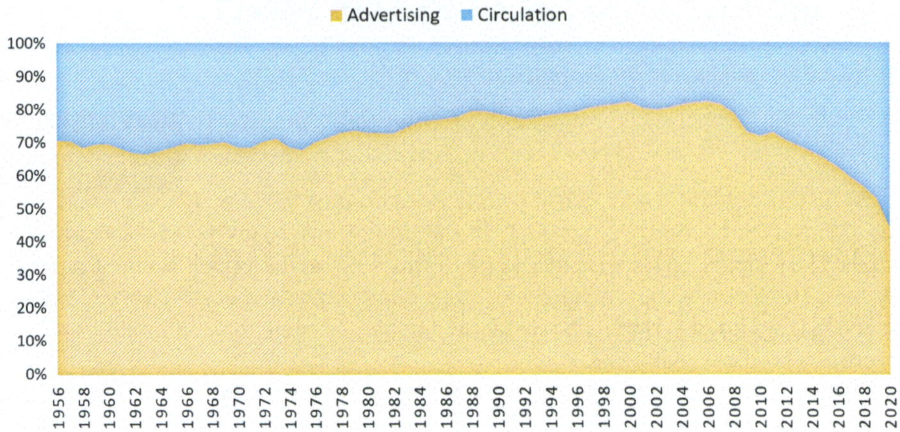

FIGURE 2.2

Changes in the relative proportions of advertising and sales revenue in the US newspaper industry (1956–2020). *From Pew Research Center, 2024. Newspapers fact sheet. https://www.journalism.org/fact-sheet/newspapers/ accessed 01.05.25.*

consumers. Furthermore, as news consumer numbers decline, advertisers lose incentive to place ads with the media outlet. Therefore under normal circumstances, news media reflect the interests and preferences of their consumers in content creation rather than those of advertisers.

However, in reality, there are times when the revenue gained by catering to advertisers' preferences exceeds the revenue lost from alienating news consumers. For example, if a news media outlet alters its coverage to be more favorable to a particular corporation and receives increased advertising revenue of 100 over a certain period, while the revenue lost from a decline in news consumers over the same period is 50, the media outlet might shift its editorial stance in favor of the advertiser.

Such practices are more likely to occur over the short term, particularly when news consumers are less aware of changes in editorial tone. Theoretically, this can happen when advertisers offer substantial compensation in exchange for favorable coverage, less critical reporting, or even the omission of certain stories.[14]

Additionally, in two-sided or multisided markets, there are also "network effects" or "network externalities," in which the value of a product increases as more people use it. For example, even if App A's messaging features are inferior to App B's, if more people use App A, its value increases (due to the network effect), and more

[14] The phenomenon of news media adjusting reporting biases to align with advertisers' preferences is discussed in greater detail in Section 9.3, The Two Faces of Advertisers.

people are inclined to use it. These network effects become more intricate in multi-sided markets.[15]

Such network effects can arise among news consumers who engage with ideologically aligned media outlets. For example, within a community where a large number of people regularly consume a left-leaning news outlet, individuals may continue to rely on that outlet—even if its quality is objectively low—due to the reinforcing effects of shared consumption. This, too, can be regarded as a form of network effect.

References

Anderson, S. P., Gabszewicz, J. J., 2006. The Media and Advertising: A Tale of Two-Sided Markets. In: Ginsburgh, V., Throsby, D. (Eds.), *Handbook of the Economics of Art and Culture*, Vol. 1. Elsevier, Amsterdam, pp. 567–614.

Armstrong, M., 2006. Competition in Two-Sided Markets. RAND Journal of Economics 37 (3), 668–691.

Curran, J., Seaton, J., 2018. Power Without Responsibility: Press, Broadcasting and the Internet in Britain, 8th ed. Routledge, London. https://doi.org/10.4324/9781351212298.

Engels, F., 1940. The part played by labour in the transition from ape to man. In: Marx, K., Engels, F. (Eds.), Dialectics of nature. International Publishers, pp. 170–180. (Original work written in 1876).

Gabszewicz, J., Resende, J., Sonnac, N., 2015. Media as Multi-Sided Platforms. In: Picard, R.G., Wildman, S.S. (Eds.), Handbook on the Economics of the Media. Edward Elgar Publishing, pp. 3–35.

Gans, H. J., 1979. Deciding What's News: A Study of CBS Evening News, NBC Nightly News, Newsweek, and Time. Pantheon Books.

Gentzkow, M., Shapiro, J. M., 2006. Media bias and reputation. Journal of Political Economy 114 (2), 280–316. https://doi.org/10.1086/499414.

Gentzkow, M., Shapiro, J. M., 2008a. Competition and truth in the market for news. Journal of Economic Perspectives 22 (2), 133–154. https://doi.org/10.1257/jep.22.2.133.

Gentzkow, M., Shapiro, J.M., 2008b. Market forces and news media in Muslim countries. In: Islam, R. (Ed.), Information and Public Choice: From Media Markets to Policy Making. World Bank, Washington, DC, pp. 107–120.

Gentzkow, M., Shapiro, J. M., 2010. What Drives Media Slant? Evidence from US Daily Newspapers. Econometrica 78 (1), 35–71.

Grossman, S. J., Hart, O. D., 1980. Disclosure laws and takeover bids. The Journal of Finance 35 (2), 323–334. https://doi.org/10.2307/2327390.

Herman, E.S., Chomsky, N., 1988. Manufacturing Consent: The Political Economy of the Mass Media. Pantheon Books, New York.

Kahneman, D., 2002. Maps of bounded rationality: a perspective on intuitive judgment and choice. Nobel Prize Lecture, 8 December 2002.

Kamenica, E., Gentzkow, M., 2011. Bayesian persuasion. American Economic Review 101 (6), 2590–2615. https://doi.org/10.1257/aer.101.6.2590.

[15] For a discussion on media as a multi-sided platform, refer to Gabszewicz, Resende, and Sonnac (2015).

Lai, C. S. L., Fisher, S. E., Hurst, J. A., Vargha-Khadem, F., Monaco, A. P., 2001. A forkhead-domain gene is mutated in a severe speech and language disorder. Nature 413 (6855), 519–523. https://doi.org/10.1038/35097076.

Matsuoka S., 2000. Jōhō no rekishi o yomu [Reading the history of information]. Tokyo: NTT Shuppan.

McManus J. H., 1994. Market-Driven Journalism: Let the Citizen Beware? Sage.

Milgrom, P., Roberts, J., 1986. Relying on the information of interested parties. The RAND Journal of Economics 17 (1), 18–32. https://doi.org/10.2307/2555625.

Nerlove, M., Arrow, K. J., 1962. Optimal Advertising Policy Under Dynamic Conditions. Economica 29 (114), 129–142. https://doi.org/10.2307/2551549.

Pew Research Center, 2024. Newspapers fact sheet. <https://www.journalism.org/fact-sheet/newspapers/> (accessed 01.05.25.).

Reuters Institute for the Study of Journalism, 2020. *Digital News Report 2020*. Retrieved from https://www.digitalnewsreport.org/.

Rousseau J.-J., 1998. Essay on the Origin of Languages and Writings Related to Music (J.H. Moran, Trans.). University Press of New England.

Stephens, M. (2010). A History of News (third ed.). Translated into Korean by Lee In-Hee. Seoul: Communication Books. [Original work published 2007].

Stigler, G. J., 1961. The economics of information. Journal of Political Economy 69 (3), 213–225. https://doi.org/10.1086/258464.

Tversky, A., Kahneman, D., 1983. Extensional versus intuitive reasoning: The conjunction fallacy in probability judgment. Psychological Review 90 (4), 293–315.

CHAPTER

3 The Development of the News Market and the Transformation of Journalism

Chapter Outline

Journalism is intelligence and civilization itself.[1]
—Honoré de Balzac

Except for certain underdeveloped regions of the world, most of modern humanity enjoys a level of material prosperity unprecedented in history. This affluence can be traced primarily to the Industrial Revolution, which drastically lowered production costs and enabled mass production. The information abundance we experience today is, in many ways, a parallel phenomenon. Since the advent of movable metal type in the West, the cost of producing, storing, and transmitting information—as well as the price consumers must pay to access it—has fallen steadily and significantly over time.

[1] Balzac, H. de. (1981)

The Economics of News Media. DOI: http://dx.doi.org/10.1016/B978-0-443-45044-0.00005-2

In the digital era, the price of many forms of informational content has dropped to zero or near zero, while the volume of available content has exploded. Compared to prehistoric times—when acquiring knowledge from across a river could mean risking one's life because of poisonous plants or predatory animals—it is hardly an exaggeration to say that news and information have become the most devalued goods in the history of humankind.

3.1 THE SPIRAL EVOLUTION OF "INFORMATION DEMOCRACY"

From an economic perspective, the supply of goods or services is determined by production costs and market prices. When market prices fall below production costs, suppliers have little incentive to offer those goods or services—unless they are willing to incur losses. Conversely, even essential goods or services remain out of reach if their prices exceed what consumers can afford.

This principle holds true in the news market as well. The supply of information is directly influenced by the cost of collecting, processing, and distributing it. Just as rare minerals are expensive due to the difficulty of extracting them, information becomes more valuable and scarce the harder it is to obtain. If there were no way to store information, the cost of storing it would be prohibitively high. And if human memory were the only available means of storage, information could simply vanish with the passage of time. Moreover, the transmission of information requires communication and transportation infrastructure, and the development level of these systems also directly affects the cost and price of information.

In short, the higher the cost of collecting, storing, and transmitting information, the more expensive information becomes—turning it into a privilege reserved for the few who can afford it. Under such conditions, a genuine market for news can hardly emerge, and actual news consumers remain extremely limited. Various factors can lower the costs of collecting, storing, processing, and delivering information, but none are as decisive as media technology. This is because every stage of the information lifecycle—from production to consumption—depends entirely on media systems. Let us begin by examining how this played out in the distant past.

The Drastic Reduction in the Cost of Information Supply

In primitive societies, information was as scarce as any other resource accessible to humans. Gathering and transmitting new knowledge was often a life-threatening endeavor. Even exploring areas just a few dozen kilometers away required overcoming the formidable hazards of the natural environment. As Posner (1980) notes, the cost of acquiring information in such contexts was inevitably high.

Moreover, even when individuals risked their lives to obtain new knowledge, there was no medium other than oral language to preserve it. Human memory served as the sole means of storing information.[2] Since information had not yet become a regularly exchanged commodity, it was difficult to assign to it a clear market value. Still, given its rarity and the absence of effective storage mechanisms, its implicit price would have been extraordinarily high. Consequently, both the production and consumption of news in early societies remained extremely limited.

Yet because such information was vital for the survival of both individuals and communities, it was not monopolized by a privileged few. Knowledge was commonly shared, and everyone acted simultaneously as both a producer and a consumer of information, with no clear distinction between the two roles.

With the advent of written media, information was no longer confined to the limitations of human memory. Among the three main costs of handling information—collection, storage, and transmission—the cost of storage dropped significantly thanks to the invention of writing. Yet the benefits of reduced storage costs accrued almost exclusively to a literate elite. Although the total volume of information held by a society expanded dramatically, its fruits were concentrated in the hands of the ruling classes.

In contrast to the oral media era—when information was communally shared—this marked the beginning of an era in which a small minority monopolized access to the growing body of knowledge and information. While written texts and news may have existed, most members of society remained illiterate, making such content effectively inaccessible to them.

As societies advanced through antiquity and the medieval era, both scientific knowledge and social organization improved, leading to the gradual increase in the quantity of information collected, transmitted, and stored. Technological development, written media, transportation infrastructure, and political systems all contributed directly to lowering the costs of information collection, transmission, and storage. Still, the cost of producing and delivering information remained high, and news markets largely remained in the dark. It was not until the printing revolution—when the costs of producing and disseminating information fell even further—that a functioning news market could truly begin to emerge.

The printing revolution enabled the mass distribution of news and information through printed materials. Soon after, modern newspapers began to appear, giving rise to the first modern news market: the newspaper market. By the 20th century, the era of mass media had fully arrived with the emergence of broadcasting. Throughout this process, the cost of supplying news dropped sharply, the number of professional news providers increased substantially, and the news market expanded rapidly.

The simultaneous surge in both news providers and news consumers resembled two sides of the same coin. Previously, news consumption had been limited

[2] The longest body of information preserved through human memory and oral transmission is the Kyrgyz three-part Epic of Manas, recited by bard Sayakbay Karalaev, comprising approximately 503,500 lines—more than 20 times the length of Homer's Iliad and Odyssey combined, and about 2.5 times longer than the Mahabharata.

to a privileged few, but thanks to the dramatic advances in media and information-communication technologies, access to news was extended to virtually every member of society. The result was a news market populated by a vast number of both producers and consumers—one that resembled a textbook example of a free and competitive market. However, this period did not last long.

As newspapers and broadcast media grew in scale, entry barriers began to emerge in the news market. The need for large-scale infrastructure investments acted as a significant barrier to entry, limiting the proliferation of newspapers and broadcast outlets and constraining competition among news providers to within a manageable range. At the same time, the influence of mass media like newspapers and television grew exponentially—far surpassing that of previous generations of news producers.

In the digital age, the cost of storing and distributing news and information declined once again, and this time even more dramatically. In the digital realm, the price of informational content such as news became, in many cases, virtually zero. Simultaneously, the monopolistic structure of mass media—built on massive initial investments and high entry barriers—began to collapse. Digital infrastructure tore down those barriers, ushering in an era in which everyone could be both a consumer and a producer of news. As a result, the monopoly of traditional media—newspapers and broadcasters—over the supply of news was broken, the power of news providers diminished, and the power of news consumers grew accordingly.

In this way, advances in media technology and shifts in the cost of acquiring (or supplying) information led to what can be described as the "spiral evolution" of information and knowledge democratization. Fig. 3.1 on the following page illustrates this process. In the era of primitive oral media, everyone was both a supplier and a consumer of information, and information was shared equally by all. But with the invention of writing came an era in which the dominant classes monopolized most of the knowledge and information produced within a society.

The arrival of print media began to erode that monopoly, and by the time of the mass media era, the dominant class's exclusive control over information consumption had been dismantled. Yet the production and distribution of news and information became concentrated in the hands of newly emerging mass media monopolies.

In the subsequent digital media era, traditional mass media and the newly empowered public—now acting as both suppliers and consumers of content on digital platforms—began to coexist. As a result, the monopolistic nature of information production weakened significantly, and the democratization of access to information advanced rapidly.

Fig. 3.1 illustrates the historical progression of media and how it has transformed the flow and distribution of information and knowledge from exclusive control by the few to widespread accessibility among the many.

- In the *Oral Media Era*, information was exchanged face-to-face within small communities, limiting its reach. The *Text Media Era* marked the beginning

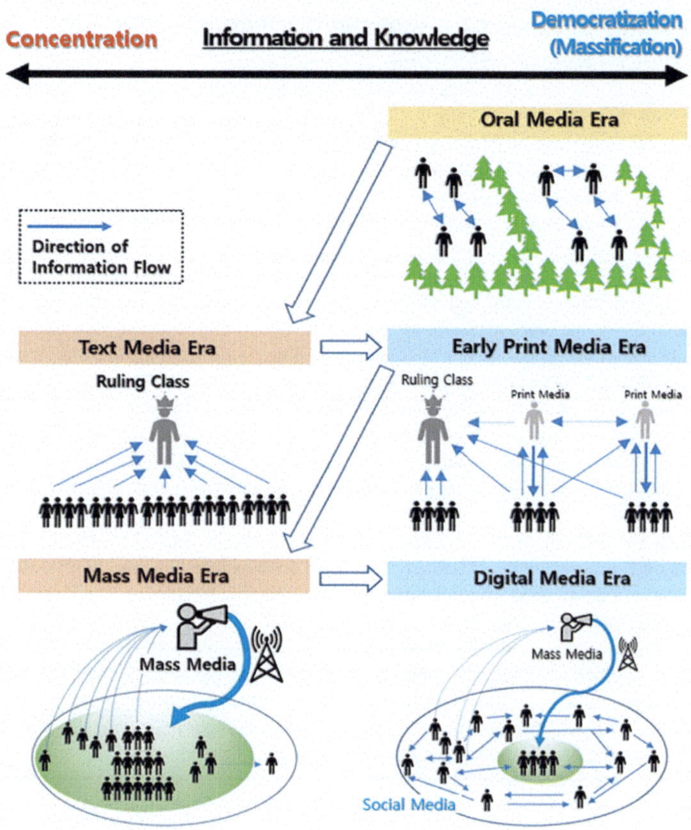

FIGURE 3.1

Media development and the democratization of information and knowledge.

of information monopolization, where literate elites controlled the flow of information in a one-way, top-down manner.

- With the rise of the *Early Print Media Era*, the number of information producers increased, and more people gained access to printed materials, allowing broader dissemination and interaction. However, the power to control information still largely resided with the elite.
- In the *Mass Media Era* (newspapers and broadcasting), media organizations held exclusive control over production and distribution. Information flow remained one-way, from a few producers to the general public.
- The *Digital Media Era* ushered in a radical change. With digital technology and the internet, anyone can be both a producer and a consumer of information. Communication became multidirectional and interactive, marking a significant shift toward the democratization of information and knowledge.

[More to Explore] News as a Commodity: Information Goods

What are the defining economic characteristics of news as a good?

From an economic standpoint, news can be classified as an information good—a type of good that derives its value from the information it conveys to the consumer. Information goods encompass a wide range of content, including books, magazines, music, video, and the output of newspapers and broadcast media. A defining characteristic of information goods is nonrivalry in consumption: one person's use of the good does not diminish its availability to others. This implies that the traditional law of supply and demand, which presumes scarcity, applies imperfectly to such goods.

Information goods typically involve high fixed costs of production but negligible or zero marginal costs for additional consumption. For instance, once a newspaper is printed or a broadcast is transmitted, adding one more reader or viewer incurs little to no extra cost. This nonrivalrous nature of information goods has served to dramatically amplify the effects of technological advances in media and information and communication technologies (ICT), particularly by further reducing the marginal cost of producing and delivering informational content.

Historically, most information goods were excludable, meaning access could be restricted to paying customers. However, this property has become increasingly variable. Depending on the supplier and distribution method, some information goods now exhibit nonexcludability, whereby no consumer can be prevented from accessing the good once it is provided. Subscription-based platforms such as Netflix or pay-TV channels remain excludable, whereas free-to-air broadcast channels and open-access online content are examples of nonexcludable goods. Excludability is a defining feature of private goods, but information goods may function either as private or public goods, depending on how they are produced and distributed.

Finally, information goods are also classified as experience goods, whose quality and value cannot be fully assessed until after consumption. In markets for experience goods, reputation plays a key role in guiding consumer choice. Patients must choose a doctor before treatment, and audiences must decide whether to engage with a news outlet without prior knowledge of its specific content—often relying on reputational signals from others.

3.2 THE BIRTH OF MASS MEDIA AND JOURNALISM

Like the supply and consumption of all goods and services, the provision and consumption of news have evolved in accordance with the prevailing economic conditions of each era. Both the form and content of news have been shaped by the media through which news is delivered, and by the economic conditions faced by news providers. Journalism—the act of reporting and commenting on facts or events through mass media—is no exception. This is because mass media itself, the prerequisite for journalism, is a product of advances in media technology and changes in economic circumstances. Consequently, the fate of journalism has never been independent of the technological and economic structures that sustain the news market.

As will become evident in the following sections, journalism has manifested in various forms depending on the conditions of the news market, and has evolved in ways that reflect those conditions. What follows examines how news providers have adapted to the changing news market since the emergence of the modern newspaper, considering both the corporate dimension and the professional logic of journalism.

Before proceeding to the modern era, it is helpful to briefly review the state of news provision before the rise of modern newspapers. Even before industrialization, early forms of what would later resemble newspapers existed in both the East and the West. In ancient Rome, records of Senate proceedings and decisions of public assemblies were engraved on metal or stone and displayed in public locations.[3] In Tang dynasty China, hand-written bulletins on silk were produced by the central government and delivered to regional officials. Similar forms of manuscript newsletters continued to exist in both Eastern and Western societies, but access to such information was limited to government officials and elites wealthy enough to bear the considerable costs.[4]

The technical breakthrough that allowed manuscript newsletters to evolve into modern newspapers was the invention of movable metal type by Johannes Gutenberg (1397–1468) in fifteenth-century Germany. Initially, printed materials were mostly pamphlets, but the first publication resembling a modern newspaper appeared in 1605 in Strasbourg, a city near the French-German border. Newspapers gradually spread across Europe, and in 1702, England saw the publication of its first daily newspaper, *the Daily Courant*.

However, the newspaper industry remained relatively stagnant for the next two centuries. Even during the Industrial Revolution, which began in the mid-eighteenth century, printing technology saw little advancement. Newspaper publishers continued to use flatbed presses that differed little from those in Gutenberg's time. These presses were highly labor-intensive, and both the number of pages and the total volume of output were severely constrained. The lack of efficient long-distance transportation also limited the geographic reach of newspaper distribution. Most newspapers circulated fewer than 100 copies, and their revenues depended almost entirely on a small number of fixed subscribers.

3.2.1 INNOVATIONS IN PRINT TECHNOLOGY AND THE TRANSFORMATION OF NEWSPAPERS

Leading up to the late 19th century, at the tail end of the Industrial Revolution, the newspaper industry began to experience a series of technological innovations in printing. New papermaking technologies significantly lowered the cost of newsprint. In 1814, the steam-powered press was introduced, and by 1846, the rotary press—which used rotating cylinders instead of flat plates—marked the beginning of the

[3] These posted notices were called Acta or Acta Diurna.

[4] The Kaiyuan Za Bao (Bulletin of the Kaiyuan Era) from the 8th century was a type of official gazette. In the collection and distribution of information—early forms of what would become newspapers—China was ahead of the West.

transition away from flatbed printing. These innovations raised printing capacity from a few hundred copies per hour to several thousand.

Simultaneously, improvements in transportation infrastructure, including the expansion of railroads and canals, dramatically enhanced distribution capabilities. Industrialized urban centers attracted large populations, leading to a steep decline in the cost of news production and delivery, alongside a rapid increase in the pool of potential news consumers.

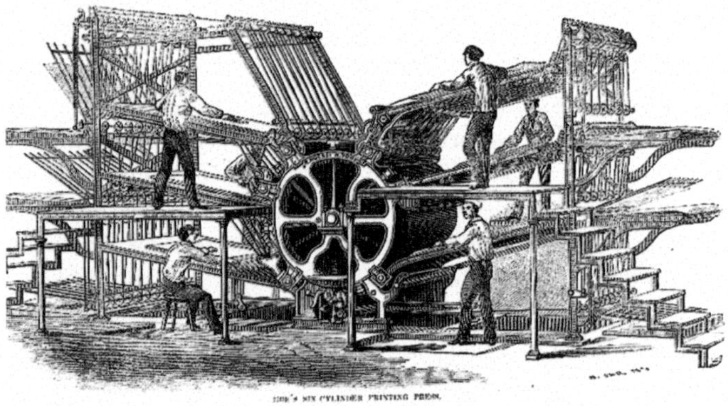

Rotary press from the 1860s.

Public domain image via Wikimedia Commons.

As mass production became feasible at low cost, the entire newspaper business model underwent a fundamental transformation—two centuries after the emergence of the modern newspaper. The change extended well beyond hardware improvements such as rotary presses, encompassing also the physical format of newspapers and their volume of production. It also redefined the economic structure of newspapers and gave rise to modern journalism. From this period onward, the content of newspapers began to reflect the economic and market conditions in which they operated.

This transformation also reshaped the organizational structure of newspaper firms. In earlier periods, newspapers were often run by just a few individuals who handled all aspects of production and distribution. The publisher was also the reporter, editor, and salesperson. By the 1850s, however, major newspapers in the United States and Europe had expanded to employ up to a hundred people.

A clear division of labor emerged during this period between those responsible for reporting and editing the news and those engaged in printing, sales, and administration. This was also the era in which the journalist first emerged as a distinct class of professional, devoted exclusively to news gathering, reporting, and editing. Although many journalists today perceive their role as independent of the financial conditions of their employers, the profession of journalism itself arose from, and remains rooted in, the broader economic and corporate context of the newspaper industry.

At the same time, substantial entry barriers began to emerge in the industry. Steam-powered presses were vastly more expensive than manual ones. As press performance improved and newspapers began printing more pages at higher volumes, the demand for capital—both human and physical—rose accordingly. Investment in labor for editorial production, printing, and distribution also increased significantly. The capital intensity of the business made it increasingly difficult for new entrants to launch newspapers without considerable financial backing.

With the emergence of such high and substantial entry barriers, competition among suppliers was no longer driven toward unrestrained or unlimited rivalry, but was instead contained within a manageable level. Moreover, the high fixed costs associated with printing equipment and labor meant that the cost of producing the first copy of a newspaper was exceptionally high. However, as circulation increased, these fixed costs were spread across a larger number of units, substantially lowering the average cost per copy. In this context, the newspaper industry became increasingly subject to economies of scale, with profitability largely determined by the scale of output.

3.2.1.1 The Rise of Objective Journalism

> *Though we often talk about covering the news objectively as an ethical or professional norm, objective news coverage is a commercial product that emerges from market forces.*[5]
>
> **—James T. Hamilton**

The introduction of rotary printing technology, which made large-scale printing feasible, brought a dramatic drop in newspaper prices in the United States during the 1830s. The turning point came in 1833, when The Sun, a New York-based newspaper, lowered its price to one penny, i.e., one cent, per issue, down from the standard six cents. This period marked the advent of the so-called "penny press" era,[6] characterized by the rise of low-cost, mass-market newspapers. Scholars of journalism describe this as a transformative moment when two key developments reshaped the press.

The first was a change in the business model of newspapers. As prices fell, the number of consumers who could afford to buy newspapers increased exponentially. Penny press newspapers became smaller and easier to carry, and were often sold on the street by newsboys. Lower prices attracted a wider audience, which in turn further reduced the marginal cost per unit. Newspapers also began to carry commercial advertisements on a regular basis. As their reader base expanded, newspapers were

[5] Hamilton (2004, p. 37)

[6] Also known as the "penny paper." In the United States at the time, a 1-cent coin was commonly called a penny.

able to raise advertising rates and increasingly derived more of their revenue from advertisers than from readers. This commercial model—anchored in mass circulation and advertising revenue—remains largely intact to this day.

The second development was the emergence of a new journalistic norm—namely, the rise of professional and objective journalism. Before the penny press, newspaper readers were typically a small group of politically committed elites who could afford expensive, partisan papers. Newspapers often served as direct organs of political parties and maintained strong editorial partisanship. However, as inexpensive newspapers began to reach a mass audience, publishers attuned to economies of scale found it increasingly unnecessary—and even counterproductive—to cater to a small number of ideologically driven readers. Instead, their survival depended on attracting as many readers as possible.

Political alignment and partisan readers were no longer essential to the survival of newspapers. To secure their new source of revenue—namely, a larger and more diverse readership—newspapers had to weaken the partisan editorial stance they had previously maintained. This shift laid the foundation for the pursuit of objective journalism as a professional ideal. Alongside it, the emergence of objectivity as a standard of news quality further stimulated the growth of the news market.

Rotary press of the Toledo Blade newspaper in Ohio, 1890s. It could print 48,000 eight-page newspapers per hour

Public domain via Wikimedia Commons.

Journalists during this era also began to conceive of themselves as professionals serving the public interest. The rise of professional journalism was closely linked to the structural expansion of newspaper organizations, which began to include specialized roles dedicated to reporting and editorial work. As the news market grew, journalists faced growing pressure to justify their role and legitimacy within the media system. In this context, objective journalism and professional journalism developed in a mutually reinforcing relationship. The idea that objectivity required professional expertise, and that the pursuit of public interest required an objective stance, became deeply embedded in the institutional logic of modern journalism.

3.2.1.2 Newspapers' Differentiation Strategies

As time went on, newspaper circulation—and thus the size of the readership—increased substantially. By the late 19th century, urban populations in both the United States and Europe were able to purchase daily newspapers that were printed in the tens of thousands at low prices. With newspapers being the sole form of news media at the time, the industry came to be seen as a highly profitable business—"the goose that lays golden eggs," as it were.

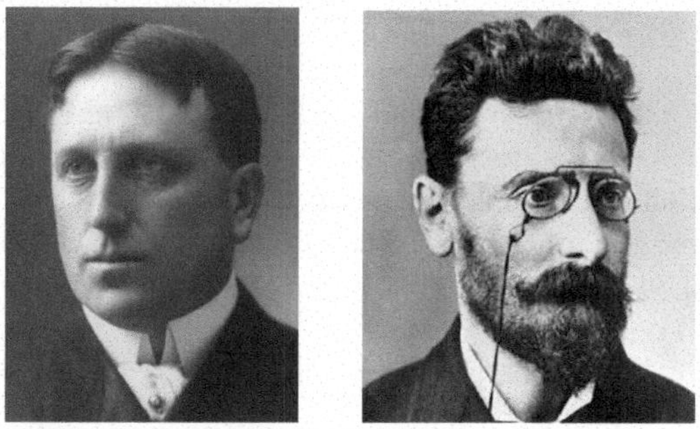

William Randolph Hearst and Joseph Pulitzer, two legendary American press barons.
Public domain via Wikimedia Commons

In this context, newspaper firms began to pursue profit maximization by differentiating their product—namely, the editorial tone and content of their newspapers—to align with the preferences of targeted consumer groups. These differentiation strategies expanded the overall readership of the newspaper market and further fueled the growth of the industry.

In Britain, leading newspapers adopted distinct editorial tones and content strategies to appeal to specific social classes. *The Times*, for example, catered to elite readers, whereas *The Daily Telegraph* targeted the rising middle class.

In the United States, media magnates such as William Randolph Hearst (1863–1951) and Joseph Pulitzer (1847–1911) ushered in the era of yellow journalism[7] through sensationalized reporting. In contrast, many other newspapers began to differentiate themselves by adopting less sensationalistic and less partisan editorial styles, influenced by the principles of objective journalism. The result was a segmentation of the newspaper market into mass-circulation popular papers and more sober, opinion-leading papers.

[7] The term derives from the "Yellow Kid" comic strip and the sensational style of reporting associated with the fierce circulation war between Pulitzer and Hearst.

Adolph Ochs.

Public domain via Wikimedia Commons.

One of the most notable examples of the latter was *The New York Times* under Adolph Ochs (1858–1935), who acquired the paper in 1896. Facing financial difficulties at the time, Ochs reduced the paper's price from three cents to one cent, while simultaneously promoting high-quality journalism. Under his leadership, the paper's readership, which had been under 10,000 at the time of acquisition, grew to over one million within two decades.

The newspapers of this period also responded swiftly to changes in reader demand by diversifying the range of information they provided, revising their formats, and redesigning headlines and layout styles. Until the 1870s, many American newspapers consisted primarily of editorials, political speeches, serialized fiction or poetry, and limited advertising. But by the early 20th century, newspapers had greatly expanded their reporting sections and topical coverage. As mass production gave rise to a flood of consumer goods, newspapers began publishing more content aimed at consumers. The expanding social and economic roles of women also brought increased coverage of fashion, household management, and family issues. Newspapers enhanced their visual appeal as well, using multicolumn headlines and varied layouts to attract attention at newsstands. These developments illustrate how economic changes exerted a profound influence on both the form and content of journalism.

In many respects, the late 19th and early 20th centuries marked the golden age of newspapers in both Europe and the United States. The range and depth of information expanded, newspapers employed product differentiation strategies to meet diverse consumer preferences, and circulation increased exponentially. The number of newspapers also reached historic levels: in 1914, for instance, there were 80 daily newspapers published in Paris alone, including *Le Figaro*.

3.2.2 THE EMERGENCE OF BROADCASTING AND THE NEWSPAPERS' COUNTERACTION

The first half of the 20th century saw the rise of radio, followed by the emergence of television in the mid-20th century. Both radio and television reached far larger audiences than newspapers and did so more rapidly. In the advanced news media markets of the Western world, the era in which newspapers served as the sole channel for news came to an end.

The first regular radio broadcast began in the United States in 1920. Within just two decades, by 1940, more than 80% of American households owned a radio. The diffusion of television occurred even more quickly. Following the launch of the world's first regular television service by the BBC (British Broadcasting Corporation) in the United Kingdom in 1936, NBC began regular television broadcasting in the United States in 1939. By 1960, television penetration in the United States had reached 90% of households—just 21 years after NBC's first broadcast.

However, the ownership and operational models of broadcasting diverged sharply between Europe and the United States. These differences would go on to shape the distinctive media environments and news markets of the two regions. In much of Western Europe, nonprofit public broadcasting systems—funded by license fees and government subsidies—became the dominant model. In contrast, the US adopted a commercial broadcasting model, where free-to-air content was funded primarily through advertising revenue. As a result, American broadcast journalism developed in a more sensationalist direction compared to its European counterparts and became more susceptible to the influence of advertisers.

3.2.2.1 The Shift in Newspapers and Journalism's Arc

The emergence of broadcasting had a significant impact on the newspaper industries of many countries. The rise of radio and television advertising diverted substantial revenue away from newspapers, leading to declines in profitability and growing financial distress for many print outlets. This impact was especially pronounced in the United States, where commercial broadcasters—operating as for-profit enterprises—aggressively sought to expand their audiences. In the years following World War II, hundreds of newspapers that had fallen into financial difficulty were forced to cease publication. In many small and mid-sized cities, only one newspaper survived.

At the same time, major newspaper companies with relatively greater financial capacity began to grow through mergers and acquisitions.[8] The goal was to consolidate multiple papers under a single corporate umbrella to improve bargaining power in the advertising market against the growing dominance of broadcast media. As a result, large media corporations emerged, and by the 1960s, nearly one-third of all US newspapers were owned by newspaper chains—corporations that owned and operated multiple titles. This trend accelerated further, and by 2000, more than 90% of American newspapers were controlled by major newspaper chains (Abernathy, 2016).

To finance these acquisitions, newspaper chains raised significant amounts of capital through stock offerings. The number of shareholders—motivated by profit expectations—grew rapidly. This raised growing public concern over whether newspapers

[8] Although the US government maintained a strict antitrust policy, it often approved newspaper consolidations under joint operating agreements, provided that separate newsrooms were maintained to ensure diverse viewpoints.

would continue to fulfill their journalistic mission, or whether they would instead prioritize shareholder interests such as stock prices and dividends. These concerns became too widespread for newspaper companies to ignore.

Faced with public anxiety over the commercialization of journalism and with increased competition from broadcast news, many newspapers began to embrace investigative journalism as a strategic response. Leading newspaper chains such as The New York Times Company and Knight Ridder made major investments in their newsrooms. They recruited experienced investigative journalists and provided the institutional support needed to conduct in-depth reporting. Journalists with proven track records in producing impactful investigative stories became highly sought after, with their market value rising accordingly.

The investigative reports produced during this period were of significant social value and were difficult to replicate under the time constraints of broadcast news (Whitaker, 2019). As investigative journalism gained recognition and popularity among news consumers, it gradually spread beyond newspapers to include wire services and television broadcasters as well.

Reflecting its growing importance, the Pulitzer Prize, established in 1917, recognized investigative reporting in related categories from 1953. Some of the most iconic Pulitzer-winning investigations include the 1970 exposé on the My Lai Massacre[9] during the Vietnam War and the 1972 Watergate investigation that led to the resignation of President Richard Nixon. These and many other groundbreaking stories helped elevate the status and influence of newspapers in the second half of the 20th century.

Victims of the My Lai Massacre, March 1968

US Army photo by Ronald L. Haeberle. Public domain via Wikimedia Commons.

[9] Reporting on the concealed massacre of civilians in My Lai, a village in South Vietnam, in March 1968 during the Vietnam War. Seymour M. Hersh, who broke the story, was later recruited by The New York Times, where he went on to produce other major investigative reports, including the 1986 exposé on the Soviet Union's downing of Korean Air Flight 007 in 1983.

Investigative journalism not only reinforced the credibility of the press but also drew strong interest from news consumers. Over time, it became one of the most valued products in the American newspaper industry. Its influence extended internationally as well, with news organizations in other countries adopting similar practices. To this day, investigative journalism remains one of the most respected and impactful forms of news production worldwide.

As was the case with its initial rise and growing recognition, the decline of investigative journalism was also driven primarily by changes in the economic environment surrounding newspaper organizations. Toward the end of the 20th century, with the onset of the digital era and stagnation in the growth of the newspaper industry, news organizations began to lose interest in investing in investigative journalism. Above all, the high costs associated with employing top-tier journalists and supporting long-term investigative projects were increasingly seen by media executives as unattractive investments. Instead, it became more cost-effective to hire less experienced journalists to produce rapid reports on daily events that required little sustained investigation.

At the same time, as advertising became an increasingly dominant source of revenue, the influence of large corporate advertisers in the newspaper market grew substantially. In this context, investigative reporting that exposed corporate wrongdoing began to recede.

Commenting on this shift, journalism scholar Robert McChesney wrote in his 2004 book *The Problem of the Media* that "investigative journalism, once the hallmark of a vibrant press in a free society, now belongs on the endangered species list" (McChesney, 2004, p. 81). Similarly, Marion Just and colleagues observed in 2002 that "despite its value, investigative reporting is in steady decline" (Just, Levine and Regan, 2002).

Leading media outlets such as *The New York Times*, *The Washington Post*, and *The Guardian* have continued to support investigative reporting efforts. However, the surge of enthusiasm that once spread throughout print and broadcast media during the late 20th century had largely dissipated by the early 21st century in most parts of the world.

In response to this decline, a wave of nonprofit investigative journalism organizations emerged in the 21st century. Notable examples include *WikiLeaks* (founded in 2006), *ProPublica*[10] in the United States (2007), *Mediapart* in France (2008), and *Newstapa* in South Korea (2012). The rise of these nonprofit outlets—now familiar names in the field—cannot be separated from the broader retreat of investigative journalism once practiced by mainstream media.

[10] ProPublica is one of the most prominent nonprofit investigative journalism outlets today. Declaring independence from "money and power" in the public interest, it is funded by donor contributions. Its team of over 100 journalists produces investigative reports that are distributed free of charge to more than 90 partner media organizations including The New York Times, CNN, and The Los Angeles Times.

While many of these independent nonprofit organizations have achieved a degree of operational stability, most have not experienced substantial growth. Their financial foundations—reliant on donations and philanthropic support—have typically allowed them only to sustain small newsrooms. As a result, they have filled only a part of the void left by the withdrawal of investigative reporting from commercial newsrooms.

In sum, from the birth of journalism to the present, the emergence and decline of various journalistic forms have been shaped first and foremost by changes in the economic conditions facing the news media. From partisan journalism to professional journalism, from objectivity-based reporting to investigative journalism, every rise and fall has reflected the strategic responses of media organizations adapting to new market conditions. And because the structure of media markets differs across countries, journalism itself has taken distinct forms in different national contexts, reflecting the particular environments in which it has evolved.

3.2.2.2 *Coexistence and Growth*

The emergence of broadcasting brought dramatic change to news markets that had previously been dominated by newspapers alone. Among democratic nations, Western Europe and East Asia experienced relatively stable transitions, whereas the United States—the world's largest news market—underwent a far more competitive restructuring shaped by the logic of survival of the fittest. Still, both the new medium of broadcasting and the surviving newspapers continued to grow, as the overall mass media market expanded.

Fig. 3.2 and Fig. 3.3 illustrate the US case. In 1940, the total circulation of US newspapers averaged 36.75 million copies (with 41.13 million on weekdays and 32.37 million on weekends). By 1990, that figure had risen to 62.48 million. Subscription revenues grew from $1.604 billion in 1960 to $11.22 billion by 2003. Advertising revenues grew even faster, from $3.68 billion in 1960 to an all-time high of $49.435 billion in 2005 (Pew Research Center, Newspapers Fact Sheet; Fig. 3.3). These figures indicate that, up to the early 2000s, newspapers in the US were able to expand, consolidate, and coexist successfully with broadcasting, which at the time was considered a "new media" platform.

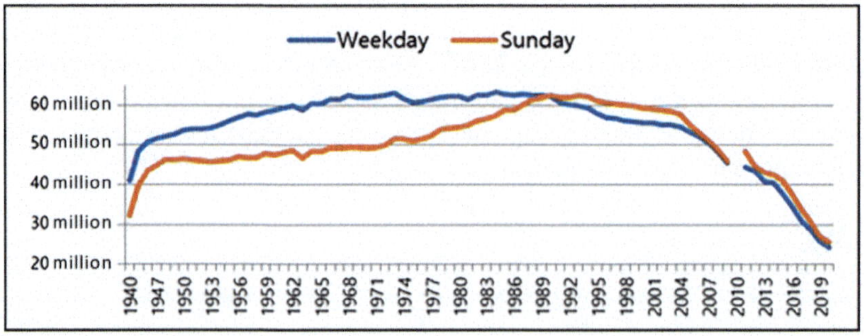

FIGURE 3.2

Changes in US newspaper circulation (1940–2020).

Pew Research Center, https://www.journalism.org/fact-sheet/newspapers/

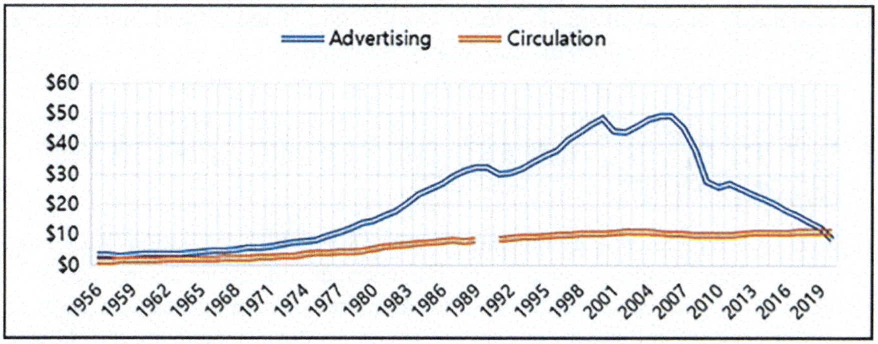

FIGURE 3.3

Trends in US Newspaper Industry Revenue (1956–2020, unit: billion USD).
Pew Research Center, https://www.journalism.org/fact-sheet/newspapers/

The nature of this coexistence varied across regions. Europe, with its predominantly public-service broadcasting systems, differed significantly from the United States, where commercial broadcasting prevailed. In countries where freedom of the press had only recently been restored, the emergence of broadcasting did not necessarily hinder the newspaper industry's recovery. Examples include post-fascist Germany and Italy, post-militarist Japan, and numerous developing nations emerging from colonialism or military rule.

In fact, while the American newspaper industry faced contraction, many newspapers in democratic countries across Europe and Asia were being newly established or revitalized. France's *Le Monde* (founded in December 1944) and Germany's *Die Welt* (April 1946) grew into internationally respected dailies. Japan's *Asahi Shimbun* and *Yomiuri Shimbun*, founded in the 19th century, each reached a circulation of around ten million by the late 20th century, making them the most widely read newspapers in the world. These outlets enjoyed a period of prosperity before the full onset of the digital media era. One reason newspapers in these countries sustained longer periods of growth was that the competitive pressure between broadcasting and newspapers was not as severe as it was in the United States.

Transnational media empires also began to emerge. In India, the Jain family, owners of *The Times of India*, launched other publications and regional editions, building a media empire that extended across Asia. In Australia, Rupert Murdoch inherited two newspapers in the 1950s and over the following four decades acquired major film studios, television networks, and leading newspapers in the United States and the United Kingdom, establishing what would become the largest global media conglomerate of its time.

As with all human and natural cycles, decline often begins at the peak. By the late 20th century, the rise of digital media swept across global news markets like a tsunami, disrupting the coexistence once enjoyed by newspapers and broadcasters.

Traditional media entered an era of tectonic shifts, in which neither scale nor even the pursuit of investigative journalism could ensure survival.

3.3 THE ICT REVOLUTION AND THE SEISMIC SHIFT IN THE NEWS MARKET

The digital information and communication technology (ICT) revolution, led by the internet, has shaken traditional media—both newspapers and broadcasting—at their very core. Neither newspapers, with centuries of history, nor broadcasting, with over half a century behind it, had ever experienced such upheaval. The decline of legacy media was universal; while its pace and sequence varied by country, the downward trajectory was unmistakable.

3.3.1 THE MISJUDGMENT AND FALL OF LEGACY MEDIA

As previously shown in Fig. 3.2, the US newspaper industry enjoyed decades of expansion before its sharp reversal. Circulation, which had peaked at 62.48 million in 1990, plummeted to 25.04 million by 2020—dropping below even 1940 levels. The rate of decline only accelerated: while annual losses averaged 500,000 copies before 2000, that figure rose to 1.5 million between 2005 and 2010, and surpassed 3 million per year after 2010.

These steep circulation losses soon translated into financial collapse. After reaching its peak in the early 2000s, subscription revenue began to fall, and advertising income—once the industry's main source of revenue—underwent a dramatic decline. Although digital advertising's share grew from 17% in 2011 to 39% in 2020, total advertising revenue (print and digital combined) continued to shrink (Pew Research Center, Newspapers Fact Sheet).

The 2008 global financial crisis further accelerated this downward spiral. Major newspaper chains filed for bankruptcy, and newsrooms downsized or closed entirely. According to researchers at the University of North Carolina at Chapel Hill, one in five US newspapers disappeared between 2004 and 2018, leaving behind vast "news deserts"[11] with little or no local coverage (Abernathy, 2018). Ultimately, the newspaper industry revenue fell from its $60.2 billion peak in 2005 to just $19.9 billion in 2020—only one-third of its former size. Advertising income, which had taken 30 years to grow from $8 billion in 1975 to its peak, returned to 1970s levels in just half that time.

While television has fared somewhat better, the proportion of people who receive news through newspapers and television has declined steadily. According to the

[11] According to more recent data from the same institution, average weekday circulation—including both print and digital editions—fell to approximately 20.9 million in 2022, down 8% from the previous year and 32% from 2017. Sunday circulation declined by 10% year-over-year, indicating continued structural contraction in the industry.

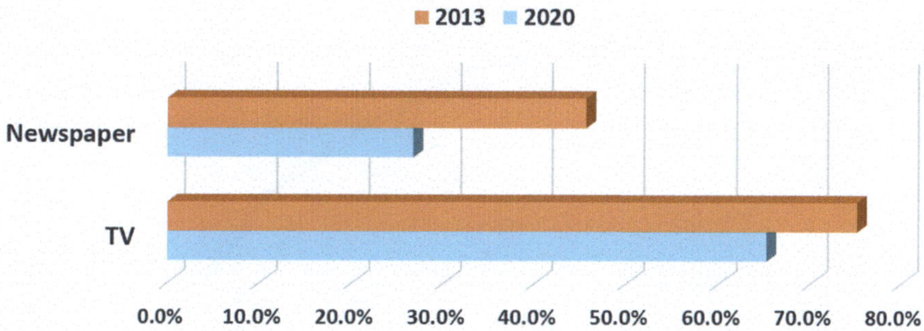

FIGURE 3.4

Trends in newspaper and TV news usage (average across 35 major countries).
Reuters Institute for the Study of Journalism, Digital News Report 2013; 2020. https://reutersinstitute.politics.ox.ac.uk/sites/default/files/2020-06/DNR_2020_FINAL.pdf

Reuters Institute for the Study of Journalism's Digital News Report, in 35 major countries surveyed, the percentage of people who reported getting news from TV and newspapers in the past week fell from 75% and 46% in 2013 to 65% and 27%, respectively, in 2020 (Fig. 3.4). This unprecedented shift was merely a matter of time across the globe. Even in Japan—long considered the final stronghold of traditional media—the daily circulation of newspapers dropped from 53.71 million in 2000 to 35.09 million in 2020, a decline of more than one-third (Fig. 3.5).[12] In place of traditional media, the space has been overtaken by real-time news from platforms like Google, Facebook, blogs, podcasts, and YouTube.

Despite the growing dominance of digital media, many believed at the turn of the 21st century that newspapers and broadcasting would continue to coexist with the new platforms. Few anticipated the extent or intensity of the disruption that would follow. Neither industry seriously entertained the possibility that new media might actually replace the old. Even those who expected peaceful coexistence rarely foresaw the scale and intensity of the disruption that would accompany it.

In the 1990s, as the internet emerged as a new tool of civilization, most newspapers and broadcasters offered their content online for free. The disruptive potential of digital substitution (Gentzkow, 2007) was not fully understood; traditional media companies focused instead on the promise of new advertising revenue streams. However, this hope proved to be little more than wishful thinking. The idea that increased digital consumption would inevitably lead to decreased demand for print

[12] Only Indian newspapers—representing the world's second-largest newspaper market—temporarily defied this trend. From 40 million copies in 2006, their circulation surged to over 60 million in 2016 across 8,000 titles. However, even in developing countries, the decline of traditional media is only a matter of time.

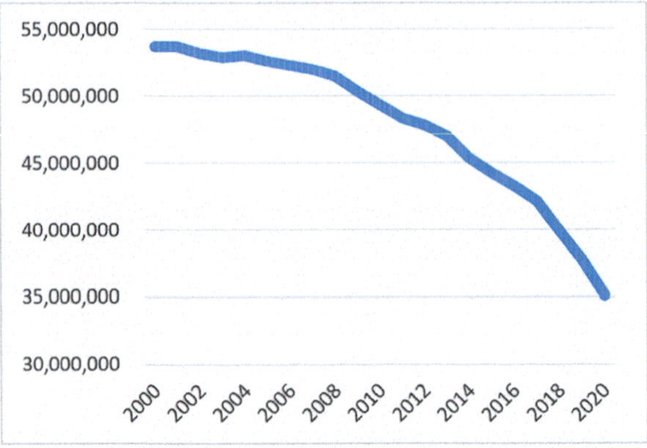

FIGURE 3.5

Daily newspaper circulation in Japan (as of October each year).

The Japan Newspaper Publishers & Editors Association. (n.d.). Newspaper circulation: Total average circulation of newspapers in Japan. Retrieved May 29, 2025, from https://www.pressnet.or.jp/english/data/circulation/circulation01.php

and linear broadcast was poorly grasped. Across the globe, many journalists and executives believed that traditional media would ultimately survive. They mistook subjective optimism for rational prediction. It did not take long for that illusion to collapse.[13]

Digital ICTs transformed daily life and reshaped how people consume media. These changes have steadily eroded the material foundations of newspapers and broadcasting. As the media infrastructure weakened, so too did the superstructure: the journalistic paradigms that had defined an era—objective journalism, professional journalism, and investigative journalism—began to fade into the background.

3.3.2 THE VICIOUS CYCLE OF SHRINKING IN LEGACY MEDIA

Many traditional media companies failed to recognize the substitutive relationship between online and offline news—and paid a steep price. Though many later regretted having rushed to provide their content online for free, by then it was too late. Free internet services may have been necessary to expand influence, but had media executives foreseen today's landscape, they might have opted for collusion (paid services) rather than competition (free services). However, long accustomed to the dominant

[13] The growing demand for online news has accompanied a sharp decline in the demand for print newspapers. By 2020, the average weekday circulation of daily newspapers in the US and Japan had dropped to 44% and 65%, respectively, of their 2000 levels. This trend continues to accelerate.

power of mass media, traditional media were blinded by complacency and failed to anticipate the approaching digital future.

In the US alone, the 1990s saw the rise of major internet portals, beginning with America Online (AOL) in 1991, followed by Netscape, MSN, Lycos, Yahoo, and eventually Google. E-commerce platforms such as Amazon and eBay also emerged in the late 1990s, followed by the rise of social network services like Facebook in the 2000s. These digital platforms steadily pulled audiences away from newspapers and television toward their own ecosystems. Around 2010, in many parts of the world, online news consumption began to overtake that of print newspapers.

In digital spaces, users freely exchanged information and opinions. Anyone with content—not necessarily large printing presses or broadcast infrastructure—could compete with established media. The era of mass media dominance began to fade. As audiences moved online, advertisers followed. Globally, platforms like Google and Facebook began to siphon off the advertisers that had once sustained traditional media. According to the market research firm eMarketer, in 2017, Google and Facebook together accounted for approximately 60% of all US digital advertising revenue and captured 99% of that year's growth in the digital ad market (Whitaker, 2019).

Meanwhile, newsrooms—an indicator directly tied to the quality of journalism—saw steep cutbacks. In the US, between 2008 and 2018, total newsroom employment was cut in half. Newspaper newsroom staff, in particular, declined from a peak of 74,410 in 2006 to just 30,820 in 2020 (Fig. 3.6). If the number of media outlets signals diversity of opinion, then newsroom size correlates with news quality. The sharp

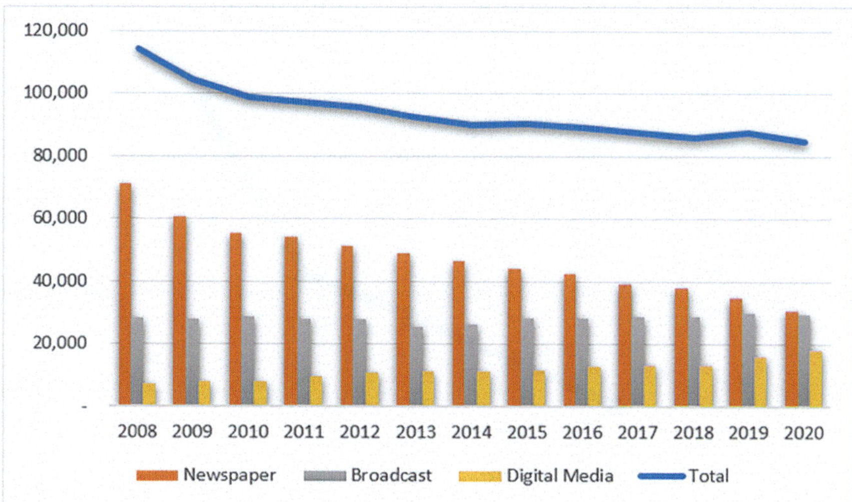

FIGURE 3.6

Trends in newsroom employment in the US news industry.

Pew Research Center, https://www.journalism.org/fact-sheet/newspapers/

decline in staffing raised concerns not only about the quality of journalism but also about the long-term viability of legacy media, which had long claimed superiority in quality.

This marked the first time since the advent of modern newspapers that newsroom journalists themselves began to disappear. When computer typesetting systems were introduced, traditional typesetters and compositors—those who selected type and assembled printing plates—were eliminated. Yet at that time, newsroom staff were unaffected or even expanded, and the quality of newspapers actually improved. Today, however, the reduction in newsroom personnel is directly resulting in the deterioration of journalistic quality. A vicious cycle has set in: "shrinking newsroom staff → declining quality → reduced demand (and revenue) → budget cuts → further staff reductions."

This growing cycle of decline suggests that journalism itself has entered an unpredictable era. The gradual disappearance of journalists—the core of the newsroom—signals not just an economic crisis but a structural and existential one for journalism as a profession. French economist Julia Cagé observed that "in the digital age, news organizations are desperately chasing revenue just to stay alive" (Cagé, 2016). Media scholar Anya Schiffrin similarly noted, "We had hoped that more competition would lead to better journalism—but the opposite has occurred" (Schiffrin, 2018).

These diagnoses highlight the severity of the economic unraveling that has accompanied the digital age—not only for legacy media institutions, but also for the traditional forms of journalism they supported, such as investigative reporting and objectivity-based journalism. As this economic foundation collapses, trust in journalism itself continues to erode (see Fig. 3.7).

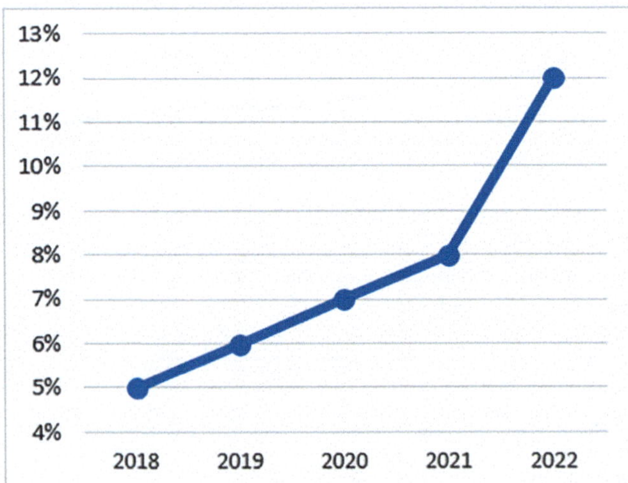

FIGURE 3.7

Percentage of news disengagement (2018–2022) (*Average across 46 countries surveyed by the Reuters Institute*).

Choi, J. & Park, Y. (2022). Digital news report 2022: Korea.

3.3.3 IS COEXISTENCE BETWEEN OLD AND NEW MEDIA POSSIBLE?

Today, most news consumers have moved away from print newspapers and traditional broadcasts, favoring online sites and platforms like YouTube for news and informational content. In 2018 over 200 million users visited European news websites each month. The *Daily Mail* and *The Guardian* led with around 20 million and 16 million monthly visitors, respectively. Turkey's *Hürriyet* and *Milliyet*, as well as Germany's *Bild*, also exceeded 10 million monthly users. The trend is similar in most other countries.

Amid this shift, a few global news companies—such as the Guardian Media Group and the New York Times Company—have successfully adapted to digital business models, acquiring substantial numbers of paid online subscribers. Since the mid-2010s, these companies have seen digital subscription revenue (including donations) surpass that of advertising and print circulation, and this trend continues to grow.

However, the success of *The New York Times* and *The Guardian* can be attributed to several conditions that are often overlooked: (1) they operate on a global scale beyond the confines of a single national market; (2) they streamlined operations by divesting noncore subsidiaries[14] and focusing resources on digital and flagship brands; and (3) despite the growth in digital subscriptions, declines in advertising revenue mean total revenue still falls short of their peak years.

The situation is vastly different for most traditional media companies, which lack the scale and strategic positioning of these leading outlets. These organizations continue to struggle for viability across the globe. Two structural reasons help explain this bleak outlook:

First, when broadcasting entered the news market once dominated by print, there was still a clear distinction between traditional news content and entertainment or educational programming. Broadcast content outside of news did not directly compete with newspapers. In the digital era, however, the convergence of text, audio, and video has created a multidimensional competitive environment in which all forms of old and new media now contend. As illustrated in Fig. 3.8, the boundary between traditional news and entertainment has become increasingly blurred. At the same time, as shown in Fig. 3.7, the number of individuals—especially among the younger generation—who are disengaged from news is growing.

Second, the digital realm houses virtually all past and present informational content, accessible at any time. Broadcasting has become merely one subset of the larger video content market, which is now fully consumer-centered. As media storage,

[14] The New York Times Company, the parent company of The New York Times, was once a diversified media conglomerate that owned as many as 18 newspapers—including the International Herald Tribune and The Boston Globe—as well as several radio stations. However, it has since streamlined its holdings, selling The Boston Globe in 2011 and ceasing publication of the International Herald Tribune in 2013, to concentrate its efforts on The New York Times.

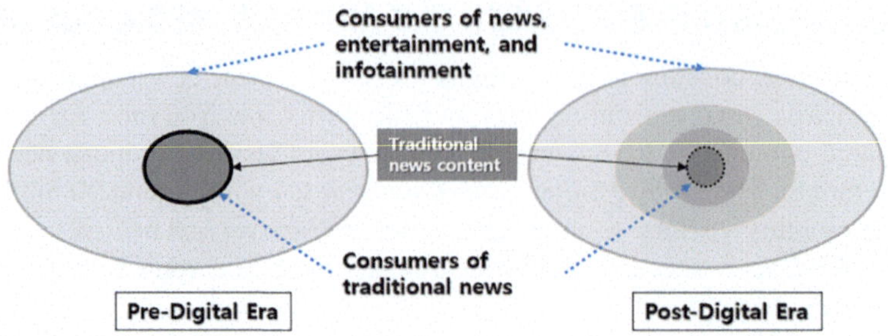

FIGURE 3.8

Changes in content consumption patterns.

distribution, and consumption have shifted to prioritize user control and accessibility, it is unclear how long mass media—rooted in supply-side logic—can remain viable.

Although there is significant pessimism regarding the coexistence of traditional and new media, coexistence remains possible—provided that legacy media can successfully adapt to this transformed media consumption environment. Looking back to the 20th century, newspapers initially stood alone, and later coexisted with broadcasting. As discussed in Section 3.2.2, newspapers managed this coexistence by "scaling up" and embracing investigative journalism.

To coexist with new media powered by digital technologies, traditional media must once again transform. While it is difficult to predict the exact nature of this transformation, it will certainly be driven by economic imperatives.

3.3.4 THE FUTURE OF NEWS MEDIA SHAPED BY ECONOMIC FORCES

Economic drivers in the news market have continuously reshaped the structure and conditions of the media industry. They have not only given rise to journalism—the normative framework for producing and distributing news—but also driven its transformation. Modern journalism, in particular, emerged from the foundation of mass media, making the decline of mass media synonymous with a crisis in journalism.

The core problem facing mass media in the digital era is the collapse of its business model. The effective price of content has fallen to nearly zero, and once prices drop, they rarely recover. Although many news organizations have attempted to implement paywalls and monetize digital content, only a handful—such as *The New York Times*—have achieved anything close to meaningful success. Warning lights have long been flashing for advertising revenue, the main source of income for mass media. For most of the 20th century, newspapers and broadcasters earned revenue by exposing ads to audiences of hundreds of thousands or even millions. Today, however, more effective and diverse digital advertising platforms dominate, leaving little room for traditional media to reclaim their former glory.

The structural reason for all of this is the shift from a "linear two-sided market" dominated by mass media to a "multidimensional multisided market" led by digital platform companies (Fig. 3.9). Emerging technologies like artificial intelligence,

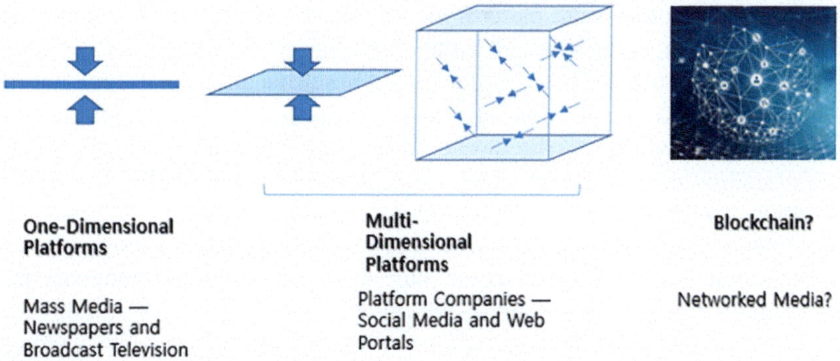

FIGURE 3.9

Evolution of news and information platforms.

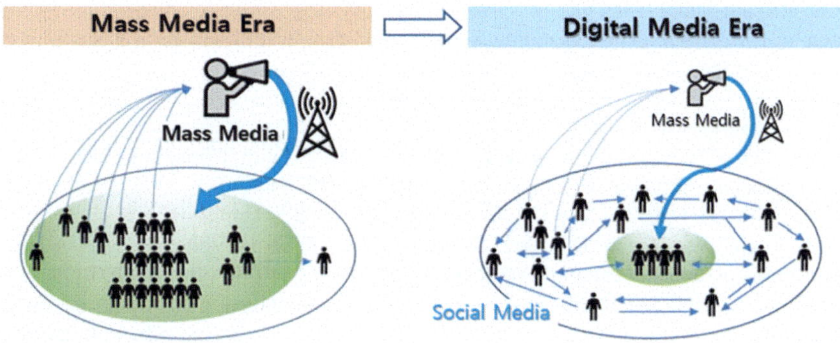

FIGURE 3.10

The era of "one-to-many" and "many-to-many" communication.

blockchain, and the metaverse continue to evolve and disrupt the news industry. Although we cannot yet see where these developments will lead, it is clear that they will continue to reshape how information is gathered, stored, processed, and distributed.

Despite these profound changes, most journalism scholars and practitioners still regard traditional media as the most credible news providers. This is largely because, while numerous new players have entered the news market, none have yet matched the institutional capacity or credibility of legacy media. Nevertheless, if shrinking newsrooms and declining competitiveness are not reversed, the continued erosion of traditional media's relevance seems inevitable.

In the digital age—characterized by many-to-many communication facilitated by social media—the one-to-many model that defined mass media is no longer as effective (Fig. 3.10). This shift in communication dynamics further weakens the role of legacy media.

History offers a consistent pattern: the printing press gave birth to newspapers, telecommunications enabled broadcasting, and digital ICTs opened the era of the internet and social media. News producers did not drive any of these revolutions—they simply adapted. Those who successfully adjusted to technological and economic shifts survived; those who did not faded into obscurity. The same holds true today. For traditional news media of the 20th century to survive in the 21st, they must clearly understand and respond to the evolving economic drivers of the news market. This insight is even more fundamental than theoretical discussions of journalism itself. What must remain constant is not journalism per se, but our understanding of the economic forces that create and transform it.

REFERENCES

Abernathy, P.M., 2016. "The Rise of a New Media Baron and the Emerging Threat of News Deserts." Center for Innovation & Sustainability in Local Media. University of North Carolina at Chapel Hill.

Abernathy, P.M., 2018. "The Expanding News Desert." Center for Innovation & Sustainability in Local Media. University of North Carolina at Chapel Hill.

Balzac, H. de (1981). Monographie de la presse parisienne. Paris: J. E. Hallier/Albin Michel.

J. Cagé, Saving the Media. (2016),

Gentzkow, M., 2007. "Valuing New Goods in a Model with Complementarity: Online Newspapers.". American Economic Review 97 (3), 713–744.

Hamilton, J.T., 2004. All the News That's Fit to Sell. Princeton University Press.

Just, M., Levine, R., Regan, K., 2002. Investigative journalism despite the odds: watchdog reporting continues to decline. Columbia Journalism Review 41 (4), 102–105.

R. McChesney, 2004. The Problem of the Media: US Communication Politics in the Twenty-First Century.

Pew Research Center, Newspapers Fact Sheet. Available from: https://www.pewresearch.org/journalism/fact-sheet/newspapers/.

Posner, Richard A., 1980. A theory of primitive society, with special reference to law. The Journal of Law and Economics 23 (1), 1–53. 0022–2186. https://doi.org/10.1086/466951.

Reuters Institute for the Study of Journalism, 2013. Digital News Report 2013. Retrieved from https://www.digitalnewsreport.org/.

Reuters Institute for the Study of Journalism, 2020. Digital News Report 2020. https://reuters-institute.politics.ox.ac.uk/sites/default/files/2020-06/DNR_2020_FINAL.pdf.

Reuters Institute for the Study of Journalism, 2022. Digital News Report 2022. Retrieved from https://www.digitalnewsreport.org/.

Schiffrin, Anya, 2018. Introduction to special issue on media capture. Journalism 19 (8), 1033–1042. 1464–8849. https://doi.org/10.1177/1464884917725167.

E. Whitaker, 2019. What History Teaches Us: How Newspapers Have Evolved to Meet Market Demands. Available from: https://www.cislm.org/what-history-teaches-us-how-newspapers-have-evolved-to-meet-market-demands/.

CHAPTER

The Role of News Media for Democracy

4

CHAPTER OUTLINE

Our Republic and its press will rise or fall together.[1]
—Joseph Pulitzer

What would the world look like without news media? In such a case, individuals would have to personally observe and gather all the information necessary for their lives. While this may be feasible in a small village society, it is virtually impossible in modern society. Even if individuals or small groups attempted to collect information themselves, there would be clear limits to what they could gather, and sharing it with others would not be easy. The process of acquiring and transmitting information is riddled with numerous obstacles.

[1] This quote is widely attributed to Joseph Pulitzer and has been frequently cited in journalism discourse. However, no definitive primary source has been identified.

The Economics of News Media. DOI: http://dx.doi.org/10.1016/B978-0-443-45044-0.00013-1

Imagine trying to find a lost child in a massive shopping mall so crowded that there is barely room to move—bumping into people, jostled from all sides, and constantly pushed around. The amount of friction would be overwhelming. In a similar vein, economists refer to the effort that individuals must exert to acquire and exchange information without mass media as *information frictions*.[2]

News media dramatically reduce these information frictions. By collecting and distributing information on behalf of individuals, news media significantly lower the effort required to obtain information. Moreover, the degree of information frictions is critically influenced by the level of development in information and communication technology (ICT).[3] The more advanced the ICT infrastructure, the fewer individuals suffer from information frictions. Thus as ICT continues to evolve, the frictions individuals face will decline, and their dependence on news media will likely diminish. However, for now, the magnitude of information frictions that would arise in the absence of news media remains enormous. Accordingly, news media are still an indispensable part of individual and societal functioning.

Starting with this chapter, we examine various economic theories and empirical studies on news media and news markets that help reduce information frictions, organized by topic and area. As a first step, this chapter focuses on the role that news and journalism play in democratic political processes.

Information conveyed through the news is essential not only for individual survival but also for the effective functioning of society. At the societal level, shared information enables collective action and is indispensable for members of the community engaged in decision-making. News, by delivering such information, serves as the very foundation that sustains democratic systems.

Scholars and journalists have made this point. Herbert Gans, a renowned sociologist and former president of the American Sociological Association, stated on the first page of his book *Democracy and the News* (2003) that "the democratic process can only be truly meaningful if these citizens are informed. Journalism's job is to inform them." Anthony Lewis (1927–2013), a two-time Pulitzer Prize–winning columnist for *The New York Times*, similarly argued that "The theory of democracy is that the citizens are the ultimate sovereign. But in today's world, individuals cannot personally observe events and reach decisions in a forum, as in ancient Athens. They necessarily depend on the press to be informed."[4] Jack Fuller, another Pulitzer Prize–winning journalist, stated that "The central purpose of journalism is to tell the truth so that people will have the information that they need to be sovereign."[5]

[2] The concept of "information frictions" was first introduced by George Stigler (1961), in a paper titled "The Economics of Information."

[3] Compared to ancient times—when media consisted only of the spoken word, transportation relied on horses at best, and communication technology was limited to signal fires or drums—the level of information frictions people experience in today's digital age has decreased dramatically.

[4] Lewis (1997, p. 62), as also discussed in Gans (2003, p. 1).

[5] Quoted in Gans (2003, p. 1).

Economists have made similar points. Joseph Stiglitz, the 2001 Nobel laureate in economics, described the news media as part of the system of checks and balances essential to democracy (Stiglitz, 2017). Giacomo Corneo also noted that news enables collective decisions within society (Corneo, 2006).

These are far from the only voices in this field. Numerous scholars have studied the relationship between democracy and news or journalism, and they are unanimous in asserting that journalism has a profound impact on democracy and that "democracy without news" is unimaginable. The fundamental role of the news media is to provide sovereign citizens with the information they need to make informed decisions. This function is essential for the proper operation of democratic systems.

Before examining the economic theories and empirical research on the role of news media in democracy, let us first consider what sets the economics approach apart from other social sciences in this area.

4.1 THE ROLE OF MEDIA IN THE POLITICAL PROCESS: THEORETICAL DEVELOPMENTS AND ECONOMIC APPROACHES

In the 1930s, fascist dictators, such as Adolf Hitler in Germany and Benito Mussolini in Italy, effectively used the media for political propaganda. Radio usage was rapidly spreading at the time. These circumstances led sociologists and communication scholars to begin investigating the influence of mass media on political processes. Somewhat surprisingly, early research findings concluded that mass media had either no significant effect or only a limited one in changing people's minds. These results gave rise to the interpretation that the role of media was not so much to change people's opinions but to reinforce preexisting attitudes.

A representative study was conducted by Lazarsfeld et al. (1944), scholars of sociology and communication, who surveyed approximately 3000 voters in Ohio during the 1940 US presidential election to examine whether—and why—their initial candidate preferences had changed. The results showed that while radio and print media did have some direct influence on voters' choices, the overall magnitude of the impact was small.

A few years later, psychologists (Hovland, Lumsdaine and Sheffield, 1949) conducted a study on the effectiveness of wartime propaganda during World War II. In line with Lazarsfeld et al.'s earlier findings, they concluded that the propaganda films distributed by the US military failed to significantly influence either soldiers or civilians.

Adopting a more specific perspective, later research suggested that media can have a substantial impact on individuals. One of the most well-known theories from this wave is the agenda-setting theory, developed by journalism scholars Maxwell McCombs and Donald Shaw. This theory posits that media coverage of certain issues makes people perceive those issues as important (McCombs and Shaw, 1972). The priming effect—proposed by Shanto Iyengar and Donald R. Kinder, which holds that people evaluate political actors based on issues emphasized in the media—can be seen as conceptually aligned with agenda-setting theory (Iyengar and Kinder, 1987).

Equally influential is the framing theory, which argues that news media shape public interpretation and opinion by presenting issues within specific frames. This theory builds upon sociologist Erving Goffman's work on "frame analysis" (Goffman 1974). For example, during the COVID-19 pandemic and the height of social distancing measures, public reactions to mass rallies held by labor or religious groups could differ depending on whether such events were framed as matters of "freedom of assembly" or "public safety." According to the framing theory, the frame employed by media outlets influences how audiences interpret the news and form opinions.

The implications of these theories can be summed up by a well-known quote: "The press may not be successful much of the time in telling people what to think, but it is stunningly successful in telling its readers what to think about" (Cohen, 1963, p. 13).

In the study of the media's role in democratic political processes, disciplines such as sociology, political science, psychology, communication, and media studies have produced rich and extensive bodies of research. Economic studies on media have built upon these foundations, but they also exhibit distinct characteristics. Andrea Prat and David Strömberg, two leading scholars in the political economy of media, describe these characteristics as follows (Prat and Strömberg, 2013). While the explanations may initially seem complex, their meaning will become clearer as we proceed through this book.

First, economic research tends to focus on the informational role of mass media. Information influences people's voting behavior, and most of the information that voters rely on during elections is provided by news media.

Second, economists emphasize the (economic) outcomes resulting from information provision. Unlike scholars in other disciplines who may focus on political competition or institutional dynamics, economists are primarily interested in tangible outcomes such as policy changes and the provision of public goods that voters care about.

Third, economists often use major tools from modern economics—such as contract theory,[6] game theory, and decision theory[7]—to model and analyze interactions

[6] Contract theory studies optimal decision-making and contract structures in situations involving information asymmetry between parties. It posits that social welfare improves when contracts are transparent and satisfy all involved parties. A well-known application is the principal-agent problem, where the agent—who promises to act on behalf of the principal—may act in self-interest due to having more information. In political economy and media economics, voters (or news consumers) are typically modeled as principals, while politicians act as agents.

[7] Decision theory provides mathematical and statistical tools for identifying optimal choices under uncertainty by assessing the probabilities of different states of the world and the expected utilities associated with each action.

among the agents involved in and around the news market, including media organizations, voters, and politicians. These theories provide a concise framework for understanding complex strategic interactions.

Fourth, in empirical research, economists emphasize identifying causal relationships that stem from the media market. For instance, they investigate how the entry of a new media outlet or the launch of a new news channel affects political and social outcomes.

4.2 IS MORE INFORMATION ALWAYS BENEFICIAL TO PEOPLE?

Is the principle that "more is better" always true? One of the first questions raised by economists studying the informational role of mass media—a question that may initially sound naïve—was whether citizens actually benefit from having access to more information. Put differently, should the so-called right to know be satisfied without limitation? While poverty in material goods or information is generally painful, an overabundance of either can produce side effects.

The theoretical foundation economists use to assess the value of "more information" is contract theory, notably advanced by Finnish economist Bengt Holmström, the 2016 Nobel laureate in economics. In his seminal work, Holmström (1979) mathematically proved that in any situation involving moral hazard on the part of the agent, the more information the principal has about the agent's performance, the more the agent's economic rent—that is, the extra payoff the agent can extract thanks to private information—can be reduced, thereby increasing the principal's benefit.

Elected officials and politicians are, in effect, agents entrusted by the sovereign public. Thus the economic insights into moral hazard—where agents use private information unknown to the principal to maximize their own benefit—align closely with *the principle of open government*,[8] which holds that all government activity should be open to citizen and media scrutiny. These insights help explain both the effectiveness of information provided by news media and the economic rationale behind the emergence of freedom of information laws in democratic societies.

Of course, even under this principle of openness, not all information qualifies as appropriate for disclosure. Detailed personal information about ordinary citizens or data that could jeopardize national interests cannot be deemed suitable for public release. If the utility of information does not accrue entirely to voters, but instead can be used by others in ways that threaten the public interest or the well-being of citizens, disclosure should not be the default. This includes information that falls under

[8] The concept of open government was first codified in 18th-century Sweden. In the United States, the Freedom of Information Act (FOIA), enacted in 1966, formalized the principle of open government.

John Stuart Mill's "harm principle" or the US Supreme Court's "rule of clear and present danger,"[9] as well as information that may benefit hostile states.

Nonetheless, in advanced democracies, there is a strong political will to promote information disclosure and transparency. In these societies, even when exceptions to disclosure are recognized as unavoidable, there is a broadly shared social consensus that such exceptions must not be exploited as a cover for moral hazard by political agents such as government officials and politicians.

Then, if we exclude such sensitive or potentially harmful information, is it always beneficial for citizens to have access to more information? Economists have gone beyond the general belief that more information is better and have sought to answer this question more concretely. They have analyzed whether the timing and content of information actually help realize representative democracy. Their conclusion is that some information may, in fact, harm democratic outcomes.

This insight originated from a study by Eric Maskin and Tirole (2004), Nobel laureates in economics in 2007 and 2014, respectively, who examined whether public responsibilities should be entrusted to elected or unelected officials. According to their findings, although elected officials often possess more information than voters, they tend to ignore information unknown to voters and make policy decisions based only on what voters know. This is because their primary objective is reelection, and they try to curry favor with voters to serve their own interests. The power of voters to elect officials ends up encouraging pandering behavior. However, Maskin and Tirole point out that when politicians adopt policies designed to appease voters rather than to pursue the best outcomes, the result is clearly detrimental to the public.

Is there a way to reduce the risk of politicians pandering to voters? Andrea Prat, a leading scholar in the political economy of media, has offered an answer. According to Prat (2005), it is always beneficial for voters to know the "outcomes" of political actions, but it may be harmful for them to be informed about actions that are still in progress and whose outcomes are not yet known.

Prat argues that the more voters know about the performance resulting from politicians' actions, the better. This allows voters to evaluate politicians based on the utility they generate. However, when actions are still underway and their outcomes are unknown, disclosing such information may induce politicians to pander to voters in harmful ways. Politicians, by nature, want to appear competent in the eyes of voters. When certain information does not help them project competence—and when voters are unaware of it—politicians may deliberately ignore such information.

For example, if a politician knows that the likelihood of an enemy state possessing chemical weapons is low, but voters do not, the politician may choose to ignore this information and initiate a war, later publicizing a military victory. The US escalation of the Vietnam War—following the fabricated 1964 Gulf of Tonkin

[9] The "rule of clear and present danger" was established by US Supreme Court Justice Oliver W. Holmes (1841–1935) in 1919 as a standard for limiting freedom of speech or the press. It is based on John Stuart Mill's "harm principle," which asserts that individual liberty may be restricted to prevent harm to others.

incident[10]—and the 2003 Iraq War—justified by false claims about weapons of mass destruction[11]—are both examples of such behavior.

Similarly, in quite a few cases, when investigative authorities such as prosecutors or police leak allegations to the public—before guilt or innocence has been determined or even before formal charges have been filed—such actions can be understood in the same context, particularly when they appear aimed at shaping public perception of guilt in advance of judicial judgment or to serve institutional or political interests.

When politicians' actions are revealed to voters before outcomes are known, two adverse effects follow: (1) all politicians pander to voters, making it difficult for voters to meaningfully compare their performance, and (2) pandering by politicians typically results in socially undesirable outcomes. These risks are especially pronounced when there is a long lag between the disclosure of an action and the realization of its consequences.[12]

The economic insight that disclosing political actions before their results are known can be harmful is supported by actual institutional practices. In Sweden, which has the longest history of freedom of information laws, citizens do not have the right to access information about a government decision before it is implemented. Other countries with such laws similarly allow exemptions for information related to ongoing decision-making processes.

In short, when politicians compete for public attention, information about the outcomes of their actions is always beneficial to voters. But information about ongoing actions with unknown outcomes can encourage pandering and ultimately harm voter interests.

That said, economists also emphasize that over the long run, all information should eventually be disclosed. Even when action-related information is withheld to reduce pandering, the duration of nondisclosure should not be unnecessarily prolonged. According to theories by Bengt Holmström, Oliver Hart, Eric Maskin, and Jean Tirole, with few exceptions, more information is almost always beneficial to citizens. This principle is reflected in real-world institutions: freedom of information

[10] In August 1964, the US government claimed that the USS Maddox had been attacked by North Vietnamese forces in the Gulf of Tonkin. This led to a full-scale war, beginning with the bombing of North Vietnam in February 1965. However, later declassified documents showed that the alleged second attack had been misrepresented. Despite the war's devastating toll—including millions of deaths and the eventual US withdrawal in 1973—President Lyndon Johnson won reelection just 3 months after the announcement, defeating Barry Goldwater by 486 to 52 in the Electoral College.

[11] In 2002, President George W. Bush claimed that Iraq possessed weapons of mass destruction, a claim backed by CIA reports. In March 2003, the United States, United Kingdom, and Australia launched a war against Iraq, but no such weapons were found. A 2016 inquiry concluded the intelligence had been exaggerated or manipulated. The war caused massive casualties, yet Bush was reelected in 2004, defeating John Kerry.

[12] Based on insights from economists like Prat, one might argue that when the outcome of political actions is uncertain, media reports—especially those involving unproven allegations—should remind the public of the presumption of innocence. Yet this is often neglected.

laws, open government initiatives, and efforts to minimize exceptions to disclosure. Numerous empirical studies by economists also confirm the benefits of more information.

At the same time, the idea that "more information" about politicians and governments benefits voters also implies that politicians and governments have incentives to reduce the information available to the public. Indeed, the phenomenon of media capture, in which political actors suppress negative coverage by the press, arises from precisely such incentives. Media capture is discussed in detail in Chapter 9, "Media Capture and Media Power," and Chapter 10, "Empirical Studies: Various Media Capture Cases Around the Globe."

4.3 IS MEDIA BIAS HARMFUL TO DEMOCRACY?

What impact does the supply of biased news by media outlets have on the main actors of democratic systems—namely, politicians and voters?[13] Chan and Suen (2009) have studied how media bias affects the political positioning and policy choices of political parties. They assume that news media provide two distinct types of information that help voters make decisions. The first type consists of fact-based, straightforward reporting of policies proposed by political parties. In this format, there is minimal room for manipulation or distortion by media bias. The second type includes more interpretive content—such as background analysis and critical commentary on party policies—which is harder to verify and more prone to reflecting the ideological or political bias of the media.

According to their findings, when only the first, bias-free type of news is available, political parties tend to differentiate their platforms as much as possible in order to gain voter support. This leads to polarization, as parties adopt increasingly extreme positions. In contrast, when the second type of news—including critique and analysis—is also available, biased news can still perform a useful social function. The presence of critical (albeit biased) reporting gives parties an incentive to adopt more centrist policies in order to avoid harsh criticism. Chan and Suen therefore argued that increasing the number of independent news voices—those not controlled by political powers or parties—is one way to encourage more moderate policy positions. In short, the more critical and biased news coverage there is, the less political polarization occurs.[14]

The implication of their argument is that even biased reporting is not necessarily harmful to the democratic decision-making process. A similar perspective is shared by Duggan and Martinelli (2011), who argue that "balanced news media that provide equal coverage of all issues can, in fact, be worse for voters than partisan outlets."

[13] Theoretical and empirical discussions on media bias are addressed in detail in Chapters 5 through 8.

[14] Chan and Suen note that this role of the media is subtle and may be difficult to verify through empirical research.

In an earlier study, Chan and Suen (2008) had already suggested that biased news media can paradoxically lead political parties to adopt less-biased policies. Their model suggests three key mechanisms: (1) political parties are primarily influenced by media outlets that share similar ideological leanings, (2) "mildly partisan" media are more effective than "completely neutral" media in reducing the partisanship of political platforms, and (3) extremely biased media have little impact on aggregate political outcomes. Moreover, the two scholars argue that having a diverse array of media outlets with different ideological biases is desirable, as it allows news consumers with varying beliefs to find sources that match their preferences. For example, while liberals may see Fox News as heavily biased, many conservative viewers regard it as a trustworthy source. In the absence of Fox News, these consumers might seek even more extreme right-wing media or cease consuming news altogether.

By contrast, Bernhardt et al. (2008) offer a more cautionary perspective. They argue that politically polarized news consumers and biased media can lead voters to select the "worst" rather than the "lesser evil" in elections. They present the following scenario: left-wing consumers derive greater utility from reading favorable news about left-wing politicians and unfavorable news about right-wing politicians. Consequently, left-leaning media avoid reporting negative stories about left-wing candidates. However, left-wing consumers are aware of this omission and assume that left-wing politicians are, on average, as corrupt as typical politicians. Ironically, this dynamic enables a more corrupt left-wing politician to win an election because the lack of negative reporting causes voters to perceive him or her as no more corrupt than less corrupt alternatives. In some cases, a relatively clean left-wing politician may even lose due to the absence of information highlighting their integrity. The same logic applies symmetrically to right-wing consumers and media.

In this way, partisan news consumption and media polarization can eliminate the electoral distinction between more and less corrupt politicians. Bernhardt and his coauthors contend that "partisan media fail to treat the politicians they support in proportion to their actual levels of corruption," thereby distorting voter choices. They further argue that such distortions are more likely when ideological preferences among news consumers are more polarized. Applied to real-world contexts, this suggests that landslide victories by either left-wing or right-wing parties in legislative elections may reflect a highly imbalanced ideological distribution among voters at the time. These electoral outcomes may also result in a higher number of corrupt candidates winning seats within the victorious party.

Finally, Prat and Strömberg (2013) have emphasized that the quantity of information voters receive depends on how media bias is expressed. According to them, when the media display bias by suppressing unwelcome news or providing false information, the informational content available to voters decreases. On the other hand, when media exhibit bias by focusing on issues and facts that resonate with their audience, the amount of information voters acquire increases.

4.4 EFFECTS OF NEWS CONSUMPTION ON POLITICAL BEHAVIOR AND ACCOUNTABILITY

Earlier, we noted that while providing more information to voters is generally beneficial, exposing political actions when outcomes are still uncertain may encourage politicians to pander to voters. We also examined some unintended effects of biased media reporting on democratic outcomes. In this section, we turn to the question of how individuals' news consumption influences electoral outcomes and the political accountability of elected officials. By political accountability, we refer to the responsibility and obligation that politicians owe to voters for their actions in office.

In the economic framework, the main actors in this context are politicians, voters (as news consumers), and news media. Voters aim to elect politicians who maximize their individual utility; politicians, in turn, seek to attain elected office and enjoy the resulting political rents; and news media aim to maximize their profits through the production and dissemination of news content.

Given this setup, how do news media choose which stories to report? According to Prat and Strömberg (2013), who synthesized existing theoretical and empirical research, news media are more likely to report on certain issues when the following conditions are met:

1. *The group of news consumers interested in the issue is large*
2. *This consumer group has significant potential in terms of advertising revenue*
3. *The issues that interest this group possess high journalistic news value*
4. *The cost of delivering news to this group is relatively low*

Under these conditions, mass news media are more likely to increase coverage of issues that attract the attention of such consumer groups.

Regarding the first condition—the size of the news consumer group—a study by Lisa George and Joel Waldfogel (2003) presents an important economic mechanism. Their empirical research shows that the greater the number of consumers with similar preferences, the more likely it is that the market will supply news tailored to those preferences. For example, in US regions with a higher proportion of Black residents, local newspapers provided more frequent coverage of policy issues relevant to Black voters, which in turn increased newspaper readership among Black residents. In this way, a larger news consumer group leads to a stronger reflection of their preferences in news content, reinforcing a self-reinforcing cycle of greater media supply and increased news consumption.

This kind of feedback loop may also occur—albeit with some variation—with the other three conditions: groups with high advertising value, issues with high journalistic newsworthiness, and environments with low delivery costs. As news supply increases, news consumption tends to rise as well. This enhances advertising effectiveness, increases the frequency of coverage for high-value issues, and expands the scale of distribution, which in turn lowers the marginal cost of news delivery.

Previously, we explained that as voters gain access to more information, it becomes easier for them to hold politicians accountable, which increases the likelihood of better policy outcomes. So what happens when the above conditions are satisfied and news media increase their coverage of particular issues?

According to theoretical models and empirical studies, the emergence of new media outlets or an increase in coverage of specific issues leads to changes in voters' political judgments and behaviors. When the media expand coverage of topics relevant to a specific consumer group, that group's voter turnout tends to rise, and politicians respond by making greater efforts to appeal to them. At the same time, the incidence of political corruption tends to decline. In the remainder of this section, we examine these dynamics in greater detail.

[More to Explore] Preference Externalities and Network Effects

The phenomenon in which the presence of news consumers alters the content of news reporting, which in turn increases news consumption within that same group, can be explained in economics through the concept of *preference externalities*. This concept refers to the idea that the greater the number of consumers who share similar preferences, the more likely it is that goods or services aligned with those preferences will be supplied in the market, thereby increasing the utility of individuals with such preferences.[15]

Thus in markets where preference externalities are at work, the larger the size of a specific consumer group, the greater the range of options and satisfaction available to its members. The empirical findings by George and Waldfogel (2003)—which showed that news supply increases for topics of interest to demographically large groups—illustrate this mechanism well. However, when a market becomes disproportionately concentrated around consumer groups with homogeneous preferences, preference externalities can reduce the overall diversity of the news media at the market level.

A related but distinct concept is that of *network effects*. Whereas preference externalities involve the indirect influence of other consumers—through producers' responses—on one's utility, network effects describe how the media consumption choices of people in one's social environment directly affect one's own media choices. For example, in communities where a large number of people consume media with a particular political orientation, individuals may continue to consume the same media outlet—even if it is of low quality—simply because it is widely consumed by others.

In summary, both preference externalities and network effects share the common feature that "the presence or behavior of others affects one's utility." However, network effects operate through the direct influence of other consumers' behavior on one's own choices, while preference externalities operate through the indirect influence of other consumers' presence via the producer's response. The distinction is summarized in Table 4.1.

Continued

[15] For example, if I am a Black reader living in an area with a large Black population, the local newspaper is more likely to report on news and content relevant to the interests of Black readers. As a result, my news consumption experience becomes more satisfying, and my utility increases.

Table 4.1 Comparison of Preference Externalities and Network Effects

Concept	Preference Externalities	Network Effects
Core idea	The larger the group with similar preferences, the greater the likelihood of a market supply of matching goods.	The value of the product or service increases as more users adopt it.
Mechanism of influence	Indirect—affects the supply structure of goods and services	Direct—enhances the perceived or actual value of use
Examples	Newspapers, broadcast media, niche media markets	Telephones, social networks, messaging apps, platforms, partisan news media

4.4.1 VOTER TURNOUT

Economic research on the relationship between information and voter turnout has evolved steadily in both theoretical and empirical dimensions. The theoretical foundation was laid by Anthony Downs, whose *An Economic Theory of Democracy*—the title of his influential book and theory—remains widely cited. Based on rational choice theory, Downs explained voter behavior as a decision-making process in which individuals weigh the benefits of voting against the associated costs.

Building on this model, Riker and Ordeshook (1968) introduced the concept of a "sense of citizen duty," suggesting that voters may still participate in elections even when the expected material benefits are minimal.

In the 1990s, economists such as Matsusaka (1995) expanded the framework by incorporating decision theory to account not only for the quantity but also the content of information supplied to voters and its impact on turnout. Feddersen and Pesendorfer (1996, 1999) analyzed strategic abstention by voters, while Krishna and Morgan (2011) showed that greater information availability can not only increase turnout but also reduce voter bias.

These theoretical insights have been supported and extended by various empirical studies. On the whole, the evidence suggests that increases in both the amount of information and news consumption tend to raise levels of electoral participation, that is, voter turnout. However, in line with some of the theoretical literature, empirical studies also point out that the relationship between media-provided information and turnout is not straightforward. Instead, the quality and distribution of information are critical variables. This body of work emphasizes that enhancing voters' access to information is not sufficient on its own; it is equally important to ensure that the information is objective and balanced.

In what follows, we first examine economic theories and general perspectives on how information supply affects voter turnout. We then turn to empirical research that focuses specifically on the role of news media in information provision and its relationship to turnout.

4.4.1.1 Theoretical perspectives

In economic models, voting is framed as a rational decision in which individuals weigh the benefits and costs of participation. While early models focused on a simple cost-benefit calculus—where the benefit is the preferred candidate's victory and the cost includes time, effort, and information acquisition—subsequent research has introduced more nuanced considerations, including strategic abstention, information framing, and media environments.

A foundational contribution came from Anthony Downs (1957), who within the framework of rational choice theory, proposed that the expected utility of voting could be expressed as:

$$U = P_{tie} * B - C$$

Here, P_{tie} is the probability that an individual's vote will be decisive, B is the benefit derived from the preferred candidate winning, and C represents the cost of voting, including the cost of acquiring information. A rational voter will vote only if $P_{tie} * B > C$, i.e., if the expected benefit exceeds the cost ($U = P_{tie} * B - C > 0$) This implies that as the cost of acquiring information falls, voters are more likely to participate due to the higher expected utility.

However, Downs' model struggled to explain why individuals continue to vote even when P_{tie} is vanishingly small—a common situation in large elections. Riker and Ordeshook (1968) provided a well-known answer to this question. They stated:

> *A person votes if the expected utility of voting is positive. That utility includes not just the instrumental benefit from affecting the outcome of the election, but also the satisfaction from fulfilling a sense of citizen duty.*

They formalized this idea by introducing the concept of citizen duty (D) into the voter's expected utility function, represented as:

$$U = P_{tie} * B - C + D$$

Here, the D term captures a variety of psychological benefits: a sense of civic responsibility or citizen duty, personal satisfaction derived from participating in the democratic process (such as the belief that one is contributing to the support of democracy), and the social pressure experienced when family, friends, or coworkers expect one to vote. Even within this revised model, the implication remained that an increase in information could lead to higher voter turnout, as more information may enhance voters' sense of political efficacy and stimulate their sense of civic duty.

Since the 1990s, however, a growing body of theoretical work has argued that it is not only the amount of information but also the content—including the framing of how information is presented—that affects turnout. Matsusaka (1995) directed attention to the term P_{tie} in the expected utility function, $U = P_{tie} * B–C$. He argued that as voters become better informed, the value of P_{tie} could change. If more information makes the election seem close, then P_{tie} increases and turnout may increase. But if the information suggests a landslide victory for one candidate, then $P_{tie} \rightarrow 0$, and the voter may abstain. In other words, Matsusaka emphasized that turnout does not always increase with more information, but depends on whether the information increases voters' certainty about the election outcome. He argued that both the content of the information and the way it is framed shape voters' motivations to participate. Information supply has nonneutral effects and consequences, shaping outcomes in a particular direction.[16]

Feddersen and Pesendorfer (1996) used game theory to explain strategic abstention by uninformed voters. In their model, uninformed voters are those who believe that informed voters—those with greater political knowledge—are more likely to make correct choices. For an uninformed voter who is inclined to vote for Candidate A, the expected utility of voting is as follows:

$$U_A = P(\text{A wins}) - P(\text{B wins}),\ U_{\text{abstain}} = 0$$

Thus the voter will vote only if $U_A > 0$, that is, if their action is expected to have a positive effect. However, their expected utility conditional on voting for A is as follows:

$$U_A = P(\text{A wins} \mid U \text{ vote for A}) - P(\text{B wins} \mid U \text{ vote for A})$$

If $U_A < 0$, then the voter believes that voting for A would not change the outcome and may even distort the result in favor of the less preferred Candidate B. In this situation, abstaining becomes the rational choice. Feddersen and Pesendorfer argued that uninformed voters abstain not because they are apathetic but because they recognize that uninformed participation may dilute or distort the outcome produced by informed voters. Their decision reflects the logic: "My vote is unlikely to improve the outcome, but it could distort it—so I'd rather abstain."[17]

In a follow-up paper, Feddersen and Pesendorfer (1999) analyzed the effect of information asymmetry among voters on turnout. They argued that as the level of information asymmetry, denoted by θ[18], increases, the probability that uninformed voters will turn out to vote (P_U) decreases. This is because the higher the information gap, the more likely uninformed voters are to believe that their vote is unnecessary or potentially harmful. In contrast, the probability of turnout among informed voters

[16] Levine and Palfrey (2007) provided empirical evidence that while increased information can lead to higher voter turnout, it can also result in higher abstention rates in elections where the outcome is perceived as certain.

[17] This perspective suggests that when informed voters constitute the majority, it may be more rational for uninformed voters to abstain, and that even with low overall turnout, the election outcome can still be correct or socially desirable.

[18] The parameter θ, which takes a value between 0 and 1, represents both the probability that a given voter is uninformed and the proportion of uninformed voters in the overall electorate. A value of $\theta = 0$ indicates that all voters are informed, whereas $\theta = 1$ implies that no voter possesses information. An increase in θ reflects a growing concentration of information among a smaller subset of the electorate.

(P_I) increases since informed voters believe that uninformed individuals will abstain, making their own votes more decisive.

In expected utility terms, as θ increases, P_{tie} increases for informed voters and decreases for uninformed voters. That is, the marginal impact of the informed voter's ballot on the outcome—ΔP_{tie}—becomes more significant. Informed voters may reason: "If I don't vote, uninformed voters may make the wrong choice" or "As θ increases, the uninformed are more likely to abstain, and the responsibility to influence the result falls increasingly on people like me."

Based on this model, the authors concluded that higher information asymmetry leads to higher rates of abstention among uninformed voters, greater electoral dominance by informed voters, and that reducing this asymmetry through information provision could serve as an important policy tool to increase turnout.

4.4.1.2 Empirical evidence on news media and voter turnout

General information provision. Economists generally argue that, with few exceptions, greater access to political information—particularly through increased exposure to news media—leads to higher voter turnout. This theoretical prediction has been consistently supported by a wide body of empirical research.

Lassen (2005) presents robust evidence that improved access to information, specifically through better Internet infrastructure, significantly boosts voter turnout. Similarly, Degan and Merlo (2011), using a dynamic discrete choice framework within a structural econometric model, show that voters' gradual accumulation of political information over time increases their likelihood of participating in elections.

Political scientists Green and Gerber (2019), known for their experimental and econometric approaches, have conducted and synthesized numerous field experiments demonstrating that providing voters with political information can substantially raise turnout levels. Across these studies, a consistent finding emerges: media exposure enhances information acquisition, which in turn promotes electoral participation.

The remainder of this section will examine empirical studies by economists that investigate the relationship between news media and voter turnout, focusing on several different types of media.

The advent of broadcast media. Strömberg (1999; 2004a) analyzed how the spread of radio in the 1920s and 1930s affected voter turnout and public policy in the United States. Before the advent of radio, rural voters—who lacked access to newspaper delivery—were largely excluded from timely political information. But by the 1930s, radio had become widely available across the country, including in previously underserved rural areas. During this period of expanded radio access, gubernatorial election turnout in the United States rose by approximately 5.5 percentage points.

A study by Oberholzer-Gee and Waldfogel (2009) provides further evidence from a different context. Between 1994 and 2002, several US regions introduced Spanish-language television news programming. In those areas, Hispanic voter turnout increased by 5 to 10 percentage points relative to non-Hispanic voters. Notably, the introduction of Spanish-language television prompted 27% of previously nonvoting Hispanic individuals to participate in elections.

Prat and Strömberg (2005) offer additional evidence from Sweden, where the introduction of commercial television in the late 1980s and early 1990s led to measurable gains in both political knowledge and civic engagement among viewers compared to nonviewers.

Collectively, these studies show that the introduction of broadcast media significantly improved access to political information and raised voter turnout—particularly among groups that had previously been politically marginalized.

The rise of print media. The long-term impact of news media on voter turnout has also been documented in historical studies. Gentzkow et al. (2011) examined the relationship between newspaper market entry and exit and voter turnout in the United States over a span of 136 years (1869–2004). They found that newspapers exerted a strong and positive influence on political participation. Specifically, the entry of one additional newspaper into a market was associated with a 0.3 percentage point increase in turnout in both presidential and congressional elections. This effect was particularly robust for the 59-year period from 1869 to 1928, during which newspapers were the only major political information source, as radio and television had not yet emerged.

A similar pattern is observed in the Italian context. Drago et al. (2014) analyzed all newspapers circulated in Italian municipalities with populations over 15,000 from 1993 to 2010. They found that the entry of a new newspaper into a local media market increased turnout in municipal elections and also improved the administrative performance of local governments. Extending the historical lens further, Cagé and Rueda (2016) studied the long-term effects of print media in 19th-century sub-Saharan Africa. Their findings indicate that regions more exposed to print media disseminated by Protestant missionaries developed higher levels of social trust, education, and political participation.

In short, print media—especially newspapers—have historically played a vital role in disseminating political information and stimulating voter engagement over extended periods of time.

Media content and voter participation. Scholars have offered differing views on how the nature of media content affects political engagement. Markus Prior (2007), a political scientist who frequently employs economic frameworks, argues—consistent with Gentzkow (2006) and Campante and Hojman (2013)—that entertainment-oriented media can lead to political disengagement and lower voter turnout. As the proliferation of cable television and the Internet has expanded the range of media choices, the opportunity cost of consuming political news has increased.[19] Consequently, more individuals

[19] In the past, there were few alternatives to consuming news, meaning that the opportunity cost of following political news was relatively low. By contrast, today's media environment is saturated with entertainment content that offers immediate gratification. As a result, consuming political news now requires forgoing a wide array of more enjoyable alternatives—implying that the opportunity cost of political news consumption has risen substantially.

opt for entertainment content, thereby exacerbating information inequality and uneven political participation. Prior contends that this shift has contributed to declining voter turnout, especially among politically uninterested citizens.

In contrast, Dyck et al. (2013) argue that embedding political information in entertaining formats can enhance engagement, particularly among passive voters. Their empirical analysis shows that, in the early 20th century, muckraking magazines combined political information with entertainment content to inform the public about policy issues, thereby increasing political engagement. According to them, this effect stems from the media's ability to lower the cost of political information acquisition for passive voters by embedding it in entertaining formats, thus encouraging broader political participation.[20]

Another study by Gerber et al. (2009) found that newspaper readership increased voter turnout regardless of readers' ideological orientation. In a field experiment conducted during the 2005 Virginia gubernatorial election, two groups of voters were randomly assigned subscriptions to either the liberal-leaning *Washington Post* or the conservative *Washington Times*. Regardless of the newspaper's ideological slant, readers were more likely to vote than nonreaders.

Taken together, these findings suggest that media content—not just access—plays a critical role in shaping political participation. The design, tone, and framing of media content can either facilitate or hinder voters' engagement in the democratic process.

4.4.2 WHEN EVERYONE KNOWS THAT EVERYONE KNOWS: COMMON KNOWLEDGE

Until now, we have explored economic theories and empirical findings suggesting that news media influence political participation by providing information. This effect becomes more powerful because news media serve a function beyond merely delivering information: they help create what is known as common knowledge.

Common knowledge is consistently defined across fields such as philosophy, psychology, and economics as a state in which everyone knows a given fact P and everyone knows that everyone knows it.[21] In economics, this concept has been formalized

[20] Dyck and his coauthors argue that profit-maximizing media can help reduce voter abstention by addressing the rational ignorance problem highlighted by Anthony Downs—namely, that as the number of voters increases, the influence of any individual voter on the electoral outcome diminishes, making abstention a rational choice.

[21] Scholars in cognitive science, psychology, and epistemic logic classify knowledge representation into five levels: Private Knowledge (Level 1: A knows P), Mutual Knowledge (Level 2: A and B both know P), Mutual Awareness (Level 3: A knows that B knows P and vice versa), Higher-Order Knowledge (Level 4: Each party knows that the other knows that they know P and so on), and Common Knowledge (Level 5: Everyone knows P, and knows that everyone knows it, infinitely). This hierarchy clarifies how individual awareness evolves into shared understanding capable of influencing group coordination and collective behavior. See De Freitas et al. (2019).

Table 4.2 Definition and Key Contributions on Common Knowledge Across Disciplines

Field	Key Scholars	Core Contribution
Philosophy/epistemic logic	David Lewis (1969)	Formulated the classic definition: "Everyone knows P, everyone knows that everyone knows P," and so on
Economics/ game theory	Robert Aumann (1976)	Provided a formal mathematical structure of common knowledge and analyzed its role in strategy and equilibrium
Psychology/cognitive science	De Freitas et al. (2019)	Investigated the cognitive and behavioral mechanisms underlying common knowledge through experiments
Political science/ communication	Michael Chwe (2001)	Argued that mass media and public rituals generate common knowledge, enabling collective action

mathematically within the framework of game theory, where it is used to analyze how individual strategic choices and collective behaviors are shaped. For a summary of key contributions across disciplines, see Table 4.2.

When common knowledge is established within a community, even individuals who had remained silent may gain the incentive to act. For example, when information about a corrupt high-ranking official spreads informally, most people do not immediately take action simply because they are aware of it. However, the situation changes once the information is widely and publicly reported by the news media. At the moment when "everyone knows it, and everyone knows that everyone knows it," public attitudes shift from passive awareness to active engagement. People join protests, demonstrations, or vote not just because they possess information but because news coverage turns it into common knowledge—creating the expectation that others will act as well.

In the digital era, not only mass media but also social media play a similar role by connecting dispersed knowledge and perceptions across individual users and thereby facilitating the formation of common knowledge. In some respects, social media may even be more effective than traditional mass media in this process. In fact, there are numerous cases where social media has created common knowledge that triggered collective action.

For instance, during the Arab Spring (2010–11), protest images shared on social media helped shape the perception that "others are also outraged," leading to mass mobilization. In the 2014 Hong Kong Umbrella Movement, social media replaced censored news outlets by delivering real-time protest updates and messages of solidarity, giving many citizens a sense that "everyone knows this." In the 2020 George Floyd incident in the United States, the rapid spread of video footage on social media created a shared belief that "everyone has seen it," which contributed to global

Table 4.3 Traditional Versus Social Media in Common Knowledge Formation

Aspect	Traditional Media	Social Media	Effects on Common Knowledge Formation
Government censorship	Vulnerable	Decentralized and resistant	✓ Enables rapid information spread ✕ Risk of unverified dissemination of false information
Mode of communication	One-way delivery	Interactive and real-time sharing	✓ Facilitates quick empathy and awareness ✕ Reinforces confirmation bias, limits exposure to dissenting perspectives
Visibility of group response	Limited feedback	Visible via likes, comments, shares	✓ Promotes a sense of "everyone has seen it" ✕ May remain confined within in-groups
Formation of focal points	Formal reporting	Symbolic, short content (memes, hashtags)	✓ Can spark collective action ✕ Risk of oversimplification and loss of context

protests. Table 4.3 summarizes the contrasting roles of traditional media and social media in the formation of common knowledge.

However, it is important to note that social media also raises concerns about fragmentation, misinformation, and ideological polarization.

In short, from national electorates to small online communities, both mass media and social media help transform individual knowledge into a shared structure. This transformation forms common knowledge, which provides the cognitive and informational foundation for individuals to engage in strategic collective action.

[More to Explore] From Information to Influence: Common Knowledge and News Media

A fact P is common knowledge if everyone knows P, everyone knows that everyone knows P, and so on ad infinitum.

(Aumann, 1976)

This is the standard definition of common knowledge used in economics and other disciplines. When common knowledge is formed among individuals, expectations and strategies shift, and silence may turn into action. Collective political protests, consumer movements, and acts of civil resistance are often triggered at such turning points. This is because common knowledge gives rise to the belief that "others will now act as well." In game-theoretic coordination games,[22] this

[22] A coordination game is a situation in game theory where players benefit from making the same or compatible choices, and success depends on mutual expectations.

point marks the shift in expectations that moves the equilibrium toward action. A frequently used puzzle[23] helps illustrate this mechanism.

Q. On an island where there are no mirrors, people can see everyone else's eye color but not their own. The rule of the island is: if someone comes to know they have blue eyes, they must leave the island that night. One day, an outsider visits and announces to all, "There is at least one person on this island with blue eyes." Exactly N days later, N people with blue eyes all leave at once. Why?

A. Each person can see others' eye colors but not their own. If there is only one blue-eyed person, they see no other blue-eyed person and deduce it must be them—so they leave on the first night. If there are two, each sees only one and waits to see whether the other leaves on Day 1. When no one does, they both realize the truth and leave on Day 2. If there are N, this process continues: seeing (N−1) blue-eyed people who don't leave, each deduces they must be the Nth, and all N depart together on Day N.

This puzzle demonstrates not only the meaning of common knowledge but also its power: people may already possess individual knowledge, yet only when that knowledge becomes common does behavior shift. In this puzzle, the outsider who creates the common knowledge functions much like news media in the real world—serving not merely as an information provider, but as a social mechanism that reshapes expectations and triggers action.[24]

4.4.3 POLICY IMPROVEMENT AND REDUCTION IN CORRUPTION

Increased news consumption affects not only voter turnout but also government policy. This pattern is evident in David Strömberg's earlier research showing that the introduction of radio in the United States led to higher turnout. According to Strömberg (1999, 2004a), as radio listenership increased, urban-rural inequalities in news access declined, and federal government spending increased. Rural areas, where turnout increased more dramatically than in urban areas, received 20% more social assistance funding than urban areas of comparable size. The expansion of radio weakened politicians' urban bias and shifted the government's responsiveness to rural voters.[25]

Other scholars have studied the relationship between news consumption and the responsiveness of government policy. Besley and Burgess (2002) analyzed how

[23] This puzzle is widely known as the Blue-Eyed Islander Puzzle and is formalized in the epistemic logic literature (Halpern & Moses, 1990). It illustrates how common knowledge—not mere information—triggers collective action.

[24] A notable application of this concept to media and collective behavior appears in Chwe (2001), who argues that mass media and public rituals function as mechanisms for generating common knowledge. He emphasizes that it is not merely shared information but the shared awareness of mutual awareness that enables coordination—highlighting how media can catalyze strategic behavior by shifting players from fragmented beliefs to unified expectations, as modeled in coordination games.

[25] Strömberg (2004b) also developed a theoretical model to explain how the shift in the primary source of political information—from newspapers to broadcast media—led to increased government spending on poor and rural voters.

Indian state governments responded to food shortages between 1958 and 1992. Wealthier states were not necessarily more responsive. Instead, states with higher newspaper circulation responded more quickly to food crises, highlighting the role of media exposure in holding governments accountable.

Olper and Swinnen (2013) examined how television access affected agricultural taxation and subsidies. Their cross-country study of 69 countries showed that increased TV penetration correlated with lower agricultural taxes in poorer countries (where farmers are the majority) and reduced subsidies in wealthier countries (where farmers are a minority). This suggests that broader media access led to policy shifts benefiting larger segments of society.

The absence of media coverage can also reduce voter awareness and dampen political activity. Snyder and Strömberg (2010) analyzed 161 local newspapers covering 385 congressional districts in the United States from 1991 to 2002. Districts with less overlap between newspaper circulation and congressional boundaries received less coverage of their representatives. In those districts, voter awareness was lower, members of Congress were less active, and federal spending was lower. This underscores the importance of local media in fostering political accountability.

In their book *Corruption and Reform: Lessons from America's Economic History*, Gentzkow et al. (2006) documented a dramatic decline in political corruption in the United States between 1870 and 1920. During that time, newspaper circulation in the top 100 US cities grew from 1.37 million to 20.5 million. Copies circulated per person tripled from 0.194 to 0.606. The authors argue that the rise of the press as a provider of information was a plausible explanation for the decline in corruption.

Ferraz and Finan (2008) found that in Brazil's 2004 local elections, incumbent mayors who had been audited and whose audit results were made public were about 20% less likely to be reelected. The effect was especially pronounced in municipalities with radio stations, suggesting that media amplification reinforced accountability. In Uganda, economists Reinikka and Svensson (2005) conducted a field experiment showing that newspaper campaigns informing parents about education grants led to reduced corruption and less misappropriation of public funds.

These studies collectively demonstrate that increased media access and news consumption can significantly influence government accountability, public spending, and corruption levels.

4.4.4 MEDIA'S SENSATIONALISM BIAS AND ITS IMPACT

News selection and production by media outlets are heavily influenced by audience preferences, a phenomenon commonly referred to as news values.[26] Among these criteria, unexpectedness and human interest frequently lead to sensational reporting, one of the most common practices in modern journalism. Empirical studies in

[26] "News value" is briefly explained in Footnote 3 of Chapter 2. Among various newsworthiness criteria, "unexpectedness" or the unusual is one of the most important factors in modern journalism.

economics have shown that the media prioritize stories based on their novelty rather than the actual suffering involved.

For instance, events such as famines or volcanic eruptions are significantly more likely to be covered by the news than chronic hunger or droughts, even if the latter are more widespread or deadly. This is because famines and eruptions are perceived as more unusual and thus more newsworthy. (Chronic hunger refers to prolonged and severe malnutrition, whereas a famine is defined as a sudden and acute food crisis.) This pattern of coverage can distort public perceptions and ultimately affect government policy, often leading to inefficient or misaligned responses.

Among the economists who have provided theoretical and empirical explanations of this dynamic are Amartya Sen, the first Asian recipient of the Nobel Prize in Economics (1998), and Jean Drèze of Belgium. In their coauthored book, *The Political Economy of Hunger*, Drèze and Sen (1991) argued that democratic societies with a free press tend to respond more effectively to famines than to endemic hunger. This is because famines are far more newsworthy, which leads to greater media coverage and, in turn, stronger governmental responses.

Eisensee and Strömberg (2007) extended this analysis by empirically examining how disaster coverage in the US media affected the government's foreign aid responses. They analyzed approximately 5212 natural disasters that occurred globally between 1968 and 2002. On average, these disasters claimed 63,000 lives annually and affected 125 million people each year. However, they found that US government aid was not proportional to the scale of the disaster. The authors attributed this discrepancy to the variation in media coverage.

According to their study, in years when the Olympic Games were held, media coverage of natural disasters declined as outlets allocated more attention to the Games. This decline in coverage led to a corresponding decrease in US disaster aid. In addition, the criteria for disaster coverage varied sharply depending on geographic location. For a disaster in Africa to receive the same level of coverage as a similar event in Eastern Europe, it had to result in approximately 50 times more deaths. Disparities were also observed between types of disasters: a drought had to cause over 2,000 times more fatalities than a volcanic eruption to be covered at the same level.

As a result, US aid to victims of droughts or disasters in Africa was significantly lower than aid directed toward volcanic eruptions or events in Eastern Europe, not because of objective differences in suffering, but because of how these events were covered by the media. These findings offer strong empirical evidence that the quantity and prominence of media coverage exert a causal influence on policy decisions.

In summary, the core function of news media in democratic societies is to provide citizens with information about governments and public policy. For voters to make informed electoral choices, they need to know who is proposing which policies, who is responsible for their implementation, and what the outcomes are. News media are the main channel through which this information is disseminated. This, in turn, raises political participation (such as voter turnout), improves policy outcomes by holding politicians accountable, and enhances the welfare of voters through more responsive and effective policy.

However, these findings also imply the reverse: those who (1) lack access to news media, (2) are affected by issues deemed to have low news value, (3) live in areas where news production is costly, or (4) are not attractive to advertisers may be systematically excluded from media attention. Such exclusion often leads to being neglected by policymakers and marginalized from public services and welfare provisions.

Moreover, when discussing the democratic role of the media, it is important to consider the role of technological change. As noted in previous chapters, media functions are deeply shaped by media technology. The successive innovations in printing technology in the late 19th century, followed by the emergence of radio and television in the 20th century, brought profound changes to how the media operated. Now, in the ongoing era of the digital revolution, we are once again witnessing a fundamental transformation in the media's role within democratic political processes.

References

Aumann, R.J., 1976. Agreeing to disagree. The Annals of Statistics 4 (6), 1236–1239. https://doi.org/10.1214/aos/1176343654.

Bernhardt, D., Krasa, S., Polborn, M., 2008. Political polarization and the electoral effects of media bias. Journal of Public Economics 92 (5–6), 1092–1104. https://doi.org/10.1016/j.jpubeco.2008.01.006.

Besley, T., Burgess, R., 2002. The political economy of government responsiveness: theory and evidence from India. The Quarterly Journal of Economics 117 (4), 1415–1451. https://doi.org/10.1162/003355302320935061.

Cagé, J., Rueda, V., 2016. The long-term effects of the printing press in sub-Saharan Africa. American Economic Journal: Applied Economics 8 (3), 69–99. https://doi.org/10.1257/app.20140379.

Campante, F.R., Hojman, D.A., 2013. Media and Polarization: Evidence from the Introduction of Broadcast TV in the United States. Journal of Public Economics 100, 79–92.

Chan, J., Suen, W., 2008. A spatial theory of news consumption and electoral competition. Review of Economic Studies 75 (3), 699–728. https://doi.org/10.1111/j.1467-937x.2008.00495.x.

Chan, J., Suen, W., 2009. Media as watchdogs: the role of news media in electoral competition. European Economic Review 53 (7), 799–814. https://doi.org/10.1016/j.euroecorev.2009.01.002.

Chwe, M.S.Y., 2001. Rational Ritual: Culture, Coordination, and Common Knowledge. Princeton University Press.

Cohen, B.C., 1963. The press and foreign policy. Princeton University Press.

Corneo, G., 2006. Media capture in a democracy: the role of wealth concentration. Journal of Public Economics 90 (1–2), 37–58. https://doi.org/10.1016/j.jpubeco.2005.08.002.

De Freitas, J., Thomas, K., DeScioli, P., Pinker, S., 2019. Common knowledge, coordination, and strategic mentalizing in human social life. Proceedings of the National Academy of Sciences 116 (28), 13751–13758. https://doi.org/10.1073/pnas.1905518116.

Degan, A., Merlo, A., 2011. A structural model of turnout and voting in multiple elections. Journal of the European Economic Association 9 (2), 209–245. https://doi.org/10.1111/j.1542-4774.2010.01013.x.

Downs, A., 1957. An economic theory of political action in a democracy. Journal of Political Economy 65 (2), 135–150. https://doi.org/10.1086/257897.

Drago, F., Nannicini, T., Sobbrio, F., 2014. Meet the press: how voters and politicians respond to newspaper entry and exit. American Economic Journal: Applied Economics 6 (3), 159–188. https://doi.org/10.1257/app.6.3.159.

Drèze, J., Sen, A., 1991. Political economy of hunger: volume 1: Entitlement and well-being. Clarendon Press.

Duggan, J., Martinelli, C., 2011. A spatial theory of media slant and voter choice. The Review of Economic Studies 78 (2), 640–666. https://doi.org/10.1093/restud/rdq009.

Dyck, A., Moss, D., Zingales, L., 2013. Media Versus Special Interests. The Journal of Law and Economics 56 (3), 521–553.

Eisensee, T., Strömberg, D., 2007. News droughts, news floods, and U.S. disaster relief. Quarterly Journal of Economics 122 (2), 693–728. https://doi.org/10.1162/qjec.122.2.693.

Feddersen, T.J., Pesendorfer, W., 1996. The swing voter's curse. American Economic Review 86 (3), 408–424.

Ferraz, C., Finan, F., 2008. Exposing corrupt politicians: the effects of Brazil's publicly released audits on electoral outcomes. Quarterly Journal of Economics 123 (2), 703–745. https://doi.org/10.1162/qjec.2008.123.2.703.

Gans, H.J., 2003. Democracy and the News. Oxford University Press.

Gentzkow, M., 2006. Television and voter turnout. Quarterly Journal of Economics 121 (3), 931–972.

Gentzkow, M., Glaeser, E.L., Goldin, C., 2006. The Rise of the Fourth Estate: How Newspapers Became Informative and Why It Mattered. In: Glaeser, E.L., Goldin, C. (Eds.), Corruption and Reform: Lessons from America's Economic History. University of Chicago Press, Chicago, pp. 187–230. https://doi.org/10.7208/chicago/9780226299594.003.0007.

Gentzkow, M., Shapiro, J.M., Sinkinson, M., 2011. The effect of newspaper entry and exit on electoral politics. American Economic Review 101 (7), 2980–3018. http://pubs.aeaweb.org/doi/pdfplus/10.1257/aer.101.7.2980. https://doi.org/10.1257/aer.101.7.2980

George, L., Waldfogel, J., 2003. Who affects whom in daily newspaper markets? Journal of Political Economy 111 (4), 765–784. https://doi.org/10.1086/375380.

Gerber, A.S., Karlan, D., Bergan, D., 2009. Does the media matter? A field experiment measuring the effect of newspapers on voting behavior and political opinions. American Economic Journal: Applied Economics 1 (2), 35–52. https://doi.org/10.1257/app.1.2.35.

Goffman, E., 1974. Frame analysis: An essay on the organization of experience. Harvard University Press.

Green, D.P., Gerber, A.S., 2019. Get out the vote: how to increase voter turnout. Bloomsbury Publishing USA.

Halpern, J.Y., Moses, Y., 1990. Knowledge and common knowledge in a distributed environment. Journal of the ACM 37 (3), 549–587.

Holmström, B., 1979. Moral hazard and observability. The Bell Journal of Economics 10 (1), 74–91.

Hovland, C.I., Lumsdaine, A.A., Sheffield, F.D., 1949. Experiments on mass communication. Princeton University Press.

Iyengar, S., Kinder, D.R., 1987. News That Matters: Television and American Opinion. University of Chicago Press, Chicago.

Krishna, V., Morgan, J., 2011. Overcoming ideological bias in elections. Journal of Political Economy 119 (2), 183–211. https://doi.org/10.1086/660731.

Lassen, D.D., 2005. The effect of information on voter turnout: evidence from a natural experiment. American Journal of Political Science 49 (1), 103–118. https://doi.org/10.1111/j.0092-5853.2005.00113.x.

Lazarsfeld, P., Berelson, B., Gaudet, H., 1944. The people's choice: how the voter makes up his mind in a presidential campaign. Duell, Sloan and Pearce.

Levine, D.K., Palfrey, T.R., 2007. The paradox of voter participation? A laboratory study. American Political Science Review 101 (1), 143–158.

Lewis, A., 1997. Democracy and the Free Press: Are They Incompatible? Bulletin of the American Academy of Arts and Sciences 51 (3), 49–63.

Lewis, D., 1969. Convention: A philosophical study. John Wiley & Sons.

Maskin, E., Tirole, J., 2004. The politician and the judge: accountability in government. American Economic Review 94 (4), 1034–1054. https://doi.org/10.1257/0002828042002606.

Matsusaka, J.G., 1995. Explaining voter turnout patterns: an information theory. Public Choice 84 (1–2), 91–117. https://doi.org/10.1007/BF01047803.

McCombs, M.E., Shaw, D.L., 1972. The agenda-setting function of mass media. Public Opinion Quarterly 36 (2), 176–187. https://doi.org/10.1086/267990.

Oberholzer-Gee, F., Waldfogel, J., 2009. Media markets and localism: does local news en español boost hispanic voter turnout? American Economic Review 99 (5), 2120–2128. https://doi.org/10.1257/aer.99.5.2120.

Olper, A., Swinnen, J., 2013. Mass media and public policy: global evidence from agricultural policies. The World Bank Economic Review 27 (3), 413–436. https://doi.org/10.1093/wber/lht008.

Prat, A., Strömberg, D., 2013. The Political Economy of Mass Media. In: Acemoglu, D., Arellano, M., Dekel, E. (Eds.), Advances in Economics and Econometrics: Tenth World Congress, Volume II. Cambridge University Press, Cambridge, pp. 135–187. https://doi.org/10.1017/CBO9781139060028.004.

Prat, A., 2005. The wrong kind of transparency. American Economic Review 95 (3), 862–877. https://doi.org/10.1257/0002828054201297.

Prat, A., Strömberg, D., 2005. Commercial television and voter information. CEPR Discussion Papers. 4989.

Prior, M., 2007. Post-Broadcast Democracy: How Media Choice Increases Inequality in Political Involvement and Polarizes Elections. Cambridge University Press.

Reinikka, R., Svensson, J., 2005. Fighting corruption to improve schooling: evidence from a newspaper campaign in Uganda. Journal of the European Economic Association 3 (2), 259–267. https://doi.org/10.1162/1542476054472883.

Riker, W.H., Ordeshook, P.C., 1968. A theory of the calculus of voting. American Political Science Review 62 (1), 25–42. https://doi.org/10.1017/S000305540011562X.

Snyder, J.M., Strömberg, D., 2010. Press coverage and political accountability. Journal of Political Economy 118 (2), 355–408. https://doi.org/10.1086/652903

Stigler, G.J., 1961. The economics of information. Journal of Political Economy 69 (3), 213–225.

Strömberg, D., 1999. The Political Economy of Public Spending. Ph.D. Dissertation, Princeton University.

Strömberg, D., 2004a. Radio's Impact on Public Spending. The Quarterly Journal of Economics 119 (1), 189–221.

Strömberg, D., 2004b. Mass Media Competition, Political Competition, and Public Policy. The Review of Economic Studies 71 (1), 265–284.

CHAPTER

5 Theories of Media Bias: The Inescapable Shackles

Chapter Outline

Akira Kurosawa, the great director, created a cinematic masterpiece in film history with "Rashomon" (1950). The film depicts how the truth behind the incident of a samurai's wife being assaulted by a bandit, and the samurai found dead with a sword in his chest, becomes shrouded in mystery. This is because the samurai, his wife, the bandit, and a woodcutter, who witnessed the event, all recount different versions of the truth. Although four versions of the "plausible truth" emerge, the "real truth" is never revealed. Even if there is only one truth, the way people experience and understand it varies from person to person. The film dramatically illustrates how truth can be distorted due to human self-interest.

The Economics of News Media. DOI: http://dx.doi.org/10.1016/B978-0-443-45044-0.00004-0

Most people believe that the mainstream news media are biased. They think the media are biased toward specific political forces, interest groups, or ideologies. This reality is not just based on people's subjective feelings. News media are indeed biased. All news media differ in the way they select and present facts. Most tend to one side of the political or ideological spectrum.

So, can media bias be eliminated or disappear entirely? What is its inherent nature? In this chapter, we will introduce various theories by economists on why "media bias" occurs. Economists suggest that media bias arises due to news consumers' limited ability to verify news content fully or because of the biases of news consumers or the news suppliers (journalists and media owners). These perspectives are both intuitive and intriguing. It is also noteworthy that the biases of news consumers, which are a primary driver of media bias, vary across different eras and societies.

The final section of this chapter offers a concise overview of media bias as analyzed by communication scholars. Through this, readers can gain a clearer understanding of the differences between how communication scholars and economists approach media bias.

5.1 WHAT IS MEDIA BIAS?

On December 2, 2003, during the Iraq War, US forces engaged in a battle in the Iraqi city of Samarra. The global media giants Fox News, *The New York Times*, and Al Jazeera reported the event as follows (Gentzkow and Shapiro, 2006, p. 281):

> *Fox News: In one of the deadliest reported firefights in Iraq since the fall of Saddam Hussein's regime, US forces killed at least 54 Iraqis and captured eight others while fending off simultaneous convoy ambushes Sunday in the northern city of Samarra.*
> *The New York Times: American commanders vowed Monday that the killing of as many as 54 insurgents in this central Iraqi town would serve as a lesson to those fighting the United States, but Iraqis disputed the death toll and said anger against America would only rise.*
> *Al Jazeera: The US military has vowed to continue aggressive tactics after saying it killed 54 Iraqis following an ambush, but commanders admitted they had no proof to back up their claims. The only corpses at Samarra's hospital were those of civilians, including two elderly Iranian visitors and a child.*

All three media outlets based their reports on the same basic facts. However, through selective omission of facts, word choice, and the degree of trust placed in information sources, each media outlet conveyed fundamentally different interpretations of the event. In short articles ranging from only 40 to 48 words, the news media each filtered the reported facts and framed the event differently.

The reports differed from the very beginning in how they conveyed the number of casualties in the battle with US forces. Fox News used the phrase "at least 54," *The*

New York Times said "as many as 54" while noting that the death toll was disputed, and Al Jazeera reported that there was "*no proof to back up*" the US military's claims.

There were also differences in the facts included in the articles. Al Jazeera mentioned that "the only corpses at Samarra's hospital were those of civilians, including two elderly Iranian visitors and a child," a fact not mentioned by either Fox News or *The New York Times*. Similarly, neither *The New York Times* nor Al Jazeera included the fact reported by Fox News that US forces "captured eight others." The portrayal of the adversaries also varied. Fox News referred to them simply as "Iraqis," while *The New York Times* called them "insurgents."

Looking at the overall context, Fox News emphasized the US military's achievements, describing the battle as "In one of the deadliest reported firefights in Iraq since the fall of Saddam Hussein's regime." *The New York Times*, on the other hand, reported that "Iraqis disputed the death toll" and conveyed the anger of Iraqis, while Al Jazeera prompted its readers to consider the innocent deaths of civilians.

In this way, the reports from the three media outlets revealed inherent biases in their reporting. *The New York Times* and Al Jazeera, which were critical of the US invasion of Iraq, showed their bias just as clearly as Fox News, which was not. Even globally respected media outlets known for their high quality and credibility are not free from reporting bias. Many people desire unbiased news, but the reality is far from that. So, how do people perceive media bias? And are these biases something that can be eliminated from the news media?

5.1.1 THE TWO NATURES OF MEDIA BIAS

5.1.1.1 *Opposing biases*

A prominent characteristic of people's perceptions of media bias is that they can hold completely opposite views about the bias of the same news story or news outlet. This is like someone standing on the east side of a building along an east-west road claiming that it is on the west side, while someone on the west side insists it is on the east side.

This polarized perception of media bias is more pronounced among people with differing political views. It is especially evident in countries with strong two-party systems, such as the United States or South Korea, where liberal and conservative parties are well-established, and where those with similar biases tend to reinforce each other's views.

Bernard Goldberg, a prominent journalist formerly with Columbia Broadcasting System, published a book in 2001 criticizing the liberal bias of television news (Goldberg, 2001). Conservative media commentator and columnist Ann Coulter also claimed in her book that left-wing forces had taken over the media (Coulter, 2002). Goldberg's book reached the top of *The New York Times* bestseller list for nonfiction in November 2001, and Coulter's book held the number one spot in the same category for 8 weeks in 2002.

However, around the same time, economist Paul Krugman (Nobel Prize in Economics, 2008) wrote a column in *The New York Times* pointing out the conservative bias in the American media (Krugman, 2002). Also, renowned historian and journalist Eric Alterman, in his 2003 book, argued that the idea of a liberal media bias is merely a myth and that the media as a whole leans conservatively. In particular, he sharply criticized the views of Goldberg and Coulter that the media have a liberal bias (Alterman, 2003). Alterman's book also became a bestseller.

The opposing perceptions of media bias are so common that they can be considered an everyday occurrence, especially among those with clear political views. Such partisan perceptions of the media are continuously reproduced not only by political forces but also by partisan news outlets, influencers, and even NGOs[1] that monitor media bias. The more politically polarized a society is, the greater the opposing perceptions of media bias become. In highly politically polarized countries, it is very common for people to interpret media reports through the lens of their political affiliations.[2]

Generally, people evaluate media bias based on their own perspectives, without recognizing their own biases. This means that people's perceptions of bias in a news story or news outlet differ to varying degrees. As a result, it is clear that such perceptions of media bias are far from objective.

5.1.1.2 Persistent bias

The reason why news consumers perceive bias differently is due to human limitations. Unless humans completely transcend their limitations through awakening, they cannot completely rid themselves of their biases. If humans cannot escape their biases, the biases perceived in news media reflecting these personal biases become a "persistent bias" that doesn't disappear. Moreover, news media cannot ignore the needs of biased news consumers. This means that unbiased news never existed in the past and cannot exist in the future. For instance, even if media watchdog organizations meticulously monitor, thoroughly expose, and effectively keep certain news outlets in check for their biases, there will always be some bias in news media.[3] Just as having doctors does not eliminate all diseases, media watchdogs cannot eliminate all bias.

---

[1] In the United States, organizations that monitor media bias include those with a liberal perspective, such as the Center for Media and Democracy, Fairness and Accuracy in Reporting, and Media Matters for America. On the other hand, organizations with a conservative perspective include the Media Research Center and Accuracy in Media. Additionally, there are groups with a relatively nonpartisan stance, such as Ad Fontes Media, the Center for Media and Public Affairs, and FactCheck.

[2] Partisan mindset activates what is known as "hostile media perception," where people believe that news is written unfavorably toward their own side and favorably toward the opposing side. This phenomenon refers to the tendency of individuals not to accept media messages at face value but to perceive their fairness differently based on their partisan positions. It describes the tendency of people with clear opinions on an issue to believe that the media is more supportive of views that oppose their own.

[3] Nevertheless, it is always beneficial for media watchdog organizations to monitor news media and provide news consumers with information about hidden biases.

According to a study by renowned journalism scholar John Merrill, *Time* magazine displayed different biases toward the three US presidents who served between 1945 and 1963. The magazine showed a strong negative bias toward Truman, a strong positive bias toward Eisenhower, and a more neutral tone toward Kennedy (Merrill, 1965). After this study caused a stir, the editors of *Time* claimed that the magazine had become fairer over time (Severin and Tankard, 1992). However, contrary to these claims, a study found that *Time*'s political bias continued to follow similar patterns as in the past, while its circulation increased by 40% during the period when the editors claimed the magazine had become fairer (Fedler et al., 1979). The periods examined in these studies correspond to the mid-20th century, when American news consumers' trust in mass media was at its peak. Yet, even during these times, media bias persisted.

These studies on *Time*'s reporting bias suggest that media bias does not disappear even when subjected to scrutiny and evaluation by external observers. In reality, the display of bias by news media around the world has not fundamentally changed over a long period. This is because media bias, in many cases, has a positive effect on expanding the news audience and increasing the influence and revenue of news media (Anand et al., 2007).

Thus, a "human without bias" or a "news media without bias" is like a "vacuum without air." Just as a vacuum exists only in theory or in laboratories, so too does unbiased news exist only in theory. People's perceptions of bias are diverse, and bias in news media will never disappear. Furthermore, as mentioned earlier in Section 4.3, it is important to remember that media bias is not always harmful, just as not all bacteria are harmful to the human body.

On the contrary, when news consumers have no bias, they can become easy targets for those seeking to manipulate public opinion. This creates an ideal setting for power or media to shape public opinion as if working on a blank canvas. If we think of bias as air, polluted air should be purified, but air itself cannot—and should not—be eliminated.

5.1.2 THE DEFINITION OF MEDIA BIAS IN ECONOMICS

So far, we have explained two fundamental characteristics of media bias: first, that media bias is perceived differently by different people and second, that it is a persistent attribute that does not disappear. From here, let's explore how to concretely define such media bias and examine the perspectives of economists on why media bias occurs.

Economists began studying media bias later than scholars in journalism and media communication, but their contributions have been significant to the extent that journalism scholars have acknowledged their impact. Moreover, economists have increasingly conducted both theoretical predictions and empirical analyses, not only on the causes but also on the effects of media bias.

In fact, renowned communication scholar S. Robert Lichter, in a book summarizing academic findings on media bias, noted that "in recent years, economists have played an increasingly significant role in developing new models of media bias" and stated that "recent changes in journalism can at least partially be explained by economic incentives." He particularly emphasized that "it becomes even more significant that news consumers are drawn to news that reflects their own views and consider news that challenges their opinions to be biased, as their utility is maximized when the bias provided by news suppliers aligns with the bias desired by consumers" (Lichter, 2017, p. 8).

In the study of media bias, the economist who first had a significant impact on journalism and communication scholars was James Hamilton. In his 2004 book, *All the News That's Fit to Sell*,[4] he argued that news media's differentiation of political biases in coverage resembles how firms in other markets differentiate products to appeal to varying consumer preferences (Hamilton, 2004). For example, news with a progressive perspective gains popularity among people who share similar views, while news with a conservative perspective is welcomed by conservative news consumers. Hamilton explained that news media maximize profit and demand by differentiating their bias to target news consumers with different preferences.

How, then, do economists define media bias? Before introducing their definitions, let us briefly examine the various forms in which media bias appears. Prat and Strömberg (2013), in their study of the role of news media in democratic political processes, categorized media bias into four types: "facts bias," "framing bias," "issue bias," and "ideological stand bias."[5] They explained that issue bias depends on which issues the media choose to cover, facts bias refers to which aspects of an issue are included or excluded, framing bias concerns how those facts are presented, and ideological stand bias reflects how the issues are commented on. Gentzkow et al. (2015), summarizing economic research on media bias, proposed a simpler typology with two categories: "distortion" and "filtering of information." Generally, Prat and Strömberg's "facts bias" and "framing bias" correspond to "distortion," while "issue bias" and "ideological stand bias" fall under "filtering of information." Based on Gentzkow et al.'s simpler categorization, let's concretely explain these biases.

First, "distortion" includes cases where specific facts are not reported at all or when reporting does not align with the facts. This bias involves deliberately omitting important facts or distorting, manipulating, or fabricating the facts themselves. Therefore, identifying such bias is relatively easy. For example, in the reports on the US military's battle in Samarra, if Fox News had reported that "there were no civilian corpses" or if Al Jazeera had reported that "the people killed by the US military

[4] The title of this book is derived from the slogan *All the News That's Fit to Print*, which was adopted by Adolph Ochs when he acquired *The New York Times* in 1896.

[5] Another economist, Sobbrio (2014), presents a similar classification of bias. He categorizes media bias into four types: "selective omission of information," "framing," "issue selection/agenda setting," and "slanted endogenous information acquisition."

were not Iraqi insurgents," then at least one of these reports would constitute outright distortion.[6]

The second type, "filtering of information,"[7] is the act of selectively choosing facts during the reporting process. This type of bias is relatively hidden because it is embedded in the news along with summaries of facts. It is the bias that journalists consciously or unconsciously incorporate into the news and is prevalent in news media. To explain the bias resulting from filtering in the context of the Iraq battle reports, Fox News reported "the capture of eight Iraqis," *The New York Times* reported "the anger of the Iraqis," and Al Jazeera uniquely reported on "the corpses at the hospital." Each news outlet filtered different facts. The differing expressions regarding the number of people killed by the US military, "at least 54" (Fox News) versus "as many as 54" (*The New York Times*), can be broadly seen as information filtering related to the possibility of the actual number being higher or lower than 54.

In practice, bias arising from information filtering is an inherent characteristic of news suppliers and can occur even unintentionally. Anthony Downs, an economist who explained democracy from an economic perspective, described it as follows:

> *...information is necessarily gathered by means of certain principles of selection: rules employed to determine what to make use of and what not to. Different persons use different rules, but everyone must use some rule—even random selection follows a rule. Therefore, all information is by nature biased because it is a selection of data from the vast amount extant, others of which could have been selected... all such selection is evaluative to some extent. In short, there is no such thing as purely objective reporting of any situations or events.*[8]
>
> **(Downs, 1957, p. 212).**

While there are differences in how economists categorize and describe media bias, their fundamental understanding of media bias is not significantly different. Therefore, although economists may use varying terms to describe forms of media bias, their perspectives are not mutually exclusive. Furthermore, in practice, the biases we observe in the media often result from a combination of these different forms of bias. Gentzkow, Shapiro, and Stone, who categorized media bias into "distortion" and "information filtering," proposed the following definition of media bias,

[6] Economists who have studied media bias caused by "outright distortion" include Milgrom and Roberts (1986b), Mullainathan and Shleifer (2005), Baron (2006), Besley and Prat (2006), Gentzkow and Shapiro (2006), and Bernhardt et al. (2008).

[7] Economists who have defined media bias in terms of "filtering of information" include Strömberg (2004b), Chan and Suen (2008), and Duggan and Martinelli (2011). The first person to conceptualize the idea of "filtering of information" was the renowned linguist Samuel I. Hayakawa (1906–1992), a Japanese-American who also served as a US Senator. He defined "slanting," a term synonymous with bias, as "the process of selecting favorable or unfavorable details about what one is attempting to describe" (Hayakawa, 1964, p. 13).

[8] The legendary American journalist Walter Lippmann also stated in his book *Public Opinion* (1922) that every news article, except for sports scores presented in numerical form, undergoes a process of selection and omission in some way.

which captures various types of bias recognized by economists. This is an economic definition of media bias that most economists generally agree upon:

> *It is such systematic differences in the mapping from facts to news reports—that is, differences which tend to sway naive readers to the right or left on political issues—that we will call bias.*
>
> **(Gentzkow et al., 2015, p. 625).**

Such media bias was evident in the coverage of the US military battle in Samarra by Fox News, *The New York Times*, and Al Jazeera, and it is a phenomenon that readers frequently encounter in news media. Furthermore, Gentzkow et al. argued, "Despite its negative connotations, bias as we have defined it need not be socially harmful. In some cases—outright distortion or needless omission—the consequences for consumer information, at least, will be unambiguously negative, and it is meaningful to talk about a benchmark of 'unbiased' reporting. In other cases—filtering or selection—an efficient market may supply different varieties of bias, and there is no meaningful notion of unbiasedness" (Gentzkow et al., 2015, p. 643). In other words, media bias does not disappear and is not always socially harmful.

5.2 WHY DOES MEDIA BIAS ARISE?

So why do systematic differences in the way facts are presented in news—what we call media bias—occur?

This question is related to the fact that just as people perceive different biases in the same news, they also often have opposing opinions about the causes of bias and the entities responsible for it. For example, many progressive politicians, civic group members, and media scholars in the United States often attribute media bias to "media owners" or "advertisers," believing they influence reporting to serve their financial and political interests. On the other hand, many conservative politicians, interest groups, and commentators blame "journalists" or "media organizations" themselves, arguing that individual reporters and media outlets push liberal agendas. This difference in perception naturally stems from the fact that progressives perceive conservative bias, while conservatives perceive liberal bias in media coverage. This kind of opposing perception, as introduced in the section "Opposing biases," is common in other countries as well.

However, economists have a different perspective on why the media becomes biased. They believe that media bias can be caused not only by media owners or individual journalists as news suppliers but also by news consumers—readers and viewers—as well as external entities like politicians and large corporations outside the news market. They see media bias as not being exclusive to any particular ideological camp.

According to economists, on the supply side of news, media bias can arise from media owners or journalists. Additionally, when power or financial influence captures media companies or journalists, the resulting news may reflect the biases desired by those in power or with financial clout. On the demand side, media bias can emerge as news media try to align themselves with the biases of their consumers, such as readers and viewers. While economists have not yet found definitive evidence on whether the supply side or demand side is the primary cause of media bias, they generally agree that with increased market competition, demand-side influences—such as those of readers and viewers—tend to play a more dominant role.[9]

Now, let's take a closer look at each of the causes of media bias as discussed by economists.

5.2.1 VERIFIABILITY OF NEWS

The persistence of media bias, despite thorough monitoring of news media, and the differing perceptions people hold regarding its direction and degree have already been explained. Drawing from these empirical characteristics of media bias, Anand et al. (2007) explored the causes of media bias in their study, demonstrating that consumers' inherent limitations in verifying news content drive the occurrence of media bias.

They argued that if news content were composed solely of facts that could be completely verified by news consumers, news media would report only facts, leaving no room for bias. This is because it would be unwise for news media to distort or filter facts that can be easily verified by news consumers. However, when unverifiable facts appear in news content, consumers focus more on the opinions embedded by media outlets. The scholars believed that the news media introduce bias through such opinions. In other words, the inherent nature of news, which does not consist solely of verifiable facts, is what leads to media bias.[10]

To support their argument, the scholars pointed to the fluctuating quality of news media. For instance, certain news outlets sometimes maintain an appearance of objectivity, when at other times they convey significant bias. The reason for this dual phenomenon, they argued, lies in the fact that information is not always fully verifiable.

According to Anand, Di Tella, and Galetovic, the reality that news consumers cannot fully verify the content of the news provides news suppliers with the "leeway" to add opinions or interpretations to their news content. This leeway is a necessary condition for the occurrence of media bias. The sufficient condition for media bias to arise, on the other hand, is the awareness of news consumers' biases when news media fill this leeway with their own biases. To maximize profits, news media must

[9] "Understanding the origin of slant is potentially important for regulatory reasons. However, at this stage, the evidence is mixed" (Prat and Strömberg, 2013, p. 182).

[10] This perspective on bias aligns closely with the definition provided by the renowned communication scholar Denis McQuail (1935–2017). He defined bias as the inherent subjectivity that arises when the media, beyond the realm of reporting reality as it is, include editorial opinions and interpretative articles that freely incorporate subjective judgments and evaluations. This nonobjectivity, according to McQuail, constitutes bias (McQuail, 2005).

attract more consumers, and to do so, they must reflect the biases favored by consumers in their reporting.

The scholars developed an economic model of "media bias" based on the assumption that the information included in news cannot be fully verified and that news consumers each have their own biases. In this model, news consumers assign relative weights to information and opinions in news content based on its verifiability.[11] That is, when news is highly verifiable, consumers assign more weight to the information, and when news is less verifiable, they assign more weight to opinions (or interpretations). Anand and his colleagues explained that media bias is the result of news media differentiating their products based on facts that are difficult to verify.

According to this view, the more verifiable the news content, the smaller the bias gap among media outlets. For instance, in scandal reports involving one of two opposing political camps, the bias gap between partisan media is typically large. However, the more easily verifiable the facts of the scandal, the smaller the reporting bias difference between left- and right-leaning media outlets. The scholars' perspective is convincing in that news reports on events like sports matches—where the truth of the facts can be easily confirmed—tend to be less biased.

Anand and his colleagues also attributed news consumers' distrust of journalists to media bias, which emerges inversely to the verifiability of news. They stated, "As long as the news item in question is not fully verifiable, customers will observe how different media firms reach drastically different conclusions (editorials), starting from the same piece of information. Not surprisingly, viewers will find suspect what most journalists have to say, with the exception of the one he/she usually watches."[12] Thus the scholars explained that simply asking people about media bias is hardly the way to infer bias.

5.2.2 THE DESIRES AND LIMITS OF NEWS PROVIDERS

The most common perception among the public is that media bias arises from the news media and journalists who produce and supply the news. There is ample justification for this belief. From media owners to editors and frontline journalists, each actor in the news production process carries personal biases shaped by their interests, beliefs, or experiences. The extent to which these biases affect individual articles or broader news coverage depends on the person's role and level of editorial authority. In practice, media bias arises from news providers' intention to influence the

[11] In news products, information and opinions each possess attributes of vertical differentiation, while opinions can be seen as attributes of horizontal differentiation. For more on these two types of differentiation, refer to Section 6.3, where news media compete through differentiation based on bias and quality.

[12] The British political philosopher Onora O'Neill states, "The press are skilled at making material accessible, but erratic about making it assessable. This may be why opinion polls and social surveys now show that the public in the UK claim that they trust newspaper journalists less than any other profession." (O'Neill, 2002, May 1).

behavior of news consumers or from their unconscious cognitive and professional limitations.[13]

The existence of bias attributable to news providers can be easily confirmed through examples of misinformation. Imagine a scenario where a news media outlet claims to have uncovered new facts and reports them. However, if this discovery is later proven to be inaccurate or contains false information (whether intentionally or not), the root cause of this misinformation is likely to be a bias resulting from the journalists' political leanings, professional interests, lack of expertise, or cognitive limitations. Such bias led the journalists to misunderstand or intentionally distort the facts, ultimately crossing a line that should not have been crossed.

The media bias driven by supply-side factors includes biases stemming from the interests, biases, and human limitations of journalists and media owners, as well as those resulting from the capture of news providers by external forces, such as politicians, governments, large corporations, and interest groups outside the news market. This phenomenon is known as "media capture."

To elaborate further, political powers or large corporations might physically threaten or economically entice media owners, executives, desk editors, or journalists to adjust the facts, tone, or context of news in a way that aligns with those media capturers' interests. Common examples include preventing the reporting of unfavorable news or encouraging the publication of favorable news. The frequent political (ideological) bias observed in public broadcasting in many countries is likely related to media capture by political powers. Similarly, the phenomenon of news media reporting in favor of conglomerates or refraining from negative coverage of them can be attributed to advertising influence over the media.

The level of competition among news providers also affects both the extent and direction of media bias. Consider a news market with varying levels of competition: a monopoly with only one media outlet, a duopoly with two dominant players, an oligopoly with several providers controlling the market, and a competitive market with many outlets. In a monopoly, most media bias reflects the preferences of the sole news provider, with little consideration for consumer preferences. However, as competition intensifies—from duopoly to oligopoly to full competition—news outlets face increasing pressure to cater to audiences and market forces, resulting in different forms and degrees of bias. The supply-side media bias described above is illustrated in Fig. 5.1.

Next, let's examine in greater detail the principles behind media bias driven by the news suppliers, such as journalists and media owners. Some other supply-side biases, influenced by the degree of competition and media capture, will be briefly discussed in this chapter and covered in greater depth in other parts of this book.[14]

[13] Refer to Section 2.2, "The Destiny and Limits of News Providers".

[14] Bias resulting from competition is explored in detail in Chapter 7, *The Virtues and Vices of Competition in News Market*, while bias resulting from media capture is examined in depth in Chapter 9, *Media Capture and Media Power*.

FIGURE 5.1

Media bias due to supply factors.

5.2.2.1 *Journalists*

David Baron, a political economist at Stanford University, believed that news consumers always want "less biased" news. If that were true, then the intense competition among media outlets should have eliminated or minimized their biases. However, as discussed in section "Persistent bias," media bias has always persisted, even amid fierce competition among media outlets. Baron identified the reason as follows (Baron, 2006).

Baron reasoned that although news media, as profit-seeking companies, display political bias, they would not pursue political bias at the expense of profits. Since news media are profit-driven enterprises, there must be a profit motive behind their political bias. In this context, Baron focused on the journalists employed by these media firms.

Generally, the executives or owners of news media cannot ignore the demands or preferences of news consumers, as they are profit-driven enterprises. However, individual journalists are not as conscious of consumers as the owners or executives. For journalists, their reputation or career development often matters more than the profit their media outlet generates. For this reason, Baron believed that journalists report news in ways that benefit their career advancement, and this tendency leads to media bias.

According to Baron, journalists are likely to gain fame by reporting in a biased manner in a specific direction, as bias can make articles more compelling. For example, a report claiming that "GMOs (genetically modified organisms) are harmful" is more likely to appear on the front page of a newspaper, while an article stating that "GMOs are not harmful" might be relegated to a less prominent section. In such situations, journalists are inclined to choose biased news within permissible limits.[15] On the other hand, news consumers prefer less biased news because bias diminishes accuracy.

Baron proposed that news media might allow a certain degree of biased reporting by journalists. He noted that the more news media restrict journalists' discretion regarding bias, the higher the wages they must pay. Conversely, allowing some discretion reduces labor costs. In other words, while news media companies can control reporting bias by limiting journalists' discretion, doing so requires paying higher wages. By giving journalists some leeway, media firms can lower labor costs and increase profits.

Therefore according to Baron, profit-maximizing news media firms seek to reduce labor costs by expanding journalists' discretion regarding bias. As a result, media bias arises from journalists who prioritize career advancement and are willing to sacrifice current wages for future opportunities.

Baron's model also implies that competition among news media can increase bias. The pressure to cut costs due to competition leads news media to grant journalists greater discretion to report with bias, minimizing the wages paid to them. Consequently, if other conditions are the same, Baron's view suggests that highly biased, low-quality media outlets can still generate sufficient profits.

5.2.2.2 *Media owners*

Unlike David Baron, who argued that media owners allow journalists' biases for greater profits, Harold Demsetz (1930–2019) and Kenneth Lehn, two pioneers of the New Institutional Economics school, believed that media firm owners are willing to tolerate lower profits if they can infuse their ideological views into media content. In other words, media owners might pursue ideological objectives even at the cost of reduced profits (Demsetz and Lehn, 1985).

Simon Anderson and John McLaren of the University of Virginia took this idea a step further. They explored media bias driven by the political motivations of media owners, proposing that these owners seek both commercial profits and political influence. Building on this notion, Anderson and McLaren developed a theoretical model in which media owners derive utility not only from profits but also from influencing the political choices of news consumers (Anderson and McLaren, 2012).

In this model, media owners influence public opinion by withholding certain information from news consumers for their political gain. This is possible for the following reasons: news consumers do not know all the information available to news media. Media owners (through the journalists they hire) omit information from news reports, thereby embedding their desired bias. Even if news consumers are aware of the owners' political leanings, they are still influenced by the bias created through

[15] The worst outcome of journalists' attempts to attract the attention of both news consumers and other journalists can be news that crosses the line from acceptable bias into misinformation or disinformation. In extreme cases, this may result in fabricated news.

omitted facts. When information is not reported, news consumers cannot discern whether it was unavailable or deliberately hidden by the media.

Anderson and McLaren argue that while media owners can use their outlets to advance their political interests, competition among media outlets can serve as a check on this behavior. According to them, competing news outlets strive to meet the demands of news consumers. If consumers demand accuracy, the media will seek to reduce bias and improve accuracy to avoid losing their audience. Therefore, as long as news consumers desire accurate reporting, increased competition effectively mitigates media bias caused by media owners' political interests. Conversely, a reduction in competition has the opposite effect. Furthermore, media owners who infuse their political biases into their outlets cannot offer diverse and differentiated news to consumers. Thus in a market where media owners intervene in content, increased competition is more desirable, according to the two scholars.

In general product or service markets, decreased competition results in lower quality and higher prices. In contrast, in news markets where media owners embed their biases into the news, reduced competition can lead to distorted democratic decision-making and social choices. This suggests that the negative effects of mergers and ownership concentration in news markets are likely to be more severe than in other markets, as they can lead to greater distortions in democratic decision-making and public opinion.

5.2.3 CONSUMER DEMAND FOR BIASED NEWS

Among journalists, the idea that news consumers want the truth is often treated as a matter of faith—accepted widely and unquestioningly, much like a guiding belief in religious communities. It is both a belief and a moral imperative. But is it really so? If news consumers truly desire the truth, how can they determine the authenticity of news? Especially when one of the fundamental criteria they use to judge the truthfulness of news is their own inherent confirmation bias? How does the confirmation bias of news consumers affect their ability to evaluate truthfulness in news?

Economists have grappled with similar questions. If news consumers value accurate news, economic logic suggests that increased competition among news media should eliminate bias. After all, it would be impossible for news outlets that distort the news with biases disconnected from consumer demands to survive in a competitive market. However, media bias persists even amid fierce competition. This reality has led economists to explore the seemingly irrational behavior of consumers who seek biased news and to investigate the mechanism behind this demand for biased news.[16]

[16] "The implicit starting point of any demand-driven rationale for media bias is rooted in the idea that if viewers always (and only) value full accuracy in news reports, in fairly competitive media markets any supply-driven media bias should fade away" (Sobbrio, 2014).

5.2.3.1 News consumers seeking "satisfaction" over "truth"

Confirmation bias refers to the tendency to accept information that aligns with one's preexisting thoughts or beliefs while ignoring or rejecting information that contradicts them. It is a universal cognitive bias that affects both the selection and interpretation of information. Simply put, people tend to see only what they want to see. Although news consumers claim to seek "truth," they assess whether something is true or not through the prism of their own "bias." So, what exactly is the "truth" that news consumers who are gripped by confirmation bias desire?

If you were to receive news about your spouse's infidelity along with news denying it, or see a report predicting a sharp drop in the stock you own alongside one saying the opposite, which news would you believe? For ordinary people, the answer is clear. Before confronting a dispute between truth and falsehood, people first encounter news they want to believe and news they would rather not believe. And they tend to consider the former to be "the truth."[17]

Moreover, throughout human history, there have been many instances when even falsehoods, if aligned with many people's confirmation bias, were accepted as truths not just for days or years but for decades or even centuries. During the Age of Discovery, what European explorers discovered was the American continent. However, due to the confirmation bias held by most Europeans at that time, the existence of a "New World" was beyond their imagination. As a result, from Christopher Columbus's discovery of the continent in 1492 until Amerigo Vespucci announced in 1503 that it was a New World, the Americas were considered to be part of the Indies for at least a decade.[18]

There is an even more prominent example. The geocentric theory proposed by the Greek astronomer Ptolemy in the 2nd century, which claimed that the sun revolves around the earth, remained an unchallenged truth for 1400 years until Copernicus proposed the heliocentric theory in the 16th century. Even then, it took hundreds of years for most people to accept the heliocentric model as "the truth." The primary reason for this prolonged transition was the confirmation bias that people held regarding the geocentric model. Regardless of how truthfully the news is reported, if it neither aligns with nor successfully overcomes the consumers' bias, it is not only unlikely to be chosen by the consumer, but even less likely to be accepted as "the truth." In essence, while news consumers claim to seek true news, they first look for news that aligns with their own beliefs. Only when they can overcome their biases can they open their eyes to the "truth."

Moreover, human desires for news are paradoxical. While rational thinking and judgment are emphasized, most people instinctively pay attention to sensational news that appeals to their emotions. Fast news is rarely accurate, and accurate news

[17] Economists Rabin and Schrag (1999) demonstrated that people can end up believing in false hypotheses due to confirmation bias, even when exposed to an infinite amount of information.

[18] The Americas were actually first discovered by Norsemen from Northern Europe around AD 1000. Columbus's achievement was the discovery of a West Indies route from Europe to the American continent.

is rarely delivered quickly; however, most people want news that is both fast and accurate. Sometimes emotions and confirmation bias overwhelm rationality, and the desire for quick information surpasses the desire for accurate information. This contradictory set of desires among news consumers exerts a compelling force on news media and journalists, who must capture their audience's attention. Just as newspapers cannot exist without readers, news media that disregard consumer desires cannot survive in the news market. This is why media bias arises from news consumers.

5.2.3.2 The utility of "confirmation news"

News consumers prefer "confirmatory news" that aligns with their preferences or biases, rather than the most objective and accurate news. Communication scholars also commonly believe that people enjoy and trust stories that align with their beliefs (Severin and Tankard, 1992). Psychologists have also explained from multiple angles that people tend to selectively use empirical evidence (Lord et al., 1979), remember information consistent with their beliefs better than contradictory information (Bartlett, 1932), and universally possess confirmation bias in various forms (Nickerson, 1998). This consumer behavior in news consumption leads to media bias from news providers.

In this context, Gentzkow et al. remarked in their literature review on economic theories of media bias, "The other potential driver of bias is demand from consumers themselves" (Gentzkow et al., 2015, p. 633).

Economists, in particular, have made efforts to rationally understand "seemingly irrational human behaviors" (Tirole, 2002; Caplan, 2000). Matthew Rabin and Joel Schrag drew attention by demonstrating that people are less likely to trust data that contradicts their beliefs and, therefore, less likely to incorporate it into updating their beliefs (Rabin and Schrag, 1999). This means that people interpret new information in a way that reinforces their preexisting biases. Sendhil Mullainathan also argued that people tend to ignore information unless it is substantial enough to challenge their broader set of existing beliefs (Mullainathan, 2002).

Economists have two main perspectives on why humans prefer confirmatory news. The first is the "psychological utility" that people gain from consuming news. It is the view that news consumers derive direct satisfaction from consuming news that aligns with their confirmation bias. For example, people find it pleasurable to encounter news that reassures them that their beliefs are correct and others' beliefs are wrong. On the other hand, encountering news that challenges one's existing beliefs inevitably requires reevaluating related matters, which involves effort. For this reason, people tend to avoid news that contradicts their confirmation bias.

Thus economists who see news consumers' preference for confirmatory news as a matter of psychological utility think that consumers prefer news closer to their political ideologies or views (Yariv, 2002; Mullainathan and Shleifer, 2005; Yang, 2022; Gabszewicz et al., 2001), derive utility from positive news about the political parties they support and negative news about opposing parties (Bernhardt et al., 2008), or prefer news that helps them avoid cognitive dissonance (Schulz and Weimann, 1989).

The second explanation from economists for humans' preference for confirmatory news is "expected utility." In economics, expected utility refers to the rational (probabilistic) utility one can expect to gain from an action in an uncertain future. Rational individuals compare the expected utilities of different actions and choose the one with the highest expected utility, according to expected utility theory. Based on this theory, it is rational for consumers to make choices (and take actions) based on information that aligns with their prior beliefs or preferences in uncertain situations (Calvert, 1985; Suen, 2004). In other words, news consumers seek information that increases the expected utility of their choices and actions. This information is what we call "confirmatory news," which satisfies their confirmation bias.[19]

Therefore when news consumers prefer confirmatory news due to psychological utility, they are seen as irrational. However, when they prefer confirmatory news due to "expected utility," they are viewed as highly rational.

5.3 THE DIVERSITY OF NEWS CONSUMER BIAS ACROSS TIME AND SOCIETIES

News consumer bias, a primary driver of media bias, changes over time and varies across societies, even within the same era. Political conflicts, wealth distribution, and long-standing customs within a society all shape the nature of news consumer biases. Just as people's lifestyles, ways of thinking, and cultures vary across different times and societies, so too does the attitude of news consumers toward the news. It would be unusual for the patterns of political bias in a society with intense political conflicts to be the same as those in a relatively stable society. Moreover, such biases among news consumers are constantly changing. This is because societal shifts—such as changes in political power, ideology, or economic conditions—are consistently reflected in the biases of news consumers.

5.3.1 BIAS VARIES BY COUNTRY

The Reuters Institute for the Study of Journalism conducts an annual survey and analysis of news consumers' perceptions and usage patterns in major countries around the world and publishes these findings in the *Digital News Report*. According to the *Digital News Report 2020*, skewed news consumption, like in South Korea or Brazil, is among the most severe in the world. South Korea has one of the highest percentages in the world, with 44% of its news consumers favoring "news that aligns with my perspective," while only 4% prefer "news that offers a different perspective."

[19] Studies on media bias by economists who assume that news consumers desire biased news from the perspective of expected utility include Gentzkow and Shapiro (2006), Chan and Suen (2008), Burke (2008), Strömberg (2004b), and Duggan and Martinelli (2011).

As shown in Fig. 5.2, South Korean news consumers exhibit "extreme" news consumption behaviors compared to those in other countries.

This exclusive consumption of news that aligns with their own views—where individuals seek to confirm their beliefs while avoiding opposing opinions—is the most pronounced in countries like South Korea and Brazil. This indicates that in South Korea, there is significant pressure on news media from consumers demanding coverage that aligns with their biases. Consequently, news media with a moderate viewpoint are relatively the least welcomed. While this survey was conducted in 2020, there has been little change in this pattern since then.

Many South Koreans may think, "Why would anyone read news that opposes their own views? It would only cause stress, so it's understandable that few people would want to do so." However, if they think this way, it's probably because they live in South Korea. Shifting our focus to countries like Finland and Norway in Northern Europe offers a different picture. In the same survey by the Reuters Institute, only 11% of people in Finland and 12% in Norway preferred "news that aligns with my perspective," which is just a quarter of the figure for South Korea. Even more noteworthy is that 12% of people in Finland and 17% in Norway favored "news that offers a different perspective," which is higher than the percentage of people who preferred news that aligns with their views. The Finnish and Norwegian people, who are more inclined to learn about others' views than to reinforce their own, demonstrate greater openness to differing opinions.

The differences in news consumers' biases and their attitudes toward the news in each country, as illustrated in Fig. 5.3, result in varying ideological positioning of news media across nations.

The selective consumption of news that aligns with one's own views while avoiding news that contradicts them is easily observed in countries like South Korea and Brazil, as shown in Fig. 5.2. This phenomenon is the result of continuous political polarization and the accumulation of biased reporting by news media taking advantage of it. It is difficult to definitively say which came first—exclusive news consumption or polarized, biased reporting by news media. However, there seems to be little room for disagreement that the two phenomena have mutually influenced each other.

In summary, as illustrated in Figs. 5.2 and 5.3, the differing ideological positioning of news media in each country is closely related to the attitudes of their news consumers. However, this situation is not set in stone. Germany could someday resemble Spain, and Brazil could become more like Switzerland. As mentioned earlier, as time passes and political and economic landscapes shift, along with changes in technology, environment, and culture, people's perceptions and biases also change.

5.3.2 BIAS VARIES BY ERA

It is not easy to objectively verify how political biases change over time. To observe changes in the biases of an entire society over different periods, consistent survey questions must be accumulated over a long duration. Due to this, although it is

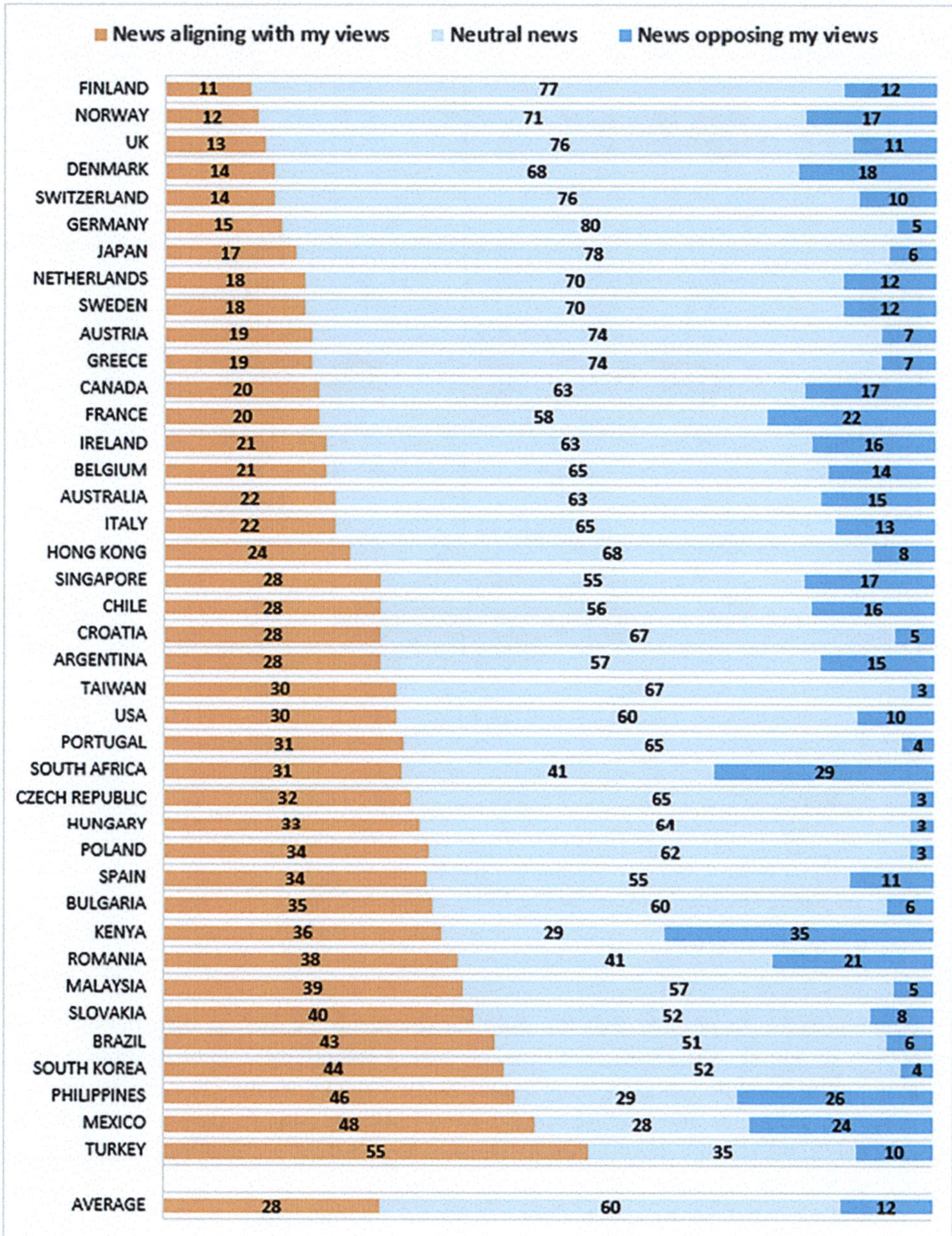

FIGURE 5.2

News preferences of consumers by country (40 countries) unit: %.

Based on Reuters Institute for the Study of Journalism. Digital News Report 2020.

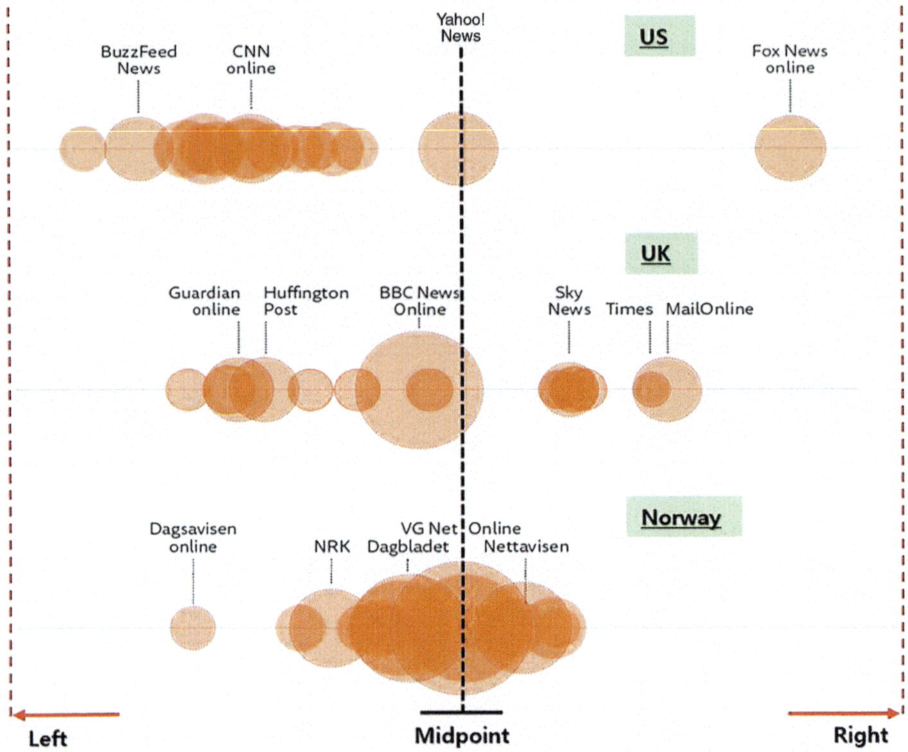

FIGURE 5.3

Ideological bias of major online news media outlets in the United States, the United Kingdom, and Norway. Note: The size of the *circles* representing news media brands indicates their relative market share in the online news market.

From Reuters Institute for the Study of Journalism. Digital News Report 2017.

common sense to assume that the political (or ideological) bias distribution of a society or nation would shift over time, providing objective evidence to support this assumption is challenging. In many countries, such data does not yet exist. However, in the United States, the Pew Research Center has been conducting relevant surveys for over 20 years, allowing for comparisons of Americans' political bias distribution across different periods.

In 2017, the Pew Research Center released findings from seven surveys conducted over the past two decades, using the same set of 10 questions since 1994 to assess how Americans' ideological (or political) biases have changed.

According to these findings, the number of Americans with consistently liberal or conservative biases has steadily increased over this period. There has been a rise in the number of Americans displaying partisan attitudes toward the two major political parties,

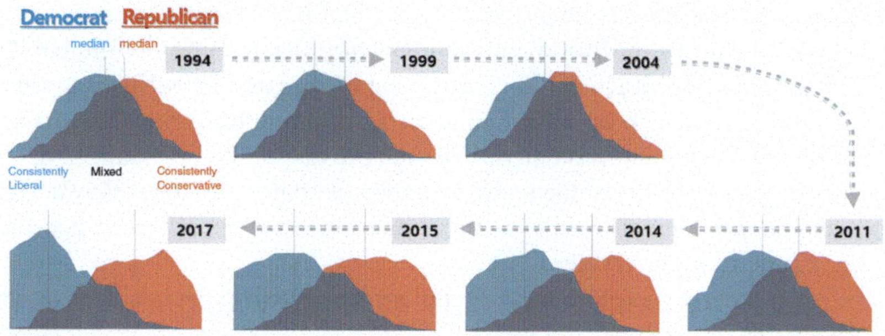

FIGURE 5.4

Trends in political polarization among American news consumers (1994–2017). Note: The "median" represents the person with the median ideological stance among each party's supporters.

From Pew Research Center (Oct 20, 2017).

the Democrats and Republicans. As seen in Fig. 5.4, in 1994, a substantial moderate segment existed among American news consumers, and political polarization had not significantly intensified. In contrast, by 2017, when Donald Trump took office as President, political polarization had reached a level so severe that the nation seemed split in two.

In recent years, countries like South Korea, Brazil, Slovakia, and Romania have faced severe political polarization, similar to the deep divisions observed in the United States. However, in these countries as well, during periods when political polarization was less pronounced—like the early 2000s or the 1990s in the United States—the distribution of political biases among news consumers was likely different from what it is today.

Likewise, in these countries, political polarization may ease in the future, leading to changes in the distribution of people's political biases. Conversely, countries that are currently less polarized might move in the opposite direction. People's thoughts and biases continue to change everywhere around the world. And the biases of news media will likely change in tandem with, or in response to, the evolving biases of news consumers.

5.4 MEDIA SCHOLARS' VIEWS ON MEDIA BIAS

The definitions and understandings of media bias among media scholars are much more diverse than among economists. Such diversity not only aids in explaining and understanding various types of media bias but also provides a rich reservoir of concepts and typologies that can inform future research in the economics of news media. However, it also has a drawback, as there is no clearly standardized academic definition of media bias.

In fact, media scholars themselves have noted that "Media bias is a concept the widespread use of which belies equally widespread disagreement about its meaning, measurement, and impact" (Lichter, 2017, p. 1) and that "[media] bias is yet to be defined clearly, let alone received much serious empirical attention" (Entman, 2007, p. 163). Even though media bias is a core subject of research in media or journalism studies, a universally accepted definition is difficult to pinpoint among media scholars. Consequently, discussions on media bias are broader and more nuanced in media and journalism studies. This is due to the tendency of economics to employ deductive methods and rational models, while media studies tend to adopt inductive approaches grounded in empirical observation.

Here, we will briefly explore media scholars' perspectives and debates on media bias, with a focus on S. Robert Lichter's (2017) work, "Theories of Media Bias."

5.4.1 OBJECTIVITY AND IDEOLOGICAL BIASES

As explained in section "The rise of objective journalism" of Chapter 3, objective journalism emerged when the prevalent partisanship among newspapers hindered corporate growth, and reducing this partisanship helped attract a broader readership. Objective journalism is a school of thought that argues news media should remain unbiased and objective when dealing with political and public issues. Based on this, American journalists and scholars established professional norms and identities that distinguish journalistic reporting from partisan manipulation of information (Kaplan, 2009). Since then, objectivity in news has been regarded as synonymous with fairness, balance, and impartiality, serving as a criterion for assessing media bias.

However, the view that "news must be objective" has been a subject of debate among journalism scholars from the very beginning. Many scholars criticized the journalistic norm of objectivity as an unattainable ideal, subjective convention, or a mask for personal or political interests.

Notably, a considerable number of media scholars have argued that mass media have ideological biases. One group of scholars asserts that mass media have a conservative bias, while another group claims that they have a liberal bias. These conflicting claims by prominent scholars raise fundamental doubts about the objective journalism professed by mainstream news media and journalists.

5.4.1.1 Conservative bias

A group of sociologists and media scholars argue that mass media have a "conservative bias." They claim that news media play a crucial role in shaping public consciousness, thereby maintaining the interests and hegemony of the dominant social class. The most representative figure of this view is the well-known linguist and sociologist Noam Chomsky. Together with his colleague Edward Herman, Chomsky emphasized in their book, Manufacturing Consent: *The Political Economy of the Mass Media*, that media distort reality in ways that manipulate public consent, ultimately serving the interests of the ruling elites (Herman and Chomsky, 1988).[20]

[20] Chomsky and Herman argued that mass media serve as propaganda organs for the ruling class through five types of filtering. These filters are (1) corporate ownership, (2) advertising, (3) sourcing, (4) flak, and (5) anticommunism and fear.

Although the primary role of the press is to monitor and check power, Chomsky and Herman argue that, in reality, the press functions more as a propaganda tool for power and interest groups rather than holding them accountable.

Ben Bagdikian (1920–2016), a journalist and former professor, also argued that media owners and advertisers shape the production of news in ways that systematically favor the wealthy and the powerful (Bagdikian, 1983; Bagdikian, 2004). Communication historian Robert McChesney likewise attributed the decline in the quality of modern journalism in the United States to capitalism, arguing that dissenting voices that challenge the status quo are excluded from public discourse by dominant media (McChesney, 1995; McChesney, 2008).

These theories that support the claim of conservative media bias generally treat the media as a tool used by the ruling class or elites to control society. Some scholars even argue that while journalists sometimes play the role of a "watchdog" rather than a "lapdog" in relation to the powerful, they tend to defend the system when fundamental threats to the social order arise (Olien et al., 1995).

5.4.1.2 *Liberal bias*

On the other hand, some communication scholars argue that news is an explicit or implicit product of journalists' liberal biases. This view is based on survey results of journalists' ideological views and on the observed ideological differences between journalists and the general public. However, these scholars tend not to emphasize the influence of media owners in the news production process.

Robert Lichter, Stanley Rothman, and Linda Lichter conducted surveys on journalists' ideological leanings and compared the results to the news they produced. They concluded that news reflects the liberal biases of journalists (Lichter et al., 1990). Similarly, Thomas Patterson and Wolfgang Donsbach's research on journalists from five Western democratic countries (the United States, the United Kingdom, Germany, Italy, and Sweden) pointed out that although journalists self-define as adhering to objectivity and political neutrality, they remain partisan actors who incorporate their political beliefs into the news (Patterson and Donsbach, 1996). The claim of liberal bias among journalists and news media has also been supported by scholars like Andrew Kohut (1942–2015) and Jim A. Kuypers.

While numerous scholars have clearly identified journalists as having liberal tendencies, they have generally failed to verify whether these tendencies are reflected in the news produced. This is because they have been unable to objectively demonstrate the anticipated liberal bias of journalists through analyses of election coverage or other such content (Niven, 2002; D'Alessio and Allen, 2000). However, as empirical studies by 21st-century economists indicate that US news media exhibit a liberal bias, the debate on media bias within journalism studies has been reignited.

5.4.2 NONIDEOLOGICAL STRUCTURAL BIASES

Media scholars have identified various biases arising from the inherent characteristics and operating environment of news media and journalism. These biases are structurally embedded in the processes of news production and distribution. The following list of 10 nonideological structural biases proposed by Andrew R. Cline helps illustrate what structural biases entail (Cline, 2009):

- *Commercial bias*: News media prioritize stories that are likely to generate profit.
- *Temporal bias*: News media are inclined toward reporting recent events.
- *Visual bias*: TV broadcasting focuses on visual depictions of news, as news without visual support receives less attention.
- *Bad news bias*: Good news is perceived as boring. The bias toward reporting bad news often presents the world (especially politicians) as more dangerous and negative than it is. This is also known as the "Media Negativity Bias."[21]
- *Narrative bias*: News media frame news as a clear narrative with a beginning, middle, and end, often requiring a protagonist and antagonist. However, many real-world events are ambiguous. News media tend to impose clear causality on these events.
- *Status quo bias*: Mainstream news media do not question the existing social systems.
- *Fairness bias*: The journalistic ethic of fairness leads to mechanically balancing positive and negative information about individuals or issues. For example, if politician A announces a positive achievement, the media will seek a negative comment from politician B.
- *Expediency bias*: Journalists prioritize gathering information that is fast, easy, and cheap to obtain. For instance, as deadlines approach, journalists gather readily available information from well-known sources.
- *Glory bias*: Many journalists, particularly TV reporters, aim to be the central figures or characters in the news they cover, which distorts the facts.
- *Class bias*: Journalists were initially members of the working class. However, throughout the 20th century, they became highly educated members of the middle class or higher. News media also target wealthier audiences over lower-income groups. As a result, most journalists are closer, politically and culturally, to the middle class and elite than to the poor and working class.

In summary, structural biases are those embedded in the production and distribution processes of news, regardless of the political biases of consumers or providers. The overlap among these biases and their wide variety complicates the development of overarching theories about them (Lichter, 2017). For instance, even the "bad news bias," a tendency of journalists to focus on critical rather than positive reporting, can appear as a "fairness bias"; if it's a video news segment, it may fall under "visual bias"; and if the news contains facts that challenge the existing system, it might give an impression of "status quo bias" or "class bias."

[21] Scholars have attributed this bias to the professional attributes of journalists. The concepts of cynicism and conflict-oriented framing proposed by Jamieson and Waldman (2003) are examples.

References

Alterman, E., 2003. What Liberal Media? The Truth About Bias and the News. Basic Books.
Anand, B., Di Tella, R., Galetovic, A., 2007. Information or opinion? Media bias as product differentiation. Journal of Economics & Management Strategy 16 (3), 635–682.
Anderson, S.P., McLaren, J., 2012. Media mergers and media bias with rational consumers. Journal of the European Economic Association 10 (4), 831–859. https://doi.org/10.1111/j.1542-4774.2012.01069.x.
Bagdikian, B., 1983. The Media Monopoly. 1st ed. Boston: Beacon Press.
Bagdikian, B., 2004. The New Media Monopoly. Beacon Press, Boston.
Baron, D.P., 2006. Persistent media bias. Journal of Public Economics 90 (1–2), 1–36.
Bartlett, F.C., 1932. Remembering: A Study in Experimental and Social Psychology. Cambridge: Cambridge University Press.
Bernhardt, D., Krasa, S., Polborn, M., 2008. Political polarization and the electoral effects of media bias. Journal of Public Economics 92 (5–6), 1092–1104.
Besley, T., Prat, A., 2006. Handcuffs for the grabbing hand? Media capture and government accountability. American Economic Review 96 (3), 720–736.
Burke, J., 2008. Primetime spin: media bias and belief-confirming information. Journal of Economics & Management Strategy 17 (3), 633–665.
Calvert, R.L., 1985. The value of biased information: a rational choice model of political advice. The Journal of Politics 47 (2), 530–555. https://doi.org/10.2307/2130895.
Caplan, B., 2000. Rational irrationality: a framework for the neoclassical-behavioral debate. Eastern Economic Journal 26 (2), 191–211.
Chan, J., Suen, W., 2008. A spatial theory of news consumption and electoral competition. The Review of Economic Studies 75 (3), 699–728.
Cline, A., 2009. Bias. In: Eadie W., ed., 21st Century Communications. Thousand Oaks, CA: Sage; 479–486.
Coulter, A., 2002. Slander: Liberal Lies About the American Right. Crown Publishers.
D'Alessio, D., Allen, M., 2000. Media bias in presidential elections: a meta-analysis. Journal of Communication 50 (4), 133–156. https://doi.org/10.1111/j.1460-2466.2000.tb02866.x.
Demsetz, H., Lehn, K., 1985. The structure of corporate ownership: causes and consequences. Journal of Political Economy 93 (6), 1155–1177. https://doi.org/10.1086/261354.
Downs, A., 1957. An economic theory of political action in a democracy. Journal of Political Economy 65 (2), 135–150. https://doi.org/10.1086/257897.
Duggan, J., Martinelli, C., 2011. A spatial theory of media slant and voter choice. The Review of Economic Studies 78 (2), 640–666.
Entman, R.M., 2007. Framing bias: media in the distribution of power. Journal of Communication 57 (1), 163–173. https://doi.org/10.1111/j.1460-2466.2006.00336.x.
Fedler, F., Meeske, M., Hall, J., 1979. Time magazine revisited: presidential stereotypes persist. Journalism Quarterly 56 (2), 353–359. https://doi.org/10.1177/107769907905600219.
Gabszewicz, J.J., Laussel, D., Sonnac, N., 2001. Press advertising and the ascent of the 'Pensée Unique'. European Economic Review 45 (4–6), 641–651. https://doi.org/10.1016/S0014-2921(01)00139-8.
Gentzkow, M., Shapiro, J.M., 2006. Media bias and reputation. Journal of Political Economy 114 (2), 280–316.
Gentzkow, M., Shapiro, J.M., Stone, D.F., 2015. Media bias in the marketplace. In: Handbook of Media Economics. Elsevier, 623–645. https://doi.org/10.1016/b978-0-444-63685-0.00014-0.
Goldberg, B., 2001. Bias: A CBS Insider Exposes How the Media Distort the News. Regnery.

Hamilton, J.T., 2004. All the News That's Fit to Sell. Princeton University Press.

Hayakawa, I.S., 1964. Language in Thought and Action. Harcourt, Brace, and World, New York.

Herman, E.S., Chomsky, N., 1988. Manufacturing consent: the political economy of the mass media. New York: Pantheon Books.

Jamieson, K.H., Waldman, P., 2003. The Press Effect. Oxford University Press.

Kaplan, R., 2009. The origins of objectivity in American journalism. The Routledge Companion to News and Journalism Studies. pp. 25–27.

Krugman, P., 2002. American Media and Conflicts of Interest. The New York Times.

Lichter, S.R., 2017. Theories of media bias. In: Kenski, K., Jamieson, K.H. (Eds.), The Oxford Handbook of Political Communication. Oxford University Press.

Lichter, S.R., Rothman, S., Lichter, L.S., 1990. The Media Elite: America's New Powerbrokers. Hastings House.

Lord, C.G., Ross, L., Lepper, M.R., 1979. Biased assimilation and attitude polarization: the effects of prior theories on subsequently considered evidence. Journal of Personality and Social Psychology 37 (11), 2098–2109. https://doi.org/10.1037/0022-3514.37.11.2098.

McChesney, R., 1995. Telecommunications, Mass Media, and Democracy: The Battle for the Control of US Broadcasting, 1928–1935. Oxford University Press.

McChesney, R., 2008. The Political Economy of Media. Monthly Review Press.

McQuail, D., 2005. McQuail's Mass Communication Theory, fifth ed. Sage.

Merrill, J.C., 1965. How time stereotyped three U.S. presidents. Journalism Quarterly 42 (4), 563–570. https://doi.org/10.1177/107769906504200406.

Milgrom, P., Roberts, J., 1986b. Price and advertising signals of product quality. Journal of Political Economy 94 (4), 796–821.

Mullainathan, S., 2002. Thinking Through Categories [Working paper]. Harvard University.

Mullainathan, S., Shleifer, A., 2005. The market for news. American Economic Review 95 (4), 1031–1053. https://doi.org/10.1257/0002828054825619.

Nickerson, R.S., 1998. Confirmation bias: a ubiquitous phenomenon in many guises. Review of General Psychology 2 (2), 175–220. Available from: https://journals.sagepub.com/home/RGP. https://doi.org/10.1037/1089-2680.2.2.175.

Niven, D., 2002. Tilt? The Search for Media Bias. Praeger.

O'Neill, O., 2002, May 1. Shoot the Messenger: The Media Are Always Calling for Transparency, but Who Are They Accountable To? The Guardian Retrieved from: https://www.theguardian.com/comment/story/0,3604,707820,00.html.

Olien, C.N., Donohue, G.A., Tichenor, P.J., 1995. Conflict, consensus and public opinion. Public Opinion and the Communication of Consent. pp. 301–322.

Patterson, T.E., Donsbach, W., 1996. News decisions: journalists as partisan actors. Political Communication 13 (4), 455–468. https://doi.org/10.1080/10584609.1996.9963131.

Prat, A., Strömberg, D., 2013. The political economy of mass media. In: Advances in Economics and Econometrics. Cambridge University Press, 135–187. https://doi.org/10.1017/cbo9781139060028.004.

Rabin, M., Schrag, J.L., 1999. First impressions matter: a model of confirmatory bias. The Quarterly Journal of Economics 114 (1), 37–82.

Reuters Institute for the Study of Journalism. Digital News Report 2017. https://reutersinstitute.politics.ox.ac.uk/sites/default/files/Digital%20News%20Report%202017%20web_0.pdf.

Reuters Institute for the Study of Journalism. Digital News Report 2020. https://reutersinstitute.politics.ox.ac.uk/sites/default/files/2020-06/DNR_2020_FINAL.pdf.

Schulz, N., Weimann, J., 1989. Competition of newspapers and the location of political parties. Public Choice 63 (2), 125–147. https://doi.org/10.1007/bf00153396.

Severin, W.J., Tankard, J.W., 1992. Communication Theories: Origins, Methods, and Uses in the Mass Media.

Sobbrio, F., 2014. The political economy of news media: theory, evidence and open issues. In: Forte, F., Mudambi, R. (Eds.), A Handbook of Alternative Theories of Public Economics. Edward Elgar Publishing, pp. 278–320.

Strömberg, D., 2004b. Mass media competition, political competition, and public policy. The Review of Economic Studies 71 (1), 265–284.

Suen, W., 2004. The self-perpetuation of biased beliefs. The Economic Journal 114 (495), 377–396. https://doi.org/10.1111/j.1468-0297.2004.00213.x.

Tirole, J., 2002. Rational irrationality: some economics of self-management. European Economic Review 46 (4–5), 633–655. https://doi.org/10.1016/s0014-2921(01)00206-9.

Yang, S., 2022. Media bias with asymmetric media quality. Applied Economics Letters 29 (19), 1810–1814. https://doi.org/10.1080/13504851.2021.1963401.

Yariv, L., 2002. "I'll See It When I Believe It: A Simple Model of Cognitive Consistency." Cowles Foundation Discussion Paper, 1352. New Haven, CT: Yale University.

CHAPTER

6 News Quality: Double Standards and Objective Criteria

Chapter Outline

What is striking is the fact that what I regard as "trash journalism" may be seen by someone else as "real journalism," and what I consider to be "real journalism" may, in turn, be dismissed by another as trash.[1]

—Joon Man Kang

Just as consumer preferences guide choices between goods or services, confirmation bias plays a similar role in news consumption—it shapes an individual's selection of news and media. However, bias is not the only factor at play. Quality is another key determinant in the choices made by news consumers. Given the same price and bias, quality becomes the decisive factor in consumer choice. Consider the following: if regular milk and organic milk were offered at the same price, or if economy and

[1] Kang, J. (2020, November 22).

The Economics of News Media. DOI: http://dx.doi.org/10.1016/B978-0-443-45044-0.00009-X

business class seats on a plane were equally priced, the average consumer would not hesitate to choose the organic milk or the business class seat. The reason is simple: organic milk is considered higher quality than regular milk, and business class offers superior quality to economy. In this way, while preferences are inherently subjective and differ across individuals, quality—at least from an economic perspective—is viewed as an objective criterion.

But what does "quality" mean in the context of news or news media? To news consumers, the notion of quality in news is hardly foreign. In fact, consumers engage in informal assessments of news quality on a routine basis. Many dismiss sensational tabloid magazines as low-quality "yellow papers," while viewing globally respected publications like *The New York Times* as "quality papers." The rise of digital journalism has also brought new terminology that reflects growing awareness of low-quality content. Consider the terms *churnalism*,[2] used to criticize the unchecked copying of press releases or previously published stories, and *clickbait*,[3] which refers to sensationalized headlines crafted to attract clicks on digital platforms. Another telling example is the Korean slang term *giregi*—a portmanteau of "journalist" and "trash"—which expresses deep public contempt toward journalists perceived as unethical or sensationalistic. Clearly, judgments about the quality of news are deeply embedded in the daily habits and vocabulary of modern news consumers.

However, while such impressionistic assessments may come naturally to the public, they pose a more complicated challenge for economists. Before one can evaluate quality, one must first define it—and doing so requires a deep understanding of both human behavior and the nature of news itself. Scholars, in particular, are expected to define and explain news quality using clear and objective criteria. Yet the nature of news as a commodity is highly unusual. Unlike most goods, news is composed of intangible elements, and each article can be seen as a unique product in itself. This makes the task of defining quality in news especially difficult.

Perhaps the most formidable obstacle in assessing news media quality is that audiences often judge it through the lens of their own bias. For example, individuals with conservative leanings may find it difficult to view liberal-leaning media outlets as high quality and vice versa. It is often only when comparing outlets that share similar ideological orientations that consumers begin to perceive differences in quality. This subjective variation in quality perception makes it difficult to establish a universally accepted standard—something that, by definition, quality should entail.

In this chapter, we address the challenge of defining and evaluating news quality by examining how consumers make objective assessments despite these subjective biases. First, we explore the everyday contexts in which people judge the quality of news or news media as either high or low. Then, we turn to how economists have

[2] Churnalism: A term that refers to the practice of turning press releases or promotional materials into news stories with little or no original reporting. It is a blend of "churn out" (to mass-produce) and "journalism."

[3] Clickbait: Content that is designed to attract attention and encourage clicks, often through sensational headlines or images, but offering little real value. It is a blend of "click" and "bait."

defined and analyzed news quality from a more rigorous theoretical perspective. Finally, we examine how media firms leverage both quality—an objective basis for consumer choice—and bias—a subjective one—to segment the market and maximize profit. Furthermore, Section 6.4 provides an overview of how journalism scholars have approached the issue of news quality.

6.1 THE PUBLIC'S PERCEPTION OF NEWS QUALITY

People routinely compare products and make judgments such as "Product A is better than Product B." Yet what qualifies as "better" often depends on individual preferences. John may believe B is better than A, while Jane may insist otherwise. One person may prefer a smooth wine, another a tannic one. On airplanes, some passengers choose window seats, while others prefer the aisle. These examples illustrate how subjective preferences shape what each person considers "better."

By contrast, there are cases where one option is widely considered "better" by most people. For instance, business class is generally perceived as superior to economy class, and organic milk is typically viewed as better than regular milk. When the price is the same, the preferred option becomes obvious. This is because the standard for comparison is objective.

Consumers evaluate and compare goods or services using both subjective preferences (tastes) and objective criteria. The more complex a product or service is in terms of features and components, the more difficult this evaluation becomes. Consider the difference between choosing a bicycle and choosing a car. When buying a car, consumers must assess not only major categories such as exterior design, interior features, driving performance, convenience, and safety systems but also a host of details—color, seat material, engine power, acceleration, handling, navigation systems, the number of airbags, and so on. Comparing and judging these numerous features based on both subjective taste and objective standards is not easy.

For this reason, consumers make extensive efforts to evaluate and compare their options. But ultimately, they tend to stop at a satisfactory threshold of comparison and make a decision.[4] Often, their judgments based on subjective preferences and objective criteria are blurred together, leading them to conclude broadly that one product is simply "better."

The phrase "better" is often used as shorthand for "better quality," but in most cases, it reflects a combination of objective quality and subjective taste. The same is true for news. When news consumers say that a particular article or outlet is "better" or "higher in quality," they are synthesizing judgments based on both their bias—a

[4] In behavioral economics, this human tendency is referred to as satisficing. The concept was first introduced by Herbert Simon, who argued that individuals do not always pursue utility maximization through fully rational calculations. Instead, they tend to settle for an option that is "good enough" once it meets a satisfactory threshold. Simon coined the term satisfice as a blend of satisfy and suffice to describe this behavior.

form of subjective preference—and objective standards of quality. With that in mind, let us now examine some of the typical criteria that ordinary people use when determining what counts as "better news."

Trust

People generally regard news as higher in quality when they believe it is trustworthy. For this reason, trust in news serves as a broadly accepted criterion for assessing news quality—one that is rarely disputed. Here, the term "broadly accepted" refers to something that applies universally across individuals. It differs from "objective," which implies viewing or evaluating something from a third-party perspective, independent of personal relationships or interests.

How, then, do news consumers form trust in news and news media? According to a 2021 report by the Reuters Institute for the Study of Journalism (Toff et al., 2021),[5] people tend to rely heavily on prior experiences and impressions of news media brands when assessing trustworthiness. This suggests that both confirmation bias—the subjective tendency to trust information that aligns with one's existing beliefs—and the reputation of a news outlet play major roles in shaping trust. Consumers' individual biases, which differ from person to person, lead them to trust different news sources—and that trust, in turn, drives the perception of those sources as high quality. As discussed earlier, this inevitably results in varied perceptions of quality, as each consumer brings a different bias to the evaluation.

However, trust in news is shaped not only by subjective factors such as confirmation bias but also by relatively objective elements—such as the format and style in which news is presented, the so-called mode of delivery—that have a significant impact on consumer trust. News that is clearly structured, logically written, and free of ambiguity tends to inspire greater trust. Consumers also place more trust in news that is in-depth, supported by statistics, graphics, or other visual aids, and that presents multiple perspectives on an issue. Conversely, news media that display excessive advertising—such as intrusive pop-up ads—are perceived as less trustworthy. These findings suggest that the way news is delivered plays an important role in shaping trust, which in turn influences whether the media outlet and its content are perceived as high in quality. News presentation—or what may be called the ability to deliver news effectively—can be considered an objective criterion for assessing news quality, insofar as it allows for a certain degree of observation and evaluation independent of bias.

These findings show that people form trust in news based on both subjective criteria—such as confirmation bias—and objective criteria, such as the clarity, depth, and professionalism of the news presentation. To put it simply, people are more likely to perceive news as trustworthy and high in quality when it aligns with their own

[5] This study engaged 132 news consumers across four countries—Brazil, India, the United Kingdom, and the United States—through focus group interviews with 70 participants and in-depth individual interviews with 62 participants. It aimed to examine the criteria and rationale people use to determine whether they trust the news.

beliefs. But at the same time, they also tend to trust news that is logically coherent, factually complete, and accompanied by quantitative or visual evidence—more so than news lacking those qualities.

"The more, the better"

People generally assume that, all else being equal, news with more information is "better." In other words, the higher the information density—how much information is conveyed within a given amount of time or space—the more valuable the news is perceived to be.

The *Oxford English Dictionary* defines information either as "facts provided or learned about something or someone" or as "what is conveyed or represented by a particular arrangement or sequence of things." The first definition emphasizes the qualitative aspect of information—its meaning and content—while the second reflects a quantitative dimension, suggesting that information, as a structured sequence, can be measured.

Information density

In the past, it was impossible to measure information density. The dominant perspective viewed information solely through a qualitative lens, focusing on meaning rather than measurable structure. However, the advent of the digital age enabled a shift. As most forms of information became digitized, it became possible to quantify them in bits or bytes, regardless of the medium. Once information could be measured in this way, its density—the amount of information delivered per unit of time or space—could also be calculated, and this metric began to serve as a proxy for information quality.

Importantly, this transformation was not driven by technology alone. In fact, prior to the 1960s, major dictionaries contained no definitions of information that reflected a quantitative understanding. The rise of the so-called information society in the latter half of the 20th century marked a turning point in how information was conceptualized.

This shift coincided with the emergence of a new ontological perspective: that information could exist prior to interpretation, not only as something understood or assigned meaning. One of the earliest and most influential proponents of this view was Tom Stonier. He argued that information exists as a physical resource independent of human perception and that it is measurable even before it is interpreted or understood (Stonier, 1990). This view provided a theoretical foundation for the quantitative treatment of information in the digital age.

Consider the old Chinese proverb, "A hundred hearings are not worth one seeing," or its English counterpart, "A picture is worth a thousand words." These sayings show that even in predigital societies, people recognized a qualitative difference between auditory and visual information. What they lacked was a way to quantify that difference. Today, however, we can express the qualitative distinction between audio and video formats in terms of information density, measured as the number of bytes transmitted per second.

Just as audiovisual content is generally more effective than purely auditory content, information that can be experienced through multiple sensory channels—sight, hearing, touch, smell, and taste—is often perceived as richer and more appealing. The greater the degree of sensory realism, the more vivid and immersive the information becomes.

For example, if the same message is delivered in both a text article and a video, each taking 1 minute to consume, most people would likely choose the video. Even within visual formats, three-dimensional video, virtual reality, or four-dimensional (4D) films[6] are typically preferred over traditional video because they engage more senses and convey a larger volume of information. In short, the more sensory channels information can engage, the higher its information density. For ordinary consumers, information that contains the same message is often judged to be of higher quality when it is denser in measurable terms.

This growing emphasis on information density reflects how the quantitative dimensions of information have become increasingly central in the digital age. Yet, it is important to recognize the limitations of viewing information purely through a quantitative or physical lens. While information's quantitative properties have grown increasingly prominent in the digital age, we must be cautious not to overlook an essential point: information cannot be fully understood or evaluated solely as a physical entity like matter or energy. This reductionist view misses a core aspect of information's role in society—its semantic and qualitative dimensions.

This is particularly true for information that contributes to individual or collective decision-making, rather than mere entertainment. In such contexts, information is not just a string of data; it carries meaning and intent, shaping how people think, communicate, and act. Meaningless information—information stripped of its semantic content—cannot facilitate communication, let alone decision-making. In this sense, a comprehensive understanding of information in modern society must account for both its quantitative and qualitative characteristics. Only by integrating these dual aspects can we accurately assess the value and function of information in the contemporary world.

[More to Explore] Beyond Meaning: Information as Being and as Quantity

Ontological perspective: Tom Stonier's redefinition of information. Tom Stonier posed a fundamental ontological challenge to conventional understandings of information. He bridged the conceptual gap between information as something interpreted (qualitative) and as something measurable (quantitative). In his 1990 book, *Information and the Internal Structure of the Universe*, Stonier argued that information is not merely a component of knowledge or a subject of human interpretation—it is the third fundamental entity in the universe, alongside matter and energy. "Information exists. It does not need to be perceived to exist. It does not need to be understood to exist. It requires no intelligence to interpret it. It does not have to have meaning to exist. It exists" (Stonier, 1990: 21).

[6] A 4D film is a motion picture enhanced with physical effects that correspond to the events on screen. These effects—such as moving seats, wind, mist, or scent—are synchronized with the visual content, offering a highly immersive sensory experience.

That is, information exists even before it is observed or interpreted. Much like the patterns etched into a stone exist regardless of whether anyone notices or interprets them, information, in this view, is an objective physical entity. This redefinition separates information from subjective meaning and allows it to be treated as a measurable, material resource and a fundamental factor of production in the modern economy. It represents a departure from the traditional view of information as merely "meaning conveyed" and recasts it as quantifiable content.

Stonier's work stands out as a rare example of using the language of economics to explore problems in physics and philosophy. His ideas have influenced fields as diverse as information economics, information society theory, philosophy of information, information physics, and digital humanities. Notably, his ontological framework helped lay the philosophical groundwork for understanding information density as a standard of news quality in the digital era.

Mathematical definition of information quantity. The mathematical theory of information was established by Claude Shannon (1948), who, in his 1948 paper *A Mathematical Theory of Communication*, defined information in terms of its capacity to reduce uncertainty. According to Shannon, the amount of information is inversely related to the probability of an event: the less likely an event is to occur, the more information its occurrence conveys.

Let s be a specific event and p_i be the probability of the i-th event occurring. The information content $I(s_i)$ of that event, measured in bits, is defined as:

$$I(s_i) = \log_2\left(\frac{1}{p_i}\right)$$

Under this formula, rare events carry more information. If an event is highly probable, it provides little new information when it occurs because its occurrence was expected. Conversely, if an event is unlikely, its occurrence resolves a large amount of uncertainty and thus carries more information.

Shannon's framework laid the foundation for modern digital communication, including data compression, error correction, and storage technologies. It has since influenced fields such as economics, linguistics, and biology. Information, in this sense, is not about meaning alone—it is about novelty, unpredictability, and the reduction of uncertainty. Shannon's definition has become the conceptual basis for related ideas such as information density, compression, and selection.

Satisfaction of instinct and reason

Information that people perceive as "better" often appeals to a greater number of senses—but more broadly, it appeals to human instinct. News that satisfies instinctual desires can take many forms, just as human instincts themselves are diverse. Common examples include news about extramarital affairs or pornographic content. Few people openly express favorable attitudes toward such material, yet most are more drawn to content that stimulates instinctual curiosity than to content that is culturally refined or intellectually elevated. If this were not the case, it would be difficult to explain why sensationalistic media continue to thrive.

Still, no one calls a tabloid magazine high quality, just as no one would describe a program about traditional music as low quality. That is because the concept of quality in these cases carries sociocultural or ethical meaning. Nonetheless, in reality, people are more likely to glance at news about a celebrity's affair than to focus on dry economic reporting. The extent to which news or information satisfies basic human desires is rarely discussed openly, yet it is undeniably a significant—if overlooked—criterion in how people evaluate news. In this sense, the ability of news to fulfill instinctual needs shared by all humans can be seen as a universal and objective standard of quality.

At the same time, the extent to which news appeals to reason also serves as an objective basis for assessing news quality. This has long been considered one of the most important standards in news evaluation. While people often rely on emotion rather than reason and tend to trust information that aligns with their confirmation bias rather than critically assessing its truthfulness, they still seek news that makes sense and follows logic. Indeed, when choosing among news stories that share the same ideological slant, people will regard those composed of coherent facts and reasoning as "better" than those filled with irrational claims. The same can be said of the types of news cited as trustworthy in the 2021 Reuters Institute study (Toff et al., 2021) introduced earlier: logically written stories, in-depth coverage, data-driven reports with statistics and graphics, and articles that incorporate diverse perspectives. These forms of reporting clearly align with the people's rational desire for understanding.

To summarize, people tend to regard trustworthy news as high-quality news. While trust grows when the bias in the news aligns with one's own biases, such confirmation bias varies across individuals and therefore cannot serve as an objective standard. In contrast, people also trust news that is delivered in a clear and understandable manner, regardless of bias. Furthermore, they value news that satisfies their senses through high information density and appeals to both their instincts and reasoning. Factors such as effective presentation, information richness, and the ability to fulfill both instinctual and rational needs are qualities that nearly all people recognize as hallmarks of better news—and thus, they serve as objective criteria for evaluating news quality.

6.2 ECONOMIC PERSPECTIVE OF NEWS QUALITY

In journalism studies, high-quality news is generally understood to be the product of journalists who pursue truth without prejudice. It is even more desirable when there are thoughtful news consumers who actively seek to overcome their own confirmation bias. For this reason, journalism scholars have long contributed to the discourse on news quality by proposing concrete normative standards for ideal news producers and consumers.

However, there is often a significant gap between normative ideals and real-world practice. Economics begins by attempting to understand the world as it actually is. When it comes to journalism, economic analysis focuses less on ideals and more on the reality that journalism is a livelihood. News media companies must survive in competitive markets, and individual journalists are not free from the economic imperatives of the media organizations they work for.

Accordingly, while journalism studies tend to focus on the ideal standards and normative expectations of news providers, economics evaluates news quality primarily through the lens of the market and the behavior of news consumers. In particular, the perceptions and evaluations of news consumers are essential to the economic understanding of news quality.

In economics, quality is often classified into two types: vertical quality and horizontal quality. Vertical quality refers to attributes that are universally recognized as better or worse, for example, the resolution of a television screen. Horizontal quality, by contrast, reflects individual preferences; one person may prefer a strawberry milkshake, while another may favor chocolate. In the context of news consumption, horizontal quality corresponds to consumers' personal biases and preferences, such as political orientation, stylistic inclinations, or interest in particular topics.

In this section, however, we focus on vertical quality, that is, qualities that are generally perceived in the same way across consumers. Concepts such as clarity, depth of information, factual accuracy, and information density in news fall under this category. While personal preferences undoubtedly influence how news is received, the standards we discuss here aim to assess news quality on a more objective and commonly shared basis.

6.2.1 "ACCURATE REPORTING ABILITY" AND "HONEST REPORTING ATTITUDE"

Many economists have traditionally regarded accuracy as the primary standard for evaluating the quality of news media. In their view, accuracy depends on the news media's ability to observe the facts of nature and society. In this context, David Baron defined news media quality as "the ability to investigate the true state of the world" (Baron, 2006). Building on this, Gentzkow and Shapiro (2006) added the notion of honest reporting, meaning that high-quality media report facts as they are, without intentional distortion. According to their framework, high-quality news outlets directly observe reality and report it honestly, while ordinary outlets observe noisy signals and report them strategically, that is, with bias (Gentzkow et al., 2015). The assumption is that the difference between high- and low-quality media lies in their levels of accuracy and honesty and that this difference can be recognized by fully rational news consumers.

However, this way of understanding quality raises several important concerns. Under such a framework, higher quality becomes synonymous with lower bias. Reporting "the true state of the world" accurately implies the absence—or near absence—of unintentional bias, and "honest reporting" implies the absence of intentional bias. Yet, as discussed earlier, news consumers often evaluate quality based on their own biases. That is, even if a news outlet is highly biased, it may still be regarded as high quality by those whose biases align with it. The assumption of a fully rational news consumer is also far removed from reality. For these reasons, many scholars have raised critical perspectives on defining news quality solely in terms of accuracy and honesty. Their critiques can be summarized as follows:

1. Traditional economics assumes rational agents, but in the real world of the news market, the behavioral economics perspective—that humans are only boundedly rational—is more appropriate.[7] According to behavioral economist Kahneman (2002), humans process information through two distinct systems: one based on intuition and instinct and the other on deliberative reasoning. The former leads people to seek news that satisfies confirmation bias and instinctual interests, while the latter reflects a desire to pursue truth through rational thought.
2. If news consumers are only boundedly rational, then the accuracy of news becomes difficult to evaluate objectively. People with different cognitive limitations perceive quality differently. When multiple interpretations of the same news exist, the classic economic notion that "(vertical) quality differences are recognized similarly across consumers" no longer holds.
3. Even if a news organization possesses a high level of skill in investigating "the true state of the world," bias-free reporting is impossible as long as the agents are human. As the eminent economist Anthony Downs noted, "All information is inherently biased due to the filtering process during collection."[8] In other words, even honest reporting cannot eliminate unintended bias.
4. The implicit conclusion of defining quality as accuracy is this: higher (or lower) quality equals lower (or higher) bias. Under this logic, any change in bias becomes a change in quality, making it unnecessary to distinguish between the two. However, in practice, bias and quality are often seen as separate attributes. For example, *The New York Times*—a globally respected broadsheet—and the *Daily Mirror*—a British tabloid—are often considered to have comparable levels of political bias.[9] Yet few would argue that the two are equal in overall quality. From writing standards and author credentials to photo quality, graphic design, font choice, layout, and even website usability, the differences in quality between these outlets are widely recognized.[10]

---

[7] For a detailed discussion of bounded rationality, see Sections 1.1.2 The Economic Theories on Human Choice and 2.1.2 Multifaceted News Consumers.

[8] For Anthony Downs' comment on the inevitability of bias in information collection, see Section 5.1.2 The Definition of Media Bias in Economics.

[9] According to Ad Fontes Media, a neutral media watchdog based in the United States, *The New York Times* and the *Daily Mirror* both rank near −8 on a left-right ideological spectrum ranging from −42 (far left) to 42 (far right), indicating a similar degree of left-leaning bias.

[10] Even among news outlets with similar levels of political bias, objective quality differences can be observed. For example, a video-based report may offer greater clarity than a plain-text version; a story with logical coherence and contextual depth is more informative than one that is poorly reasoned; and a well-structured, graphically supported article is often more effective than a lengthy, monotonous one.

[More to Explore] What Is "Accuracy"?

In economic models, the concept of accuracy is typically treated as a theoretical assumption used to explain the behavior of news media. Separately, however, journalism studies also make extensive use of the concept as a normative standard for how the press should convey truth. This normative understanding draws on two philosophical theories of truth.

First, correspondence theory holds that reported facts must correspond to events that actually occurred. Second, coherence theory maintains that reported facts must be placed within an appropriate context and connected in a meaningful way.

Accuracy is a fundamental value in journalism, but it alone does not guarantee truth. To illustrate this limitation, scholars often invoke the example of looking out the window of a moving train. Even if a person accurately describes the shape and distance of an object at a specific moment, that description may no longer represent the truth once the train has moved on. In the same way, a report that seemed accurate yesterday may no longer be so today—something that happens frequently in journalism.

Recognizing this inherent limitation, journalism scholars often describe the pursuit of truth as a process or an ongoing journey of understanding, rather than a fixed endpoint. Because merely describing things accurately is not enough to convey the whole truth, journalism is seen as continually striving toward, but never fully attaining, objective truth.

For this reason, it is extremely difficult—even for economists—to empirically verify accuracy in journalism. This is fundamentally different from identifying and studying clear factual errors. In this sense, the concept of accuracy used in economic models should be understood not as an empirically measurable indicator, but as an abstract construct intended to support theoretical modeling.

6.2.2 INFORMATION PRESENTATION ABILITY

Can the quality of news media be defined in a way that is more realistic and logically coherent than the traditional approach that equates quality with accuracy? The recent literature has proposed an alternative definition (Yang, 2020, 2021, 2022):

1. News consumers are boundedly rational. According to behavioral economics, rational understanding of information requires effort—a kind of cost. When news providers offer coherent contexts, well-structured factual relationships, and effective visual aids, they help reduce the cognitive effort required for rational understanding. News that lowers the cost of comprehension in this way is perceived as higher quality.
2. News quality and bias can be treated as independent dimensions. Even among news outlets with similar political leanings, quality can vary significantly. For instance, although *The New York Times* and the *Daily Mirror* are evaluated as similarly left leaning, many consumers perceive a significant quality gap between them. News that is logically structured, persuasive, and grounded in solid evidence is easier to understand and more compelling. Likewise, news enhanced with visual elements tends to be preferred over verbose, text-heavy reports. These are all objective attributes that enhance perceived quality.

Based on these premises, we may define the quality of news as "an ability to help the reasoning of boundedly rational consumers, independently of media bias" (Yang, 2022, p. 1811). That is, news that is presented in a way that reduces the cognitive effort required for rational inference is considered higher in quality.

This definition of quality can be extended to account for features unique to the digital era. For example, online portals that allow side-by-side comparisons of different outlets' coverage are more useful to consumers than individual media homepages. Tools such as "most-read articles" or intuitive interfaces that improve access to information are also welcomed by readers. Infrastructure-level features like server speed and stability can further influence consumers' evaluation of media quality. Thus from a digital perspective, news media quality may be redefined as "a news provider's ability to reduce the consumers' disutility or increase utility in interpreting information by better delivering information through news" (Yang, 2020, p. 3).

Deliverability is a broader concept than presentation ability: while the latter refers to the structuring and narration of content itself (such as coherent writing or the use of graphics), deliverability also includes infrastructural and interface-level features—such as server speed, navigation design, and side-by-side comparison tools—that affect how easily news can be accessed and comprehended.

This approach moves the evaluation of quality away from debates about truth or bias. It also challenges the assumption that less biased news is necessarily closer to the truth. News with extreme bias can still be true, while politically neutral reports may be false. Most people intuitively treat bias-free information as truthful, but history suggests otherwise. For example, heliocentrism once seemed like an extremely biased claim but is now accepted as a scientific fact. Truth may lie anywhere along the ideological spectrum. By emphasizing deliverability over accuracy, news quality becomes observable and measurable. Elements like coherent logic, structured facts, graphics, and even server infrastructure can be evaluated objectively.

This perspective allows us to understand how consumers choose news by weighing both bias and quality. It resembles how airline passengers weigh personal preferences (window vs. aisle) against objective differences (economy vs. business class) when choosing a seat. As has been noted several times already, most news consumers tend to regard news media that share similar biases with themselves as high quality. However, this is not because bias and quality belong to the same category, but rather because they conflate the two in their perception. This perceptual bias is metaphorically illustrated in Fig. 6.1, where bias (ink) alters the perceived quality (water).

In sum, the alternative perspective defines news and media quality as a matter of deliverability or presentation capacity. More broadly, it encompasses a range of provider capabilities that enhance consumers' access to and comprehension of information.[11] Moreover, this definition is not based on abstract concepts such as "truth" or "accuracy," which are difficult to determine objectively, but rather on objective

[11] Mullainathan and Shleifer (2005: 1031) wrote, "Audiences want news to explain, interpret, persuade, and entertain. Thus, media do not simply provide information—they tell stories." In doing so, they acknowledged the role of presentation ability as part of the media's function. However, the two scholars did not treat this expressive capacity as an objective capability independent of media bias. This was for two reasons: first, they did not assume significant differences in presentation ability across media outlets, and second, they regarded such ability solely as a means for media to more effectively infuse their bias into the news.

attributes and criteria that ordinary news consumers use in real life to judge which news or news media are "better."

6.3 MEDIA COMPETING IN BOTH BIAS AND QUALITY DIFFERENTIATION

The New York Times is widely regarded as one of the most influential and prestigious news media outlets in the world. Employing thousands of journalists, it consistently ranks at the highest level globally in most of the quality-determining factors previously discussed, including reporting accuracy, expressive clarity, and delivery capacity.

By contrast, there exist small-scale, YouTube-based media outlets that are incomparable to *The New York Times*. Operated by just a few individuals, these media tend to produce crass and sensational content, often heavily biased and lacking in professional quality.

In this respect, *The New York Times* represents a "high-quality–low-bias" outlet, while such YouTube-based media exemplify "low-quality–high-bias" journalism. What is noteworthy, however, is that both types of news media—despite being polar opposites in terms of quality and bias—succeed in the market by differentiating their news products in distinct ways.

Like any other business, news media must attract and retain consumers in order to remain sustainable. They pursue differentiation from competitors and strive to maximize profit. In economics, this process is typically classified into two forms: vertical differentiation and horizontal differentiation. Vertical differentiation involves variations in objective value—such as product quality, function, or price—whereas horizontal differentiation refers to differences based on consumers' subjective preferences. The latter can be illustrated by individual taste: for instance, whether one prefers vanilla or chocolate milkshakes.

More specifically, vertical differentiation refers to offering greater functional or price value than competitors. A typical example is providing a product of similar quality at a lower price or a higher-quality product at the same price. Even higher-priced products can qualify as vertically differentiated if consumers perceive them to offer superior value. In such cases, all consumers would agree on which product is objectively better.

However, vertical differentiation requires investment. Media outlets without sufficient resources are structurally unable to deliver high-quality content. On the other hand, well-capitalized outlets are more likely to invest in quality improvement if they believe it will generate higher returns.

Horizontal differentiation, by contrast, is accessible even to low-resource outlets. It does not depend on producing better quality but rather on embedding features that competitors do not offer—features that appeal to specific consumer preferences. Just as some people prefer chocolate milkshakes while others favor vanilla, or some prioritize fashion while others seek comfort, horizontal differentiation targets consumer

FIGURE 6.1 When bias colors perception of quality.

The fact that people seem to perceive media quality based on how closely its bias aligns with their own is akin to judging the color of tinted water: although the color is determined by the respective amounts of water (quality) and ink (bias), people tend to overlook the amount of water and focus solely on the concentration of ink (bias).

tastes rather than objective superiority. In news media, horizontal differentiation typically manifests in the form of ideological or political bias, but it can also include targeting particular regions, age groups, or worldviews.

Most news media combine both vertical and horizontal strategies to compete in the market. Fig. 6.2 illustrates how media outlets differentiate themselves along these two axes: quality (as a form of vertical differentiation) and political bias (as a form of horizontal differentiation). The chart, produced by Ad Fontes Media—a US-based media watchdog claiming to maintain nonpartisan standards—draws on more than 25,000 pieces of content published by over 200 English-language news outlets. It evaluates each outlet's reliability (as a proxy for quality) and its political or ideological bias.[12]

In this chart, the horizontal axis measures political bias, ranging from extreme left (−42) to extreme right (42), while the vertical axis measures quality or reliability, ranging from pure factual reporting (64) to highly manipulated or misleading content (0). The distribution of outlets roughly takes the shape of an inverted "V." When evaluated against a centrist baseline, high-quality media generally exhibit minimal ideological bias, whereas low-quality outlets tend to display more extreme positions. This overall pattern broadly corresponds to public perception.

However, several noteworthy exceptions exist. Some outlets share a similar degree of political bias but differ significantly in terms of reliability, while others exhibit comparable reliability scores despite diverging ideologically.

For instance, Bloomberg News and The Bulwark both show mild left-leaning biases (−2.66 and −2.73, respectively) yet differ substantially in reliability (45.72 vs. 34.15). Similarly, both *The New York Times* and the *Daily Mirror* display a

[12] Ad Fontes Media employs a methodology that quantifies the bias and quality of news content through analysis panels composed of evaluators with liberal, conservative, and centrist orientations.

comparable political bias (around −8), but they differ markedly in their perceived quality. Conversely, National Broadcasting Company (NBC) and *The Wall Street Journal (WSJ)* are nearly identical in reliability scores (45.80 and 45.34), yet differ in political bias (−6.90 for NBC, +5.17 for the *WSJ*).

These cases clearly demonstrate how news outlets strategically differentiate themselves along both the quality and bias dimensions to position themselves in the competitive media marketplace.

6.4 MEDIA SCHOLARS' VIEW ON NEWS QUALITY

Scholars in journalism have long examined the concept of news quality from two broad perspectives. One centers on how news quality is perceived and evaluated by news consumers. This approach parallels the framework employed by economists, who emphasize consumer behavior. The other focuses on the standards that news producers should uphold in pursuit of journalistic ideals. This producer-centric perspective typically leads to discussions about the normative principles that journalists should observe. Among these, the producer-side approach enjoys a longer history and a more extensive body of literature. This is arguably due to the academic roots of journalism studies, which originated in the normative practices of journalists themselves. Below, we examine both perspectives on news quality, as presented by journalism scholars.

6.4.1 DEMAND APPROACH

Journalism scholars (Lacy and Rosenstiel, 2015: 14) defined "demand-side news quality" as "the extent to which news or journalism satisfies the diverse needs and desires of individual consumers." However, they also noted that this relativistic approach—where consumers subjectively perceive quality based on personal criteria—implies that news quality may be inherently immeasurable in any objective sense.

According to Lacy and Rosenstiel, variation in how consumers perceive news quality stems from differences in individual needs and preferences. For instance, a news report on road maintenance might be considered high quality by someone living near the affected area but irrelevant to those residing elsewhere. Consumers also assess the adequacy of media coverage by comparing it to their own interests. Given their diverse biases, they may disagree on what constitutes accuracy or fairness in reporting. Furthermore, a distinction often arises between personal and societal value: a news story may affirm a consumer's biases and therefore be deemed high quality on a personal level, while being socially useless or even harmful. In short, individual needs and the broader societal impact of news can diverge, resulting in widely differing perceptions of news quality (Lacy, 1989).

Various journalism scholars have offered distinct criteria for the kinds of needs and desires that high-quality news should meet. Purcell (2010) and her colleagues outlined five types of news-related needs: (1) information about family, friends, and local communities; (2) information that enables civic responsibility; (3) information

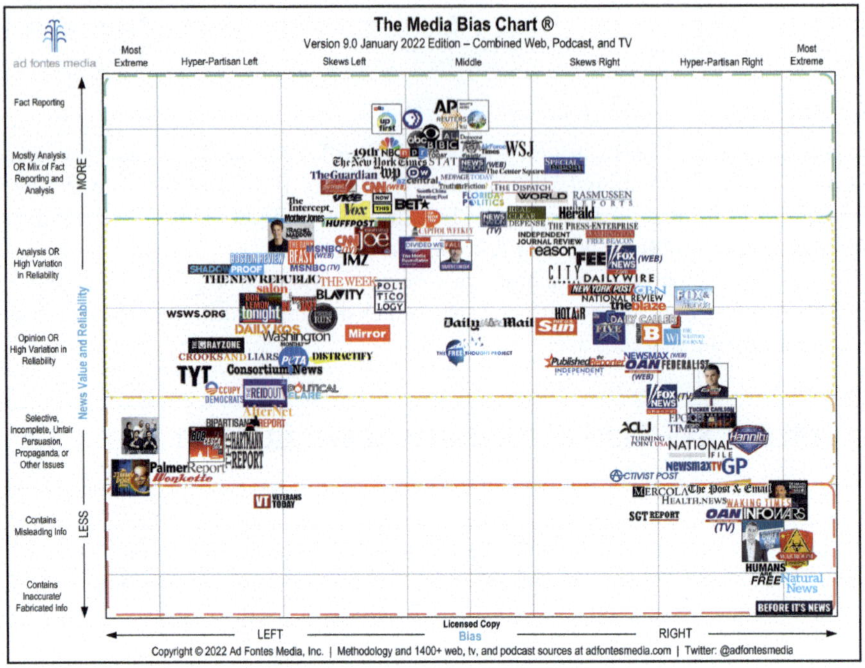

A

B

C

FIGURE 6.2

Chart of media bias and reliability by Ad Fontes Media.

(A) Reproduced with permission from Ad Fontes Media, Media Bias Chart 9.0. https://adfontesmedia.com.

(B) Reproduced with permission from Ad Fontes Media, Media Bias Chart 9.0. https://adfontesmedia.com.

(C) Reproduced with permission from Ad Fontes Media, Media Bias Chart 9.0. https://adfontesmedia.com.

that helps people manage their lives; (4) news that offers diversion, emotional stability, or entertainment; and (5) job-related information. Building on this, Rosenstiel and colleagues (2015) later categorized these needs into eight more granular criteria.

6.4.2 PRODUCT APPROACH

Research grounded in the producer perspective is both historically rich and extensive. Representative contributions include those by journalism ethicist John Merrill, who evaluated media quality based on both "internal factors" such as the professionalism of journalists and editors, and "external factors" like the extent to which news coverage influences policymakers (Merrill and Lowenstein, 1971). In the late 1980s, Bogart (1989) conducted a survey of editors at 746 daily newspapers, generating a ranked list of 23 factors for evaluating newspaper quality. These included diversity of political columnists, the ratio of images to text, and readability (Bogart, 1989). In the 2000s, influential media theorist Denis McQuail (2005) proposed five core values that high-quality news should serve: liberty, equality, diversity, truth and informational quality, and social order and solidarity.

The most widely cited producer-side framework, however, is the "Ten Elements of Journalism" articulated by Bill Kovach and Tom Rosenstiel in 2001. These principles include independence from factions, a discipline of verification, functioning as an independent monitor of power, and reporting that is both comprehensive and proportional (Kovach and Rosenstiel, 2021). These ten principles received widespread endorsement from both academic and professional communities. They are also regarded as a systematized and evolved version of the five responsibilities outlined by the 1947 Hutchins Commission on the Freedom of the Press.[13]

It is important to note that producer-oriented standards of news quality often vary by country, reflecting differences in newsroom practices and media culture. Even outlets that embrace similar standards differ in their priorities for those standards. Furthermore, producer-centric perspectives generally treat audiences as passive recipients of news. As a result, such views may be increasingly outdated in the digital era, where news consumers exert unprecedented influence. Defining quality solely from the producer's viewpoint has limited utility for economists, who typically take the consumer's perspective as foundational.

[13] The Commission on Freedom of the Press, commonly referred to as the Hutchins Commission after its chair, Robert Hutchins (1899–1977), was established in 1942 to examine the responsibilities of the press in a democratic society. Its 1947 report asserted that "mere reporting of the fact is not sufficient; the truth about the fact must be reported." The Commission outlined five essential responsibilities of the press: (1) "A truthful, comprehensive, and intelligent account of the day's events in a context which gives them meaning"; (2) "A forum for the exchange of comment and criticism"; (3) "The projection of a representative picture of the constituent groups in society"; (4) "The presentation and clarification of the goals and values of the society"; and (5) "Full access to the day's intelligence" (Chafee, 1947).

The Ten Elements of Journalism Proposed by Kovach and Rosenstiel.

1. Journalism's first obligation is to the truth.
2. Its first loyalty is to citizens.
3. Its essence is a discipline of verification.
4. Its practitioners must maintain independence from those they cover.
5. It must serve as a monitor of power.
6. It must provide a forum for public criticism and compromise.
7. It must strive to make the significant interesting and relevant.
8. It must present the news in a way that is comprehensive and proportional.
9. Its practitioners have an obligation to exercise their personal conscience.
10. Citizens have rights and responsibilities when it comes to the news as well—even more so as they become producers and editors themselves.

6.4.3 CONTRASTING APPROACHES TO NEWS QUALITY: ECONOMICS VERSUS JOURNALISM STUDIES

The most fundamental difference between economic and journalistic approaches to news quality is that economists do not draw a rigid distinction between the producer and consumer perspectives. Rather, economic analysis begins with a unified concept of quality and focuses on the strategic interactions between producers and consumers in the marketplace.

Whereas journalism scholars discuss quality in terms of normative ideals, ethics, and social roles expected of news producers, economists start from the premise that quality is what consumers collectively recognize as "better." They then examine how producers pursue differentiation strategies and the outcomes of those efforts.

Furthermore, the economists' approach contrasts even with journalism scholars who emphasize consumer perspectives. Economics favors simplified models that enable generalized and scalable analysis. In contrast, journalism studies tend to break down quality into a more detailed taxonomy of consumer-relevant attributes.

Ultimately, these differing approaches underscore the complementary strengths of the two disciplines. While journalism studies provide normative depth and empirical nuance, economics offers parsimonious models for understanding behavior and outcomes in the media marketplace.

References

Baron, D.P., 2006. Persistent media bias. Journal of Public Economics 90 (1–2), 1–36. https://doi.org/10.1016/j.jpubeco.2004.10.006.

Bogart, L., 1989. Press and the Public: Who Reads What, When, Where and Why in American Newspapers. Lawrence Erlbaum Associates.

Chafee, Z., 1947. A Free and Responsible Press: A General Report on Mass Communication: Newspapers, Radio, Motion Pictures, Magazines, and Books, vol. 10. University of Chicago Press.

Gentzkow, M., Shapiro, J.M., 2006. Media bias and reputation. Journal of Political Economy 114 (2), 280–316. https://doi.org/10.1086/499414.

Gentzkow, M., Shapiro, J.M., Stone, D.F., 2015. Media bias in the marketplace. In: Handbook of Media Economics. Elsevier, 623–645. https://doi.org/10.1016/b978-0-444-63685-0.00014-0.

Kahneman, D., 2002. Maps of bounded rationality: a perspective on intuitive judgment and choice. Nobel Prize Lecture 8 (1), 351–401.

Kang, J., 2020, November 22. Would anyone still read print newspapers? Hankyoreh. (in Korean). https://www.hani.co.kr/arti/opinion/column/970947.html.

Kovach, B., Rosenstiel, T., 2021. The Elements of Journalism: What News People Should Know and the Public Should Expect, Revised and Updated third ed. Three Rivers Press.

Lacy, S., Rosenstiel, T., 2015. Defining and Measuring Quality Journalism. Rutgers School of Communication and Information.

Lacy, S., 1989. A model of demand for news: impact of competition on newspaper content. Journalism Quarterly 66 (1), 40–48. https://doi.org/10.1177/107769908906600105.

McQuail, D., 2005. McQuail's Mass Communication Theory, 5th ed. Sage.

Merrill, J.C., Lowenstein, R.L., 1971. Media, Messages, and Men: New Perspectives in Communication. D. McKay Company.

Mullainathan, S., Shleifer, A., 2005. The market for news. American Economic Review 95 (4), 1031–1053.

Purcell, K., 2010. Understanding the Participatory News Consumer. Pew Research Center.

Rosenstiel, T., et al., 2015. How millennials get news: Inside the habits of America's first digital generation. Media Insight Project, pp. 1–40.

Shannon, C.E., 1948. A mathematical theory of communication. Bell System Technical Journal 27 (3), 379–423. https://doi.org/10.1002/j.1538-7305.1948.tb01338.x

Stonier, T., 1990. Information and the Internal Structure of the Universe. Springer.

Toff, B., et al., 2021. Listening to What Trust in News Means to Users: Qualitative Evidence From Four Countries. Reuters Institute. Retrieved from: https://reutersinstitute.politics.ox.ac.uk/listening-what-trust-news-means-users-qualitative-evidence-four-countries.

Yang, S., 2020. Media bias with digital intermediary. International Telecommunications Policy Review 27 (4), 1–23. https://doi.org/10.37793/itpr.27.4.1.

Yang, S., 2021. Media Capture and Media Bias in the Digital Age [Ph.D. dissertation]. Yonsei University.

Yang, S., 2022. Media bias with asymmetric media quality. Applied Economics Letters 29 (19), 1810–1814. https://doi.org/10.1080/13504851.2021.1963401.

CHAPTER

7 The Virtues and Vices of Competition in News Markets

Chapter Outline

Let her and Falsehood grapple;
who ever knew Truth put to the worse, in a free and open encounter?
—John Milton, Areopagitica (1644)

I have seen enough of the unadulterated falsity of the newspapers
for the last forty years to be satisfied
that nothing in them is to be believed,
and that we are safer without than with them.
—Thomas Jefferson, Letter to Joseph C. Yancey (1816)

It is widely assumed that free competition within the media inherently reveals the truth. Indeed, throughout human history, the contributions of a free press have been invaluable. However, both in the past and present, the press has often brought profound disappointment to the public, leaving numerous blemishes on its record. Although media freedom was hard-won through bloodshed, the media has often indulged this freedom by inundating the public with sensational and peripheral

The Economics of News Media. DOI: http://dx.doi.org/10.1016/B978-0-443-45044-0.00008-8

news, frequently dividing public opinion with extreme political bias. At times, it has betrayed public trust by spreading significant misinformation and fake news, causing turmoil in society. These aspects of the media reveal the dual nature of freedom and competition, reminiscent of Dr. Jekyll and Mr. Hyde.

Economists have studied this reality of free media competition through theories and empirical evidence. Does free competition among media outlets consistently yield "truth," or is this expectation overly optimistic? How does the competition among news providers affect the quality and quantity of the information supplied? In this chapter, we explore economists' theoretical perspectives on these questions, focusing on two broad categories. First, we examine the dysfunctions and adverse effects caused by "too much competition" and "too little competition" among news media outlets, and consider measures to improve these issues. Then, we introduce the differing views of scholars on whether competition among news media outlets truly leads us to the truth.

7.1 THE DILEMMA OF THE NEWS MARKET: MARKET FAILURE AND GOVERNMENT FAILURE

What we expect from the market is the optimal allocation of resources. In the context of the news market, this role involves ensuring the equitable distribution of essential information among members of society. However, it is often observed that the news market fails to meet these expectations. These situations can be broadly categorized into two types.

One occurs when excessive competition leads to a surge in sensational "soft news," misinformation, and disinformation, resulting in a lack of the substantive information essential for democracy and informed voting decisions—often referred to as "hard news." The other occurs when the news market becomes increasingly concentrated, leading to insufficient competition and a decline in information diversity. In other words, too little competition undermines the diversity of public opinion and media plurality.[1]

So, how should we address the issue of insufficient information supply? If excessive competition is the problem, competition needs to be alleviated. Conversely, if monopolies dominate the market, a more competitive environment must be fostered. This leads us to consider the role of government intervention, or regulation.

However, opinions among scholars are deeply divided on government intervention aimed at controlling the dysfunctions of competition or enhancing its positive effects. While some argue that regulation is necessary, others argue that regulation

[1] Diversity of public opinion refers to the coexistence of various perspectives and opinions freely expressed by members of society. Media plurality ensures that these diverse viewpoints are represented across multiple media channels. The issue of insufficient competition in the news market is revisited in Section 9.4 Media Power.

is ineffective and only creates further issues. This reflects the traditional economic debate over "market failure" and "government failure," which is also a prominent theme in the political economy of the news media. Let us first examine the situation where excessive competition results in insufficient news supply.

7.1.1 TOO MUCH COMPETITION AND INSUFFICIENT INFORMATION SUPPLY

Soft news appeals to human instincts, garners interest, and has a strong entertainment component. Gossip news is a typical example. In contrast, hard news refers to practical news essential for daily life, typically covering topics like politics, economics, international relations, and welfare. In a democratic society, crucial information for people's political choices and social participation is mostly contained in hard news. People also form their views on personal and social issues through hard news. In contrast, soft news primarily satisfies curiosity.

There is little disagreement among economists regarding the social efficacy of hard news. Many scholars, including Downs, who explained democracy through economics, and Posner, a leading law and economics scholar, all assert that society benefits greatly when people engage with hard news (Downs, 1957; Posner, 1986). They argue that, for people to make the best decisions for society, it is better to watch news rather than entertainment and, among news, to consume politically significant hard news rather than soft news such as car chases or celebrity scandals (Gentzkow and Shapiro, 2008). This perspective aligns with the view among political scientists that soft news is "weakening the foundation of democracy by diminishing the public's information about public affairs and its interest in politics" (Patterson, 2001, p. 2). Economists generally summarize the supply and consumption of soft and hard news as follows:

- *News consumers instinctively prefer soft news.*
- *However, society benefits more when news consumers consume hard news rather than soft news.*
- *Competition among news providers drives them to produce the news that consumers want.*
- *News providers who are relatively less bound by competition tend to produce more hard news.*
- *Public or government-funded media, as well as private media that pursue the public interest, are less bound by competition, whereas other private media are more engaged in it.*

In summary, these points suggest that the more intense the competition among news media, the more soft news is produced and the less hard news is supplied, even though the latter has greater social value. Empirically, Hamilton (2004) found that political news, a representative example of hard news, decreased on American television networks after competition among cable channels intensified in the early 1980s.

Political scientist Zaller (1999) also argued that the news quality of Britain's public broadcaster, the British Broadcasting Corporation (BBC), was higher than that of American private broadcasters engaged in fierce competition and that monopoly newspapers in noncompetitive regions provided higher-quality news than competitive television broadcasters.

Economist Cagé (2020), who studied the French newspaper market over 70 years from 1944 to 2014, stated that when the number of newspapers increased, and competition intensified, the number of journalists and articles per newspaper decreased, along with a reduction in the supply of hard news. Cagé concluded that this reduction ultimately contributed to a decline in voter turnout.

Concerns about insufficient information supply from excessive competition among media outlets have grown in the digital age. With the advent of digital platforms, the entry barriers of the news market, such as massive newspaper printing facilities or broadcasting equipment, have disappeared, making it irrelevant for media outlets to compete in the investment of news-producing capacity or the price of delivering news. Instead, competition to capture consumers' attention with sensational and stimulating content has intensified. While media theorists considered the "open marketplace of ideas" as a stage where truth triumphs, in reality, it has turned into a space that is flooded with sensational soft news.

The only solution to the insufficient hard news supply due to the increase in soft news is to reduce competition in the news market. Therefore, economists who focus on the failure of the news market argue that competition should be mitigated through measures such as the introduction of public media, which is less influenced by market competition.

Ineffectiveness and risks of reducing competition through policy

In contrast, economists critical of government interference in the competition argue that the same applies to the news market. Even if the production and supply of hard news are increased through policy intervention, there is no guarantee that consumption will increase, and only side effects are likely to occur. Gentzkow and Shapiro's (2008) arguments are as follows:

First, even if the supply of hard news increases, news consumers may not consume it, or the information contained in the news may not be absorbed by consumers. The American public television station PBS's news program, *NewsHour*, is often cited as an example of high-quality journalism. However, it has a relatively small audience compared to Fox News or CNN. This suggests that even if more programs like *NewsHour* are aired, there may be little impact on actual news consumption due to consumer neglect.

It is also very difficult to reduce the supply of interest-oriented and entertainment-focused content or to limit its consumption. Achieving this would require either converting private media companies to public or government-owned ones or regulating all major media content. Even if a policy to reduce soft news and increase hard news were feasible, it would be ineffective if people continued to watch only soft news.[2] Moreover, even if consumers watch more practically beneficial news, if it is not easily understood or quickly forgotten, its effectiveness would be diminished. In such cases, even if a news media outlet, supported by the government, provides a large amount of information through specialized coverage of economic issues, it may not improve citizens' knowledge and decision-making.

Second, it is not easy to determine what constitutes socially beneficial news. For example, it is challenging to assess whether a story about a distant war or sensational crime news in one's own neighborhood is more useful. Similarly, the Monica Lewinsky scandal, which began in 1998 as soft news, later escalated into the hard news of a presidential impeachment—illustrating how the boundary between soft and hard news can sometimes blur. Over time, there may be a consensus on what constitutes necessary or useful news. However, news is a complex, multidimensional product. It is extremely challenging to provide producers of such news with real-time standards for judging whether the news is useful or to offer appropriate incentives for supplying useful news.

Third, apart from the case of the BBC in the United Kingdom, there is little empirical evidence to support the claim that public media or policy regulation improves the supply of hard news, especially political news. On the contrary, government-controlled media in many countries are associated with less democratic governments, lower levels of media freedom, and less independent reporting. In these cases, governments use media to strengthen their own power rather than to address market failures.[3] Even in the United States, government intervention has shown no success. After the Federal Communications Commission (FCC) introduced the Fairness Doctrine in 1949, which required broadcasters to present opposing political views fairly, political debates on the radio sharply declined (Hazlett and Sosa, 1997).

To summarize Gentzkow and Shapiro's view, restricting competition in the news market has uncertain effectiveness but carries high costs. Moreover, policies to restrict competition in the news market cannot be free from the influence of governments or political powers seeking to manipulate the news. The two scholars pointed out that government intervention attempts in the United States occurred when information was most crucial for democratic decision-making, such as during the Watergate scandal or the World Wars. They also noted that media under government intervention was least accurate when political stakes were highest.

[2] The news is a non-rival good, meaning that one person's consumption does not reduce the amount available for others. Therefore, even if the production of soft news decreases, the amount consumed by people may not necessarily decrease.

[3] Djankov et al. (2003) stated that high levels of public ownership of media are, in fact, associated with less press freedom and fewer political and economic rights. See Section 10.4.1. Inferior Societies.

7.1.2 TOO LITTLE COMPETITION AND INSUFFICIENT INFORMATION SUPPLY

Excessive competition in the news market can be problematic, but insufficient competition poses even more serious issues. Consider a country where a single media outlet monopolizes the news market. There is no competition among media outlets, and news consumers have no choice but to rely on the news selected and provided by the monopolistic media. This scenario is evident in authoritarian countries with a limited number of government-controlled media outlets.

In the United States, the world's largest news market, continuous mergers and acquisitions in the media industry over the past several decades have intensified the concentration of the news media market. In particular, the advent of television broadcasting in the mid-20th century further accelerated the trend of mergers and chain-building in the newspaper industry.[4]

Consequently, concerns about the negative effects of this increasing concentration in the news media industry have been continuously raised. Bagdikian (2000), a journalist and journalism scholar, emphasized in his book *The Media Monopoly* that media concentration threatens freedom of expression and independent journalism.

Earlier, American legal scholar Ingber (1984, p. 1) argued that while freedom of the press has been believed to create a neutral marketplace of ideas and lead to the discovery of truth, press freedom alone does not guarantee an environment where new ideas, awareness, and values can flourish. He pointed out that news consumers may struggle to distinguish accurate from inaccurate reporting, calling for "efforts to reform and correct these market defects." Concerns about the flaws of the news media market, which lead to market concentration, have been raised by many others and were recognized by the FCC as a core reason for government regulation of the broadcasting industry (Federal Communications Commission, 2003).

Ineffectiveness of policies for promoting competition

However, some economists believe that it is inappropriate for the government to intervene in the news market through concentration regulations or other measures. They argue that even if concentration in the news media advances through mergers and acquisitions, there will always be sufficient competition in a free news market. Let's revisit the arguments of Gentzkow and Shapiro (2008), who oppose intervention in the news market. Their perspective is as follows:

First, the news market is both a "product market" and an "information market." In most product markets, competing firms are substitutes from the consumer's perspective. However, in the news market, which combines features of both information and product markets, competitors in each can be distinct. For example, *The Washington Post* in the eastern United States and the *Los Angeles Times* in the western United States are not competitors in the product market but can be competitors in the information market.

The scope of the information market is much broader than that of the product market. In the information market, even small media outlets that may be insignificant as

[4] See section 3.2.2.1. The Shift in Newspapers and Journalism's Arc.

product market competitors can play important roles. Leading media outlets like *The New York Times* are influenced by the reporting of smaller media outlets. Especially in the digital age, news spreads rapidly through online platforms, and small media outlets can even win Pulitzer Prizes. The unique nature of the news market as an information market implies that evaluating competition in the news market solely based on market share in the product market is inappropriate.

Second, totalitarian states have significant media concentration to the extent that they meaningfully reduce the spread of information. However, such extreme concentration occurs not because of a lack of government intervention but due to excessive government intervention.

Third, even if media concentration deepens, it is not possible to completely block the dissemination of specific news or information. No individual has the power to prevent certain reports to the extent that the US president does. Yet, Richard Nixon's efforts to block the reporting of the Watergate scandal ultimately proved futile. Moreover, in today's era of numerous media outlets, including online news media, the speed of information dissemination has become much faster than in the past.

In summary, while markets do not always yield optimal outcomes, Gentzkow and Shapiro argue that even in democratic societies, media concentration does not pose a significant obstacle to the spread of truth.

[More to Explore] The Paradoxical Coexistence of Over- and Under-Competition

In South Korea, the three major newspapers—*The Chosun Ilbo*, *JoongAng Ilbo*, and *The Dong-A Ilbo*—have collectively held a market share of 50%–70% for several decades, all with a conservative bias. Meanwhile, the television broadcasting market was an oligopoly dominated by public broadcasters such as KBS and MBC. When these dominant newspapers created subsidiaries to enter television broadcasting in 2011, public opinion became sharply divided, and conflicts intensified. Conservatives backed the new channels, whereas progressives strongly opposed them. However, an interesting point is that both sides cited the harms of monopolization, or "too little competition," as their reasons for supporting and opposing these new channels.

Conservatives argued that the new channels would break the monopoly in broadcasting and promote competition. In contrast, progressives worried that the three conservative newspapers would deepen monopolization in the news and public opinion markets by expanding into broadcasting. These opposing views, when combined, indicate that the new channels would promote competition in broadcasting but deepen monopolization in the public opinion market.

Now, over a decade later, competition in broadcasting has increased noticeably, but broadcast content quality has not improved. This serves as an example of "too much competition" resulting in an inadequate news supply, as discussed earlier. Meanwhile, conservative media's influence on public opinion has undeniably grown since the channels launched. In South Korea, where public broadcasters' bias is heavily influenced by the ruling power, conservative bias in the news market tends to expand during conservative administrations. This is a clear example of "too little competition" causing insufficient news supply.

7.1.3 THE LIMITS OF THE LIBERTARIAN VIEW OF INTERVENTION IN THE NEWS MARKET

Some readers of this book may sympathize with economists like Gentzkow and Shapiro, whose arguments are compelling in many respects. Based on the classical principle of "press freedom"—that truth and falsehood should compete openly in the marketplace of ideas—government intervention in the news market may appear both futile and inappropriate.[5]

Director (1901–2004), a pioneer of law and economics, argued that the market for ideas precedes all other markets and that if there is one area where laissez-faire should be preserved above all, it is in this very market (Director, 1964, pp. 3–5).

Yet this libertarian view does not fully explain the realities of the news market, either in theory or in practice. Ronald Coase (1910–2013), a Nobel laureate in economics and the creator of the Coase theorem, argued that government intervention is unnecessary even in cases of market failure. However, even he admitted that if intervention is desirable to address externalities,[6] monopolies, or asymmetric information, then it is most needed in the market for ideas. At the very least, this implies that there is no reason to treat the news market differently from other markets for goods and services.

Silvio Berlusconi was a media mogul and former prime minister. His dominance over both private media and public broadcasters in Italy illustrates the risks of media concentration. Similarly, in South Korea, the 2011 entry of major newspapers into broadcasting is widely seen as having amplified their influence over public opinion. Historically, media concentration has reduced diversity, prompting many Western European countries—unlike the United States—to emphasize public broadcasting and strictly regulate ownership structures.

There is another reason why policy intervention in the news market is unavoidable. Unlike most markets, the boundary between the news market and its outside environment is inherently blurry. The production and consumption of news do not

---

[5] Milton (1608–1674), considered the founder of modern thought on press freedom, left the following monumental statement in his work Areopagitica: "Though all the winds of doctrine were let loose to play upon the earth, so Truth be in the field, we do injuriously by licensing and prohibiting to misdoubt her strength. Let her and Falsehood grapple; who ever knew Truth put to the worse, in a free and open encounter?" (Milton, 1644[2006]). This remark by Milton is often cited as the foundation for two core principles of modern press freedom: the open free marketplace of ideas and the self-righting process of truth.

[6] An externality occurs when an economic activity imposes costs or benefits on third parties who are not directly involved in the transaction. For example, the construction of public infrastructure like roads generates positive externalities, while activities such as pollution, including water contamination, result in negative externalities. Externalities can lead to "market failures," situations where the market fails to allocate resources efficiently due to unaccounted costs or benefits. The term externality is widely used in economics to describe these unintended effects, encompassing both positive and negative impacts.

remain confined within the market itself; rather, they continuously influence society at large—shaping elections, policy decisions, and consumer behavior. At the same time, external actors such as politicians, governments, and corporations have ongoing incentives to intervene in the news market.

In the apple market, it is hard to imagine politicians or corporations campaigning for or against a particular variety.[7] But in the news market, it is commonplace for powerful actors to promote or suppress certain information, depending on its bias or implications.

Libertarian economics rests on the belief that the "invisible hand" allows markets to self-regulate toward optimal outcomes. But in the news market, this mechanism frequently fails—especially given constant interference by external actors. The result is a market more prone to distortion than most others.

Figuratively speaking, the news media market is like a lake into which turbid streams continuously and forcefully flow from outside. Relying solely on the lake's self-purification ability while ignoring the inflowing turbid water would not be wise. One might believe that the "free market of ideas" has an infinite self-purification capacity, but belief is not science. Policy decisions on whether or not to intervene in the news market should be based on an objective understanding of reality. This understanding starts by assessing whether the news market—the "lake"—is receiving more turbid water than its self-purification can manage.

To summarize this section, both excessive competition and insufficient competition in the news market can lead to market failures. Excessive competition leads to an increase in sensational soft news, resulting in an insufficient supply of essential hard news needed by individuals and society. On the other hand, media concentration reduces the diversity of public opinion. In both cases, policy intervention to maintain an appropriate level of competition may be necessary.

Libertarian scholars caution that intervention is difficult and often counterproductive. But when excessive competition turns press freedom into sensational "turbid water," or too little competition creates "stagnant water," inaction is not an option. Especially when media capture overwhelms the market's capacity for correction, intervention becomes essential. Still, the news market is delicate—like tending to a wound on an infant. Even the right remedy must be applied with the utmost care, respecting the warnings of those who advocate restraint.

[7] Even in conventional markets, external entities such as governments sometimes intervene to encourage or discourage the consumption or production of specific goods. This can occur in the context of planned economic policies implemented even within democratic countries. An example is South Korea in the 1970s, when the government, facing a severe imbalance in the supply and demand of rice, a staple food, launched a large-scale campaign promoting the consumption of mixed grains, supported by policy measures to reduce rice demand. Although the overt influence of planned economic policies has largely faded, many governments around the world continue to provide institutional support in the energy market to increase the supply of alternative energy sources. However, these cases are fundamentally different from external interventions in the news market.

7.2 THE EFFECTS OF COMPETITION ON MEDIA BIAS

We have previously examined the various reasons behind the emergence of media bias. On the supply side, such reasons stem from journalists and media owners (or executives), while on the demand side, they relate to news consumers. Given this range of contributing factors, what role does competition among news outlets play in shaping media bias? Understanding how the degree of competition affects media bias requires integrating the perspectives of consumers, producers, and market mechanisms within a single analytical framework. Accordingly, the effect of competition on media bias serves as a primary route through which economics seeks to explain the phenomenon.

While there is no established consensus among economists on this matter, they do share a baseline understanding: competition among news outlets generally weakens the incentives of suppliers to inject their own biases into news content. Under intense competition, news providers must prioritize the preferences of consumers over their own ideological leanings in order to capture audience share. In other words, the more competitive the environment, the more dominant the demand-driven sources of media bias become relative to supply-driven ones. Thus, demand-side media bias is inextricably linked to market competition, which ultimately revolves around satisfying consumers.

With this context, we now turn to four contrasting theoretical views on the relationship between media competition and media bias:

(1) *Competition does not affect media bias.*
(2) *Competition exacerbates media bias.*
(3) *Competition alleviates media bias.*
(4) *Competition either increases or decreases media bias, depending on quality differences among news outlets.*

Among these, the fourth view is a relatively recent attempt to incorporate both the second and third views into a unified model and is still under academic scrutiny. The first view offers valuable insight into the persistence of media bias but remains limited in scope. As such, most economic research in this area has so far focused on the second and third viewpoints.

7.2.1 COMPETITION DOES NOT AFFECT MEDIA BIAS

Earlier, in Section 5.2.1 on the verifiability of news, we introduced the argument by Anand, Di Tella, and Galetovic (2007) that media bias arises because consumers cannot fully verify the content of news. If news consisted solely of verifiable facts, news outlets would report without bias. However, when unverifiable elements are present, consumers become more interested in the opinions embedded within news content, and media outlets respond by incorporating explicit or implicit bias into these opinions.

If this is the root cause of media bias, then competition does not influence its presence or magnitude. This is because, as the authors explain, "More competition does not change these results, as there is no reason to expect that the extent of verifiability inherent in the news event will change, or that it will affect the distribution of tastes." They further argue, "In general, competition does not lead to a reduction in bias unless this is accompanied by an increase in verifiability or a smaller dispersion of prior beliefs." To illustrate the point, they draw an analogy: "A free press does not eliminate bias for similar reasons that a free market does not lead to one color of cars" (Anand, Di Tella, and Galetovic, 2007, pp. 666, 636, 638). Despite more than 200 years of competitive news markets, media bias has remained consistently present, lending support to this argument.

The authors also challenge the classical liberal notion that a free marketplace of ideas leads to truth. According to them, a free press does not necessarily bring society closer to the truth when readers place little value on truth or share highly similar ideological views. In such cases, the press may even move society further away from the truth. Moreover, they suggest that even a free press is constrained in its ability to report truths that are unpalatable to its audience (pp. 638–639).

At the same time, the authors suggest that while competition per se may not affect media bias, a reduction in fixed costs of news production or growth in market demand (either in terms of consumer numbers or attention span) can lead to the emergence of more heavily biased media outlets. For example, radio—having lower fixed costs than television or newspapers—can foster more extreme ideological content. Similarly, as fixed costs for television broadcasting have fallen and the number of new channels has increased, the degree of media bias on television has also grown, according to their analysis. This aligns with the observation that many low-cost digital outlets or YouTubers in the post-digital era exhibit far more extreme biases than traditional media organizations.

Importantly, this linkage between falling fixed costs and the rise of highly biased media warrants a closer scrutiny of the intermediate variable: increased competition. Lower fixed costs—whether in broadcasting or printing—lower the barriers to market entry, intensifying competition. Therefore, it is worth asking whether the resulting extreme bias is caused directly by lower fixed costs or by the increased competition that follows. Contrary to Anand and his co-authors' position, many economists working in the political economy of media believe that competition does, in fact, directly influence media bias.

7.2.2 COMPETITION DEEPENS MEDIA BIAS

Early economic studies on media bias argued that news outlets differentiate their political slants much like firms in a product market tailor their offerings to consumers with diverse preferences. Left-leaning news appeals to left-leaning consumers, and right-leaning news appeals to right-leaning consumers; thus, media firms maximize profits by tailoring bias to the ideological inclinations of different consumer groups (Hamilton, 2004).[8]

Mullainathan and Shleifer (2005) provided a rigorous mathematical model supporting this perspective. According to their model, if consumers are rational and seek only accuracy in the news, they will reject all forms of bias. In such a market, news organizations deliver unbiased content to meet demand. Whether or not competition exists, news quality would remain at a perfect, unbiased level, and competition would influence only pricing, not content.

However, if consumers are irrational—preferring news that confirms their preexisting beliefs rather than objectively accurate reports—then the degree of media bias depends on how consumer biases are distributed across the market. If news consumers have homogeneous ideological biases, competition among profit-maximizing news outlets results in little to no difference in their slant. In fact, in societies where most news consumers think alike, media outlets tend to produce similar coverage. For example, the US media treated the US downing of an Iranian civilian aircraft as a technical error, while portraying the Soviet downing of a Korean airliner as an immoral atrocity. This is a typical example of similar treatment of similar events, aimed at ideologically aligned audiences (Prat and Strömberg, 2013, p. 169).[9] Similarly, media outlets across a nation tend to adopt a unified tone when covering territorial disputes or international sports competitions. Conversely, when news consumers are ideologically heterogeneous, media outlets polarize to opposite ends of the ideological spectrum.

These phenomena run counter to the liberal belief that a free press inevitably leads to truth. Instead, the outcomes of market-driven news production may be homogeneous bias tailored to a uniform audience, or extreme polarization reflecting diverse ideological camps. Moreover, Mullainathan and Shleifer viewed high-quality media as those characterized by greater accuracy and less bias. In this light, their model suggests that market competition results not in higher-quality news but in severely degraded information quality.[10]

Furthermore, according to their theory, as the number of news outlets increases, more ideologically tailored media emerge, audience segments grow narrower, and the accuracy of individual reports declines. However, if consumers have access to

[8] As previously discussed in Sections 5.1.2 (The Definition of Media Bias in Economics) and 6.3 (Media Competing in Both Bias and Quality Differentiation), this relates to media outlets' strategy of product differentiation.

[9] "On September 1, 1983, a Soviet fighter plane shot down Korean Air Lines Flight 007, killing its 269 passengers and crew. On July 3, 1988, a US Navy ship, the Vincennes, shot down Iran Air Flight 655, killing its 290 passengers and crew. In both cases, military officials identified a passenger plane as a possibly hostile target; in both cases, the perpetrating nation's officials claimed the shooting was justifiable under the circumstances. By de-emphasizing the agency and the victims and by the choice of graphics and adjectives, the news stories about the US downing of an Iranian plane called it a technical problem while the Soviet downing of a Korean jet was portrayed as a moral outrage" (Entman, 1991, p. 6).

[10] For the relationship between accuracy and bias in news (media), see Section 6.2, Economic Perspective of News Quality.

multiple sources, they may average out the biases and arrive at more accurate understandings.[11] This insight aligns with Thomas Jefferson's famous assertion that he would prefer "newspapers without a government" over "a government without newspapers"—provided that everyone has access to all newspapers and can read them.

Their theory resonates strongly with the real world. In most countries outside authoritarian states like North Korea or China, where the media is tightly controlled, politically polarized media systems are the norm. Media outlets commonly divide into conservative and liberal factions, and, except in "exceptional circumstances"—such as wars, natural disasters, or major international sporting events that foster national unity—they maintain clearly opposing biases.

Many scholars share Mullainathan and Shleifer's view that competition exacerbates media bias. Burke (2008) argues that when consumers engage only with outlets most aligned with their own biases, media organizations are incentivized to cater to these biases. As a result, consumers are unlikely to change their views, and competition only intensifies polarization.

Baron (2006) also links competition to increased bias, focusing on journalists.[12] He argues that as competition intensifies, media firms face cost-cutting pressures and try to limit wage growth. To offset anticipated resistance from journalists, firms may grant greater editorial discretion, especially with regard to bias.

[More to Explore] Public Interest Media Mitigating Private Media Bias

Research has shown that public interest media, funded by government subsidies, can reduce the overall level of bias in news media. Based on the model of Mullainathan and Shleifer (2005), which suggests that market competition among news media outlets leads to polarized media bias, Guo and Lai (2015) investigated the role of government intervention in addressing media bias.

According to their findings, unlike private news media that cater to consumer biases, public interest media report only the facts truthfully. When such media are introduced and supported by government funding, they can offer moderately biased news at a lower price. As a result, centrist news consumers shift toward public-interest media. In response, private news outlets—previously competing along ideological extremes—moderate their own biases to avoid losing centrist audiences.

Furthermore, Guo and Lai argue that providing subsidies to news outlets that refrain from intentional bias or implementing price regulations in the news market can have similar effects to introducing public interest media. Therefore, they conclude that introducing public interest media reduces the average level of media bias compared to a market composed solely of competing private outlets.

In addition, they argue that subsidy policies aimed at promoting truthful reporting can lower both media bias and prices in the news market. However, when ideological polarization among news consumers is severe—leaving few centrists—such policies are unlikely to have significant effects.

[11] Xiang and Sarvary (2007) argue that even when both types of consumers coexist—those who seek only unbiased truth and those who prefer confirmatory news based on their individual biases—the ideological positions of competing media tend to polarize. However, truth-seeking consumers are more likely to consume news from multiple outlets in order to verify the truth amid biased reporting.

[12] See Section 5.2.2.1 Journalists.

7.2.3 COMPETITION MITIGATES MEDIA BIAS

The view that competition exacerbates media bias provides a compelling explanation for the longstanding coexistence of conservative and progressive (or liberal) media outlets in most countries since the advent of modern newspapers. However, this perspective is at odds with the liberal ideal of a free press, which holds that open competition among news media should lead to the revelation of truth, much like the view that competition does not affect media bias. It also fails to account for the reality of news markets, where fierce competition among outlets can lead to a convergence of divergent reports around shared facts, gradually revealing the truth.

Gentzkow and Shapiro (2006) provided a logical explanation for this phenomenon of convergence. Like many others, they argued that consumers prefer "confirmatory news" that aligns with their preexisting beliefs and that media outlets cater to these biases. However, they added that if there exists at least one "high-quality media outlet" that gathers and reports accurate information truthfully, competing low-quality outlets—those that report with bias based on incomplete or inaccurate information—would eventually be compelled to reduce their bias. In other words, competition between high- and low-quality media can lead the latter to moderate their reporting bias.

According to Gentzkow and Shapiro, when individuals cannot directly verify the accuracy of information, they tend to regard news as high quality if it conforms to their own beliefs. From the perspective of expected utility theory, this is not irrational but a rational response. Rational consumers derive higher expected utility from information that matches their own priors or preferences in uncertain environments.[13] If such consumers are indeed rational, they also engage in Bayesian updating when exposed to new information.[14]

Moreover, news is an experience good, meaning that its quality is often revealed only through consumption. In markets for experience goods, reputation serves as a key signal of quality. The demand for news media rises as their reputation improves, which motivates competing outlets to seek better reputations among consumers.

Gentzkow and Shapiro applied this framework to explain what happens when high-quality media compete with biased, low-quality outlets. Initially, low-quality media may cater to their target audience's biases by reporting inaccurate information. But as consumers encounter accurate reporting from high-quality outlets and update their beliefs, the reputation of the biased media suffers. When the number of outlets is large or competition is intense, consumers are more likely to encounter follow-up reporting that helps them assess prior coverage. As a result, intensified competition pressures biased outlets to reduce their distortion to avoid reputation

[13] "This outcome could occur because of information-processing heuristics, coarse thinking, or a subconscious process of justification." (Gentzkow and Shapiro, 2006, p. 145). Also refer to Section 5.2.3.2. The Utility of "Confirmation News."

[14] These consumers are referred to as "Bayesian consumers." For their rational inference process, see Section 2.1.2.1. Rational Consumers.

loss and declining demand. Thus, even if rational consumers generate media bias through their own preferences, competition can act as a countervailing force that compels outlets to reduce bias.

As an empirical illustration, Gentzkow and Shapiro (2008) cited newspaper coverage of the Crédit Mobilier scandal of the 1870s,[15] one of the most notorious political-business corruption scandals in US history. In this case, partisan newspapers that initially displayed divergent coverage later converged in their reporting of core facts, driven by competitive pressures.

The scandal began with allegations of bribery involving Republican congressmen. At first, Republican-leaning papers reported cautiously, while Democratic-leaning papers were more aggressive. However, as the scandal unfolded, even Republican-aligned outlets began to cover key facts and criticize the misconduct. Gentzkow and Shapiro explained this shift by noting that readers who consumed both sides' reports had better access to the truth. If even one outlet reports accurately, and consumers can access all outlets, then the truth will eventually be revealed—consistent with broader economic theories of information dissemination.[16]

In this case, reporting by Democratic-aligned newspapers made it untenable for Republican-aligned outlets to remain silent. The latter eventually reported the scandal as well, enabling even partisan readers to learn the truth. Editors of Republican newspapers likely understood that continued denial in the face of mounting evidence would erode their credibility among readers. Indeed, this pattern of convergence under pressure is common across time and countries.

In short, when one outlet distorts or omits key information but other competing outlets report it, the distorting outlet risks losing credibility and readership. Conversely, outlets that provide uniquely accurate reporting can gain a reputation and a competitive advantage. However, for this mechanism to function, two conditions must be met: consumers must be rational and regularly update their beliefs based on new information, and they must consume news from multiple sources.

Other scholars have also supported the view that competition reduces media bias. Anderson and McLaren (2012), for instance, argued that media owners may embed political bias in coverage to serve their interests, but that such bias diminishes when competition intensifies—assuming consumers demand accuracy. Even politically motivated owners are forced to consider consumer preferences in highly competitive markets.[17]

Brocas, Carrillo, and Wilkie (2011) also found that as the number of competing outlets increases, overall bias declines. Their model examined how media outlets strategically monitor and critique one another's reporting. They found that media bias is lower in markets with more competitors—bias declines when there are four competing outlets compared to two, and even more so with six.

---

[15] A notorious corruption scandal involving politicians and railroad construction after the US Civil War.

[16] Refer to Section 2.1.2.2. Persuasion in Shaping Judgments.

[17] Refer to Section 5.2.2.2. Media Owners.

Finally, as will be discussed in Chapter 9 "Media Capture and Media Power," Besley and Prat also argued that competition reduces bias. In their framework, increased competition reduces the likelihood of media capture by political or economic elites. As a result, media distortion stemming from such capture also diminishes.

7.2.4 THE QUALITY GAP BETWEEN COMPETING MEDIA DETERMINES MEDIA BIAS

So far, we have examined three competing views on how market competition affects media bias: that competition has no effect, that it exacerbates bias, and that it mitigates bias. Interestingly, as illustrated by the examples used to support each of these views, the phenomena predicted by all three perspectives are observed in the real world.

The idea that competing media outlets differentiate themselves by adopting opposing biases aligns with many people's everyday experiences. In most countries—excluding those under authoritarian media control—news organizations are typically split along ideological lines, such as left versus right or liberal versus conservative. Conversely, we also frequently observe that competition drives media outlets to converge toward more accurate reporting, thereby narrowing the gap in media bias. In other words, both the view that competition increases divergence in media bias and the view that it reduces such divergence are supported by empirical observations.

How is it possible that these seemingly contradictory theoretical explanations can coexist? One key to understanding this lies in the different assumptions underlying the two opposing perspectives. Let us revisit those assumptions. Mullainathan and Shleifer (2005), who argue that competition intensifies media bias, assume a market in which media outlets are of equal quality. By contrast, Gentzkow and Shapiro (2006), who argue that competition mitigates media bias, assume a market where media outlets differ in quality. Given this discrepancy, the two views are not necessarily mutually exclusive.

One view posits that when two media outlets of equal quality compete, they will maximize their ideological differentiation. The other holds that when a high-quality outlet that reports accurately competes with a low-quality outlet that engages in biased reporting, the low-quality outlet will moderate its bias to remain competitive. Combining the two views leads to a straightforward conclusion: when media quality is equal across the two media outlets, competition tends to widen the gap in media bias; when there is a disparity in quality, competition narrows the gap.

There is a theoretical model that integrates these two seemingly opposing perspectives into a unified framework. According to this model, when two media outlets with differing levels of quality compete for audience share in the news market, the extent of the ideological gap between them depends on the magnitude of their quality differential (Yang, 2020; Yang, 2021, 2022).

This model differs from prior studies in two key assumptions. First, it reflects the reality that news content is effectively free in the digital space and therefore does not assume price competition between media outlets. Second, it defines media quality differently from earlier studies, which typically defined it in terms of accuracy or "less bias." However, in this model, the quality of a news outlet is defined as its ability to effectively deliver (or present) information—specifically, its ability to reduce the cognitive effort required for consumers to understand the news.

When media quality is defined not by accuracy but by delivery capacity, it becomes independent of media or consumer bias. If accuracy is the standard, perceptions of quality vary widely across individuals, as consumers subjectively judge quality based on how closely the content aligns with their own ideological predispositions. In contrast, when quality is defined by the ability to deliver news, it allows for a more objective assessment. A media outlet with high capacity for delivery presents content that is logically structured and rich in context, provides well-supported facts rather than incomplete ones, and employs visual aids to aid understanding rather than offering long and monotonous texts. These aspects are externally observable and unrelated to the outlet's political slant.

Under this definition of media quality, news consumers make choices based on two independent criteria: bias and quality. That is, while they prefer news that aligns with their own political bias (confirmation bias), they also favor news that is well presented and easy to comprehend. Consequently, among news items with similar ideological slant, consumers will always opt for the higher-quality version, and among news sources of equal quality, they will gravitate toward the outlet whose bias aligns most closely with their own.[18]

In such a setting, when two outlets share a similar ideological position, the lower-quality outlet loses audience share while the higher-quality outlet gains. This gives the low-quality outlet an incentive to maximize its bias differential, while the high-quality outlet has an incentive to minimize that difference to retain and expand its readership.

However, the two types of outlets face different levels of difficulty when it comes to altering their ideological slant. High-quality outlets face much greater costs in shifting their editorial bias. The more accurate (i.e., high quality) the outlet, and the greater the deviation from its existing bias, the more costly it becomes to produce the news. High-quality journalism is generally backed by a larger number of trained reporters. Any ideological shift would require the outlet to persuade these journalists—either explicitly or implicitly—to alter their editorial stance, compensate them for doing so, or hire new reporters whose views align with the intended shift. These are long-term and costly efforts.

For example, it would be extremely difficult—even over time—for a high-quality outlet like *The New York Times* to shift its editorial tone. To do so, it would need to

[18] Refer to Section 6.2.2 Information Presentation Ability.

justify the change to its existing newsroom staff, offer incentives, or recruit new journalists with different ideological orientations. Such actions incur significant costs, especially when the desired change in bias is large.

By contrast, low-quality outlets—typically small operations with fewer staff—can pivot far more easily. For them, altering the ideological slant of their reporting can be done at little or no cost, almost as easily as flipping a switch.

Therefore, when a high-quality outlet and a low-quality outlet compete for the same audience, the greater the quality gap between them, or the greater the cost of bias adjustment for the high-quality outlet, the larger the ideological gap between the two will be. Conversely, when the quality differential between the two media outlets is small or nonexistent, the ideological gap between them will diminish in the absence of price competition but will be maximized in the presence of price competition.

This framework thus explains both outcomes: competition may either exacerbate or mitigate media bias, depending on contextual factors. It is particularly effective in explaining the recent proliferation of highly partisan content among low-quality online outlets and YouTubers who lack the professional standards of traditional media.

Furthermore, this theory accommodates both the view of Mullainathan and Shleifer that competition increases bias—and that of Gentzkow and Shapiro—that competition reduces it. If we incorporate the assumption from Mullainathan and Shleifer—that two media outlets of identical quality compete through price—into this model, then the conclusion aligns with theirs: competition leads each outlet to maximize the differentiation of its ideological bias.

The claim by Gentzkow and Shapiro—that low-quality media competing with high-quality media reduce their own bias—can also be understood within the framework of this model, as illustrated in the following example. Suppose a left-leaning newspaper raises suspicions about a right-wing politician's alleged corruption, while a right-leaning paper reports that the evidence is insufficient. Then, new evidence emerges suggesting the politician is, in fact, innocent. In this case, the left-leaning paper's credibility declines, while the credibility—or the "information delivery capacity" (i.e., quality)—of the right-leaning paper increases. As a result, the left-leaning outlet starts losing its readership. To mitigate this loss, the left-leaning paper has two options: it can either moderate its initial bias (i.e., the corruption claim) or improve its media quality by making the claim more persuasive through stronger evidence and clearer reasoning. However, enhancing the delivery capacity—the core of quality—is not something that can be achieved in the short term. Therefore, to minimize audience attrition quickly, the left-leaning outlet is more likely to reduce the extremity of its bias.

Up to this point, we have reviewed a range of theoretical studies by economists on the effects of competition on media bias. While the focal points, assumptions, and conclusions of these studies differ, they also share some important commonalities. Let us now summarize both the similarities and differences.

First, most economists agree that competition among news providers tends to push them toward better satisfying consumer demand. This is because outlets that are more responsive to the preferences and expectations of their audiences tend to have a competitive advantage. Thus competition is generally seen as a force that reduces producer-driven bias in news media. That is, the owners, managers, or journalists of media organizations may introduce bias into news coverage in pursuit of economic or noneconomic interests. But competition can function as a constraint on such behavior, thereby improving consumers' information welfare by reducing distortions originating from news suppliers.

While Baron and a few others argue that competition can actually increase bias stemming from journalists or media firms themselves, this view is considered uncommon. Most economic models suggest the opposite.

In contrast, the effect of competition on consumer-driven media bias is much more contested among scholars. This is largely due to divergent assumptions about the nature of news consumers and the quality of media. When studies assume that consumers prefer ideologically biased news, media competition tends to exacerbate bias. Conversely, if consumers are modeled as rational actors who seek factual and balanced reporting—or if they are assumed to prefer more information over ideologically congenial content—then competition tends to reduce polarization.

Therefore, the impact of competition on consumer-driven media bias ultimately hinges on the underlying assumptions about human nature. If consumers are fundamentally irrational, seeking only what they want to believe, then competition will amplify bias. If they are capable of overcoming their preferences and can pursue accuracy and objectivity, then competition may alleviate polarization. In reality, however, human beings are rarely fully rational but are also not entirely irrational. This suggests that the behavioral economics view—where humans are only boundedly rational—should be more actively integrated into future analyses.

In addition, the behavior of news media with regard to bias also depends on how consumer biases are distributed across society. As discussed in Section 5.3, the ideological leanings of consumers vary significantly across countries and are not fixed over time. A deeper analysis of how the distribution of consumer bias affects media behavior is provided in the following More to Explore section.

[More to Explore] The Ideological Distribution of News Consumers and Media Bias Differentiation

The ideological distribution of individual biases among news consumers fundamentally affects the editorial strategies of competing news outlets as they seek to maximize profits. Most economists studying this issue assume a uniform distribution of consumers' ideological preferences, as illustrated at the top left of Fig. 7.1. This distribution implies that consumers are evenly spread across the ideological spectrum from the far left to the far right. It is one of the simplest and most neutral forms of distribution in statistics.

However, in reality, consumer ideology is rarely distributed so symmetrically. In most stable societies, individuals with extreme ideological views tend to constitute a minority. This suggests that more complex patterns—such as a unimodal distribution (middle-left panel) or a bimodal distribution (bottom-left panel)—may better reflect actual ideological landscapes. Still, it would be misleading to claim that any single form of distribution universally represents real-world consumer

Continued

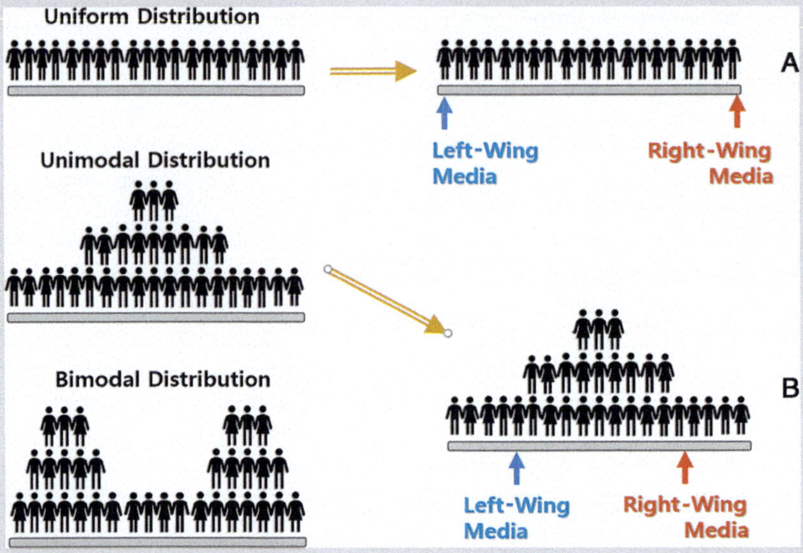

FIGURE 7.1

Consumers' distributions and media bias.

bias. For this reason, economists often rely on the simplest form—the uniform distribution—to draw theoretical implications, even if it doesn't perfectly mirror reality.

Assuming that both media outlets offer products of equal quality, the top-right panel illustrates the editorial bias strategies that news outlets adopt when consumer ideology follows a uniform distribution. According to Mullainathan and Shleifer (2005), and D'Aspremont, Gabszewicz, and Thisse (1979), profit-maximizing media firms in this setting seek to differentiate their news products as much as possible. One outlet may cater to the far left, while another targets the far right.

In contrast, the bottom-right panel shows how news outlets behave under an unimodal distribution in which most consumers are clustered around the ideological center. In such markets, firms generally reduce product differentiation as competition for the centrist majority intensifies (Neven, 1986). Accordingly, news outlets tend to adopt more moderate editorial stances when the consumer base is concentrated in the center.

Countries with such centrist-heavy ideological distributions include Norway and Finland. As a result, news outlets in these countries exhibit far smaller differences in ideological bias than do those in highly polarized societies such as the United States or South Korea (see Figs. 5.2–5.4 in Chapter 5 "Theories of Media Bias: The Inescapable Shackles").

References

Anand, B., Di Tella, R., Galetovic, A., 2007. Information or opinion? Media bias as product differentiation. Journal of Economics & Management Strategy 16 (3), 635–682. https://doi.org/10.1111/j.1530-9134.2007.00153.x.

Anderson, S.P., McLaren, J., 2012. Media mergers and media bias with rational consumers. Journal of the European Economic Association 10 (4), 831–859.

Bagdikian, B., 2000. The Media Monopoly, sixth ed. Beacon Press, Boston.

Baron, D., 2006. Persistent Media Bias. Journal of Public Economics 90 (1–2), 1–36.

Brocas, I., Carrillo, J.D., Wilkie, S., 2011. A Theoretical Analysis of the Impact of Local Market Structure on the Range of Viewpoints Supplied, 9. FCC (Federal Communications Commission) Media Study.

Burke, J., 2008. Primetime spin: media bias and belief confirming information. Journal of Economics & Management Strategy 17 (3), 633–665. https://doi.org/10.1111/j.1530-9134.2008.00189.x.

Cagé, J., 2020. Media competition, information provision and political participation: evidence from french local newspapers and elections, 1944–2014. Journal of Public Economics 185, 104077.

D'Aspremont, C., Gabszewicz, J., Thisse, J., 1979. On Hotelling's stability in competition. Econometrica 47 (5), 1145–1150.

Director, A., 1964. The parity of the economic market place. The Journal of Law and Economics 7, 1–10. https://doi.org/10.1086/466595.

Djankov, S., McLiesh, C., Nenova, T., Shleifer, A., 2003. Who owns the media? The Journal of Law and Economics 46 (2), 341–382.

Downs, A., 1957. An economic theory of political action in a democracy. Journal of Political Economy 65 (2), 135–150. https://doi.org/10.1086/257897.

Entman, R.M., 1991. Framing U.S. coverage of international news: contrasts in narratives of the KAL and Iran Air incidents. Journal of Communication 41 (4), 6–27.

Federal Communications Commission, 2003. Report and Order and Notice of Proposed Rulemaking (FCC 03–127).

Gentzkow, M., Shapiro, J.M., 2006. Media bias and reputation. Journal of Political Economy 114 (2), 280–316. https://doi.org/10.1086/499414.

Gentzkow, M., Shapiro, J.M., 2008. Competition and truth in the market for news. Journal of Economic Perspectives 22 (2), 133–154.

Guo, W.-C., Lai, F.-C., 2015. Media bias, slant regulation, and the public-interest media. Journal of Economics 114 (3), 291–308. https://doi.org/10.1007/s00712-014-0396-2.

Hamilton, J.T., 2004. All the News That's Fit to Sell. Princeton University Press.

Hazlett, T.W., Sosa, D.W., 1997. Chilling the internet: lessons from FCC regulation of radio broadcasting. Michigan Telecommunications and Technology Law Review 4, 35–70.

Ingber, S., 1984. The marketplace of ideas: a legitimizing myth. Duke Law Journal 1984 (1), 1–91. https://doi.org/10.2307/1372344.

Milton, J., 1644[2006]. Areopagitica. In: Blasi, V. (Ed.), Ideas of the First Amendment. Thomson/West, Saint Paul, MN, pp. 56–93.

Mullainathan, S., Shleifer, A., 2005. The market for news. American Economic Review 95 (4), 1031–1053. https://doi.org/10.1257/0002828054825619.

Neven, D. J., 1986. On Hotelling's competition with non-uniform customer distributions. Economics Letters 21 (2), 121–126. https://doi.org/10.1016/0165-1765(86)90049-2.

Patterson, T.E., 2001. Doing well and doing good. SSRN Electronic Journal. https://doi.org/10.2139/ssrn.257395.

Posner, R.A., 1986. Free speech in an economic perspective. Suffolk University Law Review 20 (1), 1–54.

Prat, A., Strömberg, D., 2013. The political economy of mass media. In: Advances in Economics and Econometrics vol. 2., Cambridge University Press. 135–187. https://doi.org/10.1017/CBO9781139060028.004.

Xiang, Y., Sarvary, M., 2007. News consumption and media bias. Marketing Science 26 (5), 611–628.

Yang, S., 2021. Media Capture and Media Bias in the Digital Age. Ph.D. Dissertation. Yonsei University.

Yang, S., 2022. Media bias with asymmetric media quality. Applied Economics Letters 29 (19), 1810–1814. https://doi.org/10.1080/13504851.2021.1963401.

Yang, S., 2020. Media bias with digital intermediary. International Telecommunications Policy Review 27 (4), 1–23. https://doi.org/10.37793/itpr.27.4.1.

Zaller, J., 1999. Market Competition and News Quality. Annual Meetings of the American Political Science Association.

CHAPTER

8 The Myth of Unbiased Reporting: Empirical Evidence

Chapter Outline

Unbiased news reporting is a myth, not the reality, of US media.[1]
—Andrei Shleifer, Economist.

The media is not and cannot be neutral, and we should not expect it to be.[2]
—Hans Rosling, author of Factfulness

Early in life I had noticed that no event is ever correctly reported in a newspaper.[3]
—George Orwell, novelist

[1] Shleifer (2015: 187).
[2] Rosling et al. (2018). Chapter 4. (Referenced from Korean translation; English page numbers unavailable)
[3] Orwell (1943), Section IV.

The Economics of News Media. DOI: http://dx.doi.org/10.1016/B978-0-443-45044-0.00007-6

These observations, made by prominent thinkers, highlight the persistent and widespread nature of media bias. As discussed in Chapter 5, economists often use the following definition to capture this phenomenon: "Systematic differences in the mapping from facts to news reports" (Gentzkow et al., 2015, p. 625). Among the various forms of media bias, the one most commonly perceived is political (or ideological) bias. Beyond this, there is also bias stemming from the favorable treatment of certain interest groups or individuals, such as advertisers, by news media.

However, the scope of media bias extends far beyond these categories. Even its most representative form—ideological bias—can be classified along multiple dimensions, not only the conservative-liberal (or libertarian) spectrum but also dimensions such as modernity versus tradition or individualism versus collectivism. In recent years, ideological biases related to gender and generation have also gained attention.

Media bias can also be examined based on the actors contributing to its emergence. Media owners, journalists, external actors such as political or financial forces seeking to influence the media, and news consumers themselves all play roles in creating media bias.[4]

There are multiple ways to classify bias based on how it is embedded in content. Some economists categorize bias into "factual bias," "framing bias," "issue bias," and "ideological bias" (Prat and Strömberg, 2013). Others divide it into two types: "distortion" and "filtering of information" (Gentzkow et al., 2015).[5]

Empirical studies investigating the existence of media bias in reality have been based on these diverse forms, causes, and manifestations of bias. Among these, studies conducted by economists are relatively recent and limited in scope compared to those in fields such as communication studies or political science. Despite their short history, however, many of these studies have gained recognition for their interdisciplinary approach.

One notable limitation of this body of research is that it has been predominantly led by American economists, resulting in a significant focus on the US media. Consequently, a substantial portion of the studies introduced in this book also examine the US media. Therefore when applying these empirical findings on media bias to the contexts of other countries, it is essential to account for historical and environmental differences between nations.

Most economists investigating the realities of media bias have focused almost exclusively on political (ideological) bias as the subject of their empirical research. While it is a limitation that this approach does not encompass the full spectrum of media bias, it appears understandable given that political (ideological) bias is widely recognized as the core type of media bias.

---

[4] News media consumers can include not only the audiences who consume news content but also advertisers who purchase advertising space and airtime from news media. Media bias that is directly or indirectly influenced by advertisers is discussed in Chapter 9 and Chapter 10.

[5] Some media scholars use simpler frameworks to categorize media bias, such as "emphasizing the positive aspects of favored subjects, concealing their negative aspects, highlighting the negative aspects of opposed subjects, and obscuring their positive aspects" (Van Dijk, 1998). Refer to Section 5.4.

After exploring the empirical studies on media bias presented in this chapter, readers will come to realize that the claim of delivering "unbiased news" is, in most cases, far from the truth—even for the world's most reputable media outlets. These findings may shatter our hopes and expectations, yet understanding the consistent and pervasive reality of media bias is valuable. This knowledge is beneficial not only to scholars and policymakers but also to news consumers and providers alike. Gaining an objective understanding of media bias is essential for grasping the truth about the media and for fostering societal efforts toward a better media environment. In particular, the findings of economists, derived from a value-neutral perspective, can serve as better guidance on news consumption for consumers, while offering journalists opportunities for self-reflection and introspection.

Now, let us delve into specific examples of media bias uncovered by economists.

8.1 EVEN WHEN SEPARATING OPINION FROM FACT REPORTING, POLITICAL BIAS REMAINS

Renowned newspapers such as *The New York Times* and *The Washington Post* claim to maintain a strict separation between opinion and factual reporting. This effort is evident in their news coverage, making it relatively easy to observe. But does this mean that such globally esteemed media outlets are free from bias?

Many US news media outlets, including both newspapers, openly declare their support for election candidates of specific political parties through editorials. At the same time, they assert that such partisan bias does not influence their factual reporting. However, research by economists has found that even these world-class newspapers, which generally uphold the distinction between opinion and fact in individual articles, exhibit bias toward particular ideologies or parties. This bias is reflected in the selection of issues they report on and the volume of coverage dedicated to specific issues.

Larcinese et al. (2011) analyzed the coverage of major economic issues such as "unemployment" and "inflation" by 102 major US newspapers, from 1996 to 2005. Their study found that the partisan bias expressed in newspapers' opinion sections, such as editorials, was mirrored in the volume of coverage on certain issues.

According to the study, for economic issues unfavorable to the incumbent president, newspapers that endorsed the president during the election provided less coverage, while newspapers that supported the opposition candidate offered more. Conversely, for economic issues favorable to the incumbent president, the opposite pattern was observed. The issues where bias was evident included "high unemployment rate" and "budget deficits." Notably, coverage related to "high unemployment rates" displayed significant and robust differences depending on the newspaper's partisan alignment. On the other hand, issues like "inflation" or "trade deficits" did not reveal a clear partisan bias in coverage.

Puglisi and Snyder (2011) conducted a similar analysis of 32 political scandals reported by 213 US newspapers, from 1997 to 2007. Their findings showed that newspapers demonstrated more favorable reporting of the political party they supported in their editorials. For instance, newspapers endorsing the Democratic Party reported more extensively on scandals involving Republican politicians than on those involving Democratic politicians, while newspapers supporting the Republican Party exhibited the opposite pattern.[6]

These studies reveal that many newspapers, including *The New York Times*, which claim to clearly distinguish between facts and opinions, exhibit partisan bias through their issue selection and coverage volume. This aligns with the agenda-setting theory, which asserts that "[The press] may not be successful much of the time in telling people what to think, but it is stunningly successful in telling its readers what to think about" (Cohen, 1963: 13).[7]

Empirical findings showing that newspapers report more favorably on the political parties and candidates they endorse in their editorial sections have also been presented by various political scientists. Kahn and Kenney (2002) analyzed 5529 factual and opinion articles mentioning US Senate candidates during the 1988 to 1992 election cycles. Their study found that newspapers used a more favorable tone in factual reporting for candidates they endorsed in their editorials. The researchers noted that "one of the essential elements of an impartial press is the impenetrable wall between editorial pages and the pages devoted to the news." They added, "while the political beliefs of newspaper owners and editors are articulated clearly on opinion pages, their views are not supposed to infiltrate the reporting of the news." However, their findings indicated otherwise (Kahn and Kenney, 2002: 381).

Some political scientists have also examined partisan bias in photojournalism.[8] Barrett and Barrington (2005) analyzed the visual tone of 435 photos of election candidates published in seven newspapers, including the *Chicago Tribune* and the *Cincinnati Enquirer*, during the 1998 and 2002 US congressional elections. Their study found that newspapers were more likely to feature photos that presented candidates they endorsed editorially in a more positive light than their opponents.

While professional journalism emphasizes the strict separation of facts and opinions, it has been repeatedly confirmed that even high-quality news media demonstrate bias through their selection of issues, volume of coverage, and tone of reporting.

---

[6] Galvis et al. (2016) conducted a study similar to Puglisi and Snyder (2011), examining the coverage of 121 political scandals by 159 US newspapers over a 40-year period from 1870 to 1910. Their findings revealed even clearer partisan bias in the newspapers. However, this result is perhaps unsurprising, given that newspapers and political forces had far closer personal and material ties during the late 19th century than they do today.

[7] Refer to Section 4.1.

[8] Visual images, such as photos and videos, are also representative content that reflects the biases of news providers. Due to the nature of such content, research on imagery has primarily been conducted in social sciences outside the field of economics.

8.2 THE MAIN SOURCES OF MEDIA BIAS

In Chapter 5, *Theories of Media Bias: The Inescapable Shackles*, we explored the various theoretical causes of media bias. These causes can be broadly categorized into supply-side and demand-side factors. Media bias arises on the supply side when media owners or journalists embed their own views into the news deliberately or subconsciously. On the demand side, it occurs when news media tailor their content to suit the preferences of their audience. But are these theoretical causal relationships supported by empirical evidence? The answer is that they manifest in a variety of forms.

Some scholars have focused on either supply-side or demand-side factors to identify media bias, while others have compared these factors to examine the biases each produces. However, studies investigating whether supply-side or demand-side factors dominate have yielded mixed results, depending on the methodological approaches used, such as differences in data sources, time periods, or analytical frameworks. This suggests that the media bias we perceive is often the result of a complex interplay between multiple factors rather than the influence of a single cause.

Previously, we introduced the findings of Larcinese et al. (2011), which found that even prominent US newspapers demonstrated partisanship in their coverage of certain economic issues, such as "high unemployment rates" and "budget deficits," through the volume of reporting. Interestingly, even for issues that revealed partisanship, the reasons for the newspapers' bias varied by issue. For example, political bias in coverage of "high unemployment rates" was more pronounced among newspapers than among their audiences, indicating a supply-side bias driven by the media or journalists. In contrast, bias in coverage of "budget deficits" closely mirrored the political preferences of the newspapers' audiences, suggesting a demand-side bias originating from readers.

Similarly, in the earlier section on political scandal coverage, Puglisi and Snyder (2011) showed that US regional newspapers exhibited partisanship in the volume of coverage, with the causes of bias differing between national and local political figures. For politicians at the federal level, the bias was supply-driven, as the newspapers themselves were more biased than their audiences on average. However, for local politicians, audience influence played a larger role. Newspapers in regions with more Democratic supporters covered scandals involving Republican politicians far more than those involving Democratic politicians, and vice versa.

These studies illustrate how, depending on the issue or region, either news suppliers or news consumers can have a greater influence on media bias. However, other scholars have presented empirical findings identifying either "news suppliers" or "news consumers" as the dominant factor driving media bias. Let us examine these differing perspectives in turn.

8.2.1 "NEWS CONSUMERS ARE THE ROOT OF MEDIA BIAS"

In 2010 a study that uncovered the partisan alignment between Democratic and Republican politicians and American newspapers garnered significant attention. The research identified distinct phrases used differently by Democratic and Republican politicians and examined how frequently these phrases appeared in daily newspapers. This allowed the researchers to assess the partisan bias of newspapers based on the similarity of their language to that of specific political factions.

Gentzkow and Shapiro (2010) first extracted "partisan" words and phrases used by members of the US House of Representatives in 2005. For instance, Democratic representatives used terms like "war in Iraq" more frequently, while Republican representatives preferred expressions like "war on terror." Similarly, Democrats often used phrases such as "oil companies," "tax breaks," and "middle class," whereas Republicans were more inclined to use terms like "natural gas," "death tax," and "illegal immigration."[9] The researchers then measured how frequently these partisan words and phrases appeared in 433 US newspapers during the same period.

The researchers also estimated the political preferences of newspaper audiences by region. Using postal zip codes, they categorized areas based on whether residents contributed more political donations to the Democratic or Republican parties. This allowed them to distinguish Democratic-leaning and Republican-leaning regions. In addition, they inferred the political inclinations of newspaper owners by examining political contributions made by the owners themselves, their newspapers, or the newspaper chains to which they belonged.

Their analysis revealed that in regions with more Democratic supporters, newspapers that frequently used Democratic phrases tended to have larger audiences, and the reverse was true in Republican-dominated regions. A strong correlation existed between the political biases of newspapers and the biases of their audiences.

Furthermore, after controlling for regional variables associated with audience bias, the researchers compared the bias differences between newspapers owned by the same entity and those between randomly paired newspapers. They found no evidence that newspapers owned by the same entity exhibited more similar biases than two random newspapers.

Gentzkow and Shapiro concluded that, at least in the United States, "the political bias of newspaper owners was far less significant than that of newspaper audiences in shaping media bias."[10] Additionally, their analysis found that neither the biases

---

[9] Other expressions more frequently used by Democratic representatives included "trade deficit," "private accounts," "trade agreement," "American people," "nuclear option," "African American," and "budget cuts." Meanwhile, Republican representatives were more inclined to use terms such as "stem cell," "class action," "embryonic stem," "tax relief," "Boy Scouts," "hate crimes," and "global war."

[10] Gentzkow and Shapiro's view that media owners have less influence on media bias compared to news consumers supports the argument against the necessity of media ownership and concentration regulations, which are based on the premise that owners exert significant control over news policies. For more on the harms of media ownership concentration and the need for regulation, see Section 7.1.2 Too Little Competition and Insufficient Information Supply.

of frontline journalists nor competition for newspaper sales significantly influenced media bias. They argued that media bias is more influenced by demand-side factors, such as the preference for confirmatory news among audiences, than by supply-side factors like the biases of owners or journalists.

Another study demonstrated more simply that news consumers play a dominant role in shaping media bias. Agirdas (2015) examined the US local newspaper market between 1999 and 2009, focusing on cases where rival newspapers ceased publication due to financial distress caused by the rise of online media. He found that surviving newspapers reduced their political bias when competitors with opposing biases closed down, adapting their editorial stance to attract the audience of the defunct newspapers.

However, it is challenging to generalize the above scholars' empirical findings to other countries, as there are also many cases where media bias appears to be less influenced by audiences and more determined by media owners or ownership structures. For example, in countries like Australia and the United Kingdom, newspapers[11] owned by Rupert Murdoch's News Corp tend to reflect his politically conservative stance. Conversely, outlets such as *Politiken* in Denmark and the *Hankyoreh* in South Korea display a progressive stance, shaped by their minority or employee ownership structures. Similarly, *The Guardian* in the United Kingdom, owned by a nonprofit trust, reflects the progressive values of its newsroom staff.

These cases illustrate that media bias can result from a complex interplay between news consumers and providers, underscoring the need for more context-specific research. The realities of news markets differ across countries due to factors such as traditions in media practices, levels of technological development, and cultural differences. Consequently, findings derived from one country, such as those of Gentzkow and Shapiro in the United States, may not apply universally, highlighting the importance of further research on this topic in diverse national contexts.

8.2.2 "NEWS PROVIDERS DETERMINE MEDIA BIAS"

Other economists have uncovered cases where news providers displayed their own biases, disregarding the preferences or demands of their audiences. Ansolabehere et al. (2006) found that the political bias expressed through US newspapers' public endorsements of candidates during elections often contradicted the majority political leanings of voters. They analyzed endorsements in editorials by US newspapers from 1940 to 2002, comparing the candidates (or parties) supported by newspapers with those actually supported by voters during elections. Their findings revealed that, in the 1940s and 1950s, urban voters were more likely to support Democratic

[11] The Australian in Australia, *The Times and The Sun* in the United Kingdom and *The New York Post* and *The Wall Street Journal* in the United States are all owned by Rupert Murdoch's News Corp. In particular, *The Times, The Sun*, and *The New York Post* shifted from centrist or liberal leanings to conservative positions after being acquired by Rupert Murdoch.

candidates. However, newspapers endorsed Republican candidates at twice the rate of Democratic candidates.

A few years after Ansolabehere's study, political scientists in a different study found similar results. They analyzed US presidential elections from 1940 to 1988 and reported that, while the average voter support for Democratic candidates was approximately 53%, newspapers endorsed Republican candidates more than five times as often as Democratic candidates in their editorials (Stanley and Niemi, 2013).

Since the 1960s, the Republican bias across US newspapers has gradually weakened. By the 1990s, more newspapers endorsed Democratic candidates. Yet, voter support for Republican and Democratic candidates during this period remained nearly equal. Today, newspapers endorsing Democratic candidates significantly outnumber those endorsing Republican candidates. For instance, in the 2016 US presidential election, Democratic candidate Hillary Clinton received endorsements from 243 daily publications, whereas Republican candidate Donald Trump was endorsed by only 20 (Wilson, 2020). However, the popular vote share between Trump and Clinton was nearly equal (46.1% vs 48.2%), yet it was Trump who ultimately won the presidency through the Electoral College.

However, when news providers ignore audience preferences, consumers actively seek alternatives that better align with their views. This dynamic partly explains the significant growth of partisan narratives and misinformation on social media, where the lack of alignment between traditional media and audience preferences creates opportunities for alternative sources to flourish. For example, in the 2016 election, pro-Trump fake news on Facebook was shared 30 million times, compared to 7.6 million shares for pro-Clinton fake news (Allcott and Gentzkow, 2017).[12] Similarly, in 1988, the launch of the *Hankyoreh*, a progressive newspaper in South Korea's predominantly conservative media environment under an authoritarian regime, attracted 500,000 subscribers within just a few months. This demonstrates how unmet demand can drive rapid audience shifts when alternative outlets emerge.

On the other hand, the practice of American media endorsing presidential candidates has sharply declined since the 2000s. According to the American Presidency Project at UC Santa Barbara, among the top 100 newspapers by circulation, the number of those endorsing a specific candidate dropped from 91 in 2004 to just 29 in 2024. The reasons for this change, according to media expert Joshua Benton (2024), who founded the Nieman Journalism Lab at Harvard University, include concerns over reader backlash, risk aversion in management, and the influence of major media owners.[13]

[12] Refer to Section 11.2.2.1.

[13] In the 2024 US presidential election, this trend showed signs of moderation, as traditionally pro-Democratic newspapers such as *The Washington Post and Los Angeles Times*, under the direction of their owners, refrained from making endorsements. This move can be interpreted either as a strategic response by the owners to audience preferences or as a reflection of the owners' political inclinations. For further discussion on the latter, refer to Section 9.1.3.2.

[More to Explore] Media Owners Shifting Political Bias

Otis Chandler. Larry Bessel & Kathleen Ballard/UCLA Library, CC BY 4.0, via Wikimedia Commons.

Silvio Berlusconi. European People's Party, CC BY 2.0 via Wikimedia Commons.

Until the 1950s, the *Los Angeles Times* was a staunchly conservative newspaper that supported the Republican Party, heavily influenced by the political leanings of its owners, the Chandler family. However, when Otis Chandler (1927–2006), a progressive member of the family, became publisher in 1960, the editorial stance shifted dramatically to support the Democratic Party.

This change also eliminated the paper's pro-Republican bias in factual reporting. The adjustment in bias significantly improved the paper's reputation and profitability, leading to remarkable business success (Larcinese et al., 2011). Otis's case demonstrates how a media owner can respond to consumer expectations and demands, breaking newsroom inertia.

Silvio Berlusconi, Italian media tycoon and right-wing political leader, used his ownership of television channels to provide more airtime to right-wing politicians than to their left-wing counterparts. After he came to power in 2001, even the public broadcasters shifted to favor the right. This change began when the head of news at RAI 1, the largest public broadcasting channel in Italy, was replaced with someone ideologically aligned with Berlusconi. Following this, RAI 1's flagship news program, Telegiornale 1, allocated significantly more airtime to right-wing politicians than other public or private news channels, becoming markedly more conservative (Durante and Knight, 2012).[14] This shift reflected Berlusconi's personal beliefs and political agenda. While RAI 1's audience declined, he successfully advanced his political objectives.

8.3 THE GENERAL MEDIA BIAS AND THE "TILTED PLAYING FIELD"

Empirical studies on media bias include not only research examining individual news outlets, but also investigations that seek to identify the overall political slant of an entire national press. As discussed in Chapter 5, Section 5.4, media scholars have

[14] This study is revisited in Sections 8.5.2 and 10.1.5.

long debated whether the press as a whole tends to exhibit liberal or conservative biases. Empirical research conducted by economists on the same topic offers further insights within this broader debate.

8.3.1 IS THE MEDIA IN THE UNITED STATES LIBERAL?

In 2005, at a time when competing claims that the American media leaned either conservative or liberal were at the forefront of public discourse, economists Timothy Groseclose and Jeffrey Milyo published a study measuring the ideological slant of major US news media outlets. Their research attracted considerable attention from journalists, media scholars and executives, and intellectuals, as it constituted the first systematic empirical investigation into the ideological bias of prominent US media outlets. The most widely discussed finding in Groseclose and Milyo (2005) was that "the average slant of major US news media is more liberal than that of members of Congress." At one time, books arguing that the American media leaned either liberal or conservative frequently appeared on bestseller lists; their findings sparked intense interest.

To measure the relative ideological slant of media outlets, the authors compared the similarity in think tank citations between members of Congress and news media. Specifically, they counted how often 20 major newspapers and broadcast networks, as well as members of Congress, cited various think tanks with differing ideological orientations between 1990 and 2003. Based on this data, they mapped the ideological positions of both groups on a scale ranging from extreme conservatism to extreme liberalism. Importantly, they excluded "explicit bias" found in opinion content such as editorials and columns, focusing only on factual news reporting that might contain "implicit bias."

Their findings, summarized in Table 8.1, indicated that all sampled media outlets—except for *The Washington Times* and Fox News's Special Report—exhibited a more liberal bias than the average member of Congress, who could be considered a proxy for the average US voter. Notably, *The New York Times* and CBS's Evening News were found to be significantly more left-leaning, even relative to the average bias of all media outlets. By contrast, PBS's NewsHour and CNN's News Night were closest to the ideological midpoint of American voters, while *USA Today* was the most centrist among the sampled media.

Overall, except for *The Wall Street Journal*, all newspapers' ideological slants were found to fall between the average positions of Democratic and Republican lawmakers. Groseclose and Milyo explained this somewhat surprising result by noting that "*The Wall Street Journal*, which was identified as the most liberal outlet in our analysis, reflects only the news content and excludes opinion pieces such as editorials and columns. If those were included, the paper would almost certainly appear more conservative."

Their study reignited the longstanding debate within American media scholarship regarding liberal bias in the press and fostered greater interdisciplinary engagement between economists and scholars in media and communication. While some critics

Table 8.1 Political Bias in the US News Media

News Media (Program)	ADA Score[a]
Average for Republican Members of Congress	16.1
Washington Times	35.4
Fox News' Special Report *with Brit Hume*	39.7
Average for All Members of Congress	50.1[b]
PBS Newshour *with Jim Lehrer*	55.8
CNN News Night *with Aaron Brown*	56.0
ABC Good Morning America	56.1
Drudge Report	60.4
ABC World News Tonight	61.0
NBC Nightly News	61.6
Average for News Media	62.6
USA Today	63.4
NBC Today Show	64.0
Time Magazine	65.4
US News and World Report	65.8
Newsweek	66.3
NPR Morning Edition	66.3
CBS Early Show	66.6
Washington Post	66.6
Los Angeles Times	70.0
CBS Evening News	73.7
New York Times	73.7
Average for Democratic Members of Congress	84.3
Wall Street Journal	85.1

[a]The "ADA score" refers to a numerical rating assigned by the Americans for Democratic Action (ADA), a liberal political advocacy group in the United States. Based on congressional voting records, it scores legislators from 0 (most conservative) to 100 (most liberal).
[b]Average for All Members of Congress.
**Source: Groseclose and Milyo, 2005.*

argued that the study overestimated the extent of liberalism in the press,[15] Groseclose continued to assert the left-leaning bias of American media in his subsequent work (Groseclose, 2011).

Groseclose and Milyo are not the only economists who have empirically supported the claim that US media lean liberal. Puglisi (2011) focused on *The New York Times* and its partisan leanings in favor of the Democratic Party. Drawing on the "issue ownership hypothesis,"[16] which posits that political parties are perceived by voters as more competent in handling specific issues, Puglisi examined

[15] See Gasper (2011) and Nyhan (2012) for further discussion. Both are political scientists.
[16] The concept of "issue ownership" was developed by political scientist John Petrocik. According to this idea, a party is said to "own" an issue when voters perceive it as the most competent at handling

how frequently the paper covered issues typically "owned" by either party during presidential election periods. Analyzing coverage from 1946 to 1997, he found that when the sitting president was a Republican, *The New York Times* placed greater emphasis on issues traditionally associated with Democrats—such as civil rights, healthcare, labor, and social welfare. Puglisi interpreted this as evidence that the paper exhibited a pro-Democratic bias by emphasizing issues unfavorable to Republican candidates during campaigns. Similarly, Lott and Hassett (2014) empirically argued that American newspapers overall exhibit a liberal, or pro-Democratic, bias. Focusing on how newspapers reported newly released economic indicators, they analyzed whether coverage was framed positively or negatively. Based on data from 1991 to 2004 covering 389 US newspapers, they concluded that the media tended to portray the same economic news more favorably when Democrats were in power than when Republicans were in office.[17] While there is substantial empirical support for the view that US media lean liberal, claims of a conservative bias are relatively rare in the literature. It is worth noting, however, that most economists studying the news media—such as Gentzkow and Shapiro (2010) and Hamilton (2004)—emphasize that media bias often reflects market strategies that respond to consumer preferences, rather than the ideological beliefs or intentions of news providers. For example, Gentzkow and Shapiro find that the language used by newspapers tends, on average, to align more closely with liberal positions. Yet they interpret this slant as contributing to profit maximization by matching the ideological leanings of readers.[18]

Meanwhile, the liberal slant observed in many empirical studies of US media can also be interpreted through the lens of David Baron's theory of journalist-driven media bias. According to Baron, when media firms grant journalists greater discretion to express bias, they can save on labor costs. This cost-saving incentive may lead media outlets to tolerate the ideological preferences of their reporters. In this context, if journalists in the United States generally lean liberal, media organizations may exhibit a liberal slant simply because allowing such bias helps to reduce operational costs and maximize profit.[19]

that issue. If the issues a party owns become salient during an election, that party is likely to gain an electoral advantage (Petrocik, 1996).

[17] Economists such as Groseclose, Milyo, Hassett, and Lott—who argue that American media exhibit a liberal bias—are generally regarded as conservatives. Notably, Hassett served as Chair of the Council of Economic Advisers during the first Trump administration and later as Director of the National Economic Council during the second.

[18] Gentzkow and Shapiro (2010) were previously introduced in Section 8.2.1. In their study, they measured partisan slant in US newspapers by analyzing the linguistic similarity between the vocabulary used in news articles and that used by members of Congress.

[19] See also Section 5.2.2.1.

8.3.2 CONSERVATIVE AND CENTRIST SLANTS: INTERNATIONAL AND DOMESTIC PERSPECTIVES

While much of the empirical literature has focused on liberal bias in US media, researchers have also explored whether media systems in other countries—or under different institutional conditions—exhibit similar or contrasting patterns. Some research points in a different direction—namely, that the overall media environment in other countries may lean conservative. For example, Korean communication scholars Choi et al. (2012) applied a methodology inspired by Groseclose and Milyo (2005) to empirically measure the political bias of Korean news media. Excluding opinion content such as editorials and columns, they analyzed 5,962 straight news articles and calculated bias scores based on how frequently politicians and civic organizations—categorized as progressive, centrist, or conservative—were cited as sources. Their results indicated that the Korean news media, on average, exhibited a conservative slant, with significantly greater ideological divergence among newspapers than among broadcasters.

At the same time, other empirical studies suggest that the media do not always skew toward one side of the ideological spectrum, but instead tend to adopt more centrist positions. A representative example is the study by Puglisi and Snyder (2015a), who analyzed the ideological bias of editorials published by local newspapers in the context of state-level ballot propositions in the United States between 1996 and 2012. Examining 305 newspapers, they compared the ideological positions of editorials with those of voters, interest groups, and political parties. They found that the average ideological slant of the newspapers closely resembled that of the median voter in each state. Moreover, the distribution of newspaper biases was symmetrically centered around the ideological middle, indicating that local newspapers broadly reflected moderate public sentiment.

Interestingly, in California, newspapers were found to exhibit a slightly more conservative slant than the state's median voters—a result that differed more markedly from the findings of Groseclose and Milyo, who argued that the US media lean liberal. However, it should also be noted that California voters tend to be relatively more progressive compared to the national average. In addition, newspapers were found to be more ideologically moderate than interest groups.

The study also revealed that the ideological leanings of newspapers varied depending on the issue. On socio-cultural topics such as same-sex marriage, newspapers tended to be more liberal than voters. In contrast, on economic issues such as the minimum wage or environmental regulation, they leaned more conservative than the electorate.

A similarly notable study on Australian media bias was conducted by Gans and Leigh (2012). They identified over 100 public intellectuals commonly cited in political discourse and classified them along a left–right ideological scale. Then, using citation data from 27 newspapers and broadcasters and comparing it with references made by members of parliament (MPs) between 1999 and 2007, they estimated the ideological positions of each media outlet. The results showed that, except for one outlet, all media organizations were ideologically close to the average MP, with no statistically significant differences. The authors attributed this centrist pattern to the relatively low level of competition in Australia's media market.

In the United States, an intriguing perspective comes from Ho and Quinn (2008), who compared the ideological positions of major newspaper editorials with those of Supreme Court justices. They analyzed more than 1,500 editorials published by 25 major newspapers on 495 Court rulings over 10 years from 1994 to 2004. Their findings showed that the newspapers were ideologically more moderate than the justices. Among the 21 highest-circulation newspapers, 11 papers were positioned ideologically between the two most centrist justices on the Court.

Taken together, these studies suggest that media bias does not always skew toward one ideological direction. In some cases, the media reflect moderate public preferences or occupy a more centrist position than political elites. As such, generalized claims about overall media bias must be evaluated within the institutional, cultural, and market-specific contexts of each country. These diverse cases also underscore the need for more rigorous research that examines overall bias in a society originating from news suppliers and consumers within the specific realities of each country.

8.4 THE EFFECT OF MEDIA COMPETITION ON MEDIA BIAS

The conflicting theories of economists regarding the effects of news media's competition on media bias were explored in Chapter 7, Section 7.2, and similar patterns emerge in empirical studies. Both theoretical and empirical research confirm the contrasting effects of competition.

One of the most notable studies is by Gentzkow et al. (2006), who analyzed the political bias of American newspapers over a century, from 1850 to 1950. Their findings reveal that in the 19th century, most US newspapers acted as promotional tools for politicians who financed them, exhibiting strong partisanship. However, technological advancements in the late 19th century increased competition for readership, which significantly reduced partisanship. In 1870, only 11% of urban daily newspapers in the US were politically unaffiliated, but this figure rose to 62% by 1920. The authors interpreted this shift as evidence that heightened competition diminished political bias, leading to less partisan reporting.[20]

The authors employed a creative method to track changes in newspaper partisanship. They analyzed the frequency of the word "January," a neutral term with no connection to partisanship, across all sampled newspapers. At the same time, they examined the frequency of partisan-leaning terms such as "Honest" and "Slander,"

[20] We previously discussed this study in Chapter 4, which highlighted that newspaper subscriptions in the United States increased significantly between 1870 and 1920, which substantially reduced political corruption. Refer to Section 4.4.2.

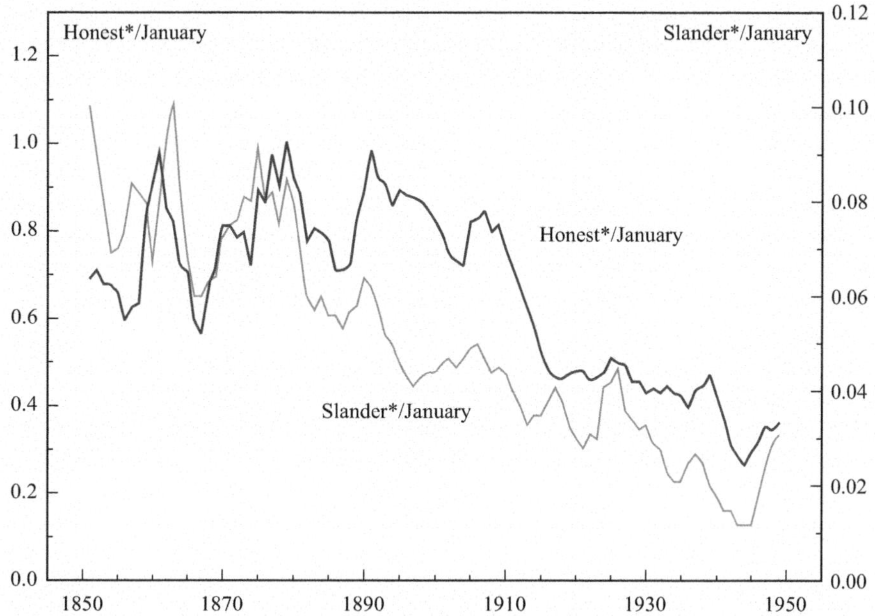

FIGURE 8.1

Changes in Partisan Bias of US Newspapers (1850–1950). Note: 3-year moving average trend. Sample newspapers vary from 10 to 50 per year.

Source: Gentzkow, Glaeser, and Goldin (2006: 195).

which were more likely to appear in partisan newspapers, and compared these frequencies to that of "January."[21]

In Fig. 8.1, the ratios "Honest*/January" and "Slander*/January" represent the frequencies of "Honest" and "Slander" relative to "January." These indicators of partisanship reveal a clear decline between 1850 and 1950. In the 1850s, the frequency of "Slander" relative to "January" was approximately 1/12. Starting in the 1880s, this ratio declined sharply, dropping to about 1/30 by the 1930s. Similarly, the relative frequency of "Honest" began to decrease noticeably in the 1890s, falling to less than half its 1890 level by the 1920s. The strong biases prevalent in American newspapers until the 1870s had significantly weakened by the early 20th century.

Galvis et al. (2016) also support this perspective with their findings on how competition influenced media bias in US newspapers between 1870 and 1910. They measure bias as the intensity with which different newspapers cover scandals. Analyzing 159 newspapers and 121 scandals, the study found that partisan newspapers gave

[21] The authors explained that among the various synonyms for "lie," they used "Slander" and its antonym "Honest" as keywords for comparison, noting that the use of "Slander" reflects editorial efforts to foster distrust toward opposing views, while "Honest" indicates an effort to promote respect.

more attention to opposition-party scandals while downplaying those involving their own party. Notably, competition significantly reduced media bias: newspapers facing two competitors exhibited, on average, only 50% of the bias seen in monopoly newspapers.

In contrast, Gentzkow et al. (2014) extended the analysis period into the early 21st century and concluded that "competition was a key driver of ideological diversity in newspapers." This finding stands in contrast to earlier studies. Using a comprehensive dataset covering 132 years (1872–2004) of circulation, business performance, and readership demographics for all English-language newspapers in the United States, the authors explored how competition influenced the ideological positioning of newspapers.

Their analysis revealed that American news consumers tended to prefer content aligned with their own views. In response, newspapers strategically differentiated themselves ideologically from their competitors to appeal to specific readership segments. This differentiation not only helped newspapers attract loyal readers but also reduced the pressure of price competition. Based on these findings, the authors argued that competition played a fundamental role in driving ideological diversity in newspapers.[22]

However, these findings do not suggest that competition universally reduces political bias or promotes diversity. The studies discussed above primarily examine American newspapers from the 19th to mid-20th century, or in some cases, into the early 21st century. While most scholars agree that political bias among newspapers generally declined over the 20th century, this decline can be attributed not only to competition but also to other factors, such as political polarization, ideological fragmentation, or economic and technological shifts.

Analyzing a period from the mid-20th century to the present, or extending the sample period further, might yield different results. Since the late 20th century, global political polarization has intensified, the role of traditional media has diminished, and digital media's influence has surged. These shifts could significantly alter the competitive dynamics among news media. Because competition among media outlets revolves around attracting consumers, the political or ideological homogeneity or heterogeneity within a society's audience fundamentally shapes news media strategies. Consequently, the effects of competition may vary greatly depending on the broader social context.

[22] The authors argued that identifying optimal competition in the newspaper market requires considering its two-sided market of readers and advertisers. They noted that price collusion on newspaper sales has minimal effect on ideological diversity and reduces consumer surplus and advertiser profits, while discouraging price competition and news differentiation. In contrast, price collusion on advertising boosts reporting diversity and economic welfare by increasing advertising revenues, lowering newspaper prices, encouraging market entry, and intensifying competition, thereby enhancing consumer surplus and bias diversity. The effect of increased advertising revenue on fostering price competition can be explained by "the seesaw principle" in two-sided markets. For more details on the seesaw principle in two-sided markets, see Rochet and Tirole (2006).

8.5 THE EFFECT OF MEDIA BIAS ON NEWS CONSUMERS

Having examined the causes and realities of media bias as observed in practice, we now turn to a central question: how does media bias influence the thoughts and behaviors of news consumers? Just as the importance of news media lies in its impact on individual lives and collective decision-making in society, the ultimate concern of media bias research is how such bias affects news consumers.[23]

8.5.1 PERSUADED NEWS CONSUMERS

One well-known area of research investigates how media bias influences voters' political choices, particularly through the lens of persuasion. A widely cited study in this domain examines the correlation between Fox News viewership and increased Republican vote share in the United States. According to DellaVigna and Kaplan (2007), the launch of Fox News contributed to an increase in Republican vote share in major American cities. Fox News entered approximately 20% of US cable television markets between the 1996 and 2000 presidential elections. The two scholars analyzed how the Republican vote share changed in these areas during this period. They found that Republican vote share increased by 0.4 to 0.7 percentage points due to Fox News viewership, and that Fox News persuaded between 3% and 8% of its viewers to vote Republican. DellaVigna and Kaplan explained that while this effect was temporary for rational voters, it could be permanent for voters susceptible to irrational persuasion.

Enikolopov et al. (2011) demonstrate the influence of media bias on political decision-making in Russia. The researchers focused on NTV, a television channel regarded at the time as the only independent broadcaster not under government control. They compared the results of the 1999 Russian parliamentary elections in regions where NTV was available versus those where it was not.

Their analysis showed that access to NTV reduced the vote share for the ruling coalition by up to 8.9 percentage points and increased the opposition's vote share by up to 6.3 percentage points, while also decreasing overall voter turnout by 3.8 percentage points. These effects were significantly larger than those found in the US Fox News studies and illustrate how independent media and media diversity can influence citizens under authoritarian regimes. However, the impact of NTV did not last long. By the 2003 election, NTV had been taken over by Gazprom, a state-controlled enterprise, and its independence had effectively vanished.

Some economists have used experimental methods to examine the effects of media bias on voter behavior. Gerber et al. (2009) conducted a field experiment ahead of the 2005 Virginia gubernatorial election. They divided participating voters into two groups, offering each group a free 12-week subscription to either the liberal

[23] For empirical studies by economists on persuasion through information provision, see DellaVigna and Gentzkow (2010).

Table 8.2 British Newspapers That Switched Endorsements in 1997

Newspaper	Endorsed Party in 1992	Endorsed Party in 1997
The Sun	Conservative Party	Labour Party
Daily Star	Proconservative	Labour Party
The Independent	Nonpartisan	Labour Party
Financial Times	Anticonservative majority	Labour Party

Source: Ladd, J.M.D. & Lenz, G.S., 2009. Exploiting a rare communication shift to document the persuasive power of the news media. American Journal of Political Science, 53 (2), 394–410. https://doi.org/10.1111/j.1540-5907.2009.00377.x.

Washington Post or the conservative *Washington Times*. Afterward, they tracked the voting behavior of these participants. Surprisingly, both groups showed an increase in support for the Democratic candidate. While the increase was slightly higher in the *Washington Post* group, the difference was not significant in qualitative terms. The researchers concluded that exposure to media itself, rather than the ideological slant of that media, was more influential.[24]

Chiang and Knight (2011) studied the 2000 US presidential election to determine how public endorsements by the 20 largest newspapers influenced voter behavior. The first finding was straightforward: readers were more likely to support a candidate endorsed by the newspaper they subscribed to. However, what stood out was that endorsements contrary to the paper's usual ideological leaning—such as a Democratic-leaning paper endorsing a Republican candidate—had a greater impact on voter preference than expected endorsements.

Political scientists Ladd and Lenz (2009) conducted a similar study using a rare case from the 1997 UK general election, during which several major newspapers switched their endorsements from the Conservative Party to the Labour Party. They examined whether readers changed their political preferences compared to nonreaders with similar ideological leanings. Table 8.2 lists the newspapers that changed their endorsements, and the results showed that many readers were persuaded by these newspapers.

Ladd and Lenz suggested that readers were influenced not only by the explicit endorsements but also by changes in slant within the news content itself.[25] This interpretation likely also applies to the findings of Chiang and Knight.

Meanwhile, other studies have shown that the media can significantly shape public perception, sometimes leading to misinformed views or even inciting violence.

[24] In the same study, the authors also found that subscribing to any newspaper led to an increase in voter turnout. For this study and other research on the relationship between news consumption and voter turnout, see Section 4.4.1.

[25] In their study, Ladd and Lenz estimated that readers persuaded to support the Labour Party ranged from approximately 10% to as high as 25% of the total readership, depending on the estimation method. This unusually large figure illustrates a rare case in which news media exerted a powerful influence on public political behavior. For a more detailed explanation, see Section 10.4.1.

Gentzkow and Shapiro (2004) found that viewers in Muslim countries who watched Al Jazeera were more likely to hold distorted views about terrorism and the 9/11 attacks. They analyzed survey data from 10,000 respondents across nine Muslim countries—including Lebanon, Kuwait, Saudi Arabia, and Pakistan—and found strong correlations between media consumption and beliefs. For instance, those who watched Arab news channels or received education in schools with little Western influence were less likely to believe that the 9/11 attacks were carried out by Arab terrorists. They were also more likely to consider the attacks morally justified and to hold more negative views of the United States. The researchers argued that these perceptions were strongly shaped by the media consumed.

David Yanagizawa-Drott (2014) examined the role of radio broadcasts during the 1994 Rwandan genocide, in which at least 500,000 people were killed. His research revealed that extremist Hutu-run radio stations incited hatred toward the Tutsi population and encouraged violence. As a result, an estimated 51,000 Hutu civilians—roughly 10% of all perpetrators—were incited by these broadcasts to participate in the genocide. These findings underscore how media, in the absence of pluralism, can play a decisive role in triggering mass violence.

8.5.2 PROACTIVE NEWS CONSUMERS

News consumers are not merely passive recipients who are persuaded by the media. According to studies by economists, they exhibit active responses—such as canceling subscriptions or selectively consuming news—when media content does not align with their own biases.

One empirical study that investigated such consumer behavior was conducted by Durante and Knight (2012). The two scholars analyzed changes in news bias on Italian public broadcasting during the government of Silvio Berlusconi. After Berlusconi's center-right coalition came to power in 2001, the ideological slant of Italy's public television channels generally shifted from left to right. As the bias of the channels they were watching changed, so too did the viewing patterns of the audience. Viewers with left-leaning political tendencies moved to other public channels that remained left-leaning. Although public broadcasters remained less right-leaning than private ones, right-leaning viewers increasingly tuned into public channels. Trust in public broadcasting also diverged: it rose among right-leaning viewers and declined among those on the left. In relation to these findings, Durante and Knight explained that when a channel's bias shifts, viewers partially offset the impact by switching to alternative channels or programs.[26]

[26] A similar phenomenon occurred in South Korea at the end of 2023. After the conservative government replaced the president of KBS (the national public broadcaster), several radio programs and hosts were removed, which led to a sharp decline in audience engagement. The number of views on KBS Radio's official YouTube channel dropped from 5.34 million during the week of November 6–12, 2023, to around 1 million by the end of the year (Keum, 2023).

Another striking study investigated East German citizens' attitudes toward state-run media under the communist regime, as well as West German media, which operated freely. German economists Kern and Hainmueller (2009) analyzed the effects of West German television broadcasts on East Germans during the period of national division. The results challenged common assumptions. It is often presumed in democratic societies that when people in authoritarian regimes are exposed to foreign media from democratic countries, the legitimacy of their regime will erode. This assumption is based on the idea that they will distrust domestic media and place more trust in foreign sources. However, Kern and Hainmueller's findings told a different story.

The authors obtained and analyzed survey data that had been collected covertly by East Germany's Central Institute for Youth Research (Zentralinstitut für Jugendforschung) in November 1988 and February 1989—shortly before the fall of the Berlin Wall. The data pertained to East German citizens' television consumption, particularly their access to West German programming. Surprisingly, those who watched West German television reported greater satisfaction with life in East Germany and with the communist regime. Explaining this unexpected finding, Kern and Hainmueller noted that the West German broadcasts played only a minimal role in delivering political information that could not be obtained from state-controlled communist media. Instead, they primarily served as a form of entertainment for East German viewers.

8.6 HOW DO ECONOMISTS MEASURE MEDIA BIAS?

Most people easily perceive news media as biased, but it is not so easy to objectively measure such media bias. The first challenge is defining what the bias is "with respect to." Should bias be judged against "truth?" Or against neutrality and fairness? Or perhaps against the average ideological preferences of the audience?

Even if we settle on one of those standards, challenges persist. In empirical research, concepts like truth, neutrality, or fairness are difficult—if not impossible—to determine objectively. For this reason, empirical studies in economics often measure *relative media bias* across outlets. It may be hard to assess whether Newspaper A is conservative or liberal in an absolute sense, but it is far easier to assess whether it is more conservative or liberal compared to Newspaper B.

Riccardo Puglisi and Snyder (2015b), who have conducted several empirical studies on media bias, categorize methods for measuring bias. The methods described there correspond to those used in the empirical studies introduced earlier.

The first method is to measure *explicit bias*. In countries like the United States, newspapers often express their support for specific political parties or candidates in their editorial pages during elections. This type of content is the most straightforward to use when measuring media bias, at least in such political environments.

The next set of methods addresses *implicit bias*—that is, the bias embedded in news coverage that media outlets do not openly declare. This hidden bias tends to be of greatest concern to the general public. Even when journalists and media companies insist that their reporting is fair and impartial, many consumers remain skeptical.

Scholars who study such hidden bias empirically generally rely on one of three major approaches. The first is the *comparison approach*. This method measures media bias by comparing news content to that of other actors whose ideological positions are already known. A common technique is to compare the vocabulary used by news outlets with that of politicians from various political camps. Outlets that use language similar to conservative politicians are considered right-leaning, while those using language similar to liberal politicians are viewed as left-leaning.

The second is the *issue intensity approach*. This method measures how frequently a media outlet covers topics that are favorable to a particular political ideology or party. Media that disproportionately report on issues favorable to conservatives are deemed right-leaning, while those that focus more on liberal-friendly topics are classified as left-leaning.

The third is *tone measurement*. This method evaluates the tone or sentiment of news coverage. If a news outlet consistently describes a party or its policies in a favorable (or unfavorable) tone, the outlet is considered biased in that direction. Tone—encompassing style, language, and atmosphere—is notoriously difficult to measure objectively. As a result, tone measurement has been less commonly used in empirical economics research. However, the development of big data analytics may make objective tone measurement more feasible in the future, just as facial recognition technologies are increasingly able to quantify what was once thought to be purely subjective human expression.

Lastly, there is *multidimensional bias*. Most empirical studies to date have treated media bias as a one-dimensional phenomenon—typically along a left–right ideological spectrum. But ideology is rarely so simple. Socio-political cleavages, such as modernity versus tradition, or individuality versus community, also reflect ideological differences. Nonetheless, public concern over media bias usually centers on the political left–right axis, especially in countries marked by deep partisan polarization.

Still, in ideologically pluralistic societies, the conventional left–right dimension may be insufficient. In mid-20th-century America, for example, social divisions over civil rights and race were often more significant than divisions between the Democratic and Republican parties. Even today, traces of this pattern remain. In the American South, many Democratic voters were economically moderate progressives but held extremely conservative views on race.

More recently, South Korea has seen the emergence of multidimensional conflict. Gender conflicts between young men and women, and generational tensions between older Koreans and the so-called MZ generation (Millennials and Gen Z), now rival the traditional left–right divide. These divisions have increasingly shaped the editorial lines of news outlets as well.

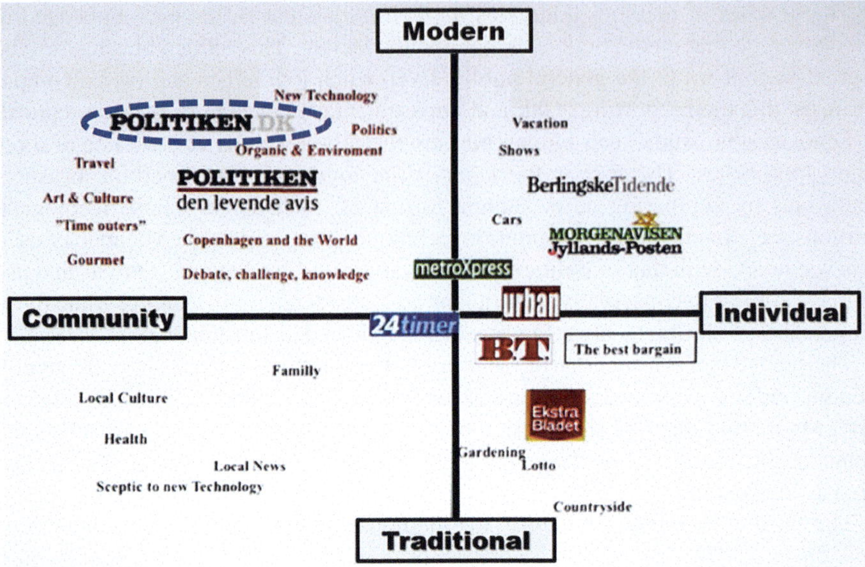

FIGURE 8.2

Two-dimensional ideological positioning of Politiken.

Source: Introduction material by Politiken (2013).

Fig. 8.2 illustrates how Denmark's largest newspaper, *Politiken*, positioned itself ideologically in a 2013 promotional material. Unlike more polarized societies such as the United States, Korea, or Brazil, Denmark is relatively moderate in its political landscape. *Politiken*, accordingly, placed itself not on a one-dimensional left–right scale, but in a two-dimensional space defined by "modern vs traditional" on the vertical axis and "individual vs community" on the horizontal axis. As shown in the figure, *Politiken* identified itself with modernist and communitarian values, favoring contemporary ideas over traditional ones and collective responsibility over individualism. This illustrates how the ideological leanings of news media, which reflect those of the societies they serve, can be multidimensional. Therefore the actual bias exhibited by media outlets is also likely to be multidimensional.

References

Agirdas, C., 2015. What drives media bias? New evidence from recent newspaper closures. Journal of Media Economics 28 (3), 123–141. https://doi.org/10.1080/08997764.2015.1063499.

Allcott, H., Gentzkow, M., 2017. Social Media and Fake News in the 2016 Election. Journal of Economic Perspectives 31 (2), 211–236.

Ansolabehere, S., Lessem, R., Snyder Jr., J.M., 2006. The orientation of newspaper endorsements in U.S. elections, 1940–2002. Quarterly Journal of Political Science 1 (4), 393–404. https://doi.org/10.1561/100.00000009.

Barrett, A.W., Barrington, L.W., 2005. Bias in Newspaper Photograph Selection. Political Research Quarterly 58 (4), 609–618.

Benton, J., 2024, November 4. The Washington Post isn't alone: roughly 3/4 of major American newspapers aren't endorsing anyone for president this year. Nieman Lab. https://www.niemanlab.org/2024/11/the-washington-post-isnt-alone-roughly-3-4-of-major-american-newspapers-arent-endorsing-anyone-for-president-this-year/.

Chiang, C.-F., Knight, B., 2011. Media bias and influence: evidence from newspaper endorsements. The Review of Economic Studies 78 (3), 795–820. https://doi.org/10.1093/restud/rdq037.

Choi, S.K., Yoo, S.J., Yang, S.E., 2012. Competition in the news market and media bias: measuring the bias in the quotation of news sources. Journal of Information and Communications Policy Research 19 (2), 69–92.

Cohen, B.C., 1963. The Press and Foreign Policy. Princeton University Press.

DellaVigna, S., Gentzkow, M., 2010. Persuasion: Empirical Evidence. Annual Review of Economics 2 (1), 643–669.

DellaVigna, S., Kaplan, E., 2007. The Fox News effect: media bias and voting. The Quarterly Journal of Economics 122 (3), 1187–1234. https://doi.org/10.1162/qjec.122.3.1187.

Durante, R., Knight, B., 2012. Partisan Control, Media Bias, and Viewer Responses: Evidence from Berlusconi's Italy. Journal of the European Economic Association 10 (3), 451–481.

Enikolopov, R., Petrova, M., Zhuravskaya, E., 2011. Media and political persuasion: evidence from Russia. American Economic Review 101 (7), 3253–3285. https://doi.org/10.1257/aer.101.7.3253.

Galvis, Á.F., Snyder, J.M., Song, B.K., 2016. Newspaper market structure and behavior: partisan coverage of political scandals in the United States from 1870 to 1910. The Journal of Politics 78 (2), 368–381. https://doi.org/10.1086/684597.

Gans, J.S., Leigh, A., 2012. How partisan is the press? Multiple measures of media slant. Economic Record 88 (280), 127–147. https://doi.org/10.1111/j.1475-4932.2011.00782.x.

Gasper, J.T., 2011. Shifting Ideologies? Re-examining media bias. Quarterly Journal of Political Science 6 (1), 85–102.

Gentzkow, M., Glaeser, E.L., Goldin, C., 2006. The Rise of the Fourth Estate: How Newspapers Became Informative and Why It Mattered. In: Glaeser, E.L., Goldin, C. (Eds.), Corruption and Reform: Lessons from America's Economic History. University of Chicago Press, pp. 187–230.

Gentzkow, M., Shapiro, J.M., 2004. Media, education and anti-Americanism in the Muslim world. Journal of Economic Perspectives 18 (3), 117–133. https://doi.org/10.1257/0895330042162313.

Gentzkow, M., Shapiro, J.M., 2010. What Drives Media Slant? Evidence from US Daily Newspapers. Econometrica 78 (1), 35–71.

Gentzkow, M., Shapiro, J.M., Sinkinson, M., 2014. Competition and ideological diversity: historical evidence from US newspapers. American Economic Review 104 (10), 3073–3114. https://doi.org/10.1257/aer.104.10.3073.

Gentzkow, M., Shapiro, J.M., Stone, D.F., 2015. Media Bias in the Marketplace: Theory. In: Anderson, S.P., Waldfogel, J., Strömberg, D. (Eds.), Handbook of Media Economics, Vol. 1. North-Holland, pp. 623–645.

Gerber, A.S., Karlan, D., Bergan, D., 2009. Does the Media Matter? A Field Experiment Measuring the Effect of Newspapers on Voting Behavior and Political Opinions. American Economic Journal: Applied Economics 1 (2), 35–52.

Groseclose, T., 2011. Left Turn: How Media Bias Distorts the American Mind. St. Martin's Press.

Groseclose, T., Milyo, J., 2005. A measure of media bias. The Quarterly Journal of Economics 120 (4), 1191–1237. https://doi.org/10.1162/003355305775097542.

Hamilton, J.T., 2004. All the News That's Fit to Sell. Princeton University Press.

Ho, D.E., Quinn, K.M., 2008. Measuring explicit political positions of media. Quarterly Journal of Political Science 3 (4), 353–377. https://doi.org/10.1561/100.00008048.

Kahn, K.F., Kenney, P.J., 2002. The slant of the news: how editorial endorsements influence campaign coverage and citizens' views of candidates. American Political Science Review 96 (2), 381–394. https://doi.org/10.1017/S0003055402000230.

Kern, H.L., Hainmueller, J., 2009. Opium for the masses: how foreign media can stabilize authoritarian regimes. Political Analysis 17 (4), 377–399. https://doi.org/10.1093/pan/mpp017.

Keum, J., 2023. Joo Jin-woo, Choi Kyung-young, etc. left; KBS Radio YouTube views drop from 5.34 million to 790,000. Media Today. [In Korean]. https://n.news.naver.com/article/006/0000121665.

Ladd, J.M.D., Lenz, G.S., 2009. Exploiting a rare communication shift to document the persuasive power of the news media. American Journal of Political Science 53 (2), 394–410. https://doi.org/10.1111/j.1540-5907.2009.00377.x.

Larcinese, V., Puglisi, R., Snyder, J.M., 2011. Partisan bias in economic news: evidence on the agenda-setting behavior of U.S. newspapers. Journal of Public Economics 95 (9–10), 1178–1189. https://doi.org/10.1016/j.jpubeco.2011.04.006.

Nyhan, B., 2012. Does the US Media Have a Liberal Bias? A Discussion of Tim Groseclose's *Left Turn: How Liberal Media Bias Distorts the American Mind.* Perspectives on Politics 10 (3), 767–771.

Orwell, G., 1943. *Looking Back on the Spanish War.* Retrieved December 27, 2024, from https://www.orwellfoundation.com/the-orwell-foundation/orwell/essays-and-other-works/looking-back-on-the-spanish-war/.

Petrocik, J.R., 1996. Issue Ownership in Presidential Elections, with a 1980 Case Study. American Journal of Political Science 40 (3), 825–850.

Prat, A., Strömberg, D., 2013. The political economy of mass media. In: Acemoglu, D., Arellano, M., Dekel, E. (Eds.), Advances in Economics and Econometrics: Tenth World Congress, Vol. 2. Cambridge University Press, pp. 135–187.

Puglisi, R., 2011. Being The New York Times: the political behaviour of a newspaper. The B.E. Journal of Economic Analysis & Policy 11 (1), 1935–1682. https://doi.org/10.2202/1935-1682.2025.

Puglisi, R., Snyder, J.M., 2011. Newspaper coverage of political scandals. Journal of Politics 73 (3), 931–950. https://doi.org/10.1017/S0022381611000569.

Puglisi, R., Snyder Jr., J. M., 2015a. The balanced US press. Journal of the European Economic Association 13 (2), 240–264. https://doi.org/10.1111/jeea.12101.

Puglisi, R., Snyder, Jr., J. M., 2015b. "Empirical Studies of Media Bias." In S. P. Anderson, J. Waldfogel, & D. Strömberg (Eds.), *Handbook of Media Economics* (Vol. 1, pp. 647–667). Amsterdam: North-Holland.

Rochet, J.C., Tirole, J., 2006. Two-sided markets: a progress report. The Rand Journal of Economics 37 (3), 645–667.

Rosling, H., Rosling Rönnlund, A., & Rosling, O. 2018. Factfulness: Ten reasons we're wrong about the world—and why things are better than you think. New York, NY: Flatiron Books. (Quoted via Korean translation: I. Chang, Trans., 2019, Seoul: Gimmyoung Publishers).

Shleifer, A., 2015. Matthew Gentzkow, Winner of the 2014 Clark Medal. Journal of Economic Perspectives 29 (1), 181–192.

Stanley, H.W., Niemi, R.G., 2013. Vital Statistics on American Politics 2013-2014. CQ Press.

Wilson, R., 2020. Biden leads newspaper endorsements - just like Clinton. The Hill. Available from: https://thehill.com/homenews/campaign/522841-biden-leads-newspaper-endorsements-just-like-clinton.

Yanagizawa-Drott, D., 2014. Propaganda and conflict: evidence from the Rwandan genocide. The Quarterly Journal of Economics 129 (4), 1947–1994. https://doi.org/10.1093/qje/qju020.

CHAPTER

Media Capture and Media Power

9

Chapter Outline

If the press reports the truth, the people will live in light;
if it degenerates into the servant of power, they will live in darkness.
—Cardinal Stephen Kim Sou-hwan

The right of the public to know all sides of a controversy
is being jeopardized by the growing concentration
of the ownership of the mass media into fewer and fewer hands,
resulting ultimately in a form of private censorship.[1]
—Supreme Court of Florida, United States

[1] *Miami Herald Publishing Company v. Tornillo*, Supreme Court of Florida, 1973. Quoted in Gentzkow and Shapiro (2008a, p. 149).

The Economics of News Media. DOI: http://dx.doi.org/10.1016/B978-0-443-45044-0.00012-X

In 1983, fifty mass media corporations dominated American audiences. By 2000, the number dropped to six. Today, the five major media conglomerates are Time Warner, Disney, News Corporation, Bertelsmann, and Viacom. This gives each of the 5 corporations and their leaders more communications power than was exercised by any despot or dictatorship in history.[2]

—Ben Bagdikian

People expect news media to fulfill their responsibility of providing essential information for human life and democracy. However, contrary to this expectation, news media are often either captured by political or financial power or become powerful entities themselves, thereby distorting information. Economists refer to the former as *media capture* and the latter as *media power*. Media capture occurs when political or financial forces control media outlets, whereas media power describes situations where media outlets manipulate political and social affairs to serve their own interests.

Media capture involves governments, politicians, political parties, and various stakeholders and groups using threats or incentives to block unfavorable reports or encourage favorable coverage. In contrast, media power refers to cases where the news media or its employees, without external intervention, shape their reports to serve their own political goals or economic interests. Both media capture and media power inevitably lead news media outlets to provide consumers with biased news, unwanted and unneeded by consumers, embedding intentional biases introduced by external forces or the media itself. These phenomena also often manifest as collusive relationships between media and power structures, such as collusion between the press and the government, politics, or business.

As a result, both media capture and media power make it difficult for news consumers to access accurate (or essential) information and for democracy to function properly. As explained in Chapter 4, voters (principals) in democratic societies obtain information about their agents—governments and politicians—through the media. Democratic political processes cannot function without the information that the media provide, as voters lack adequate information regarding their representatives' actions to hold them accountable. Both media capture and media power distort or conceal information necessary to voters. Therefore, it is important, both socially and academically, to find appropriate regulatory measures to reduce the occurrence of these two phenomena.

The standard mechanisms of media capture and media power have changed significantly in the digital era. Web portals and social media now compete with traditional mass media as key players in the production and distribution of news, reshaping the overall structure of news content production and distribution. Most information distribution and consumption has shifted from offline to online, and this accelerating trend has endangered the survival of offline, traditional media like print

[2] Bagdikian (2000).

newspapers in favor of digital intermediaries such as web portals and social media platforms. Therefore, it has become impossible to discuss media capture and media power without considering the characteristics that changed the environment of the digital age.

9.1 TRADITIONAL ECONOMIC THEORIES OF MEDIA CAPTURE

Media capture, as previously mentioned, refers to the intervention by external actors in the normal production and distribution processes of news, preventing unfavorable reporting and promoting favorable coverage. This inevitably infringes on media independence. While the term "media capture" has become increasingly popular in media studies, it originates from Capture Theory—an economic concept first introduced by George Stigler (1971), "The Theory of Economic Regulation."

According to Stigler, government agencies serve as regulators by formulating and implementing various regulations for the public interest. However, if not for the regulated entities, these agencies would not be able to maintain their structure and resources. The entities being regulated are mostly companies or interest groups, and they lobby the regulatory agencies to advance their own interests. In this process, regulatory agencies may become bodies that are excessively sympathetic or cooperative with the entities they are supposed to regulate.

As a result, regulatory agencies and policies often fail to serve the public interest. In economics, "capture" refers to a situation in which regulators, such as government agencies working for the public interest, end up serving the interests of the entities they are supposed to regulate, such as companies or interest groups. The term "capture" in "media capture" carries this same connotation.

The actors involved in media capture can vary depending on the scholars studying it. For instance, Besley and Prat (2006) identified the government (elected officials), Mungiu-Pippidi (2012) described the government or privileged groups linked by political interests, and Sobbrio (2011) pointed to lobbyists of interest groups as entities that capture media. While governments and advertisers are the most commonly cited capturers, the concept can be extended more broadly to include "special interest groups, political parties, or any actors other than consumers" (Petrova, 2008a).[3] The methods of capture range from traditional bribery and threats to sophisticated tactics like "providing information,"[4] using various incentives and punishments.

The social harms of media capture are evident and well documented across the social sciences. According to economists, media capture undermines the democratic system of checks and balances (Stiglitz, 2017), distorts collective decision-making

[3] Media capture frequently appears in economists' studies on "lobbying activities." These studies address how interest groups and lobbyists use news media to shape public opinion in their favor (Sobbrio, 2011).

[4] "The communication strategies of the activist and the industry take the form of advocacy, where they present favorable information and may conceal unfavorable information (Baron, 2005: 346)."

(Corneo, 2006), increases corruption (Brunetti and Weder, 2003), and widens wealth inequality (Petrova, 2008b).

9.1.1 COMPETITION: THE NEMESIS OF MEDIA CAPTURE—BESLEY-PRAT MODEL

Timothy Besley and Andrea Prat (2006) are among the leading economists in the study of media capture. They conceptualize media capture as the result of rational transactions between the capturers and the captured media outlets. In particular, they argue that the more intense the competition among media organizations, the less likely media capture is to occur. Their argument has been well received by economists, media scholars, and journalists alike, as it resonates strongly with the ideal of press freedom and the notion of the marketplace of ideas as a fundamental democratic value.

As a result, Besley and Prat's theory has become the benchmark model of endogenous media capture in both economics and media studies. Media capture is endogenous in that it arises not from external coercion but from the strategic and rational interactions between media outlets and powerful actors such as governments or advertisers. In other words, capture stems from economic incentives and mutually beneficial transactions between the capturers and the media. Let's briefly explain Besley and Prat's theoretical model. The theoretical model can be described as follows:

Media capturers attempt to prevent coverage of damaging news about themselves by offering economic incentives to news media. In doing so, the capturer must capture all media outlets in the market. If even one media outlet remains uncaptured and reports damaging news, all news consumers would ultimately be exposed to it. Therefore, the capture cost increases with the number of news media outlets, making capture more challenging. Besley and Prat concluded that the decisive factor in making media capture difficult is the increase in competition among media in the news market. Additionally, they explained that factors such as government ownership of media, increased media concentration, and restrictions on new media market entry all decrease market competition. This, in turn, facilitates media capture.

Besley and Prat also identified "transaction costs"[5] associated with capture deals as a significant factor affecting media capture, independent of competition among media outlets. Media capture involves not only the economic incentives given to the media but also various transaction costs. For example, the cost of delivering a bribe

[5] Transaction costs refer to the total costs involved in carrying out a transaction, excluding the price of the good or service itself. These include costs related to planning, decision-making, contract negotiation, monitoring, enforcement, and conflict resolution. The concept was first introduced by Ronald Coase (1910–2013, Nobel Laureate in Economics, 1991) in *The Nature of the Firm* (1937) and further elaborated in *The Problem of Social Cost* (1960). It was later developed and popularized by Oliver Williamson (1932–2020), who was awarded the Nobel Prize in Economics in 2009.

to achieve capture is a representative transaction cost. As these transaction costs increase, the overall cost of capture naturally rises, making capture more difficult, similar to the effect of increasing the number of media outlets.

Take the case of Silvio Berlusconi, Italy's former Prime Minister and media mogul. Consider a situation where he attempts to capture a media outlet that he owns. In this case, where the media capturer and the owner of the media being captured are the same person, transaction costs are reduced to almost zero, making capture much easier. Conversely, if it is difficult to deliver bribes, uphold mutual commitments, or maintain confidentiality, transaction costs are higher. For instance, it would be extremely difficult or prohibitively expensive for a political opponent of Berlusconi to deliver bribes to his media outlets or their key figures.

The structure of media ownership is also related to the magnitude of transaction costs in media capture. In the case of public broadcasters, unless there is an independent governance structure like that of the BBC in the United Kingdom, they can be easily captured by the ruling political power. This implies lower transaction costs. Thus, the harder it is for the government or ruling party to unilaterally appoint the CEO of a public broadcaster, the more challenging capture becomes.

Moreover, transaction costs decrease as the means of delivering bribes are more diverse. If a company that owns a news media outlet is engaged in other business sectors, a media capturer can also use monetary incentives or favorable policies related to those businesses as bribes to achieve media capture. For this reason, Besley and Prat argued that capturing media outlets within large business groups engaged in various industries is easier than capturing independent media focused solely on the news business.[6] They predicted that, all else being equal, media outlets with larger audiences and fewer unrelated businesses or affiliates would be more difficult to capture and exhibit more independent reporting. (For a mathematical understanding of the Besley-Prat model, see More to Explore.)

[More to Explore] Mathematical Understanding of the Besley-Prat Model

Let us take a closer look at the theory developed by Besley and Prat (2006), widely regarded as a foundational model in the study of media capture. To do so, we refer to a simplified version presented by Gentzkow and Shapiro (2008), structured as follows:

- There are N media outlets in the news market, and they equally share the total market revenue R, each earning R/N.
- All N media outlets can report a news item S that harms the media capturer.
- The media capturer derives a value V from preventing S from being reported—V is their motive for attempting media capture.

Continued

[6] Besley and Prat argued that when the capturer is the government, news media owned by foreign entities are less likely to be captured than those owned by domestic entities. This is because, in the case of foreign ownership, the government as the capturer has fewer benefits to offer as compensation for capture.

- If any of the N outlets report S, all consumers learn about it.
- Therefore, the capturer must either capture all N outlets or none. Failing to capture even a single outlet has the same effect as capturing none.
- The capturer offers each outlet a bribe B to suppress the news S. If even one outlet refuses, the capture attempt fails.
- If all N outlets accept the offer, the total cost of media capture becomes NB.

According to Besley and Prat, two conditions must be satisfied for media capture to succeed. First, the bribe B offered to each outlet must exceed the monopolistic return R that a media outlet would earn by being the sole reporter of a scoop. That is, $R < B$.[7] Second, the total cost of media capture NB must be less than the value V that the capturer derives from suppressing the news. This implies $B < V/N$. Taken together, the conditions for successful media capture can be expressed as follows: $\boldsymbol{R < B < V/N}$

If this condition fails, capture is infeasible. As N increases, V/N shrinks and may fall below B, violating the inequality. Thus greater competition—that is, a higher number of outlets—makes media capture harder.

As Gentzkow and Shapiro (2008:138) put it, "Just as an increase in the number of firms makes tacit collusion harder to sustain, an increase in the number of news outlets makes media capture harder to achieve." Furthermore, if we account for *transaction cost* T (borne in addition to bribes), the condition becomes: $\boldsymbol{B + T < V/N}$. If T rises significantly, the left-hand side can again exceed V/N, making capture infeasible—just as when N increases. Thus higher transaction costs also make media capture more difficult.

9.1.2 EXAMPLES OF HOW COMPETITION AFFECTS MEDIA CAPTURE

Besley and Prat's theory that the best defense against media capture is competition among media outlets has significantly contributed to a rational understanding of media capture. Gentzkow and Shapiro (2008) introduced several anecdotes that support Besley and Prat's views in practice. Let's take a look at these stories.

In April 2004, CBS's news program *60 Minutes* obtained photos and video footage showing US soldiers abusing detainees at the Abu Ghraib prison in Iraq. It was a major scoop with potentially huge political and diplomatic repercussions. Upon learning that CBS had acquired this information, the Chairman of the Joint Chiefs of Staff asked CBS anchor Dan Rather to delay the report, even if briefly, citing the safety of American hostages. Rather accepted this request and postponed the report, indicating that media capture was at play.[8]

Another example occurred in 1971, when *The New York Times* obtained the Pentagon Papers, a top-secret US government report, and began publishing articles

[7] The condition B > R ensures that no media outlet has an incentive to break the silence. If k outlets reject the offer and publish the news, each earns R/k. As more outlets are captured (k decreases), R/k increases. In the extreme case, a lone outlet earns the full R. Thus every outlet knows it could earn R by being the only one to resist. Unless the bribe B exceeds R, no outlet will agree to suppress the story.

[8] The means of capture used in this case was not material compensation. Instead, the capturer utilized the provision of information, specifically warning that "American hostages held captive would be put in danger if the report were to be released."

exposing government misconduct in the Vietnam War. The Nixon administration requested the publication to stop, citing national security concerns, and took legal action. After the third article, a federal court issued an injunction, siding with the government's claim that the papers posed a grave national security threat.[9]

Yet, these two instances of media capture by the US government did not end there. In both cases, the reports were eventually published, causing media capture efforts to fail. As predicted by Besley and Prat, competition among news media played a decisive role in these failures. In CBS's case, *60 Minutes* aired the Abu Ghraib report on April 28, 2004, after a 3-week delay, explaining the reasons for the postponement. CBS decided to proceed with the report after learning that renowned journalist Seymour Hersh[10] had obtained the same photos and was preparing to publish them in *The New Yorker*.

The Pentagon Papers case was even more dramatic. After the court banned *The New York Times* from publishing, the report's source took a copy to three TV networks and *The Washington Post*. While the networks chose not to publish, *The Washington Post* did. Expecting the same legal action from the government as against *The New York Times*, *The Washington Post* printed and distributed the newspaper before government intervention, resulting in a failed capture attempt.

As predicted by the Besley-Prat model, once a single outlet (*The Washington Post*) broke the story, the government's motivation for capture weakened dramatically. Additionally, the government's injunction against *The New York Times* led to increased revenue for *The Washington Post*, which explains why *The Washington Post* decided to defy the government's capture efforts and publish.

Another example of Besley and Prat's perspective in action is the media consolidation carried out by the military dictatorship in South Korea in 1980. At the time, the South Korean military regime used the pretext of eliminating corrupt media and those engaged in false reporting to consolidate 63 major media outlets nationwide into 44 and dismissed 933 journalists. Five news agencies were merged into one, television broadcasting was consolidated into two public channels, and local newspapers were limited to one per province.

According to Besley and Prat's view, these measures created a structural environment that made media capture easier by reducing the number of media outlets and journalists perceived as troublesome by the military regime. Furthermore, the nationalization of private broadcasters greatly lowered the transaction costs of capturing them, making the process much simpler for the government.

A similar case of media consolidation occurred in Hong Kong. Within approximately 6 months from late 2021 to early 2022, several news outlets critical of the

[9] The US government won the injunction against *The New York Times* to halt its publication but ultimately lost the main case. At that time, Supreme Court Justice Hugo Black left a famous remark: "Only a free and unrestrained press can effectively expose deception in government" (cited in Gentzkow and Shapiro, 2008a: 135).

[10] Seymour Hersh is an investigative journalist who reported on the My Lai Massacre of Vietnamese civilians by US forces during the Vietnam War.

Chinese government shut down. Although these newspapers closed voluntarily, they share the common experience of having been raided by the Hong Kong National Security Department under accusations of "incitement" (in connection with foreign forces), their assets frozen, and key executives arrested before closure. These actions by the Hong Kong government not only reduced the number of newspapers but also served as a warning of punishment for engaging in government-critical reporting.

While rewards for media compliance serve as positive incentives, punishment for noncompliance functions as a negative incentive. Negative incentives are a strategy used by capturers to pressure uncooperative media outlets into compliance. If these negative consequences, as seen with newspapers in Hong Kong, are severe enough to cause suspension or closure, even intense competition is unlikely to act as a natural deterrent to media capture. This topic, negative incentives for media capture, will be discussed in the section "Advertisers Who Punish Media for Unfavorable Coverage" of Chapter 9.

[More to Explore] Competition Eases Media Capture: Alternative Perspectives

While the prevailing view among economists holds that competition makes media capture more difficult, some studies present differing perspectives.

Trombetta and Rossignoli (2021) suggest that competition produces two opposing effects on media capture. On the one hand, an increase in the number of media outlets raises capture costs, making media capture more challenging. On the other hand, competition reduces individual news media outlets' market revenue, which lowers the capturer's cost of capture, as the cost is directly linked to the market revenue of the captured media. Trombetta and Rossignoli conclude that these conflicting effects create a "nonmonotonic"[11] relationship between competition and media capture.

Although Trombetta and Rossignoli's view is plausible, it has yet to gain significant attention from other scholars. This may be because economists often consider studies with ambiguous conclusions as starting points requiring further exploration and analysis.

Vaidya and Gupta (2016) offer a clear argument that competition can sometimes facilitate media capture. They questioned why the sheer number of news outlets has not prevented capture, if more outlets make capture more difficult. They answered that, while the capturer's burden increases with more outlets, it may decrease when some are already captured. According to them, exposing a capturer's misconduct becomes easier when multiple media outlets report diverse aspects of it. Conversely, individual media outlets have limited capacity to expose such misconduct. This difference between "many media outlets" and "individual media outlets" lowers the cost required to capture individual outlets. Furthermore, if captured media discredit the reports of uncaptured outlets and shield the capturer, the uncaptured media's ability to expose misconduct is further weakened—especially when influential television networks are among the captured.

In short, Vaidya and Gupta argued that even as competition increases, cooperation between the capturer and captured media erodes public trust in uncaptured outlets and lowers the capturer's costs, ultimately facilitating capture.

---

[11] "Non-monotonic" means that as competition increases, media capture can either increase or decrease. In mathematics, "monotonic" refers to a relationship where, as the value of the independent variable increases, the value of the dependent variable either consistently increases (or at least does not decrease) or consistently decreases (or at least does not increase). Meanwhile, Trombetta and Rossignoli argued in their study that media capture becomes easier both when competition is minimal and when it is extremely intense.

9.1.3 ECONOMIC POWER CONCENTRATION AND MEDIA CAPTURE

While Besley and Prat examined the role of media competition in preventing capture, Giacomo Corneo (2006) and Petrova (2008a) focused on economic power—specifically, the role of wealthy elites and media ownership structures in enabling media capture. Corneo analyzed how wealth concentration and patterns of media ownership influence the incentives for capture, while Petrova extended the discussion by exploring how media capture by the rich contributes to deepening economic inequality.

Together, their theories highlight how concentrated economic power can influence political and policy outcomes through the media. This perspective moves beyond viewing press freedom solely as a matter of political repression and calls for a reinterpretation of media independence in the context of capital ownership structures and socioeconomic inequality.

9.1.3.1 Wealth concentration and economic inequality

Corneo (2006) emphasizes that the media are not mere intermediaries of information but critical gatekeepers in the link between voters and policy outcomes. Since voters cannot directly observe the effects of policies, they rely heavily on media reports when casting their votes. As a result, the accuracy or distortion of media-provided information becomes central to the quality of democratic decision-making. Media outlets may deliver truthful information, but they also have the potential to collude unofficially with interest groups to distort the news. Corneo's model focuses on the structural economic incentives that make such collusion more or less likely.[12]

A key insight of Corneo's model is that the concentration of wealth within society increases the likelihood of media capture. Wealthy individuals have a direct interest in preventing policies that expand public goods, as such policies typically raise tax burdens and reduce their utility. As wealth becomes more concentrated, the rich have both a greater capacity to finance capture (i.e., pay for media distortion) and a stronger incentive to do so, since public goods expansion would more significantly affect their utility through higher taxation.

For example, the larger an individual's asset holdings, the more costly a marginal increase in the tax rate becomes. Meanwhile, the perceived benefits from public goods expansion are smaller in relative terms for the rich. Therefore, the wealthy are motivated to distort media narratives to weaken public support for redistributive policies. If the bribe they offer exceeds the revenue the media could earn by reporting the truth, the media firm has a financial incentive to comply and report a distorted

[12] Unlike Besley and Prat, who viewed an elected official (or government) as the media capturer, Corneo identifies interest groups and industrial firms as the actors in capture. Accordingly, Corneo's model includes different assumptions, whereas Besley and Prat assume that (1) voters share common interests, (2) there is a single media capturer, and (3) there are multiple news media in the market. Corneo assumes that (1) voters have diverse interests, (2) there are multiple media capturers, and (3) the market contains only a single media outlet.

version. (For a mathematical exposition of Corneo's model, see [More to Explore] at the end of this subsection.)

Petrova (2008b) extends Corneo's argument by linking media capture directly to the persistence and deepening of economic inequality. According to Petrova, public goods—such as education, healthcare, and social services—are generally more beneficial to the poor than to the rich. Since these goods are funded through taxation, their provision functions as a form of income redistribution. Like any policy, the implementation of redistribution depends on public support, which in turn depends on how well informed the public is about the policy's effects.

In democratic societies, where redistribution policies are decided through elections, the role of the media becomes especially crucial. Citizens primarily rely on media coverage to evaluate these policies. Thus any distortion of information can significantly influence voter preferences and policy outcomes. As Corneo shows, the greater the level of inequality, the more strongly high-income individuals tend to oppose redistributive policies—and they may use their influence over the media as a means to resist such policies. Petrova (2008b, p. 205) explains the mechanism as follows:

"If aggregate income stays constant, the greater inequality in the economy implies a lower income of the median voter, which leads to a higher popular demand for redistribution. This, in turn, increases incentives for those with high incomes to affect the preferences for taxation and public good provision of those with low incomes."

The wealthy may exercise this influence through investments in media companies or by directing advertising expenditures strategically. When they succeed in capturing media outlets, the resulting news coverage may lead the public to undervalue the benefits of public goods provision. Even if individuals are aware that media sources may be biased, mass media remain a powerful tool for shaping public opinion.[13]

Ultimately, Petrova concludes that when the media are captured by the wealthy, public investment in goods and services declines, redistribution decreases, and economic inequality worsens. Conversely, when media independence is stronger and less subject to elite influence, public investment tends to rise, thereby reducing inequality. Petrova supports this theoretical argument with empirical evidence, further examined in Section 10.4.

9.1.3.2 Ownership concentration in media firms

Corneo (2006) highlights how the ownership structure of media organizations influences the likelihood of media capture. According to his analysis, when media ownership is broadly dispersed, would-be capturers must negotiate with multiple stakeholders, increasing the transaction costs of capture and raising the overall compensation required. By contrast, when ownership is concentrated in the hands of a

[13] Even if news consumers are aware that certain news media are biased, they may still be influenced by those media. This is because, when certain facts are not reported, news consumers cannot know whether these facts were originally unknown or deliberately concealed by the news media (Anderson and McLaren, 2012). See Subsection 5.2.2.2 for reference.

few, transaction costs fall, and each owner stands to gain more individually from participating in capture. As a result, higher ownership concentration structurally increases the risk of media capture and reduces media independence. From this perspective, Corneo argues that promoting dispersed ownership or implementing public regulatory safeguards is essential to preserving the autonomy of the press.[14]

In addition to ownership patterns, Corneo also underscores the importance of stakeholder diversity within media organizations. Outlets with a plurality of internal actors—such as labor unions, journalists, and public investors—are more resistant to collusion with external interests. In contrast, vertically integrated media firms with owner-dominated governance are more susceptible to capture. This suggests that media independence is not merely a function of journalistic professionalism or ethical norms but is fundamentally shaped by institutional and ownership structures.

Corneo's argument can be applied to news media organizations in the United States.[15] The *Associated Press*, a cooperative owned by numerous member news organizations, disperses ownership across many stakeholders, thus making it difficult for any single entity to control the *AP*'s news agenda. Similarly, *National Public Radio* is supported by funding from local stations, the Corporation for Public Broadcasting, and individual donors, creating a diversified base that limits the influence of any single group.[16]

In contrast, media outlets like *Fox News* and *Sinclair Broadcast Group* demonstrate more concentrated ownership cases. *Fox News* is primarily controlled by the Murdoch family through *Fox Corporation*, while *Sinclair Broadcast Group* owns numerous local TV stations nationwide, with management decisions centralized under a single authority. Based on Corneo's model, it can be interpreted that such concentrated ownership structures may facilitate capture.

Then, what about *The New York Times* and *The Washington Post*, two long-standing pillars of American journalism? For much of their histories, both newspapers shared a similar ownership structure, with a dual-class stock system: the Ochs-Sulzberger family maintained controlling shares at *The New York Times*, and the Graham family did so at *The Washington Post*. While both families traditionally upheld editorial

---

[14] The renowned legal scholar and media theorist C. Edwin Baker (2007), in his book Media Concentration and Democracy, also argues that the concentration of media ownership threatens the democratic principle of diverse opinion by centralizing the formation of public opinion and discourse in the hands of a few. He warns that concentrated media power may lead to abuses and a decline in content quality. According to Baker, dispersed ownership is essential for safeguarding freedom of expression and supporting a media landscape in which diverse and socially valuable journalistic practices can flourish. He also criticizes the U.S. Federal Communications Commission (FCC) for its deregulatory policies, arguing that they undermine media diversity and harm democratic society. As policy alternatives, he proposes stricter merger regulations and legal frameworks aimed at ensuring a more decentralized media ownership structure.

[15] For a comprehensive overview of US media ownership structures, see Harvard University, Institute for Quantitative Social Science (n.d.).

[16] ProPublica is an example of a nonprofit media organization structured to resist capture; it operates with support from a broad base of foundations and individual donors rather than profit-driven shareholders. This diverse donor-backed structure may offer greater resistance to capture than dispersed ownership in commercial media.

independence, with external shareholders mainly focusing on profitability rather than editorial matters, their dispersed ownership structure and family norms supporting editorial independence have historically reduced the likelihood of capture.

However, the ownership structures of the two newspapers diverged significantly after Jeff Bezos acquired *The Washington Post* in 2013.[17] While *The New York Times*' structure remains largely unchanged, *The Washington Post* became a privately held company under Bezos's sole ownership, granting him significant influence over both business strategy and editorial decisions. The *Los Angeles Times*, a major newspaper in the western United States, is a similar case, with entrepreneur Patrick Soon-Shiong holding 100% ownership since 2018.[18]

Corneo's model encourages readers to reflect on how ownership concentration in media organizations may influence the likelihood of media capture. However, although dispersed ownership offers some protection against capture, even media organizations with concentrated ownership can maintain editorial independence. As explained later in this chapter, media capture also becomes more difficult as the influence or "media power" of a news outlet increases. For instance, capturing a newspaper with highly concentrated ownership but significant market influence may prove challenging, whereas media outlets with lower influence, despite high ownership dispersion, may be easier targets for capture. Thus when considering the capture risks associated with media ownership structures, readers should take into account the complexity and diversity of the media landscape.

Corneo also highlights that wealth concentration, rather than just media ownership concentration, may increase the likelihood of media capture. High wealth concentration could provide specific interest groups or corporations with the resources necessary to influence or control media narratives, potentially steering coverage toward their interests, thereby undermining media independence and the quality of information available to the public.

[More to Explore] Mathematical Exposition of Corneo's Model

Consider the simplified model presented by Corneo (2006). This theoretical framework illustrates how a media outlet's decision to report either truthful or distorted information depends on underlying economic conditions.

The utility of a voter i, denoted by U_i, is determined by their income y_i, the taxes they pay T_i, and the utility they derive from public goods G. Both the tax burden and the level of public goods provision depend on a policy P, which in turn is influenced by the media signal $s \in \{t, b\}$, where t stands for a truthful signal and b for a biased or distorted one. This relationship can be expressed as: $U_i = y_i - T_i(s) + G(P(s))$.

---

[17] *The Washington Post* had been under the Graham family's ownership for 80 years before it was sold to Bezos in response to declining revenues and profitability within the newspaper industry. Bezos acquired all shares, leading to its delisting from public markets.

[18] In a related instance, ahead of the 2024 US presidential election, Bezos suspended The Washington Post's practice of endorsing specific party candidates, sparking protests from both the editorial staff and readers. A similar situation unfolded at the *Los Angeles Times*, where Soon-Shiong prevented the editorial board from endorsing a presidential candidate, prompting editor Mariel Garza to resign in protest (Katzenberger, 2024.10.23).

Since a truthful signal generally leads to more efficient or welfare-enhancing policies, we assume: $G(P(t)) > G(P(b))$.

In this setup, the media firm compares its expected market revenue from reporting the truth, (t), with the sum of revenue and a bribe when reporting a distorted signal, $B + R(b)$. The media chooses distortion when the following inequality holds:

$$B + R(b) > R(t)$$

Turning to the rich (denoted by H), their utility U_H is modeled as their income y_H, minus taxes—which are a function of their asset holdings W_H and the tax rate t—plus the benefits they receive from public goods. Suppose public goods expand from level g_0 to g_1 over time, accompanied by a rise in the tax rate from t_0 to t_1. Then, the change in utility can be expressed as:

$$U_{H0} = y_H - t_0 \cdot w_H + g_0$$
$$U_{H1} = y_H - t_1 \cdot w_H + g_1$$
$$\Delta U_H = U_{H0} - U_{H1} = (t_1 - t_0) \cdot w_H + (g_0 - g_1)$$

This implies that while the expansion of public goods may increase overall welfare, the net utility for the rich can decline significantly if their asset holdings are large and the resulting tax increase outweighs the marginal gain from public goods. In other words, the larger the value of w_H, the greater the disutility from taxation, and the stronger the incentive to prevent the dissemination of truthful media coverage that could trigger such redistributive policies.

This incentive is what drives the willingness of the wealthy to offer higher bribes B to media firms, thereby increasing the likelihood of media capture.

9.2 POISONED COMPETITION IN THE DIGITAL AGE

The Information and Communication Technology (ICT) revolution ushered in the era of digital online news in the late 20th century. This shift brought soaring expectations from scholars and journalists, the most prominent of which was the belief that media capture would soon diminish. It was further expected that as media capture diminished, news would become more trustworthy.

For instance, the media historian Mitchell Stephens noted that the 20th century was an era of the most organized, effective, and brutal control of expression. But he believed that advancements in ICT in the 21st century would enable the media to provide not only far more information but also much more reliable information (Stephens, 2010: 392, 395). Similarly, Robin Foster, a media and journalism expert at the Reuters Institute for the Study of Journalism, projected that "[digital media] can help users find many more sources of news than ever before. Over time it may support new business models for high-quality news" (Foster, 2012: 5). They were not alone; countless others shared similar expectations and hopes.

The spread of this optimistic outlook was also significantly influenced by economists. Building on Besley and Prat's work, many economists predicted that intensified competition among news media would reduce media capture. Maria Petrova (2008b, p. 192), for example, explained the Internet's role in controlling media capture, stating that as the Internet increases the number of available information sources, the possibility of media capture declines. Many people, swept up in this trend of expectations, assumed that digital infrastructure, by enabling a massive increase in the supply of information, would contribute to reducing media capture and enhancing information quality.

However, these expectations turned out to be only half correct. With the digitalization of news and information content production, distribution, and consumption, news and information providers worldwide have indeed exploded since the end of the last century. Including power bloggers and influencers popular on platforms like Facebook, Twitter, and YouTube makes it difficult to measure the scale of this increase. As the number of news providers surged, the news and information markets experienced intense competition, which was in line with expectations. Yet, no evidence emerged to confirm the anticipated reduction in media capture. Unfortunately, the reality turned out to be the opposite.

> *It was assumed that the low barriers to entry for digital media would "solve" the problem of media capture by allowing the existence of so many outlets that it would be impossible to capture anyone. Scholars also assumed that more competition could even lead to higher quality news. In fact, the opposite may have happened.*
>
> (**Schiffrin, 2018**, p. 1035).

In April 2016, Columbia University's School of International and Public Affairs hosted a conference on Media Capture, with participants including prominent scholars such as Anya Schiffrin, a media studies scholar and former journalist; economist Joseph Stiglitz; and Rasmus Nielsen, Director of the Reuters Institute for the Study of Journalism at Oxford University. The scholars attending the conference unanimously agreed that the expectation that "media capture would decrease" had not materialized.

So, why has media capture increased rather than decreased in the digital era? The primary reason lies in the sharp decline in capture costs. The surge of digital infrastructure led to an explosion in the number of news media, which in turn entered a remarkable level of market competition. Consequently, the news market has been flooded with duplicated reports, and as copycat journalism became rampant, the revenue generated from original content has sharply declined. Also, media capturers could now capture original news that exposed their misconduct at much lower costs (Yang, 2021; Choi and Yang, 2021).

To explain further, the revenue that news media firms earn from original news depends on how long they can exclusively supply that news. In other words, the revenue a scoop generates is directly tied to its period of exclusivity.[19] However, this revenue from original news has drastically declined in the digital age, as widespread duplication has shortened the exclusivity period to an unmatched degree.

---

[19] News has the characteristic that its demand decreases over time after it is initially reported. Yang (2021) and Choi and Yang (2021) were the first to incorporate this characteristic, along with the "exclusivity period" of original news, into the profit function of news media firms.

Let's take news scoops, a quintessential type of original news, as an example. In the past, news media pursued scoops because they yielded significant revenue. Once a scoop was published, media outlets could enjoy monopoly profits or equivalent benefits until their competitors replicated the story. This "exclusivity period," which ensured monopoly profits, lasted a week during the era of weekly publications, a day after daily newspapers emerged, and about half a day with the advent of morning and evening editions or broadcast news.

However, things have changed drastically. In a flood of duplicated reports, it is often difficult to even find the original scoop on the internet just minutes after the first report. The more impactful the scoop, the more severe this phenomenon becomes. Intense "copycat competition" among media outlets has reduced the exclusivity period for original news to mere minutes.

As the exclusivity period for original news has shortened in this way, the profitability of original news has deteriorated beyond comparison to the past. A study in 2020 pointed out that about 25% of reported news is duplicated online within 4 minutes, posing a serious threat to the financial survival of news media (Cagé, Hervé, and Viaud, 2020). A decline in the market revenue for original news, such as scoops, also implies a reduction in the cost of capturing that news, as the cost of capture is based on the potential market revenue the media firm could earn if it refused to be captured.

Furthermore, the sharp decline in the profitability of original news may prompt media outlets to deliberately produce content intended for capture from the outset. That is, when the exclusivity period for original news becomes so short that its revenue fails to cover production costs, news media may increasingly focus on creating content not for market distribution but with the specific aim of being captured in exchange for compensation. This behavior is commonly referred to as *promotional journalism*.[20]

Additionally, factors beyond (1) the number of news media outlets or (2) the exclusivity period of original content also influence media capture conditions. These factors include (3) the share of high-quality media in the market (those capable of independently producing original content), (4) the size of the news consumer base that drives total news consumption, and (5) the rate of decline in news value (and demand) over time.[21]

When these factors are examined in the context of digital-era trends, the explosion of low-quality media has reduced the proportion of high-quality media, while the overwhelming influx of information and news has accelerated the decline in the market value of news over time. Together, these trends facilitate media capture. Conversely, the Internet and mobile revolution have dramatically improved access to news content

[20] Promotional journalism refers to the reporting practices of news media that, in exchange for monetary compensation or the expectation of such compensation, report favorable news about specific companies, interest groups, political parties, or governments or conceal unfavorable information about them. Yang (2021) and Choi and Yang (2021) were the first to interpret the principles of this phenomenon using economic theory.

[21] In the distant past, when news was scarce, its value did not diminish significantly over time. However, in today's age of information overload, where people have easy access to a vast amount of information, public interest shifts very quickly. As a result, the value of most news rapidly declines as time passes.

Table 9.1 Media Capture in the Digital Era: Key Influencing Factors

Category	Change	Media capture
(i). Number of News Media Outlets	Large Increase	More difficult
(ii). Exclusivity Period of Original News	Larger Decrease	Easier
(iii). Proportion of High-Quality Media	Large Decrease	Easier
(iv). News Consumers	Increase	More difficult
(v). Rate of Decline in News Value Over Time	Increase	Easier

and expanded the scale of news consumers and total consumption, factors that potentially hinder media capture (Yang, 2021). Table 9.1 summarizes these dynamics.

In summary, the digital age has almost removed entry barriers to the news market, resulting in an unprecedented surge in news providers and competition. This intense competition, coupled with digital infrastructure, has led to a flood of duplicated reports and declining profitability for original news. As Yang (2021, p. 33) aptly observes, "competition is no guarantee of a media sector that is free from the capturers' interference." Consequently, competition has transformed from the "nemesis" of media capture into its "accomplice." In this context, the conventional belief that competition curbs media capture no longer holds true in the digital age. Moreover, the widespread duplication of reports and declining profitability of original content have resulted in negative outcomes, including lower news quality, reduced diversity, and the rise of promotional journalism.

[More to Explore] How Shorter Periods of Exclusive News Supply Affect Media Capture

To better understand how a shorter period of exclusive supply of original news can influence the conditions for media capture, consider the following highly simplified example.

- To capture the media, the capturer must pay each outlet an amount equivalent to the market-exclusive revenue (denoted as R) that the outlet would earn from a scoop.
- In the analog era, the exclusivity period for a scoop—that is, the time before rival outlets could replicate the news—was about 300 minutes (5 hours), roughly corresponding to the interval between morning and evening newspaper editions.
- Market-exclusive revenue is assumed to be proportional to the duration of this exclusivity. Thus the outlet publishing the scoop earns R over 300 minutes.
- In the digital era, the number of media outlets has increased tenfold—from 10 to 100.
- However, in the digital environment, the time lag before news replication has shrunk dramatically. The exclusivity period has dropped to just 6 minutes—1/50 of the analog era. As a result, market-exclusive revenue has also fallen to (1/50)R.

Under these assumptions, in the analog era, a capturer needed to pay R to each of the 10 media outlets to prevent publication, resulting in a total capture cost of 10R.

If, in the digital era, the number of outlets increases to 100 while the value of R remains constant, the total capture cost would rise to 100R. In this scenario, increased media competition makes capture more expensive and therefore more difficult. However, if the rise in media competition is accompanied by a substantial decline in the value of exclusivity—due to faster replication and shorter monopoly periods—the situation changes. As the duration of exclusivity shrinks, the market value of a scoop falls accordingly. This reduces the compensation required to prevent publication.

Returning to our example, in the digital era, the capturer would only need to pay (1/50)R to each of the 100 media outlets, resulting in a total capture cost of: (1/50)R*100=2R. In other words, even though the number of media outlets has increased tenfold, the overall cost of capture drops to 2R—much lower than the 10R of the analog era.

In conclusion, while the number of outlets (i.e., media competition) has increased—making more targets for capture—the per-outlet cost of capture has decreased even more. As a result, media capture may, paradoxically, become easier. This suggests that the digital era does not automatically lead to a more democratic media environment, especially when the value of original reporting sharply declines.

9.3 THE TWO FACES OF ADVERTISERS: SUPPORTER AND CAPTURER

In the 19th century, with the emergence of cheap and mass-produced newspapers, advertisers entered the news market. It was also during this time that newspapers started to move away from overt political bias due to the introduction and growth of advertising revenue, which reduced newspapers' reliance on politically partisan sponsors and readers whose financial support had been essential for their survival before advertising. Early advertisers thus played a role in financially supporting the independence of news media from partisan influence.[22]

However, as time passed, especially in the latter half of the 20th century, concerns over the adverse effects of advertising grew. Scholars from diverse fields, including economist James Hamilton who analyzed media bias through an economic lens, media law scholar Edwin Baker, and journalist and media scholar Ben Bagdikian, identified advertisers as a source of media bias (Hamilton, 2004; Baker, 1994; Bagdikian, 2000).

The primary concern of advertisers in news media lies in maximizing the effect of their advertisements. Advertisers closely monitor not only the size and composition of the media outlet's audience but also the characteristics of the audience and even the content provided by the media outlet, as these factors are all directly or indirectly related to advertising effectiveness. As they pursue maximum ad effectiveness, advertisers have various expectations and demands for the media outlet that carries their ads. The more reliant a media outlet is on advertising revenue, the harder it becomes to ignore these expectations. However, if media reflect advertiser demands in their news content, adjustments to the content become unavoidable. In this way, advertisers, who initially helped reduce political bias, have introduced a "commercial bias" into media content (Ellman and Germano, 2009).

[22] See section "The Rise of Objective Journalism" of Chapter 3.

Over time, advertising revenue has become increasingly essential for the survival of nearly all types of news media, amplifying advertisers' influence on them. Especially since the advent of the digital age, as traditional media have experienced declining revenue streams and diminished audience influence, the balance of power between advertisers and traditional media has shifted sharply in favor of advertisers. Consequently, the increasing bargaining power of advertisers has led to an increase in commercial bias in media. Advertisers once played a positive role in enabling news media to gain independence from political forces. However, many advertisers have now become significant drivers of commercial bias in the news media.

9.3.1 ADVERTISERS MITIGATING MEDIA'S POLITICAL BIAS

First, consider how advertisers influence media content strategies through their purchasing power. Advertisers' primary concern is the effectiveness of their advertisements, which depends on the characteristics of the audience of the media outlet in which they advertise. Foremost among these characteristics is audience size; the effectiveness of an advertisement increases with the number of people who see it. Thus advertisers prefer media outlets with larger audiences, which significantly influences the content strategies of media outlets.

Jean Gabszewicz, Laussel, and Sonnac (2001) studied how the political bias of news media changes as they seek to increase their audience in order to gain more advertising revenue. According to Gabszewicz and colleagues, when a news outlet's only revenue source is sales, competing news outlets maximize political bias differentiation. By differentiating on core characteristics like political bias, these outlets can avoid direct price competition, which in turn boosts profits.

However, the situation changes when news outlets gain advertising revenue through the entry of advertisers. News outlets then seek to increase their audience to obtain more advertising income, and to achieve this, they may lower their sales prices or adjust the bias in their content. Consequently, each outlet moderates their political bias. As outlets become more similar in bias, they may end up engaging in price competition. However, the financial leeway provided by advertising revenue allows them to withstand this price competition to some extent, as explained by Gabszewicz and his colleagues. They also note that news outlets tend to moderate their political bias more actively when advertising rates are high or when consumers' political biases are relatively weak.[23]

Gabszewicz and colleagues further suggest that media outlets may increase nonpolitical content, such as soft news on culture and entertainment, to attract a broader audience. This approach helps draw less politically oriented consumers,

[23] Unlike Gabszewicz and colleagues, some argue that when newspapers achieve high advertising revenue through "price collusion" in advertising, both price competition and bias differentiation among newspapers intensify (Gentzkow, Shapiro, and Sinkinson, 2014). See footnote 22 in Section 8.4.

thereby expanding the audience exposed to advertisements. Consequently, the increased share of nonpolitical content dilutes the prominence of political bias in media.

In short, news media tend to moderate their political bias when they begin to receive advertising revenue. The views of Gabszewicz and his colleagues align well with the era of the Penny Press[24] in the 19th century, where partisan bias was significantly weakened as advertising became a major revenue source, as well as with examples of free newspapers that are entirely dependent on advertising revenue and thus exhibit minimal political bias.

Meanwhile, some scholars have explored the correlation between the size of the advertising market and the political bias of media. Gehlbach and Sonin (2014) found that as the size of the advertising market grows, political bias in news media decreases, leading to more politically independent reporting. Garcia Pires (2014) also argued that when the advertising market is small, news media differentiate their political bias as much as possible relative to their competitors, but when the advertising market is large, they minimize political bias differentiation.

[More to Explore] The Three Effects of Ad Revenue on Political Media Bias

According to Gal-Or, Geylani, and Yildirim (2012), when newspapers generate revenue from both advertising and sales, three effects on political bias emerge:

(1). Advertising revenue allows newspapers to engage in more aggressive price competition to attract readers. However, since intense price competition can significantly reduce profitability, they may further differentiate their political bias to reduce the price competition.

(2). To increase advertising revenue, newspapers aim to attract centrist readers, which naturally moderates their political bias.

(3). As newspapers further differentiate their readership profiles, advertisers can more accurately select outlets that align with their target audiences. This need of advertisers for targeting prompts newspapers to make their readership distinct from competitors.

Of these three effects, (1) and (3) increase political bias, while (2) has a moderating effect. The combined result of these effects determines the overall effect of advertisers on the political bias of media.

Gal-Or and colleagues also compared two scenarios: one in which advertisers place ads exclusively in a single newspaper and another in which they advertise across multiple newspapers. According to them, when advertisers advertise in only one newspaper, the difference in political bias between newspapers becomes even greater than when newspapers rely solely on sales revenue. Conversely, when advertisers distribute ads across multiple newspapers, the disparity in political bias diminishes, compared to when they depend only on sales revenue.

[24] Refer to Section 3.2.1.

9.3.2 ADVERTISERS DISTORTING NEWS CONTENT

If news media prioritize advertising revenue, wouldn't they naturally favor the news consumers most valued by advertisers?

According to Strömberg (2004b), media outlets tend to favor the news consumers that advertisers value most. If advertisers target affluent readers with high purchasing power, newspapers are likely to reduce coverage of issues relevant to lower-income individuals. When this occurs, politicians and parties advocating for the poor receive less media attention, making it harder for them to gain adequate support from lower-income individuals. As a result, politicians may become less responsive to the needs of the poor. Strömberg's perspective aligns with the argument by Petrova (2008b) that news media outlets are captured by affluent groups, thereby worsening economic inequality.[25]

Strömberg also noted that, in many cases, newspapers favor younger audiences because advertisers typically prioritize this demographic. Advertisers prefer those who are more responsive to ads, and since younger people generally have less established brand loyalty or purchasing patterns, they are more easily influenced by advertising than older adults.[26] Through similar mechanisms, economists widely understand that advertisers significantly influence both the content and the audience-targeting strategies of news media.

Economists consider that advertisers influence not only the overall content and consumer strategies of news media but also the coverage of individual news stories. They suggest that advertisers can directly intervene in specific news coverage that is unfavorable or favorable to their interests. From an economic perspective, this type of media capture by advertisers works in the same way as that exercised by political powers or other forces.

Indeed, many cases have come to light in which advertisers have influenced specific news stories. However, given the covert nature of media capture, there are likely many more undisclosed instances of advertiser influence. Let us examine the explanation economists have provided for why individual media outlets produce biased reports in favor of advertisers.

Germano and Meier (2013) argued that when news media generate revenue through advertising, they may engage in self-censorship regarding advertiser-related stories. This self-censorship can result in underreporting of news that might reflect poorly on advertisers, as doing so maximizes profit. Germano and Meier further explained that this tendency to underreport negative news is stronger when there are fewer owners of a given media outlet or when a single owner controls multiple media brands. This perspective aligns with the views of Corneo (2006), who argued that the media is more prone to capture as ownership becomes concentrated among fewer individuals. It also

[25] Refer to Subsection 9.1.3.1 and to Section 10.4.3 (Increasing Wealth Inequality).

[26] James Hamilton (2004), who was the first to explain different political biases in the media through the economic theory of product differentiation, also argued that newspapers are biased toward younger audiences.

aligns with Besley and Prat (2006), who, in relation to the transaction costs of capture, suggested that media outlets within larger business groups are easier to capture.

In a related study, Ellman and Germano (2009) proposed that as competition among media outlets declines, advertiser-friendly bias increases, whereas increased competition reduces such bias. According to their findings, in the case of a monopolist newspaper without competition, an increase in advertising revenue leads to less coverage of news unfavorable to advertisers, revealing a clear commercial bias. This is because, in the absence of competitive pressure from other newspapers, the monopolist newspaper becomes more inclined to favor advertisers who boost its revenue.

In contrast, in a competitive environment where multiple newspapers vie for readership, as the demand for advertising increases, the commercial bias among newspapers decreases, thereby enhancing the accuracy of reporting. This increase in advertising demand not only strengthens the newspapers' bargaining power with advertisers but also compels newspapers to monitor the reporting of competitors as they vie for readers.

[More to Explore] Punishment as a Strategy of Media Capture

In many cases, media capture is achieved not only through positive incentives—such as rewards or access—but also through negative incentives, such as punishment. Whether the capturer is the government or a private advertiser, punishments often serve as an effective tool to discipline or suppress noncompliant media outlets. Capturers may reward captured media with favorable treatment or material benefits, while punishing noncooperative outlets by reducing or withdrawing advertising, denying access to information[27], or even forcing suspension or shutdown of publication. The chilling effect of such punishment on critical media has already been illustrated in Section 9.2, with the case of newspaper suppression by the Hong Kong government.

Among various capturers, advertisers are perhaps the most frequent users of punitive strategies. Unlike political actors—who must rely on legal, institutional, or policy tools to punish critical media—advertisers can impose sanctions more easily by simply withdrawing advertising contracts. This commercial leverage requires no legal intervention but can have significant financial consequences for the targeted media outlet. Empirical examples of advertiser-driven punitive capture are discussed further in Section 10.2.1, covering industries such as tobacco, pharmaceuticals, and automotive.

Media outlets become particularly vulnerable to advertiser-led capture when (1) the advertising market is advertiser-dominated rather than media-dominated, and (2) the media outlet is heavily dependent on revenue from a small number of large advertisers. In such environments, even the

Continued

[27] Examples include the US White House's 2018 decision to revoke press credentials from a CNN reporter who asked uncomfortable questions to President Trump, and the South Korean presidential office's refusal to allow MBC journalists to board the presidential aircraft during President Yoon Suk-yeol's overseas trip in November 2022, citing their responsibility for "producing fake news." When such denials come from high-level political authorities, especially the head of state, they constitute a serious threat to the media. It is also common for large corporations and interest groups—who serve as both advertisers and news sources—to refuse interviews or access to journalists who publish critical stories.

threat of punishment—such as advertising withdrawal—can lead to self-censorship by media organizations seeking to avoid conflict with powerful advertisers.[28]

Importantly, when media capture is enforced through punitive mechanisms, increased media competition does not necessarily mitigate the risk of capture. As Ellman and Germano (2009) noted, even when competition intensifies, if advertisers retain the ability to punish uncooperative newspapers by terminating advertising relationships, then competitive pressure may fail to curb pro-advertiser bias and may even reinforce it.

Gentzkow and Shapiro (2008) further argue that when capturers adopt a strategy of punishing noncompliant media rather than rewarding compliant ones, competition may be insufficient to prevent capture. They highlight that if the punishment is severe enough to suppress critical reporting, even a large number of media outlets can be arbitrarily silenced.

9.4 MEDIA POWER

News media can exert influence over elections or public opinion through intentional reporting—this phenomenon is referred to as "media power." Media power is closely tied to media bias arising from media owners or individual journalists. It manifests when news providers manipulate content to serve personal interests or beliefs through selective reporting or framing that conveys intentional narratives.[29]

This phenomenon is not merely hypothetical; it has occurred in reality. In the late 19th century, American newspaper barons William Randolph Hearst and Joseph Pulitzer sensationalized and distorted news in their respective papers to stir public sentiment toward war with Spain, reaping commercial gains in the process. More recently, Italian media mogul Silvio Berlusconi leveraged his ownership of television channels from the 1980s onward to amplify his political influence, helping his political bloc win elections and securing three terms as prime minister over two decades. These historical examples illustrate the exercise of media power.

Media power also emerges when news outlets or journalists report on matters that affect their own professional or institutional interests. For instance, between 2014 and 2016, the vast majority of Korean news media and journalists vocally opposed the enactment of the Improper Solicitation and Graft Act, the so-called Kim Young-ran Law,[30] which extended anticorruption regulations to include journalists. Despite public polling that showed over 70% of Koreans supported the legislation, most major news outlets disregarded this sentiment. These episodes reinforced the public's

[28] For instance, in a letter addressed to all employees in September 2017, the publisher of *The Hankyoreh*, a leading independent newspaper in South Korea, wrote: "Samsung's advertising cuts are a form of coercion to pressure us into self-censorship. It is an unspoken demand that we refrain from reporting negatively on its ownership family—or else face economic consequences. Most media outlets have capitulated to this unethical and unjust pressure. This attempt to domesticate the press with capital is a direct assault on democracy." Quoted in Lee (September 22, 2017).

[29] Andrea Prat defines "media power" as the "ability to induce electoral decisions that voters would not make if media were unbiased." (Prat, 2018: 1747).

[30] The original name of the law in English is the Improper Solicitation and Graft Act.

perception—both past and present—that news organizations act to protect their own interests by influencing policy and legislation or by engaging in partisan reporting that favors particular parties or candidates.

Media power stands in contrast to the phenomenon of media capture discussed earlier. In fact, the two are inversely related; where political forces or interest groups fail to capture the media due to high capture costs, media power is more likely to arise. In societies with robust checks and balances and an independent judiciary, media capture tends to be more difficult, while the manifestation of media power becomes more likely. Paradoxically, media capture is more prevalent in less mature democracies, whereas media power tends to emerge in more developed democratic systems.

Nonetheless, both media capture and media power can severely undermine the informational welfare of news consumers and the functioning of democracy itself.

9.4.1 MEDIA CONCENTRATION AND MEASURING MEDIA POWER

The magnitude of media power is directly shaped by the market share of the media organization(s) that exercise it. In a pluralistic news market where diverse information and viewpoints are readily accessible, the harms caused by media power tend to be limited. Consider a news market in which a broad range of political, social, and cultural opinions are represented through a variety of media outlets. In such an environment, each media outlet reaches a smaller segment of the audience, while news consumers are more likely to access multiple sources. This pluralism helps contain the extent of media power.

In contrast, the risk of media power becoming harmful rises in monopolistic or oligopolistic markets where media diversity is lacking. If a society has only a single news outlet, the media power held by that outlet would be enormous. Moreover, high levels of market concentration increase the likelihood of media power being abused. Historical examples include William Hearst and Joseph Pulitzer in 19th-century America and Silvio Berlusconi in Italy from the 1980s onward. All of them exerted substantial media power through dominant market positions.

How, then, can the scale of media power be measured? The most straightforward approach is to apply standard economic indicators of market concentration, such as the Herfindahl–Hirschman Index (HHI)[31] or the Concentration Ratio (CR_k), which captures the combined market share of the top k firms. A common version is CR_3, representing the total market share of the top three firms. For example, if the top three firms account for 40% of total market transactions, then CR_3 equals 40%.

[31] The Herfindahl–Hirschman Index (HHI) was first conceptualized by the German-born economist Albert Hirschman in 1945. The index in its current form was later presented in a 1950 paper by American economist Orris Herfindahl, who applied it to the US steel industry. The name "Herfindahl–Hirschman Index" reflects the similarity of their contributions to the idea.

HHI is calculated by summing the squares of each firm's market share. A monopoly with 100% market share would yield an HHI of 10,000 (=100^2). If there are three firms with market shares of 10%, 10%, and 80%, the HHI would be 6600 (=$10^2 + 10^2 + 80^2$). With four firms at 10%, 20%, 30%, and 40%, the HHI would be 3000 (=$10^2 + 20^2 + 30^2 + 40^2$). The higher the HHI, the greater the market concentration. Typically, an HHI below 1,500 indicates an unconcentrated or competitive market, while an HHI between 1,500 and 2,500 signals a moderately concentrated market.[32]

When compared to general goods markets, the HHI levels of South Korea's media industry—ranging from approximately 760 to 946—suggest a fairly competitive market. The HHI for the Greek newspaper market in 2008 was about 1566, placing it in the range of moderate market concentration by the same standard (Psychogiopoulou et al., 2009). However, in both countries, the market share of the top three or four major newspapers has remained above 60% for decades. Similar patterns hold in other countries as well.

Consequently, no country assesses media market concentration by the same criteria used for goods markets. This is because traditional market power metrics do not fully capture the unique dynamics of the media industry (Polo, 2007). Andrea Prat (2014) explains why this distinction is necessary.

> *"Excessive concentration in, say, the milk industry may lead to lower consumer surplus through higher prices, lower quantities, and perhaps lower quality. That can happen in the media industry too, but there is an additional media-specific risk, which is by now well understood in both academic and policy circles. Unlike milk production, news production is central to the democratic process. Citizens receive political information from mass media and they use it to decide how to vote. By choosing what to report and how to report it, a media company can affect the views of its users and hence their voting decisions."* [33]
>
> **(Prat, 2014).**

Furthermore, since the advent of the digital era, traditional economic tools for analyzing concentration in the media industry have become increasingly inadequate. News markets are typically segmented by platform—print, television, radio, etc. Analyzing each platform separately makes it difficult to assess the full influence of conglomerates that span multiple platforms. Likewise, one cannot evaluate the relative influence of single-platform media organizations in the broader media landscape.

However, today, many media outlets distribute identical content across newspapers, TV, radio, and online platforms. In such a landscape, traditional supply-side measures like HHI no longer suffice to gauge comprehensive media influence. We are far removed from the era when only newspapers or newspapers plus broadcast

[32] An industry is generally classified as "moderately concentrated" when the HHI is between 1500 and 2500 and as "highly concentrated" when it exceeds 2500.

[33] In this context, Prat cited a well-known study by DellaVigna and Kaplan (2007), which found that the entry of *Fox News* increased the nationwide Republican vote share by 0.4 to 0.7 percentage points. For additional studies of this kind, see Section 8.5.

Table 9.2 Media Diversity Index (MDI) by the US Federal Communications Commission (2003)

Television broadcasting	Radio broadcasting	Newspapers	Weekly magazines	Cable internet	Other Internet sources
33.8%	24.9%	20.2%	8.6%	2.3%	10.2%

From Federal Communications Commission. (2003). "Report and Order and Notice of Proposed Rulemaking." FCC 03-127. Federal Communications Commission.

were dominant. The environment today is dramatically different. In particular, when companies across different media technology platforms merge, it becomes more important—and more difficult—than ever to measure the resulting media power and market concentration.

In the United States, where studies on media influence began earlier, the Federal Communications Commission (FCC) proposed a Media Diversity Index (MDI) in 2003 to quantify cross-platform influence (see Table 9.2). This index aimed to evaluate the impacts of cross-ownership and consolidation. However, the U.S. Third Circuit later deemed the MDI unsuitable as a standard for assessing mergers, citing "unreasonable assumptions and (factual) inconsistencies" (Prat, 2015). The ruling implied the difficulty of crafting reliable metrics for media power that spans across platforms—even after years of research by the FCC.

9.4.2 THE MEDIA POWER INDEX AND US MEDIA

Andrea Prat paved the way for effectively measuring media power in a news media environment segmented by platform. As a leading scholar on media power, Prat emphasized that the key to measuring media power lies not in how people access information (i.e., through which media platform) but in what information they actually receive. He argued that the influence of news media should be comparable across platforms. For example, one should be able to answer the following questions: "Is *The New York Times* more or less influential than CNN? Is CNN more or less influential than Yahoo News?"

Building on this line of inquiry, Prat (2018) developed the Media Power Index (MPI), which aggregates the influence that a specific media company exerts on news consumers across all media platforms. His approach began with identifying, for each news consumer, the range of media they used to consume news across various platforms. For example, one person might read the print edition of *The New York Times* and watch news on ABC, while another might consume news through *The Wall Street Journal*, the Yahoo News website, and CNN broadcasts.

After compiling such cross-platform consumption data for individual users, Prat then analyzed these data by media firm and media conglomerate to calculate each entity's MPI. (For details on the computation method, see More to Explore.) Table 9.3 presents the MPI scores calculated by Prat for the top 15 US media companies and

Table 9.3 Media Power Index of the Top 15 US Media Companies (2012)

News media company	Reach (%)	Aggregate attention	Media power index
News Corp. (Fox, WSJ)	0.311	0.181	0.221
Comcast (NBC, MSNBC)	0.268	0.133	0.153
Time Warner (CNN, Time)	0.209	0.079	0.086
ABC	0.143	0.062	0.066
NPR (National Public Radio)	0.141	0.056	0.059
Yahoo	0.126	0.054	0.057
CBS	0.087	0.035	0.036
MSN	0.094	0.032	0.033
NY Times	0.079	0.030	0.031
Viacom	0.063	0.028	0.028
PBS	0.079	0.024	0.025
Rush Limbaugh	0.063	0.021	0.022
Google	0.055	0.021	0.022
USA Today	0.047	0.019	0.020
AOL	0.031	0.013	0.013

From Prat (2018), based on data from Pew Media Consumption Survey (2012).

conglomerates in 2012.[34] According to his results, the company with the highest MPI was News Corporation, which operates Fox News and *The Wall Street Journal*. It was followed by Comcast, which owns NBC and MSNBC, and Time Warner, which owns CNN and Time magazine. *The New York Times* ranked ninth overall, and among digital-native media outlets, Yahoo News ranked highest at sixth.

A notable feature of Prat's MPI is that the four most powerful media groups are all television based. This suggests that these companies held substantial political influence and that a significant portion of the American public at the time obtained news primarily through television. Prat therefore warned that media regulators must exercise extreme caution when dealing with mergers involving major television companies.

Another striking feature was the absolute magnitude of the MPI values. Prat explained that News Corporation's MPI score of 0.221 meant it had the potential to influence 22.1% of voter preferences in an election—illustrating the profound impact that large media conglomerates can exert on a society's political processes.

[34] Prat derived the index values using data from the Media Consumption Survey conducted by the Pew Research Center, a leading US social research institute.

Such high levels of media power, as revealed by the MPI, indicate that even when a media market appears relatively competitive by traditional metrics such as the HHI, many consumers are still receiving information from a small set of dominant providers.

In short, traditional measures of market concentration—such as HHI or the Concentration Ratio (CR_k)—used for assessing general goods markets fail to capture the problem of most news consumers depending on relatively few sources. Especially in a multiplatform media environment, a more effective method for assessing media power involves collecting cross-platform consumption data at the individual level and then aggregating and analyzing it by media firm or group.

Finally, it is important to note that approaches to measuring and assessing media power vary by country. These differences arise from varying realities in media markets and industries, differing policy norms, and diverse public attitudes toward the media. As a result, methodologies range from simple market concentration metrics like HHI and CR_k to more sophisticated studies that assess political influence based on consumer surveys.

[More to Explore] Prat's Method for the Media Power Index (MPI)

Let us understand Prat's method for calculating the MPI through the illustrative example in Table 9.4. In this example, consumers who obtain information from media and make political choices are grouped into nine segments, with each group representing either 10% or 20% of the overall population of news consumers.

The media in the total news market consist of seven outlets: two television channels, three newspapers, and two websites. Each voter group consumes between one and four media outlets among these seven. For instance, Group 1 consumes only TV1, while Group 2 consumes both TV1 and Newspaper 1. In contrast, Group 9 consumes both newspapers and both websites.

In Table 9.4, the "reach" of a media outlet refers to the proportion of total news consumers who consume that outlet. For example, TV1 is consumed by Group 1 (20%) and Group 2 (10%), resulting in a total reach of 30%.

Next, "attention" refers to the degree of attention a specific media outlet receives from the entire consumer population. This is calculated by taking the proportion of each consumer group and dividing it by the number of media outlets consumed by that group. For TV1, Group 1's attention to TV1 is 20% because it consumes only TV1 (20%/1 = 20%). Group 2 consumes both TV1 and Newspaper 1, so its attention to TV1 is 5% (10%/2 = 5%). Thus the total attention to TV1 is 25% (20% + 5%). For Newspaper 1, which is consumed by Group 2 and Group 3, the total attention is calculated similarly and comes out to 15%.

Finally, the MPI is the ratio of a media outlet's attention (A) to the total attention of all other outlets combined (1 − A). That is, MPI = A/(1 − A). Therefore, with an attention of 25%, TV1's MPI is 0.333. Similarly, for Web1 with an attention of 15%, its MPI is 0.176. Prat interpreted these MPI values as indicating the potential to influence 33.3% and 17.6% of the electorate, respectively.

Table 9.4 Media Consumption Distribution and Prat's "Media Power Index (MPI)"

News consumers	Group size	TV1	TV2	Newspaper 1	Newspaper 2	Newspaper 3	Web1	Web2
Group 1	20%	■						
Group 2	10%	■		■				
Group 3	10%			■				
Group 4	10%		■					■
Group 5	10%		■		■		■	■
Group 6	10%		■		■		■	
Group 7	10%		■			■	■	
Group 8	10%					■	■	■
Group 9	10%				■	■	■	■
Reach[a]		30.0%	40.0%	20.0%	30.0%	30.0%	50.0%	40.0%
Attention (A)[b]		25.0%	14.1%	15.0%	8.3%	9.1%	15.0%	13.3%
MPI = A/(1–A)		0.333	0.164	0.176	0.090	0.101	0.176	0.152

[a] *Reach: The percentage of total news consumers who consume a given media outlet.*
[b] *Attention: The sum of [(reach of each group) × (1/number of media outlets consumed by the group)].*

9.4.3 POLICIES FOR MEDIA AND OPINION DIVERSITY

As discussed in Chapter 7, government intervention in the news market involves a complex dilemma. While intervention is often necessary to prevent the proliferation of low-quality information caused by excessive competition or to ensure the diversity of information supply, the government itself is the primary subject of media scrutiny. The very fact that the media's main object of oversight is also intervening in the media market creates an inherent dilemma. Nevertheless, policy intervention aimed at mitigating the phenomena of media capture and media power—which consistently produce negative outcomes for news consumers—is inevitable. At the same time, minimizing the side effects of such intervention is as important a task as the intervention itself in shaping effective media policy.

The central focus of policies addressing media capture and media power is straightforward. As previously examined, both phenomena are more likely to arise when the news market is characterized by high levels of concentration or monopolization. Therefore, preventing excessive market concentration is key to curbing media capture and media power. More media outlets (competition) and media diversity generally function as effective safeguards against these problems.

Media diversity, in particular, is associated with greater voter participation, increased political accountability, and the advancement of public interest. Conversely, market dominance by media outlets with a particular bias leads to a skewed media landscape, which is detrimental to the maintenance and development of a democratic society. This is why mature democracies impose regulations on excessive media market concentration.

Of course, excessive competition can also bring about negative side effects. This was discussed in Section 7.1.1 (Too Much Competition and Insufficient Information Supply) and Section 9.2 (Poisoned Competition in the Digital Age). However, easing or preventing high levels of market concentration does not necessarily trigger excessive competition. Hence, alleviating media market concentration while maintaining an appropriate level of competition remains a consistent policy goal in media and communication regulation.

Policies designed to curb market concentration and secure media pluralism generally fall into three categories: platform-specific regulations, general competition policy, and public sector involvement in the news market. The features and limitations of each category are summarized below.

First, platform-specific regulations are those applied to particular platforms, such as newspapers or broadcasting. A prime example is ownership restrictions, which exist in many countries. In France, for instance, no individual may own more than 49% of a media company. These regulations also include restrictions on cross-ownership between newspapers and broadcasters, as well as limits on foreign ownership of media. Platform-specific regulations may also involve setting caps on market share or regulating advertising practices for individual media companies.

However, with the proliferation of new platforms, the same content is now frequently delivered across various platforms. Media companies operating on different platforms often compete for the same audience. In this context, regulations limited to specific platforms have become outdated and inefficient. Consequently, there is growing support for regulating the influence of specific media entities based on cross-platform analyses rather than by individual platforms or market segments.

Second, regulations based on general competition policy refer to standard rules applied across all industries to foster a competitive environment. These rules aim to protect consumer welfare with respect to prices, quantities, and quality of products and services. They do not account for the impact of media on democratic political processes. As previously mentioned, standard economic concepts like the HHI fail to capture the essential value of media diversity (Noam, 2009; Polo, 2007). As such, general competition rules in ordinary product and service markets are ineffective when it comes to addressing media power and media capture.[35] Since these issues may not raise concerns from the perspective of general competition policy, they cannot be adequately resolved through such regulations.

Third, the public sector can participate directly in the news market, as exemplified by public broadcasters such as the BBC in the United Kingdom. In fact, outside the United States, the largest broadcast networks in most countries are publicly owned. If public media are governed by independent institutions and norms that ensure freedom from political influence, scholars generally agree that they can provide fairer and less biased news compared to private media.

However, there is scholarly disagreement over whether such institutional and normative independence from government or political forces is realistically attainable. For instance, while the BBC has been lauded for offering high-quality content and maintaining political neutrality even amid intense competition (Zaller, 1999), evaluations of public broadcasters in many other countries are far less favorable. In numerous cases, public broadcasters face repeated controversies over political bias, depending on which political faction is in power. Leadership appointments at public broadcasters often lead to internal and external political strife. Unfortunately, these situations reveal how public media lacking institutional safeguards against political interference can become easy targets for media capture or even hotbeds of unchecked media power.

Empirical studies supporting the vulnerability of public broadcasters to media capture include research by Durante and Knight (2012), who found significant shifts in bias at Italy's public broadcaster under Silvio Berlusconi's administration,[36] and the work of Djankov et al. (2003), which showed that governments in many countries exploit media not to correct market failures but to consolidate their own authority.[37]

---

[35] In the model by Besley and Prat (2006), the key determinants are N (number of media outlets), R (total market revenue), and T (transaction costs). The HHI is not directly related to N, R, or T. Thus adjusting the HHI does not alter the conditions for media capture. See [More to Explore] in Subsection 9.1.1.

[36] See Section 8.2.2 and Section 10.1.

[37] See Section 10.4.

In particular, in countries with immature democracies and low "transaction costs"[38] for media capture, large-scale public media often become tools for state-led opinion control. In this regard, Andrea Prat remarked that the BBC is perhaps the most successful example of independence, enabled by a governance structure that imposes exceptionally high transaction costs for capture. However, he also cautioned that it is unclear whether such a model can be replicated in other democracies where checks and balances are weak (Prat, 2015: 685).

References

Anderson, S.P., McLaren, J., 2012. Media Mergers and Media Bias with Rational Consumers. Journal of the European Economic Association 10 (4), 831–859.

Bagdikian, B., 2000. The Media Monopoly, 6th ed. Beacon Press, Boston.

Baker, C.E., 1994. Advertising and a Democratic Press. Princeton University Press.

Baker, C. E., 2007. Media Concentration and Democracy: Why Ownership Matters. Cambridge University Press.

Baron, D., 2005. Competing for the Public through the News Media. Journal of Economics & Management Strategy 14 (2), 339–376.

Besley, T., Prat, A., 2006. Handcuffs for the grabbing hand? Media capture and government accountability. American Economic Review 96 (3), 720–736. https://doi.org/10.1257/aer.96.3.720.

Brunetti, A., Weder, B., 2003. A free press is bad news for corruption. Journal of Public Economics 87 (7–8), 1801–1824. https://doi.org/10.1016/s0047-2727(01)00186-4.

Cagé, J., Hervé, N., Viaud, M.L., 2020. The production of information in an online world. The Review of Economic Studies 87 (3), 753–802. https://doi.org/10.1093/restud/rdz061.

Choi, J.P., Yang, S., 2021. Investigative Journalism and Media Capture in the Digital Age. Information Economics and Policy 57, 100942. https://doi.org/10.1016/j.infoecopol.2021.100942.

Corneo, G., 2006. Media capture in a democracy: the role of wealth concentration. Journal of Public Economics 90 (1–2), 37–58. https://doi.org/10.1016/j.jpubeco.2005.08.002.

DellaVigna, S., Kaplan, E., 2007. The Fox News Effect: Media Bias and Voting. The Quarterly Journal of Economics 122 (3), 1187–1234.

Djankov, S., McLiesh, C., Nenova, T., Shleifer, A., 2003. Who owns the media? The Journal of Law and Economics 46 (2), 341–382. https://doi.org/10.1086/377116.

Durante, R., Knight, B., 2012. Partisan control, media bias, and viewer responses: evidence from Berlusconi's Italy. Journal of the European Economic Association 10 (3), 451–481. https://doi.org/10.1111/j.1542-4774.2011.01060.x.

Ellman, M., Germano, F., 2009. What do the papers sell? A model of advertising and media bias. The Economic Journal 119 (537), 680–704. https://doi.org/10.1111/j.1468-0297.2009.02218.x.

Foster, R., 2012. News Plurality in a Digital World. Reuters Institute for the Study of Journalism.

[38] See Subsection 9.1.1.

Gabszewicz, J.J., Laussel, D., Sonnac, N., 2001. Press advertising and the ascent of the 'Pensée Unique'. European Economic Review 45 (4–6), 641–651. https://doi.org/10.1016/S0014-2921(01)00139-8.

Gal-Or, E., Geylani, T., Yildirim, T.P., 2012. The impact of advertising on media bias. Journal of Marketing Research 49 (1), 92–99. https://doi.org/10.1509/jmr.10.0196.

Garcia Pires, A.J., 2014. Media diversity, advertising, and adaptation of news to readers' political preferences. Information Economics and Policy 28 (1), 28–38. https://doi.org/10.1016/j.infoecopol.2014.06.001.

Gehlbach, S., Sonin, K., 2014. Government control of the media. Journal of Public Economics 118, 163–171. https://doi.org/10.1016/j.jpubeco.2014.06.004.

Gentzkow, M., Shapiro, J.M., 2008a. Competition and Truth in the Market for News. Journal of Economic Perspectives, 22 (2), 133–154. https://doi.org/10.1257/jep.22.2.133.

Germano, F., Meier, M., 2013. Concentration and Self-censorship in Commercial Media. Journal of Public Economics 97, 117–130.

Hamilton, J.T., 2004. All the News That's Fit to Sell. Princeton University Press.

Harvard University, Institute for Quantitative Social Science.(n.d.). US media ownership. The Future of Media Project. https://projects.iq.harvard.edu/futureofmedia/us-media-index.

Katzenberger, T., 2024 (October 23). LA Times Editor Resigns After Owner Blocked Presidential Endorsement. *Politico*. Retrieved from: https://www.politico.com/live-updates/2024/10/23/2024-elections-live-coverage-updates-analysis/los-angeles-times-editor-resigns-endorsement-00185196.

Lee, D.-G., 2017. Samsung is threatening democracy—yet it could be a turning point. In a company-wide email, Yang Sang-woo, CEO of The Hankyoreh, sends a message to all employees. The Hankyoreh: ON. [in Korean]. http://www.hanion.co.kr/news/articleView.html?idxno=5907.

Mungiu-Pippidi, A., 2012. Freedom Without Impartiality: The Vicious Circle of Media Capture. In: Gross, P., Jakubowicz, K. (Eds.). Media Transformations in the Post-Communist World: Eastern Europe's Tortured Path to Change, pp. 49–66.

Noam, E., 2009. Media Ownership and Concentration in America. Oxford University Press. https://doi.org/10.1093/acprof:oso/9780195188523.001.0001.

Petrova, M., 2008a. Political Economy of Media Capture. In R. Islam, ed., Information and Public Choice: From Measurement to Policymaking. 121–139. Washington, DC: The World Bank.

Petrova, M., 2008b. Inequality and media capture. Journal of Public Economics 92 (1–2), 183–212. https://doi.org/10.1016/j.jpubeco.2007.04.004.

Polo, M., 2007. Regulation for pluralism in the media markets. In: Seabright, P., and von Hagen, J. (Eds.), The Economic Regulation of Broadcasting Markets: Evolving Technology and the Challenges for Policy. Cambridge University Press, pp. 150–188. https://doi.org/10.1017/CBO9780511611124.005.

Prat, A., 2014 (August 22). Can we measure media power? World Economic Forum. Available from: https://www.weforum.org/agenda/2014/08/measure-power-of-media/.

Prat, A., 2015. Media capture and media power. In: *Handbook of Media Economics*, Vol. 1. Elsevier, pp. 669–686. https://doi.org/10.1016/b978-0-444-63685-0.00016-4.

Prat, A., 2018. Media power. Journal of Political Economy 126 (4), 1747–1783.

Psychogiopoulou E., Anagnostou D., Kandyla A., Yataganas X., Maragopoulos T., 2009. Media Policies and Regulatory Practices in a Selected Set of European Countries, the EU and the Council of Europe.

Schiffrin, A., 2018. Introduction to Special Issue on media capture. Journalism 19 (8), 1033–1042. https://doi.org/10.1177/1464884917725167.

Sobbrio, F., 2011. Indirect Lobbying and Media Bias. Quarterly Journal of Political Science 6 (3–4), 235–274.

Stephens, M., 2010. A History of News. Oxford University Press.

Stigler, G.J., 1971. The Theory of Economic Regulation. The Bell Journal of Economics and Management Science 2 (1), 3–21.

Stiglitz, J.E., 2017. Toward a taxonomy of media capture. In: Schiffrin, A. (Ed.), In the Service of Power: Media Capture and the Threat to Democracy, Columbia University Press, 9–17.

Strömberg, D., 2004b. Mass Media Competition, Political Competition, and Public Policy. The Review of Economic Studies 71 (1), 265–284.

Trombetta, F., Rossignoli, D., 2021. The price of silence: media competition, capture, and electoral accountability. European Journal of Political Economy 69, 101939. https://doi.org/10.1016/j.ejpoleco.2020.101939.

Vaidya, S., Gupta, R., 2016. Corruption via media capture: the effect of competition. Southern Economic Journal 82 (4), 1327–1348. https://doi.org/10.1002/soej.12105.

Yang, S., 2021. Media Capture and Media Bias in the Digital Age (Ph.D. Dissertation). Yonsei University.

Zaller J., 1999. Market competition and news quality. In: The 1999 Annual Meetings of the American Political Science Association.

CHAPTER

Case Studies of Media Capture Around the Globe

10

Chapter Outline

13 percent of the world's inhabitants lived in countries with a Free press, while 42 percent had a Partly Free press and 45 percent lived in Not Free environments.[1]

—Freedom House

[1] Freedom House (2017, p. 24). Freedom House, established in the United States in 1941, is a non-governmental organization dedicated to promoting democracy, human rights, and press freedom worldwide. From 1980 to 2017, the organization published an annual report on global press freedom titled Freedom of the Press. The final edition in 2017, reflecting the lowest global press freedom index in 13 years as of 2016, bore the subtitle Press Freedom's Dark Horizon.

The Economics of News Media. DOI: http://dx.doi.org/10.1016/B978-0-443-45044-0.00011-8

Media capture is a complex problem, but it is not inevitable. ... (However,) the effort so far has been miserably inadequate.[2]
—Mark Nelson

It is hard to imagine a society without crime, but a society with less crime is entirely possible. Similarly, while it may be unrealistic to expect a world entirely free from media capture, efforts to reduce it can yield meaningful results. Just as meticulous crime prevention systems can be built, policies, institutions, and practices to monitor and curb media capture can also be established. However, this task faces formidable adversaries, including political forces, powerful corporations, and entrenched interest groups collectively known as "media capturers."

As Mark Nelson, former senior editor at the Center for International Media Assistance, pointed out, many countries around the globe have failed to achieve satisfactory results in their battles against media capturers. Rasmus Nielsen (2017, p. 34), director of the Reuters Institute for the Study of Journalism, similarly observed that captured and politically instrumentalized news media—subsidized by proprietors, social and political groups, or governments—is common in most of the world. Indeed, this reality is well-documented in empirical studies by economists on media capture conducted across various regions of the globe.

Extensive research on media capture has evolved over decades, particularly in the fields of media studies and political science. Scholars such as Edward Herman, Noam Chomsky, Ben Bagdikian, and Robert McChesney have traversed both theory and empirical analysis to argue that the media is structurally captured by ruling elites.[3] Additionally, numerous empirical studies have examined media capture through various lenses, including the actors involved, methods of capture, and regional differences. Several well-known studies illustrate the diverse range of research on this topic, including studies on cases where pro-government firms acquire ownership of news media companies,[4] research on reporting differences between private media and government-captured state media (Hasty, 2005), investigations into the influence of media capital on news and other content (Bagdikian, 1983; 2004), and analyses of how information providers, such as governments, influence journalists (Gans, 1979).

However, even within empirical research, media studies scholars and economists differ in their perspectives and interpretations. For instance, economists often focus on identifying economic causal relationships related to capture, rather than emphasizing factors like coercion or violence. While these economists' approaches may appear unconventional, their efforts to uncover hidden media capture have been crucial in highlighting its varied forms across the globe. Let us now examine some representative cases of media capture identified through the work of economists.

[2] Nelson (2017, p. 158).

[3] The views of these scholars are referenced in Section 5.4.

[4] Bennett and Naim's (2015) study on the case of Venezuela and Finkel's (2015) research on the Erdogan government in Türkiye.

10.1 MEDIA CAPTURE BY POLITICAL POWER AND GOVERNMENTS

10.1.1 CASES BY COUNTRY

Captured by money: Peru

One of the most vivid accounts of media capture comes from a study that uncovered the realities of capture during President Alberto Fujimori's administration in 1990s Peru. This study garnered significant attention, particularly for its dramatic depiction of endogenous media capture, driven not by external coercion but by market forces.

McMillan and Zoido (2004) meticulously analyzed how Vladimiro Montesinos, head of Peru's secret police under Fujimori, systematically dismantled democratic systems through extensive bribery of the media, judiciary, and politicians. According to their research, the bribes Montesinos paid to a single television channel owner were 100 times greater than those paid to judges or politicians. In fact, the amount given to one television channel exceeded the total bribes distributed to all opposition politicians by a factor of five. With these enormous bribes, Peru's mainstream news media reciprocated by exclusively broadcasting favorable news about the ruling party and government while refraining from airing negative news. The sheer scale of these payments underscores the dominant importance the regime placed on controlling the media compared to other factors.

The principles of market dynamics resurfaced dramatically at an unexpected juncture, even as the grip of media capture seemed unshakable. A damning video recording of Montesinos brazenly bribing a media owner found its way to a small, independent television channel that had escaped capture. Seizing the opportunity, the channel began broadcasting the explosive footage around the clock. Viewership surged dramatically, drawing massive audiences to the channel. The pressure mounted on the captured mainstream broadcasters, leaving them no choice but to air the footage as well. Ultimately, a chain reaction sparked by a single, uncaptured channel toppled both media capture and the Fujimori regime.

The stronger the political motive, the weaker the market power, the more media capture increases: United States

Gentzkow et al. (2015) conducted a detailed study on the effect of ruling parties in state governments on daily newspapers in the United States from 1869 to 1928. They analyzed factors such as newspaper market entry and exit, circulation, pricing, and content. While no systematic evidence was found that ruling parties consistently influenced newspapers throughout the study period, significant variations emerged during certain time periods.

In the post-Civil War South (1869–1900), weakened market dynamics and strong political motives created conditions conducive to media capture. Southern newspaper markets suffered from low demand, high production costs, and limited competition. These challenges made newspapers particularly vulnerable to political influence. During Reconstruction, radical Republicans used government funds to sustain Republican-friendly newspapers, as they were deemed essential for advancing economic and social reforms. However, low literacy rates and limited public support meant these newspapers could not survive without subsidies. Market constraints further amplified political control. Southern newspapers faced low circulation rates, scarce advertising opportunities, and labor shortages, with two-thirds of prewar newspapers ceasing publication.

As Democrats regained power in the 1870s, state support for Republican newspapers disappeared, and the share of pro-democratic newspapers grew significantly. Quantitative analysis revealed that Democratic control increased pro-Democratic daily newspaper circulation by approximately 10 percentage points and weekly circulation by 19 percentage points. These changes mirrored political transitions, underscoring how government intervention shaped the press.

Gentzkow and his colleagues concluded that media capture is more likely when market forces are weak and political incentives are strong. The post-Reconstruction South highlights the intersection of political power and economic conditions in influencing media landscapes. This research emphasizes the importance of robust market competition in limiting the risks of media capture.

The more government ads, the less corruption is reported: Argentina

Di Tella and Franceschelli (2011) analyzed the effect of government advertising on news media's coverage of government corruption scandals. Their study examined Argentina's major newspapers from 1998 to 2007 and revealed that government advertising and the frequency of corruption coverage are inversely related. Newspapers receiving more government advertising gave less front-page coverage to corruption scandals, while those with more corruption coverage were allocated fewer government advertisements.

This dynamic indicates that government advertising serves as a tool to influence media content, effectively rewarding outlets that align with the government's interests. This means that newspapers closely aligned with the government are less likely to report on corruption compared to those that are not. The study underscores the distorting effects of discretionary government advertising. When governments exercise control over the allocation of advertising funds, media outlets have strong incentives to tailor their reporting to government preferences. This compromises journalistic independence and reduces the media's role in holding governments accountable.

The authors concluded that safeguarding media independence requires minimizing government discretion in advertising allocations. By ensuring that financial relationships between governments and media outlets are transparent and fair, these measures can help protect the essential role of journalism as a watchdog in democratic societies.

A similar pattern is observed in many countries. For example, in South Korea, government advertising revenue for major partisan newspapers fluctuates significantly depending on the ruling party. Under progressive administrations, newspapers with a progressive bias tend to secure more government advertising, while conservative-leaning newspapers see an increase in revenue under conservative governments. This suggests that if Di Tella and Franceschelli's study were replicated in South Korea, the findings would likely be similar.

Biased international news reporting captured by national governments: United States

Qian and Yanagizawa-Drott (2017) explored a unique approach to examining media capture by government, even under democratic regimes. They analyzed US media coverage of human rights violations committed by foreign governments from 1946 to 2010.

They found that US news media displayed differing reporting patterns based on whether the country committing the violations was a United Nations Security Council (UNSC) member or not, and whether it was an ally of the United States or not. For nonallied countries, the US media reported more extensively on human rights abuses if the country was a UNSC member. Conversely, for countries with strong alliances with the US, media coverage of human rights abuses decreased when the country was a UNSC member.

Notably, these patterns mirrored the US State Department's Human Rights Reports. The tendency was even more pronounced during the Reagan and Bush Sr. administrations (1981–92), a period known for active government influence over the media. Based on these findings, Qian and Yanagizawa-Drott concluded that even in countries like the United States, where press freedom is considered relatively high, media coverage can be influenced by the government's control over the availability and content of information. This represents a case where information provision was used as a means of media capture.

The political use of captured broadcasting: Russia, Italy, Nazi Germany

Multiple studies have shown that captured media outlets provide ruling party politicians with disproportionately greater exposure. Enikolopov, Petrova, and Zhuravskaya (2011) analyzed the frequency and duration of politicians' appearances on Russian television channels during the 1999 elections. Their findings revealed that on state-controlled television channels, pro-government politicians appeared significantly more often than opposition politicians.[5]

[5] This study also includes empirical analysis showing that viewership of NTV, which was independent of Russia's ruling powers, decreased the vote share of the ruling party and increased the vote share of opposition parties. Refer to Section 8.5.1 (Persuaded News Consumers).

Similarly, Durante and Knight (2012) examined the reporting patterns of Italian television channels from 2001 to 2007. Their study found that after Silvio Berlusconi came to power, public television channels featured ruling party politicians at higher rates.[6]

A comparable case occurred during the 1920s and 1930s in Germany under the Weimar Republic and the Nazi regime. Adena et al. (2015) studied how ruling political forces used radio to influence German voters during this period. Their study found that during the Weimar government, introducing pro-government political news on state-controlled radio significantly slowed Nazi Party support in areas with radio access. However, after Adolf Hitler's Nazi Party came to power in 1933, Nazi politicians, who had previously been largely absent from radio broadcasts, began appearing much more frequently. This led to a rapid surge in the Nazi Party's popularity.

10.1.2 DEFAMATION LAWS AND MEDIA CAPTURE

One common method of influencing news reporting is the use of policies or legal sanctions, with defamation laws serving as a prominent example. Scholars generally agree that stringent defamation laws reduce media coverage of corruption involving those with power or wealth. These laws effectively suppress the production of news targeting such corruption, producing effects akin to media capture. Legal penalties substantially increase the costs media outlets must bear when exposing corruption by powerful or wealthy entities.

Stringent defamation laws are not limited to authoritarian regimes. Debates over their legislation frequently arise even in democratic countries. For instance, they have surfaced in the United States, where the First Amendment provides strong protection for freedom of the press. A notable example is the *Sedition Act of 1798*, passed by the US Congress, which imposed fines or imprisonment on individuals accused of publishing "false, scandalous, or malicious writing" against the federal government, Congress, or the President.

The legislation was justified by the Quasi-War with France and remained in effect for three years, until 1801. During that time, 25 individuals were arrested, 15 were indicted, and 10 were convicted. However, many charges were absurdly crude, and the primary targets were newspaper editors critical of the Federalist administration (McNamara, 2009).

Back in sections 9.1.2 and 9.3.2, we discussed punitive strategies such as withdrawing advertising or applying physical coercion to media outlets that resisted capture. Such strategies by media capturers reinforce media outlets' incentives for self-censorship to avoid punishment. Strict defamation laws similarly amplify these

[6] This study is also referenced in Sections 8.2.2 (News Providers Determine Media Bias) and 8.5.2 (Proactive News Consumers).

self-censorship tendencies. Moreover, because legal sanctions apply universally across all media within a society, their negative effects are more pervasive.

Political economist Piero Stanig (2015) empirically demonstrated that stricter defamation laws lead to a reduction in critical reporting on those in power. Stanig analyzed the varying defamation laws across states in federalized Mexico and compared the extent of local newspapers' corruption reporting on public officials. His findings revealed that in states with stricter defamation laws (as of 2001), local newspapers published significantly fewer reports exposing corruption. Stanig attributed this to the "chilling effect," where defamation laws suppress freedom of expression.

A similar perspective was proposed earlier by sociologist Paul Starr, who studied the history of media development, regulation, and capture across different countries. In his book, *The Creation of the Media: Political Origins of Modern Communications*, Starr observed that countries with stricter media regulations published fewer critical reports on elected politicians and public officials (Starr, 2004: 296).

10.2 DISTORTION OF NEWS BY ADVERTISERS

Political forces or governments are not the only actors capable of capturing the media; a variety of stakeholders can also exert influence. Chief among them are advertisers who purchase advertising time and space from media outlets. Advertising revenue provides the material foundation that allows news media to resist dependence on political powers and partisan audiences. However, the more the media outlets rely on such revenue, the more advertisers can directly or indirectly influence media content. As theoretically discussed in Section 9.3, advertising revenue can reduce political bias, but at the same time may lead to content distortion as media cater to advertisers' expectations or demands.[7] Empirical studies by economists support both phenomena. This section explores empirical research that highlights the dysfunctions of news distortion caused by advertisers or advertising revenue. The positive role of advertising revenue in freeing media from political bias will be discussed in the next section on the supply and demand of media capture.

10.2.1 INDUSTRY-DRIVEN BIAS: TOBACCO, PHARMACEUTICALS, AUTOMOTIVE CASES

The tobacco, pharmaceutical, and automotive industries have long been recognized as major advertisers that have influenced news reporting over the past century. Companies in these industries leveraged their status as advertisers to shape news coverage. This subsection introduces empirical findings compiled and presented by Blasco and Sobbrio (2012).

[7] For a theoretical discussion, see Section 9.3.

Consider the tobacco companies, which for much of the 20th century were the largest advertisers in many countries. In 1954, the American Cancer Society announced a study of 187,000 men, finding that smokers had a 75% higher disease-related mortality rate than non-smokers. In particular, smokers were 16 times more likely to die from lung cancer. Yet, major American media outlets did not report this study at the time, nor for decades after. Media scholar and former journalist Ben Bagdikian (2004: 168) characterized this omission as one of the most shameful forms of money-driven censorship in American media, arguing that it represented a corruption of journalism that contributed to the deaths of millions.

Health economists Warner, Goldenhar, and McLaughlin (1992) examined 99 American magazines over 25 years (1959–69 and 1973–86) and found that those carrying tobacco advertisements were about 30% less likely to publish articles on the dangers of smoking than those that did not. The effect was even more pronounced in women's magazines, where the likelihood dropped to just 43% compared to their counterparts. Similar results were found by Kennedy and Bero (1999), who reported that newspapers and magazines carrying tobacco advertisements were more likely to dilute coverage of secondhand smoke risks by portraying the issue as "controversial."

Tobacco companies often punished media outlets that reported negatively on smoking. In 1957, when *Reader's Digest* published a medical exposé on smoking risks, the American Tobacco Company pressured its advertising agency to terminate its contract with the magazine. In 1979, after the progressive magazine *Mother Jones* reported on the addictiveness of smoking, tobacco firms, including Philip Morris, collectively pulled their ads from the publication (Enikolopov and Petrova, 2015). Such punitive actions proved to be an effective strategy for enforcing media capture. This topic is further discussed in section [More to Explore] "Punishment as a Strategy of Media Capture" of Chapter 9.

Pharmaceutical companies, like tobacco firms, have also deeply influenced media content, particularly in medical journals. According to one study, in the United States and Canada, medical journals were saturated with drug ads, even when advertising was not limited to pharmaceuticals (Fugh-Berman, Alladin, and Chow, 2006: 763). It is also a common practice for pharmaceutical companies to pay subscription fees on behalf of medical professionals, a form of sponsored subscription. These companies also penalized critical coverage. The same study reported that several large pharmaceutical firms simultaneously withdrew advertising from the *Annals of Internal Medicine* after it published a study criticizing the accuracy of pharmaceutical ads.

The symbiotic relationship between medical journals and pharmaceutical advertisers creates fertile ground for content distortion. Researchers found that many editors considered advertisers' interests when deciding whether to publish certain papers (Fletcher, 2003; Fugh-Berman, Alladin, and Chow, 2006; Wilkes and Kravitz, 1995). In some cases, articles that had received favorable peer reviews were rejected due to advertiser concerns (Dyer, 2004).

Similar patterns have appeared in the automotive industry. Before electric vehicles gained traction, car manufacturers played a major role in distorting coverage related to the climate crisis. Since the mid-1990s, a scientific consensus has existed regarding the causes and future outlook of global warming. Nonetheless, many news outlets continued to portray climate change as a controversial issue, influenced by the automobile industry (Oreskes, 2004; Oreskes and Conway, 2011).

Environmental scientists Boykoff and Boykoff (2004) analyzed climate reporting in the four leading US newspapers (*The New York Times*, *The Washington Post*, *The Los Angeles Times*, and *The Wall Street Journal*) and found serious issues. Their analysis showed that 52.6% of articles treated views for and against anthropogenic global warming as equally valid, 35.2% leaned toward the scientific consensus but mentioned counterarguments, 6.1% were skeptical of human-caused climate change, and only 5.9% clearly presented the scientific consensus.

A comparative study of media coverage in the United States and the United Kingdom during 2003 and 2006 showed that American newspapers were more likely to stray from the scientific consensus on anthropogenic climate change than their British counterparts (Boykoff, 2007). Ellman and Germano (2009) attributed this to the abundance of automobile advertisements in American newspapers.

10.2.2 ADVERTISERS' INFLUENCE ON INDIVIDUAL ARTICLES

Advertisers not only influence the overall direction of media content but can also shape the coverage and framing of individual news stories related to their own interests. A growing body of empirical research has explored this dynamic, and the results consistently show a positive correlation between advertising expenditures and favorable media coverage. That is, increases or decreases in one tend to coincide with similar changes in the other. However, the strength and presence of this correlation vary depending on the specific context of the advertiser and media outlet. In particular, when competition among advertisers is intense, economists find that the correlation between advertising expenditure and favorable news coverage disappears.

In the United States, Reuter and Zitzewitz (2006) discovered a positive correlation between mutual fund recommendations and advertising placements in financial media such as *Money Magazine*. However, they found no such correlation in more prominent national outlets like *The New York Times* or *The Wall Street Journal*. The authors interpreted this as evidence that advertisers can exert influence over news coverage when they possess greater bargaining power than the media outlet.

Rinallo and Basuroy (2009) produced similar findings using data from 291 Italian fashion firms and their advertising activity and product coverage across 123 newspapers and magazines in Italy, France, Germany, the United Kingdom, and the United States. The results confirmed that advertising positively influenced editorial coverage. However, media outlets with more diversified sources of advertising revenue were less likely to prioritize coverage of products from specific advertisers.

This suggests that when competition among advertisers exceeds competition among media outlets for ad revenue, advertising expenditure fails to influence content. It also implies that news organizations seeking independence from advertiser pressure should pursue a diversified base of advertising clients.

Further evidence of advertiser bias in Italian media comes from Gambaro and Puglisi (2015), who analyzed how Italian newspapers covered publicly listed companies and compared that to the companies' advertising expenditures in those outlets. They found that favorable coverage was associated with both current and past advertising relationships between the media and the company in question.

If governments are also considered advertisers, then the study by Di Tella and Franceschelli, introduced in Section 10.1, also serves as an example of advertiser influence on individual news content. Their findings show that newspapers receiving more government advertising were less likely to report on government corruption.

Finally, Strömberg's (2004) theoretical prediction[8]—that media outlets would exhibit bias toward the preferences of consumers valued by their advertisers—was empirically confirmed by Valentino Larcinese (2007). In his study of the UK media landscape, Larcinese found that certain outlets tended to publish more stories that appealed to audiences deemed more valuable by advertisers.

10.3 THE SUPPLY AND DEMAND OF MEDIA CAPTURE

The likelihood and intensity of media capture depend on the conditions faced by both the capturers and the media being targeted. In other words, the scope and nature of media capture can be understood through the lens of its supply and demand of capture. The demand for media capture refers to the capturers'—such as political forces, governments, or interest groups—motivation to engage in media capture. On the other hand, the supply of capture refers to the willingness of media outlets to alter their content to align with the capturers' intentions. The stronger the capturers' motivation or the greater the media's willingness to comply, the more pervasive media capture becomes.

For example, when news media outlets generate sufficient advertising revenue in the media market, their need to comply with capture decreases, thereby reducing the supply of capture. Conversely, when revenues from the news consumer market decline, more media outlets may become willing to alter their content even for relatively small rewards, increasing the supply of capture. Similarly, even an authoritarian leader who typically engages in media capture may find their motivation—the demand for capture—diminished if they need objective reporting through the media to assess policy performance or bureaucratic efficiency.

Of course, the structural factors that significantly influence the scale of supply and demand for media capture are the competition among news media and the transaction costs involved in capture deals. As these factors have been discussed extensively in other parts of this book, this section focuses on studies exploring other factors beyond competition and transaction costs.

[8] See Subsection 9.3.2.

10.3.1 THE IMPACT OF ADVERTISING REVENUE ON THE SUPPLY OF POLITICAL MEDIA CAPTURE

Advertising revenue for news media exhibits a dual nature, much like Dr. Jekyll and Mr. Hyde. The darker side, where advertising distorts news coverage, was discussed in Section 10.2. In this section, we explore the positive aspect: the role of advertising revenue in fostering and sustaining politically independent media. Specifically, advertising revenue can reduce the willingness of media outlets to succumb to capture.

This effect was first highlighted by communication scholars such as Gerald Baldasty and Richard Kaplan, who explained the reduction in partisan bias in 19th-century newspapers. These scholars attributed the decline in partisanship and the rise of objective reporting in US newspapers to economic factors, particularly the emergence of inexpensive newspapers. In Baldasty's (1992) book, *The Commercialization of News in the Nineteenth Century*, Baldasty analyzed this transition, while Kaplan (2002) provided similar insights in his 2002 publication, *Politics and the American Press*.

According to Kaplan, in the 1860s and early 1870s, US newspapers fiercely competed for readers, who were often strongly affiliated with political parties. During this period, partisan marketing strategies were more effective than politically neutral approaches for maximizing readership. However, the introduction of inexpensive newspapers in the 1870s began attracting a working-class readership that had been largely ignored by partisan newspapers. As a result, existing newspapers also began to moderate their partisanship after the 1880s, entering into competition to attract new readers who were less politically aligned.

A more systematic explanation comes from economists who identified advertising revenue as a direct cause of reduced political bias. Gentzkow, Glaeser, and Goldin (2006) argued that technological advancements in printing and changes in the newspaper business model during the late 19th and early 20th centuries allowed US newspapers to derive substantial revenue from advertising. This increased revenue enabled newspapers to free themselves economically from partisan groups and politically biased readers.[9]

Maria Petrova (2011) offered a similar perspective in her study of the revenue structures and political bias of US newspapers in the 1880s. She found that the high profitability of advertising significantly contributed to the emergence of politically independent newspapers. According to Petrova, when advertising rates were high, new politically independent newspapers were more likely to emerge, and existing partisan newspapers were more likely to distance themselves from their political affiliations.

While this perspective aligns with the earlier viewpoints as two sides of the same coin, there is also an analysis suggesting that a contraction in the advertising market exacerbates partisanship in news media. According to Julia Cagé (2020), France's

[9] Gentzkow, Glaeser, and Goldin (2006) argued that the lower the marginal production costs and the higher the marginal advertising revenues, the more independent the media would become. Other aspects of this study are discussed in Sections 4.4.2 and 8.4.

Fourth Republic (1946–58) was the period immediately after World War II, marked by the decline of industry and a stagnating advertising market. During this time, most regional newspapers in France became increasingly aligned with political parties, displaying greater partisanship than before. Cagé attributes this trend to the decline in advertising revenue, which heightened newspapers' political bias.

These empirical findings by economists collectively demonstrate that the advent and growth of advertising revenue were pivotal in enabling news media to report on politically sensitive issues more objectively and accurately after the late 19th century.[10] However, as discussed in Section 10.2, when advertising becomes disproportionately dominant in the revenue mix of news media, eclipsing the importance of consumer revenue, commercial bias driven by advertisers can once again threaten the objectivity and accuracy of news reporting.

10.3.2 CAN EVEN DICTATORS REDUCE MEDIA CAPTURE?

Even under authoritarian regimes, there are instances where press freedom is intentionally allowed, effectively reducing media capture. Several economists have offered explanations for this phenomenon. According to Russian economists Egorov, Guriev, and Sonin (2009), while dictators generally dislike a free press, it is not uncommon for certain totalitarian states to allow news media a degree of freedom. This is because even dictators require objective and independent evaluations of their policies, which free news media can provide. Such information helps dictators oversee bureaucrats effectively and achieve better policy outcomes. Failing to manage bureaucrats and implement effective policies could ultimately threaten their hold on power.

So, what factors lead a dictator to allow a certain level of press freedom? Egorov et al. (2009) examined the role of natural resource endowments. They hypothesized that in resource-rich countries, where economic prosperity is easier to achieve, dictators find it easier to maintain power, and their incentive to maximize bureaucratic performance is lower. Consequently, in such scenarios, dictators have less need for objective information from the press about bureaucratic performance, resulting in little motivation to relax media capture. Based on this hypothesis, the economists predicted an inverse relationship between abundant natural resources and press freedom. In other words, the more resource-rich a country governed by a dictator, the more tightly controlled the press tends to be. This hypothesis was consistent with their analysis of panel data from 1993 to 2007.

In summary, even in authoritarian states, dictators tend to ease media capture to evaluate and motivate bureaucrats. However, when the country is already economically prosperous, reducing the need for bureaucratic performance assessments, media capture becomes more entrenched.[11]

---

[10] Theoretical studies suggesting that advertising revenue enhances the political independence of news media are discussed in Section 9.3.1.

[11] In authoritarian regimes, honest press reporting can occasionally discourage desirable behavior among politicians, as suggested by some political scientists. Malesky et al. (2012) conducted an

[More to Explore] Dictators' Chief Motivation for Media Capture: Curbing Collective Action

What type of news is most likely to be captured by a dictator? While this topic has received little attention from economists so far, political scientists have produced some intriguing findings.

King, Pan, and Roberts (2013, 2014) provide significant insights into this question and are worth highlighting. Their two papers on content censorship by Chinese authorities have received significant attention, with over 4400 citations in academic literature to date. In their first study, the researchers collected millions of posts from approximately 1400 social media platforms across China before the government could censor them. They then identified and analyzed the posts that were removed by Chinese authorities. The findings revealed that the posts most likely to be deleted were not those critical of the state, its leaders, or its policies. Instead, posts that had the potential to incite collective action were the primary targets of censorship. This suggests that the Chinese government's top priority in media capture is to silence voices that could lead to collective action. In their second study, the researchers conducted field experiments and observed similar patterns. Messages with the potential to spark collective action were more likely to be censored than those that merely criticized the regime.[12]

The scholars' conclusion that the Chinese government's primary focus is on content related to collective action aligns with broader research suggesting that the driving motivation behind media capture by ruling powers is the stability of the regime. For example, political scientists Von Doepp and Young (2013) studied changes in press freedom across 23 African countries and found that media control intensifies when political power faces significant threats or requires extraordinary efforts to consolidate. They cited situations such as mass protests, coup attempts, or constitutional amendments aimed at expanding power as examples of circumstances where media control increases.

10.4 THE IMPACT OF MEDIA CAPTURE

Media capture undermines the proper functioning of democracy and benefits those who control the media through political or economic power. Its consequences, however, extend far beyond this. Economic research shows that captured media can foster greater corruption, widen economic inequality, promote exclusionary nationalism,

experiment in Vietnam, an authoritarian regime, where an online news outlet reported on the legislative activities of randomly selected parliamentary members. The results showed that legislators elected in regions with high internet penetration were less likely to engage in legislative activities that could embarrass regime leaders. However, these findings align with the results of Egorov et al. (2009) in that free press coverage keeps bureaucrats and elected politicians mindful of the dictator.

[12] For instance, during the 2023 Hangzhou Asian Games held in China, a photograph capturing an emotional embrace between the gold and silver medalists in the women's 100m hurdles event was reported by state media. It was later reported by overseas media that the image disappeared from major domestic outlets, as the bib numbers worn by the athletes could be associated with historically sensitive collective events.

and even incite violence and genocide. The following sections examine how captured media reshape society and influence human behavior, drawing on empirical findings by economists across four domains: "Inferior Societies," "Hatred and Violence," "Increasing Wealth Inequality," and "More Corruption."

10.4.1 INFERIOR SOCIETIES

Djankov et al. (2003) examined the negative global consequences of government ownership of the media. They analyzed patterns of media ownership in 97 countries worldwide and found that in most countries, the largest media outlets were not owned in a dispersed or competitive manner but rather by the state or by a small number of powerful families.

To evaluate the implications of this concentration, the authors tested two competing theories: the public interest theory, which posits that government ownership corrects market failures, and the public choice theory, which argues that state ownership infringes upon political and economic freedoms. The findings largely supported the latter. Government ownership of media was consistently associated with lower levels of press freedom and fewer political and economic rights.

More specifically, countries that were poorer, more autocratic, less educated, and more interventionist in economic affairs tended to have greater levels of government media ownership. These same countries also exhibited lower levels of press freedom, weaker political rights, poorer governance, underdeveloped capital markets, and inferior public health systems. The negative correlation between government media ownership and citizens' freedoms was particularly strong when the state-owned media were newspapers, rather than television broadcasters. Djankov and his co-authors noted that although these correlations do not prove direct causality, there is no empirical support for the claim that state ownership of media produces net social benefits.[13]

10.4.2 HATRED AND VIOLENCE

In Rwanda, long-standing ethnic conflict between the Hutu and Tutsi groups culminated in the 1994 genocide, during which extremist Hutu militias killed an estimated 500,000 to 800,000 Tutsi civilians and moderate Hutus over the course of 100 days. The violence was sparked by the assassination of the Hutu president in April 1994. The radio station RTLM,[14] under the control of Hutu extremists, brazenly incited hatred and violence, playing a pivotal role in fueling the genocide.

---

[13] Despite the empirical findings of Djankov et al., as discussed throughout this book, scholars widely agree that the BBC in the United Kingdom serves as a rare example of a public broadcaster that effectively addresses market failures. See Sections 7.1.1 and 9.4.3 on information supply and media diversity.

[14] RTLM was in operation from July 8, 1993, to July 31, 1994, and became infamous for inciting attacks and genocide against the Tutsi population during the Rwandan Genocide from April to July 1994. Its French name, "Radio Télévision Libre des Mille Collines," refers to Rwanda as the land of a thousand hills (mille collines).

> *"I remember RTLM broadcasting songs conveying hatred and demonising the Tutsi. The songs would openly call for our extermination."*
>
> **(Swart, 2020, June 7)**

David Yanagizawa-Drott (2014), an economist, studied the role of RTLM during the genocide. His analysis focused on the effect of a captured mass media outlet in promoting ethnic hatred and violence. Using village-level data on radio reception and incidents of violence, he found that in areas where RTLM could be heard, random acts of violence against Tutsis increased by 65%, and organized attacks rose by 77%. RTLM was estimated to be responsible for motivating approximately 9.9% of the perpetrators who were later prosecuted for genocide (about 51,000 individuals). Assuming a proportional relationship between the number of perpetrators and the number of victims, this implies that RTLM may have incited the killing of around 50,000 people. Moreover, Yanagizawa-Drott suggested that RTLM likely influenced not only civilians but also regular army units and militias. However, independent and politically uncaptured media outlets may have reduced RTLM's propaganda effects. In areas with higher literacy, independent newspapers helped counter the incitement of hate.

There is also evidence that captured media propaganda may sometimes backfire. As discussed in Section 10.1, Adena et al. (2015) found that Nazi-controlled radio broadcasting, which promoted anti-Semitic hatred after Hitler's regime consolidated power, was effective in areas with a historical predisposition toward anti-Semitism. But in areas less predisposed to such views, the propaganda had adverse effects.

In another example, DellaVigna et al. (2014) studied the effects of exposure to hostile foreign media in Croatia during the 2000s. Even though the Serbian state radio often broadcast hostile content about Croatians, many Croatians still tuned in. Ironically, the result was increased support for extreme Croatian nationalist parties, suggesting that exposure to biased or hostile media can provoke stronger nationalist reactions in targeted populations.

10.4.3 INCREASING WEALTH INEQUALITY

Petrova (2008) theorized that the wealthy segments of society may attempt to capture the media to protect their economic interests, and that such media capture can exacerbate wealth inequality. This theory was previously discussed in Section 9.1.3 (Economic Power Concentration and Media Capture). In the same study, Petrova also provided empirical evidence supporting this hypothesis.

Petrova analyzed data from 102 countries spanning from 1994 to 2003, using Freedom House's Press Freedom Index,[15] the World Income Inequality Database[16]

[15] Freedom House's Press Freedom Index scores countries from 0 (complete press freedom) to 100 (complete absence of press freedom), based on three factors: the legal environment, the political environment (e.g., editorial independence, censorship, and freedom of reporting), and the economic environment (e.g., ownership structure and state subsidies).

[16] https://www.wider.unu.edu/project/wiid-%E2%80%93-world-income-inequality-database.

compiled by the United Nations University, and additional variables such as political institutions and media access. Petrova's analysis revealed a clear inverse correlation between levels of press freedom and levels of economic inequality, as measured by the Gini coefficient. In other words, countries with higher levels of economic inequality tended to have lower levels of press freedom. Notably, this pattern was more pronounced in democratic regimes than in authoritarian ones.

Petrova argued that in democratic societies, wealthy elites are more likely to capture media outlets to influence public opinion and electoral outcomes, thereby preventing the adoption of redistributive policies such as higher taxes and increased public investment. Conversely, countries with higher levels of press freedom tended to have greater public spending on health and education—an indication that less media capture by wealthy elites enabled stronger redistributive policies.

10.4.4 MORE CORRUPTION

There is also research examining the correlation between media freedom and levels of corruption. Because reduced media capture tends to coincide with greater press freedom, this research can also be interpreted as exploring the relationship between media capture and corruption.

Swiss economists Brunetti and Weder (2003) found that societies with freer media tend to exhibit lower levels of corruption. Their empirical study showed a strong correlation between higher press freedom and lower corruption levels across many countries, and even suggested a causal relationship.

In addition, Brunetti and Weder estimated how corruption levels might change if countries with limited media freedom were to improve to the level of Norway, which is known for having one of the freest media environments in the world. The results were interesting: if Indonesia, the Russian Federation, and Nigeria improved their press freedom to Norwegian levels, their corruption levels were projected to fall to those of Singapore, the Slovak Republic, and Belgium, respectively.[17]

References

Adena, M., Enikolopov, R., Petrova, M., Santarosa, V., Zhuravskaya, E., 2015. Radio and the rise of the Nazis in prewar Germany. The Quarterly Journal of Economics 130 (4), 1885–1939. https://doi.org/10.1093/qje/qjv030.

Bagdikian, B., 1983. The Media Monopoly, 1st ed. Beacon Press, Boston.

Bagdikian, B., 2004. The New Media Monopoly. Beacon Press, Boston.

[17] Brunetti and Weder used data from Freedom House's Press Freedom Index (1996–99) for 145 countries and the International Country Risk Guide (ICRG) corruption ratings (1994–98) for 128 countries. The ICRG corruption index ranges from 0 to 6, with lower scores indicating higher levels of corruption, such as the expectation of bribes from high-level officials or pervasive illegal monetary demands.

Baldasty, G.J., 1992. The Commercialization of News in the Nineteenth Century. University of Wisconsin Press.

Bennett, P., Naím, M., 2015. 21st-century censorship. Columbia Journalism Review 53 (1), 14.

Blasco, A., Sobbrio, F., 2012. Competition and commercial media bias. Telecommunications Policy 36 (5), 434–447. https://doi.org/10.1016/j.telpol.2011.11.021.

Boykoff, M.T., 2007. Flogging a dead norm? Newspaper coverage of anthropogenic climate change in the United States and United Kingdom from 2003 to 2006. Area 39 (4), 470–481. https://doi.org/10.1111/j.1475-4762.2007.00769.x.

Boykoff, M.T., Boykoff, J.M., 2004. Balance as bias: global warming and the US prestige press. Global Environmental Change 14 (2), 125–136. https://doi.org/10.1016/j.gloenvcha.2003.10.001.

Brunetti, A., Weder, B., 2003. A free press is bad news for corruption. Journal of Public Economics 87 (7–8), 1801–1824. https://doi.org/10.1016/s0047-2727(01)00186-4.

Cagé, J., 2020. Media competition, information provision and political participation: evidence from French local newspapers and elections, 1944–2014. Journal of Public Economics 185.

DellaVigna, S., Enikolopov, R., Mironova, V., Petrova, M., Zhuravskaya, E., 2014. Cross-border media and nationalism: evidence from Serbian radio in Croatia. American Economic Journal: Applied Economics 6 (3), 103–132. https://doi.org/10.1257/app.6.3.103.

Di Tella, R., Franceschelli, I., 2011. Government advertising and media coverage of corruption scandals. American Economic Journal: Applied Economics 3 (4), 119–151. https://doi.org/10.1257/app.3.4.119.

Djankov, S., McLiesh, C., Nenova, T., Shleifer, A., 2003. Who owns the media? The Journal of Law and Economics 46 (2), 341–382. https://doi.org/10.1086/377116.

Durante, R., Knight, B., 2012. Partisan control, media bias, and viewer responses: evidence from Berlusconi's Italy. Journal of the European Economic Association 10 (3), 451–481.

Dyer, O., 2004. Journal rejects article after objections from marketing department. BMJ (Clinical Research Edition) 328 (7434), 244. https://doi.org/10.1136/bmj.328.7434.244-b.

Egorov, G., Guriev, S., Sonin, K., 2009. Why resource-poor dictators allow freer media: a theory and evidence from panel data. American Political Science Review 103 (4), 645–668. https://doi.org/10.1017/s0003055409990219.

Ellman, M., Germano, F., 2009. What do the papers sell? A model of advertising and media bias. The Economic Journal 119 (537), 680–704. https://doi.org/10.1111/j.1468-0297.2009.02218.x.

Enikolopov, R., Petrova, M., Zhuravskaya, E., 2011. Media and political persuasion: evidence from Russia. American Economic Review 101 (7), 3253–3285. https://doi.org/10.1257/aer.101.7.3253.

Enikolopov, R., Petrova, M., 2015. Media capture. In: Anderson, S.P., Waldfogel, J., Strömberg, D. (Eds.), Handbook of Media Economics, Vol. 1. Elsevier, pp. 687–700. https://doi.org/10.1016/b978-0-444-63685-0.00017-6.

Finkel, A., 2015. Captured News Media: The Case of Turkey. Center for International Media Assistance Report.

Fletcher, R.H., 2003. Adverts in medical journals: caveat lector. Lancet 361 (9351), 10–11. Available from: http://www.journals.elsevier.com/the-lancet/. https://doi.org/10.1016/S0140-6736(03)12185-X.

Freedom House, 2017. Freedom of the press 2017: press freedom's dark horizon. Retrieved from: https://freedomhouse.org/sites/default/files/2020-02/FOTP_2017_booklet_FINAL_April28_1.pdf.

Fugh-Berman, A., Alladin, K., Chow, J., 2006. Advertising in medical journals: should current practices change? PLoS Medicine 3 (6), e130. 1549–1676. https://doi.org/10.1371/journal.pmed.0030130.

Gambaro, M., Puglisi, R., 2015. What do ads buy? Daily coverage of listed companies on the Italian press. European Journal of Political Economy 39, 41–57. https://doi.org/10.1016/j.ejpoleco.2015.03.008.

Gans, H.J., 1979. Deciding What's News: A Study of CBS Evening News, NBC Nightly News, Newsweek, and Time. Pantheon Books, New York.

Gentzkow, M., Petek, N., Shapiro, J.M., Sinkinson, M., 2015. Do newspapers serve the state? Incumbent party influence on the US press, 1869–1928. Journal of the European Economic Association 13 (1), 29–61. Available from: http://onlinelibrary.wiley.com/journal/10.1111/(ISSN)1542-4774. https://doi.org/10.1111/jeea.12119.

Gentzkow, M., Glaeser, E.L., Goldin, C., 2006. The rise of the fourth estate: how newspapers became informative and why it mattered. In: Glaeser, E.L., Goldin, C. (Eds.), Corruption and Reform: Lessons From America's Economic History. University of Chicago Press, pp. 187–230.

Hasty, J., 2005. The Press and Political Culture in Ghana. Indiana University Press. https://doi.org/10.2979/3421.0.

Kaplan, R., 2002. Politics and the American Press: The Rise of Objectivity, 1865–1920. Cambridge University Press.

Kennedy, G.E., Bero, L.A., 1999. Print media coverage of research on passive smoking. Tobacco Control 8 (3), 254–260. https://doi.org/10.1136/tc.8.3.254.

King, G., Pan, J., Roberts, M.E., 2013. How censorship in China allows government criticism but silences collective expression. American Political Science Review 107 (2), 326–343. https://doi.org/10.1017/S0003055413000014.

King, G., Pan, J., Roberts, M.E., 2014. Reverse-engineering censorship in China: randomized experimentation and participant observation. Science 345 (6199), https://doi.org/10.1126/science.1251722.

Larcinese, V., 2007. The instrumental voter goes to the newsagent. Journal of Theoretical Politics 19 (3), 249–276.

Malesky, E., Schuler, P., Tran, A., 2012. The adverse effects of sunshine: a field experiment on legislative transparency in an authoritarian assembly. American Political Science Review 106 (4), 762–786.

McMillan, J., Zoido, P., 2004. How to subvert democracy: Montesinos in Peru. Journal of Economic Perspectives 18 (4), 69–92. https://doi.org/10.1257/0895330042632690.

McNamara, P., 2009. Sedition Act of 1798. Available from: https://www.mtsu.edu/first-amendment/article/1238/sedition-act-of-1798.

Nelson, M.M., 2017. What is to be done? Options for combating the menace of media capture. In: Schiffrin, A. (Ed.). In the Service of Power: Media Capture and the Threat to Democracy. Center for International Media Assistance, 143–160.

Nielsen, R.K., 2017. Media capture in the digital age. In: Schiffrin, A. (Ed.), In the Service of Power: Media Capture and the Threat to Democracy. Center for International Media Assistance, pp. 33–42.

Oreskes, N., 2004. The scientific consensus on climate change. Science 306 (5702) 1686. https://doi.org/10.1126/science.1103618.

Oreskes, N., Conway, E.M., 2011. Merchants of Doubt: How a Handful of Scientists Obscured the Truth on Issues From Tobacco Smoke to Global Warming. Bloomsbury Press, New York.

Petrova, M., 2008. Inequality and media capture. Journal of Public Economics 92 (1–2), 183–212. https://doi.org/10.1016/j.jpubeco.2007.04.004.
Petrova, M., 2011. Newspapers and parties: how advertising revenues created an independent press. American Political Science Review 105 (4), 790–808. https://doi.org/10.1017/s0003055411000360.
Qian, N., Yanagizawa-Drott, D., 2017. Government distortion in independently owned media: evidence from U.S. news coverage of human rights. Journal of the European Economic Association 15 (2), 463–499. https://doi.org/10.1093/jeea/jvx007.
Reuter, J., Zitzewitz, E., 2006. Do ads influence editors? Advertising and bias in the financial media. The Quarterly Journal of Economics 121 (1), 197–227. https://doi.org/10.1093/qje/121.1.197.
Rinallo, D., Basuroy, S., 2009. Does advertising spending influence media coverage of the advertiser? Journal of Marketing 73 (6), 33–46. https://doi.org/10.1509/jmkg.73.6.33.
Stanig, P., 2015. Regulation of speech and media coverage of corruption: an empirical analysis of the Mexican press. American Journal of Political Science 59 (1), 175–193. https://doi.org/10.1111/ajps.12110.
Starr, P., 2004. The Creation of the Media: Political Origins of Modern Communications. Basic Books, New York.
Strömberg, D., 2004. Mass media competition, political competition, and public policy. The Review of Economic Studies 71 (1), 265–284. https://doi.org/10.1111/0034-6527.00284.
Swart, M., 2020. June 7. 'Music to Kill To': Rwandan Genocide Survivors Remember RTLM. Al Jazeera. Available from: https://www.aljazeera.com/features/2020/6/7/music-to-kill-to-rwandan-genocide-survivors-remember-rtlm.
Von Doepp, P., Young, D.J., 2013. Assaults on the fourth estate: explaining media harassment in Africa. Journal of Politics 75 (1), 36–51. https://doi.org/10.1017/S0022381612000850.
Warner, K.E., Goldenhar, L.M., McLaughlin, C.G., 1992. Cigarette advertising and magazine coverage of the hazards of smoking: a statistical analysis. New England Journal of Medicine 326 (5), 305–309. https://doi.org/10.1056/NEJM199201303260505.
Wilkes, M.S., Kravitz, R.L., 1995. Policies, practices, and attitudes of North American medical journal editors. Journal of General Internal Medicine 10 (8), 443–450. https://doi.org/10.1007/BF02599916.
Yanagizawa-Drott, D., 2014. Propaganda and conflict: evidence from the Rwandan genocide. The Quarterly Journal of Economics 129 (4), 1947–1994. https://doi.org/10.1093/qje/qju020.

CHAPTER

The Digital Age and News Media 11

Chapter Outline

The historical development of the media industry and its gradual move from being primarily dominated by media operated to exercise power to being dominated by media operated to make a profit. In the twentieth century, news was a big and profitable business. In the twenty-first century, it will be a smaller and less profitable business, in large part because of the rise of digital media. In that sense, we may live in the best of times and the worst of times.[1]

—Rasmus K. Nielsen.

[1] Nielsen (2017), pp. 37, 39, 40.

The Economics of News Media. DOI: http://dx.doi.org/10.1016/B978-0-443-45044-0.00010-6

With the advent of the digital age, the scope and subject matter of the political economy of news media have expanded significantly. The boundaries between this field and adjacent disciplines, such as the economics of information[2] and network economics[3] have become increasingly difficult to delineate, given the growing areas of overlap. This is because the media industry lies at the heart of the technological innovations that define the Fourth Industrial Revolution.

In the digital age, both the production and consumption of news content differ markedly from their analog-era counterparts. Traditional perspectives and concepts regarding the production and consumption of news are also being redefined. Consequently, scholars are now compelled to reassess the validity of the achievements made by the political economy of news media during the analog era. It is a situation in which the challenges of the analog period have not yet been fully resolved, while new challenges of the digital era must be addressed.

Although studies on the news market and news media grounded in digital technology and media have become more prevalent, the history of this field remains relatively short. In fact, it is no exaggeration to say that some lines of inquiry have only just begun. As a result, there exists a substantial body of work whose academic validity has not yet been sufficiently tested. In short, the political economy of news media in the digital era is still in the process of forming its scholarly contours.

Currently, the key questions that economists have sought to answer over the past two decades concerning the digital-era news market and media can largely be summarized into the following four areas:

First, what changes have digital media and infrastructure brought to the sustainability and function of traditional media?

Second, is the fierce competition among news providers in the digital realm leading us toward a "marketplace of truth," or is it luring us into an "echo chamber of confirmation bias?"

Third, has the unprecedented abundance of information enriched our lives? To what extent have the internet and social media altered human behavior?

Fourth, how will Artificial Intelligence (AI) and algorithms—which have emerged as central topics in the production and consumption of information—affect the news media industry and market?

This chapter introduces the perspectives of economists on these questions. As mentioned earlier, however, many of these studies are relatively recent, and some of the views discussed here have not yet undergone sufficient peer evaluation within the academic community.

Moreover, the news media industry and news market continue to evolve rapidly. Facebook, once hailed as the "emperor of social media," has experienced stagnation,

---

[2] This refers to a branch of economics that analyzes the value and effects of information. It particularly focuses on outcomes and implications arising from asymmetrical information between individuals. Notable scholars in this field include Nobel laureates George Akerlof and Joseph Stiglitz.

[3] This discipline studies network effects, which means that the value or utility a user derives from a good or service increases with the number of users.

while a new platform—the Metaverse—rose to prominence only to seemingly fall out of favor within a few years. Platforms often referred to as "recommendation media," such as YouTube, Instagram, and TikTok, have each seen explosive growth in succession. However, by the time this book is published and reaches its readers—or even before a revised edition appears—these too may have become relics of the past. This breathless pace of change suggests that attempts to understand the news media and market of the digital age through academic inquiry may remain unsatisfactory for some time to come.

11.1 THE EMERGENCE OF DIGITAL MEDIA AND THE CRISIS OF LEGACY MEDIA

With the advent of the digital age came a profound crisis for traditional media. Among traditional outlets, those with relatively weaker competitiveness have already faded into history, while others continue to teeter on the brink of survival even today. In particular, newspaper media, long considered the stronghold of traditional news media, began losing ground to broadcast media in the latter half of the last century, and even more so since the emergence of digital media. Because the crisis of traditional media stems from the rise of digital infrastructure, economic reasoning and principles are essential to understanding this crisis and forecasting the future.

The top priority for traditional media companies in crisis is invariably the same: to find a new revenue model suitable for the digital era. However, their strategic responses vary. For example, *The New York Times*, *The Wall Street Journal*, and some traditional media outlets in Europe and Asia offer either all or part of their digital content behind a paywall. In contrast, most other newspapers still provide all their digital content for free. Yet it remains difficult to determine which approach is more effective.

The effectiveness of paid versus free content models varies widely depending on multiple factors, such as the characteristics and size of each newspaper's readership, the current and potential quality of its content, and the particular conditions of the news market in each country or region. In comparing and selecting among these divergent business strategies, economic thinking is invariably helpful.

Consider, for example, the introduction of paywalls for digital content from an economic perspective. With few exceptions, shifting from a free subscription model to a paid subscription model is accompanied by an increase in revenue per unit and a decrease in overall demand. A media company contemplating digital content monetization must assess how best to maximize profits in both the short and long term while accounting for these two effects.

But doing so is easier said than done. Even if revenue rises with monetization, if the paid content is not of sufficient quality to merit payment, any increase in revenue may be marginal while demand sharply declines. A drop in demand can lead to a simultaneous decline in both advertising revenue and public influence. Also, it is difficult to choose which content to place behind a paywall and set a price that maximizes revenue.

Despite these challenges, news media executives and journalists—especially those in the newspaper industry—are increasingly viewing revenues from digital subscriptions as more important than digital advertising or print subscriptions.[4] This shift appears to reflect a growing recognition that offering news content for free is not a sustainable business model. However, launching a paywall strategy without careful planning is even more reckless—akin to setting out on a journey with no destination.

Even if paywall strategies succeed in the future, a crucial point remains. As seen earlier in Sections 9.1.3 (Advertisers Mitigating Media's Political Bias) and 10.3.1 (The Impact of Advertising Revenue on the Supply of Political Media Capture), an increase in subscription revenue coupled with a decline in advertising revenue can reinforce political bias. Once dependence on subscription revenue exceeds a certain threshold, commercial bias rooted in advertiser influence may decline—but political bias may once again intensify. The recent proliferation of small YouTube channels that rely on subscriptions rather than advertising and exhibit strong partisan leanings serves as a telling illustration of this economic insight. In this way, understanding the crisis of traditional news media—and seeking viable paths forward—requires the perspective of the political economy of news media and the accumulated insights it has produced more than ever before.

11.1.1 ONLINE AND OFFLINE MEDIA AS SUBSTITUTES

There is one frequent and fundamental question that has been asked for decades: Will print newspapers—the oldest form of traditional media—eventually disappear? (The same question can be posed to the form of journalism that has been built upon print newspapers.) This question has long been the subject of debate among frontline journalists, newspaper executives, and journalism scholars. On one side, some predicted that print newspapers were "destined to vanish," while others argued that they would "still manage to survive."

In 2007, at the height of such debates within the field of journalism and media studies, a paper by an economist was published in *The American Economic Review*, the most prestigious journal in the discipline, seemingly settling the matter. Gentzkow (2007) analyzed whether online news media and traditional print newspapers are substitutes or complements from the perspective of news consumers.

His findings indicated that online and offline news products are substitutes: when demand increases for one, it decreases for the other. Surprisingly, however,

[4] In December 2021, the Reuters Institute for Journalism surveyed 246 media executives—including CEOs, editors-in-chief, and senior managers—from 52 countries about which digital revenue sources they considered most important (multiple responses allowed). Among the 217 respondents, 79% cited subscriptions, while 73% and 59% cited display and native advertising, respectively. Compared to the same survey conducted one year earlier, the importance of subscriptions had increased, while the latter two declined by 8 and 16 percentage points respectively (Newman, 2022).

Gentzkow's study received little attention from newspaper executives or journalists at the time. Many in journalism and media studies circles still assumed that print newspapers would not disappear. In fact, a substantial number of people expected that online and offline media would complement each other. This vague expectation—that digital and print media could be mutually reinforcing—was one reason many newspapers began offering their content online for free at the turn of the century. Yet Gentzkow's study demonstrated that such hopes were unfounded.

In his research, Gentzkow analyzed subscriber and user data, revenue, and cost performance for major newspapers in Washington, D.C. between March 2000 and February 2003. Based on this analysis, he explained that although leading newspapers and their online content may have appeared to be strongly complementary on the surface, in reality, online and offline news products were substitutes. Specifically, Gentzkow estimated that "in the Washington, D.C. market, online news reduced print newspaper readership by 27,000 per day and annual profits for newspapers by $5.5 million."

Importantly, he emphasized that "free online news provides substantial benefits to consumers," and "charging for online content would likely not have substantially increased newspaper profits." In short, the more digital online news media were embraced by news consumers, the more the position of traditional print newspapers eroded, and the co-prosperity of online news and print newspapers was not a viable future. When Gentzkow published this study, the crisis in the newspaper industry had not yet become as severe as it is today. But from the economist's point of view, the decline of print newspapers was inevitable as digital news consumption increased.[5]

Furthermore, Gentzkow also concluded that paywalls for digital content were unlikely to boost the profitability of news media significantly. His prediction was indirectly validated in the years that followed, as many news media outlets hesitated or failed to adopt digital subscription strategies. However, it remains uncertain whether Gentzkow's predictions—based on data from the early 2000s—still hold more than 20 years later. Since then, the structure and environment of the news market have changed, and traditional news media now face diverse circumstances. These factors make it difficult to generalize about the success or failure of digital content monetization today.

Nonetheless, one thing remains clear: traditional media companies that rush into paywall strategies either out of vague ideological conviction or by blindly mimicking others are likely to pay a heavy price—an even steeper decline.

[5] Gentzkow (2014) later suggested in an unpublished paper that the two could be complementary under certain conditions. In addition, non-economist researchers have pointed to similar possibilities in media usage behavior (Taneja et al., 2012; Pew Research Center, 2016).

[More to Explore] Mitigating Bias in Surviving Newspapers

The advent of the digital age has led to the downfall of many traditional news media outlets—especially numerous print newspapers. Among the internationally recognized daily newspapers, *The Christian Science Monitor* in the United States ceased daily publication in March 2009 due to financial difficulties and was subsequently relaunched as a weekly magazine. Similarly, the *International Herald Tribune*, which had operated as the sister daily of *The New York Times*, ceased publication in 2013. In fact, since the 1990s, a large number of local newspapers in the United States have closed their doors. According to one study, between 2004 and 2018, one out of every five newspapers in the United States disappeared (Abernathy, 2018). This raises an important question: What effect did the closure of competing newspapers have on the political bias of those that remained?

Agirdas (2015) examined 99 newspapers from 1990 to 2009, focusing on their reporting bias in coverage of unemployment—an issue generally unfavorable to the party in power. The findings revealed that in markets where newspaper competition existed, Republican-leaning newspapers reported unemployment news 17.4% more frequently when the Democratic Party was in power than when the Republican Party held office. Conversely, Democratic-leaning newspapers reported such news approximately 12.8% more often when Republicans were in office than when Democrats were. However, after competing newspapers shut down, these figures dropped sharply—to 3.5% and 1.1%, respectively. In other words, the closure of competing newspapers significantly mitigated political bias. Agirdas explained this phenomenon by suggesting that surviving newspapers moderated their political slant in an effort to attract readers who had previously subscribed to the now-defunct competitors.

11.1.2 THE DECLINE IN THE QUALITY OF LEGACY MEDIA

The superior advertising effectiveness of online media and its chain reaction

Some economists have argued that the profitability of offline media has deteriorated due to the superior advertising effectiveness of online media. Bergemann and Bonatti (2011) focused on the strong targeting capabilities of online media in reaching media consumers and studied how online and offline media compete in the news market.

According to their findings, the superior ad targeting of online media—compared to that of offline media—results in higher advertising effectiveness. Furthermore, as more consumers gravitate toward online media, advertiser demand for online platforms with strong targeting capabilities increases even more. If offline media attempt to compensate for declining ad revenue by raising advertising prices, this leads to an even greater decline in demand, resulting in lower, not higher, revenues (this is a predictable outcome of raising prices for ads with declining effectiveness). In this way, the superior targeting ability of online advertising further undermines the profitability of offline media, which are already losing audiences to digital platforms.

But does the decline in advertising revenue for offline media merely worsen their financial conditions? Angelucci and Cagé (2019) demonstrated, both theoretically and empirically, that the fall in advertising revenue experienced by traditional newspaper media following the advent of the internet also led to a decline in news quality. The two scholars proposed a theoretical model in which a decline in advertising revenue leads to a drop in content quality, lower newspaper prices, and changes in readership composition. This model was based on the intuitive assumption that newspapers, which earn income from both sales and advertising, determine the size of their newsrooms (i.e., their news production workforce) based on changes in revenue.

They tested this hypothesis using data from the French daily newspaper industry between 1960 and 1974—a period during which television broadcasting, then considered "new media," was introduced in France along with television advertising. Their analysis showed that the introduction of TV advertising led to a reduction in advertising revenue for national general-interest newspapers. As ad revenue fell, the number of journalists employed by these newspapers sharply declined. However, the amount of news content published remained the same. Because a smaller number of journalists produced the same volume of content, the quality of the news inevitably declined. Angelucci and Cagé inferred that, in response to falling ad revenues triggered by the rise of new media (television), newspapers in France either reduced their content quality or cut back on the production of "hard news" to reduce costs.[6]

This behavior by newspapers at the time offers valuable insights into today's media landscape, where digital platforms have come to dominate the advertising market. The more advertising revenue declines for traditional media, the weaker their incentives become to invest in high-quality content. In fact, traditional news media today often respond to declining ad revenues either by reducing the size of their newsrooms[7] or by increasing the volume of news produced—further confirming the real-world applicability of the theory and empirical findings presented by Angelucci and Cagé.

The paradox of competition in the digital age

As is widely acknowledged, the digital age has ushered in unprecedented levels of competition among news providers. Various outcomes of this competition in the news market have been introduced throughout this book. Among the most common assumptions is the belief that competition among media outlets leads to higher news quality. However, in the digital era, phenomena that challenge this conventional wisdom—once unimaginable—have begun to emerge. As discussed earlier in Section 9.2, one representative example is the rampant reproduction of content.

In this context, Yang (2021) and Choi and Yang (2021) explained the mechanism through which the flood of duplicated reports in the digital age has led to a decline in news content quality. Rapid advances in digital information and communication technologies have made it possible to replicate news and information in an extremely short time and release it into the market. As a result, the period during which a media

[6] The authors of this study assumed that readers have heterogeneous preferences for the "relative share of journalism-intensive content." Put simply, some readers prefer high-quality news that adheres to journalistic norms, while others prefer sensational, low-quality news that does not.

[7] According to Waldman (2011), advertising revenue for US newspapers declined by 47% between 2005 and 2009, and newspapers cut newsroom-related costs by more than one-quarter between 2006 and 2009.

firm can earn exclusive revenue from original content has shrunk dramatically compared to the analog era, and the amount of revenue has also declined significantly. Accordingly, the production of original content decreased. In turn, digital platforms became flooded with duplicated content.

More importantly, the declining profitability of original content created favorable conditions for powerful actors—those with political or financial clout—to capture original content at a lower cost. The increase in media capture, in turn, further degraded content quality. In short, intensifying competition has led to a surge in extreme levels of duplicated news, thereby undermining the overall quality of journalism.

Cagé, Hervé, and Viaud (2020) provided empirical evidence on the correlation between content duplication and news quality in the digital age. Their study analyzed all online news content produced by French news media in 2013 and found that one-fourth of news articles were reproduced online within just four minutes of initial publication. Moreover, only 32.6% of all online content was original. The majority of reproduced articles were either direct copies or contained duplicated content. The ease with which digital infrastructure enables content replication has contributed to the decline in high-quality (i.e., original) news content.

In this regard, Cagé and her co-authors argued that producing original content requires proper investment, but as replication became easier and faster, the motivation for media companies to invest in unique, high-quality journalism disappeared.

11.2 A NEW WORLD OPENED BY SOCIAL MEDIA

Social networking services (SNS) such as Facebook and Twitter, along with web portals, have been among the key drivers of the digital media era. These platforms brought the new form of media known as social media to the forefront and, in doing so, enabled an unprecedented number of individuals to participate in the collection, filtering, and distribution of news. As a result, countless individuals who had previously played only the role of passive audience members have now become information providers through social media—a "horizontal media" platform. In particular, people can now exchange information easily and quickly, even without directly accessing mass media, as long as they are connected to social media networks.[8]

Since the emergence of social media, the speed and scale at which information spreads have reached levels rarely seen in history. Corporations, organizations, and politicians have also leveraged social media to connect directly with individuals and to implement personalized advertising strategies. At the same time, many individuals find that using such platforms makes it easier to access information about the world,

[8] As of early 2025, there are approximately 5.31 billion social media users worldwide—about 64.7% of the global population and 94.2% of all internet users. The average person now spends roughly 2 hours and 40 minutes per day on social platforms, exceeding the previously estimated 2.5 hours (Kemp, 2025).

increases life satisfaction (Allcott et al., 2020), and delivers various welfare gains (Armona, 2025). This section first defines and characterizes social media and then introduces economic research exploring how the radically transformed communication environment has altered individual and social behavior.

11.2.1 AN ECONOMIC UNDERSTANDING OF SOCIAL MEDIA

In the digital media environment, social media functions as a complex platform where information consumption, content production, and social interaction converge. Reviewing economists' research on social media, Aridor et al. (2024) defined the components of the term "social media platform" as follows: "social" refers to user-generated content; "media" denotes the two-sided market structure; and "platform" signifies an algorithm-based content distribution system. In this sense, social media can be understood as a complex intermediary platform that distributes content while facilitating interaction between users through algorithms.

Because anyone can become an information producer on these platforms, the democratization of information distribution is occurring at a much faster pace than under traditional media. In the past, only media organizations or professional experts could produce and disseminate news, but now, individual users can create and distribute the content they desire via social media. This shift is also restructuring the power dynamics of the content market, especially in conjunction with the rise of the creator economy—as discussed in Chapter 3.

At the center of social media stand the platform companies. Although these firms do not produce content themselves, they serve as key intermediaries (aggregators) that control the flow of content. They determine what content is exposed to users and rely on algorithm-based content moderation and curation systems to do so. This fundamentally differs from the traditional editor-centric model of news production and has technologically and economically transformed the content distribution structure itself.

From an economic perspective, social media—like traditional media—operates under a two-sided market structure. On one side are users; on the other, advertisers. Platforms generate revenue by linking the two. Unlike legacy media, however, users on social media are both consumers and producers of content. Notably, two phenomena—network effects (where the platform becomes more valuable as more users join) and network externalities (where one user's behavior unintentionally affects others)—serve as key mechanisms reinforcing a winner-takes-all dynamic in the platform market. This is one reason why only a few global platforms dominate the market.

According to Aridor et al. (2024), the economic behaviors and decisions of social media participants can be summarized as follows:

First, content users decide how much time to allocate to social media during the day. This decision is made by weighing multiple factors: the enjoyment they derive, the useful information they obtain, the sense of social connectedness they feel, and the potential regret or self-control failure from excessive usage. This can be simplified into a utility function over time t as follows:

$$U(t) = \text{Enjoyment}(t) + \text{Information}(t) + \text{Connectedness}(t) - \text{Regret}(t)$$

This utility function also lends itself to interpretation through behavioral economics. Specifically, psychological factors such as addiction and regret may influence user decisions, thereby providing a rationale for policy intervention.

Second, content producers engage in production with expectations about how much response their content will receive. This activity can be understood as a decision-making process in which producers choose the quantity and quality of content by considering the effort (cost) required and the expected rewards. These rewards may take the form of likes, shares, or monetary income, while the costs may include time, emotional energy, and stress. In essence, content producers behave strategically in order to maximize responses with minimal input—leading to an increase in sensational content, trend-following, and clickbait-style material.

Third, platform companies, which act as intermediaries between content consumers and producers, continuously update their algorithms based on user response data and adjust their content distribution strategies accordingly. These algorithms determine which content appears and in what order by analyzing individual user interests, click histories, and time spent on the platform. This reflects a mechanism in which attention is treated as an economic resource.

Algorithms influence content producers by signaling what types of content are likely to receive higher engagement, and they influence users by determining what appears in their feed. Together, these decisions shape the broader information ecosystem. For example, Twitter scores each post based on its "engagement probability" and incorporates that score into users' timelines. Facebook and Instagram use similar algorithmic mechanisms. As a result, users are presented with content sorted not by chronological order, but by likelihood of engagement.

The longer users stay on a platform, the more advertising revenue the platform earns. Consequently, platforms tend to prioritize content that increases user dwell time. This creates a tendency for emotionally charged or sensational content to receive greater exposure. During the 2020 US presidential election, an experimental shift from algorithmic curation to a chronological feed resulted in a 26% decrease in Facebook usage time and a 13% decrease in Instagram usage time (Guess et al., 2023a). This demonstrated that algorithmic feeds have a tangible effect on extending user engagement.

Given that algorithm design is driven more by profit maximization than by technological neutrality, these systems may reduce the visibility of socially desirable content. Moreover, algorithms used in political advertising or targeted marketing serve not only to increase corporate profits. Algorithm-based advertising can deliver specific political messages with high precision, thereby influencing voter judgment and behavior. When users are repeatedly exposed to similar types of content, the overall diversity of public opinion may also decline. This is because user clicks and engagement are not merely individual choices, but structural elements that influence how the entire system operates.

Consequently, this structure has real effects on content diversity, information quality, and the nature of the public sphere. It also poses potential risks to democratic values. In addition, the fact that users' digital behavior is continuously collected and analyzed for the purpose of targeted advertising has raised growing concerns about privacy violations and surveillance capitalism.

At present, it remains unclear what specific objectives these platform algorithms are designed to optimize. For this reason, some scholars have called for reverse-engineering analysis—that is, studying algorithmic outcomes in order to infer what objective functions the platforms are prioritizing, such as user engagement, advertising revenue, long-term retention, or the suppression of harmful content (Berry and Haile, 2014).

Nevertheless, algorithm oversight and regulation remain underdeveloped. As a result, issues such as algorithmic transparency, the regulation of hate speech, political ad disclosure, and the protection of personal data have emerged as key policy concerns. Addressing these challenges requires a level of complexity and sophistication different from that of traditional media regulation. Moreover, because platforms operate across national borders, there is an increasing need for international cooperation that goes beyond the level of individual states.

Finally, social media has also had a structural impact on the processes of news production and editing. Traditional media outlets now convert content that trends on social media into news articles, and they even revise headlines and reporting methods based on social media reactions. For example, whether a topic trends on Twitter can influence whether it is covered by the news at all (Cagé, Hervé and Mazoyer, 2020), and it has also been reported that user comments can affect the headlines of articles (Leung and Strumpf, 2023). This suggests that social media now indirectly intervenes in how news is selected, produced, and edited.

In short, social media is not merely a space for content consumption, but a domain in which real-time interaction among users plays a critical role. User reactions, such as likes, comments, and shares, affect how content is disseminated. These reactions, in turn, are fed back into algorithmic design and ultimately reshape the overall user experience. Content creators perceive such reactions as their core incentives. Moreover, social media has evolved beyond being a simple technology-based content platform. It has become a complex economic system and public arena in which the interests of individual users, content producers, and platform companies intersect. Its operational mechanisms have tangible impacts on how information circulates, how social connections are formed, and how political discourse unfolds. As such, economic analysis of the social media ecosystem—viewed as a two-sided or multi-sided market—has become an essential tool for understanding its structure and designing effective policy interventions.

11.2.2 THE IMPACT OF SOCIAL MEDIA ON INDIVIDUAL LIVES AND SOCIETY

One of the defining features that distinguishes social media from traditional mass media is its low entry barrier and reliance on user-generated content. Among these, the low entry barrier weakens the efficiency of traditional gatekeeping mechanisms while providing an effective tool for whistleblowers and dissidents. It enables horizontal information flows and facilitates participation in and coordination of collective action (Zhuravskaya et al., 2020). For this reason, social media can also catalyze political turnover and revolution.

However, these same features of social media also grant equal opportunity to extremists, act as a breeding ground for misinformation, and potentially undermine mechanisms of trust. It is commonly believed that social media negatively affects mental health, fosters hate crimes, and may even bolster support for authoritarian regimes. But what do scholars find when they rigorously examine these conventional beliefs about social media's impact?

11.2.2.1 Mis/Disinformation

Many researchers studying the effects of inaccurate or deceptive content on social media have used terms like "fake news" or "false news." For example, Allcott and Gentzkow (2017) use the term "fake news" to refer to intentionally false and misleading news articles, while Vosoughi, Roy and Aral (2018) refer to such content as "false news" in their analysis of Twitter diffusion dynamics. Both terms encompass a range of inaccurate content—whether intentionally deceptive (disinformation) or unintentionally inaccurate (misinformation). In this section, we use the term "mis/disinformation" to broadly capture both forms, as is common in academic and policy discourse.

A major dysfunction commonly associated with social media is the ease with which fake news can be produced, distributed, and consumed at scale. To understand this phenomenon, one must first consider the reasons behind the proliferation of fake news on social platforms. Traditional mass media committed to high-quality journalism generally invest considerable effort into verifying the accuracy and reliability of the news they publish—although critics have argued that even this commitment has weakened in the digital era amid concerns over declining news quality. When traditional outlets publish false information, they face significant reputational costs. In contrast, individuals who participate in the production and dissemination of information on social media face little to no such costs. This asymmetry in the cost of misinformation is a major economic factor explaining why social media can serve as a hotbed for fake news, compared to traditional mass media.

A seminal study on fake news in the context of social media is that of Allcott and Gentzkow (2017). They empirically examined the extent and political impact of fake news disseminated via social media during the 2016 US presidential election between Donald Trump and Hillary Clinton. Contrary to public perception, their findings painted a more nuanced picture. Only 14% of American adults considered social media their "most important" source of election news. Of the 156 fake news stories examined, Facebook shares and views totaled 38 million and 760 million, respectively—equivalent to roughly three fake news articles consumed per adult. However, postelection surveys showed that adults remembered, on average, only 1.14 of these stories, suggesting that most fake news had low retention.

Among Clinton supporters, fake news accounted for just 1% of all news consumed. Although the figure was higher among Trump supporters—around 6%—even they consumed an average of only five fake news stories over more than five weeks. In short, the volume of fake news consumption was small relative to total news consumption.

In terms of content, pro-Trump fake news outnumbered pro-Clinton stories by a factor of 2.8, and their total shares on Facebook approached 30 million compared to 7.6 million for pro-Clinton stories. Notably, the most conservative 10% of voters—those most supportive of Trump—accounted for approximately 65% of all visits to fake news sites. Social media's tendency to create ideologically homogeneous environments appeared to amplify this pattern. Thus, fake news was not evenly consumed across the public but was disproportionately concentrated among individuals with strong political biases—especially pro-Trump leanings.

According to the political media outlet *The Hill*, Clinton received endorsements from 243 news organizations during the campaign, while only 20 endorsed Trump. Among the top 100 newspapers by circulation, 57 supported Clinton, and just 2 endorsed Trump (Wilson, 2020, October 26). Dissatisfied with what they saw as a pro-Clinton media environment, Trump supporters actively sought out (fake) news that aligned with their political views—suggesting that fake news may not have substantially changed voter preferences, as summarized in Fig. 11.1.

Allcott and Gentzkow further argue that the consumption of fake news, while widespread, was not as severe as commonly believed. Even under the strong assumption that one fake news article had the persuasive impact of a single TV campaign ad, its influence was still smaller than the margin of Trump's victory in key swing states. Their empirical findings differ markedly from the dire warnings often issued by traditional journalists or legacy media outlets.

Complementing this perspective, other empirical research has shown that the speed, reach, and depth of mis/disinformation dissemination are indeed considerable. A study by Vosoughi, Roy and Aral (2018), based on Twitter data, found that false news spread significantly faster, farther, and deeper than truthful information. In particular, political misinformation was shared up to six times faster than accurate news. While true stories reached about 1000 people on average, false ones sometimes reached over 100,000.

Strikingly, this phenomenon was driven not by algorithms but by voluntary human behavior. Mis/disinformation often elicited strong emotional reactions—such as surprise, disgust, or shock—which made it more likely to be shared. In contrast, true news tended to generate weaker emotions and less motivation to share, resulting in slower diffusion. The spread of fake news was also unrelated to users' follower

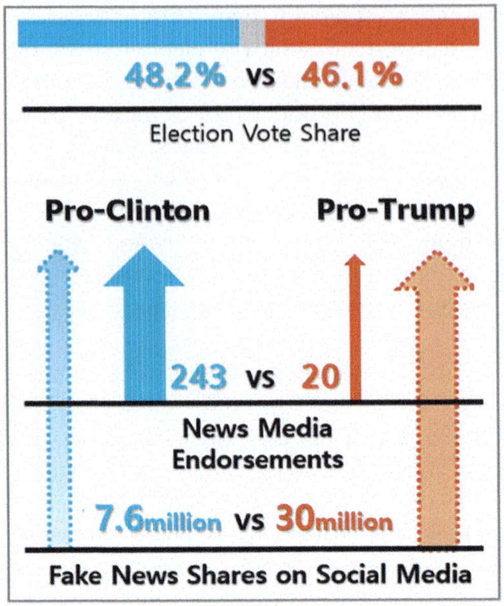

FIGURE 11.1

Contrasting biases in the 2016 US presidential election: traditional media versus fake news on social media.

counts or influence levels, suggesting that the combination of platform design and human emotional response creates an environment particularly conducive to the viral spread of mis/disinformation.

11.2.2.2 *Life, mental health, hate, and crime*

Everyday Life: In recent years, economists have published a growing body of research on how social media affects mental health and daily life. Allcott et al. (2020), in a paper titled "The Welfare Effects of Social Media," examined Facebook's influence on various aspects of everyday living.

They surveyed 3000 US adults aged 18 and over who used Facebook for at least 15 minutes a day, asking how much they would need to be paid to quit Facebook for 4 weeks. The average bid was $100. Half of the participants were randomly selected and paid to deactivate their Facebook accounts for four weeks before the 2018 US midterm elections. Remarkably, only 1% violated the agreement, with 99% abstaining from Facebook use for a month.

What happened to those who left Facebook? They spent more time with family and friends, and less time online. While online activity decreased, offline activities such as watching TV alone or socializing with others increased. Interestingly, participants did not substitute Facebook with traditional media like The New York Times.

As a result, they were less exposed to political news, their partisanship weakened, and political polarization declined.[9] They gained about an hour of leisure time per day, reported greater happiness in daily life, and significantly reduced their Facebook usage even after the experiment ended.

Mental Health: Braghieri, Levy, and Makarin (2022) also found that Facebook negatively affected college students' mental health. By leveraging Facebook's staggered rollout across US universities—starting at Harvard and expanding gradually—the researchers tracked the relationship between its adoption and students' mental health outcomes, including depression, anxiety disorders, and eating disorders.[10] They found a causal relationship between Facebook use and worsening mental health, particularly increases in depression and anxiety. Students reported more academic difficulties, partly due to unwanted social comparisons facilitated by Facebook.

In addition, Allcott, Gentzkow and Song (2022) have argued that social media use reflects "habit" rather than "addiction." While both involve repeated behaviors, addiction implies harmful consequences and a lack of control, whereas habits can be consciously regulated.

According to them, temporary incentives to reduce screen time had long-lasting effects, implying that social media use is a habit rather than an addiction. When participants were offered small incentives to stay within screen time limits, their usage declined substantially. The authors concluded that much of social media usage results from insufficient self-awareness about habit formation and lack of self-control, accounting for approximately 31% of all use.

Hate and Crime: Some studies suggest that social media increases xenophobia and hate crimes. Bursztyn et al. (2019) analyzed the causal impact of social media use on ethnic hate crimes and xenophobic attitudes in Russia. Their findings revealed significant variation across cities. In cities with preexisting nationalist sentiment, increased use of platforms like Twitter and VK (ВКонтакте)[11] correlated with rising hate crimes. Where the ideological "soil" was fertile, hate speech and violence took root more easily.

Müller and Schwarz (2023) studied whether social media could inflame minority-targeted hatred during Donald Trump's political rise. They found that after Trump began his 2016 campaign, anti-Muslim sentiment surged most sharply in the US counties with high Twitter usage. Trump's tweets about Muslims were strongly associated with increased hate crimes against Muslims. His posts spurred anti-immigrant

---

[9] That said, Facebook use cannot be definitively identified as a cause of political polarization. This is because participants in the Facebook withdrawal experiment also consumed little to no traditional media.

[10] Facebook was initially launched in February 2004 by Mark Zuckerberg and was limited to Harvard students. It gradually expanded to other US and international universities and became open to anyone aged 13 and older in September 2006.

[11] VKontakte (VK) is a social networking service created in 2006 by Russian entrepreneur Pavel V. Durov. It is widely used in former Soviet countries such as Russia, Ukraine, and Kazakhstan, and its services and business model resemble those of Facebook.

tweets by supporters and prompted conservative media—especially Fox News—to increase coverage of Muslim-related topics.

As discussed earlier, Vosoughi, Roy, and Aral (2018) found that false information spread faster and more broadly than true news on social media. Notably, this was not driven by algorithms but by users' voluntary behavior. Strong emotional reactions—surprise, disgust, shock—fueled the viral spread of mis/disinformation.

11.2.2.3 Participation and solidarity

Independent Journalism in Media-Captured Societies: Despite the dysfunctional aspects of social media—such as the spread of fake news, incitement of hatred, and negative impacts on mental health—it has emerged as the most influential medium of the 21st century due to its positive functions. Chief among these is its role in providing information that traditional mass media either overlook or deliberately ignore. In environments where traditional media are captured, social media can function as an independent watchdog, holding political and economic powers accountable.

Enikolopov, Petrova, and Sonin (2018) examined whether social media and digital platforms like blogs can fulfill journalism's traditional role of oversight in authoritarian regimes where traditional media are frequently captured by power. They noted several advantages of social media: the cost of disseminating information is much lower than for traditional mass media, while the difficulty of capturing or censoring such information is much greater. As a result, social media have emerged as a vital source of independent information in authoritarian systems and have facilitated political change. Citizens and activists use social media to expose the wrongdoing of public officials or politicians, and this public disclosure can increase transparency and accountability, even changing the behavior of those in power.[12]

In this study, the authors also analyzed whether posts from a popular anticorruption blog by Russian opposition leader Alexei Navalny had a tangible impact on political and corporate behavior. One such blog post exposing corruption in a state-owned company was shown to negatively affect the company's profits, and potentially contributed to reducing its corruption. Enikolopov and colleagues concluded that in countries with limited political freedom and heavily censored media, blogs and social media could play a crucial role in exposing and checking corruption. In short, in authoritarian regimes where traditional media fail to function properly due to media capture, social media can serve an essential watchdog function.

Civic Participation and Mobilization: Social media can also act as a catalyst for organized collective resistance when mass media, captured by political or economic power, distort the truth. During the Jasmine Revolution in Tunisia in 2010,

[12] The researchers also highlighted the negative aspects of social media. The low entry barrier that allows anyone to post on platforms like Twitter or Facebook raises concerns about the quality of the content. Moreover, many governments have utilized social media for propaganda in various ways.

which toppled a dictatorship and triggered a chain of democratization movements in neighboring Arab countries—the so-called Arab Spring—social media served as the people's primary weapon. Even today, in places like Taliban-controlled Afghanistan, military-ruled Myanmar, or authoritarian regimes like Russia and Iran, social media continues to facilitate protest participation and the organization of resistance.

One study provided empirical evidence that the spread of the social networking service VK (ВКонтакте) in Russia led to greater citizen participation in protests. According to Enikolopov, Makarin and Petrova (2020), during the surge in anti-government protests in Russia in 2011, increased VK usage led to more protest activity. Specifically, a 10% increase in VK usage raised the probability of protest occurrence by 4.6% and the number of participants by 19%. While VK helped spread anti-government information, the more decisive factor was its ability to reduce the tangible and intangible costs of organizing protests. This trend was also evident in increased pro-government demonstrations in areas with wider VK adoption.

The view that social media plays a central role in facilitating participation and coordination is shared by Fergusson and Molina (2019). They emphasized the "coordination effect" intrinsic to social media—that is, the tendency for users to express opinions and share them with others. According to their research, Facebook significantly influenced citizens' protest behavior. In less democratic regions, in particular, social media proved useful for mobilizing citizens against opposing political factions.[13] For more on the role of social media in facilitating collective action, refer to the discussion under the [More to Explore] "Dictators' Chief Motivation for Media Capture: Curbing Collective Action" of Chapter 10.

In sum, like traditional media, social media consumption brings both positive and negative effects to individuals and society. "Overall, the literature suggests that the Internet and social media have profoundly affected political and social outcomes by facilitating political mobilization, shaping attitudes, and amplifying both democratic and authoritarian tendencies" (Zhuravskaya, Petrova and Enikolopov, 2020). Unlike traditional media, social media is characterized by users consuming content for a wide range of motivations—personal satisfaction, social connection, information gathering, and emotional engagement. At the same time, it uniquely induces negative personal outcomes such as time mismanagement, regret, psychological distress, polarization, and susceptibility to misinformation. As a result, legacy media outlets and many scholars tend to emphasize the negative aspects more than the positive. While policy interventions can mitigate these harms, any regulation of social media—like that of traditional media—must strike a careful balance between freedom of expression and the intensity of regulatory control.

[13] The study found that Facebook use helped reduce social tensions. According to the researchers, Facebook and the protests it influenced allowed grievances to be aired early—before they could erupt into more violent expressions.

11.3 DIGITAL MEDIA AND CONSUMER BIAS

The case for advocacy in a courtroom would break down completely if half the jury was only allowed to hear from the defense and half the jury could only hear from the prosecution.

—Matthew Gentzkow & Jesse Shapiro

The legal scholar and behavioral economist Sunstein (2001) expressed concern that the rise of the internet could lead people to a state of extreme informational self-selection. The internet, he argued, enables an environment where people can read, see, and hear only what they want. Sunstein also predicted that this tendency would be exacerbated by exponential advances in filtering technology.

Two decades later, many believe that Sunstein's prediction has come true. On the supply side, "customizing"—the tailored provision of content to individual consumers—has become widespread. On the consumer side, the so-called "echo chamber" phenomenon appears to be cementing individual biases by reinforcing preferred narratives. But is this really the case? Often, economists' views diverge from such conventional wisdom and help clarify widespread misunderstandings. Let's examine the core issues.

11.3.1 THE POSSIBILITY OF CUSTOMIZED NEWS

Tailoring information and news content to individual consumers was unthinkable in the era of mass media, mainly because of its structurally high costs. Suppose there are three ideological groups among news consumers—left-wing, centrist, and right-wing—and a newspaper publishes 100 stories a day. Providing tailored news would mean producing each of the 100 stories in left, center, and right-leaning versions, and then distributing these customized newspapers to the respective readers.

If the ideological spectrum further fragments into far-left, left, center-left, center, center-right, right, and far-right, the number of newspaper versions required increases significantly. If we further account for readers whose ideological biases are inconsistent—for example, left-leaning on political issues but right-leaning on economic ones—the complexity and cost of producing customized content grow exponentially.

Such customization is even harder for broadcasters. Imagine airing the same event with different ideological slants at the same time to different viewers—it's practically impossible. The nature of traditional mass media, designed for the simultaneous delivery of identical content to large audiences, makes it ill-suited for tailored information.

However, if the cost barrier can be overcome, producing customized news content is not theoretically impossible. If revenues increase substantially or technological innovation dramatically reduces the cost of producing and distributing multiple ideological versions of news content, then such personalization becomes feasible. For instance, Pires (2014) argued that if the advertising market is large enough, news organizations could adopt a multi-ideology strategy.[14] A newspaper could publish left- and centrist-leaning editions, or centrist- and right-leaning ones, depending on advertising revenue.

Cost reduction through digitization also opens up new possibilities. Delivering news via websites eliminates the cost of printing different physical newspapers. If AI can generate various ideologically biased versions of the same story at the click of a button, then customized news becomes economically viable. In such a world, producing and distributing versions of a story ranging from far-right to far-left could be done cheaply, aligning with consumer preferences.

In practice, we can observe such potential in digital platform companies. Digital intermediaries—such as web portals and social networking services—are in a different position compared to traditional news providers. Even without increased ad revenue or major technological breakthroughs, they can deliver personalized content as long as they can infer individual consumer preferences. They do not need to produce their own content, but instead curate from a wide range of existing news content produced by various media with differing ideological slants.

This is why many believe that providing customized content is not particularly difficult for digital intermediaries. However, significant challenges remain. Accurately identifying each individual's preferences is an arduous task. As discussed later in Section 11.4, even the most advanced digital platforms struggle to fully understand consumer preferences. In fact, the most effective strategy to date remains Facebook's simple heuristic: "You're likely to prefer what your friends prefer."

[More to Explore] Digital Platforms and the Disappearance of News Diversity

Today, most news consumption occurs through the platforms of digital intermediaries. Among all countries, South Korea stands out as particularly notable in this regard.[15] What impact does this situation have on the ideological slant and diversity of news media? Based on the Korean context, we can examine how web portals influence the biases of news outlets using economic theory.

In South Korea, major news media outlets provide their content to web portals such as Naver and Daum in exchange for compensation. These portals, in turn, aggregate the content and offer it free of charge to news consumers on their platforms. The news articles supplied by media companies are published without any editorial modification by the portals.

Continued

[14] According to Pires, in markets that are not large enough to support multiple bias strategies, news outlets may pursue a "single-ideology strategy" instead of customizing content to reflect individual political biases, thereby maximizing differentiation from competitors.

[15] According to the Reuters Institute Digital News Report 2021, online portal usage for news stood at 72% in South Korea, 69% in Japan, 47% in Italy, 32% in Australia, 30% in the US, 19% in the UK and 15% in Finland. In the latest 2025 report, while precise percentages are not provided, South Korea remains one of the highest users of online portals for news among the 48 countries surveyed, with portals like Naver still the dominant means of accessing news online.

According to Yang (2020), when the service quality[16] of the web portal exceeds that of individual news outlets—thereby attracting more consumers to the portal—or when the fees paid by the portal are substantial, news media begin to prioritize content consumed on the portal over that on their own websites. However, the distribution of political preferences among consumers on a web portal platform differs significantly from the ideologically homogeneous audiences typical of individual news outlets. On average, consumers who favor the specific ideological stance of a given outlet represent a minority on portal platforms.

As a result, to attract a broader audience on the portal, media outlets are incentivized to moderate their original ideological slant. That is, left-leaning (or right-leaning) outlets will soften their positions to appeal to centrist or opposite-leaning audiences. This dynamic causes the ideological distance between media outlets to shrink. Moreover, the intense competition for clicks and page views may induce outlets to produce increasingly similar content, often leading to a "breaking news arms race." At times, the news market resembles a chaotic rugby match, with all players chasing the same ball.

In short, the higher the quality of the digital platform relative to news outlets—and the greater the share of media revenue that comes from the platform—the more likely it is that ideological differentiation among news outlets will diminish, leading to a decline in overall news diversity.

11.3.2 THE ECHO CHAMBER EFFECT AND POLITICAL POLARIZATION

Digital intermediaries have consistently aimed to attract more users to their platforms and keep them engaged for longer periods of time. To achieve this, they have made efforts to ensure that content consumers can more easily access and engage with the content they prefer. These efforts, along with the various functions of the digital platforms they created, have fueled public concerns about phenomena such as "echo chambers" and "filter bubbles,"[17] and the resulting political polarization.

Unlike recommendations for movies to watch or products to buy, being exposed only to news with a preferred ideological slant can have serious implications. If people only see what they want to see and hear only what they want to hear, confirmation bias can be drastically reinforced,[18] rendering the role of news media as a public forum meaningless and undermining the free market of ideas. Ultimately, the processes of public opinion formation and social consensus may become dysfunctional. To what extent, then, have echo chamber effects and political polarization materialized in the digital era?

Gentzkow and Shapiro (2011) attracted attention with an empirical study comparing the echo chamber effects observed online and offline. Their research aimed to

[16] Here, "quality of service" refers to conditions that allow easy comparison of news content, network speed, server capacity, user interface effectiveness, and the availability of reference data such as geography, age, and rankings.

[17] A "filter bubble" occurs when users are exposed only to personalized content, preventing them from encountering diverse perspectives and trapping them in selectively curated information.

[18] Flat-earthers—those who believe the Earth is flat—are one of the most symbolic examples, while racists are among the most common.

assess the degree of political polarization in digital spaces relative to that in offline spaces. The two scholars analyzed the political leanings of Americans who accessed various online news sites and compared them with the political orientations of Americans residing in specific offline geographic regions.

The results were surprising; whether the news websites had conservative or liberal leanings, the ideological similarity among the users of any given online news site was lower than the ideological similarity among residents of a specific offline region. In other words, political polarization among Americans was more pronounced when measured by residential location than by online news consumption. This suggested that the echo chamber effect might actually be stronger offline than online.

Furthermore, despite online sites producing more ideologically extreme content than any offline media outlet, Gentzkow and Shapiro's findings showed that this political polarization did not necessarily transfer to news consumers. They explained that "the effects of extremely biased websites on people's political beliefs were unclear" because visitors to such websites interpreted the site's ideological slant differently depending on their own preexisting views.

Following the rapid rise of social media, there was a surge in research investigating how these platforms might influence political polarization in society. For example, Levy (2021) conducted a large-scale field experiment involving over 30,000 Facebook users to examine whether consuming ideologically aligned news on social media intensified ideological polarization. In this experiment, Levy randomly assigned participants to follow either conservative or liberal news media on Facebook. He then collected and analyzed behavioral data, including participants' news subscriptions, Facebook news consumption and sharing behavior, news site visits, shifts in attitudes toward opposing political parties, and changes in political opinions.

The findings were twofold. First, when the content from news sites was shared on social media, it significantly affected the strategic decisions of news providers, who tended to intensify their ideological slant. Second, there was no evidence that exposure to ideologically biased news on social media led users to shift their political opinions. Interestingly, exposure to news with opposing views actually reduced users' negative attitudes toward rival political parties.

Moreover, Facebook was found to offer users relatively few opportunities to encounter content that contradicted their political views. Levy noted that this feature of the Facebook algorithm suggested that social media could potentially increase political polarization. However, given the absence of evidence showing changes in political opinions, such polarization should be understood as a possibility, not an empirical fact.

In this context, a remarkably large-scale study was conducted to examine whether Facebook and Instagram contributed to political polarization during the 2020 US presidential election. In July 2023, four papers authored by the same research team were published simultaneously in two of the world's most prestigious academic journals, *Science* and *Nature*. These studies examined the impact of social media on public understanding and opinions related to news and democracy.

The researchers involved were prominent scholars and experts in economics, political science, communication, and journalism, with each paper listing 26 to 30 co-authors—a testament to the significance of the research.[19] Notably, Facebook provided internal data on 208 million US Facebook users for this project—an unprecedented move.[20] What drew the most attention, however, was the conclusion that social media could not be held responsible for the deepening of political polarization in the United States.

The four studies, which we will refer to as Study 1 through Study 4, were all based on experiments conducted or data collected between August and December, around the time of the US presidential election. A total of 75,189 participants took part in the experiments.

In Study 1 (González-Bailón et al., 2023), the researchers provided a subset of participants (8977 individuals) with posts displayed in reverse chronological order instead of the default algorithmically curated feed. They then analyzed changes in the participants' political attitudes and behaviors. The results showed that these participants were exposed to more political and unreliable content—but less coarse or vulgar language—compared to those using the default feed. While their consumption patterns changed, there were no significant differences in their political attitudes or knowledge.

In Study 2 (Guess et al., 2023b), the researchers prevented another group of participants (8985 individuals) from seeing content that had been reshared by other users. This experiment was based on the idea that resharing had been identified as a potential driver of polarization. As a result, the volume of political news—including content from untrustworthy sources—significantly decreased. Participants' overall engagement with posts, including clicks on partisan news, also declined. Nevertheless, once again, there were no meaningful changes in political polarization.

Study 3 (Nyhan et al., 2023) reduced the exposure of a subset of participants (23,377 individuals) to content that aligned with their preexisting views by approximately one-third. As a result, these participants saw more ideologically diverse content and fewer posts containing inflammatory language. Still, there were no measurable changes in emotional polarization toward politicians, ideological extremity, or trust in false news. The researchers concluded that while exposure to ideologically congruent content is common on social media, their findings showed that reducing such exposure during the 2020 US presidential election did not lead to decreases in belief or attitudinal polarization.

[19] Experts affiliated with Meta (formerly Facebook) were involved in this research. This raised some questions about the study's objectivity. However, the researchers' credentials, the scale of the project, and the fact that the results were published in top-tier journals like Science and Nature lend credibility to the findings.

[20] One of the main challenges in studying whether social media intensifies echo chambers or political polarization has been the lack of accessible data and the difficulty of conducting large-scale field experiments (Lazer et al., 2020; de Vreese & Tromble, 2023).

In Study 4 (González-Bailón et al., 2023), the researchers analyzed the political news content that was accessible and actually consumed by 208 million Facebook users during the 2020 election period. They found that users' actual exposure and engagement revealed greater ideological separation than the pool of all available content. Conservative and liberal users consumed news differently, and most of the misinformation identified by Facebook's fact-checking system leaned conservative. Furthermore, conservative-preferred news sources had a stronger presence on the platform than those favored by liberals.

The shared conclusion across these studies is that removing Facebook's algorithm had minimal impact on users' political attitudes. While algorithms significantly shape users' experiences on social media, they appear to have limited influence on deepening echo chambers or political polarization.

Nonetheless, some caveats must be noted. These experiments were conducted only during the three-month US presidential election season, a period marked by heightened political division. The characteristics of American society should also be taken into account. Joshua A. Tucker, Director of the Center for Social Media and Politics at New York University and one of the study's lead authors, stated: "It's possible that if we did a similar study at another period of time or in another country where people were not paying as much attention to politics or not being as inundated with other information from other sources about politics, we would have found a different result," adding, "This finding cannot tell us what the world would have been like if we hadn't had social media around for the last 10 to 15 years" (Nix, Johnson and Zakrzewski, 2023).

It is also important to understand that the findings suggest social media has less impact on political polarization than widely believed—but they do not negate the normative importance of encouraging people to encounter differing views more frequently. Such exposure remains a crucial antidote to polarization, division, and hate.

11.4 ARTIFICIAL INTELLIGENCE AND ALGORITHMS

Artificial Intelligence (AI) is rapidly transforming a wide range of industries—and the news media are no exception. Often described as the defining technology of the 21st century, AI refers to systems that replicate human capabilities such as learning, reasoning, and perception. Interest in AI is growing not only in computer science and information engineering, but also in media studies. In the news sector, AI's applications can be broadly categorized into two areas: on the supply side, enabling faster and more accurate news production; and on the demand side, helping identify what types of content consumers prefer.

As with any other sector, discussions about these roles of AI within the field of economics are marked by both hope and concern. One of the most prominent economists voicing apprehension is Daron Acemoglu, one of the recipients of the 2024 Nobel Prize in Economic Sciences. He argues that if AI development continues unregulated and unchecked, it could result in a wide range of political, economic, and social harms. AI could not only infringe upon individuals' privacy and decision-making autonomy, but also lead to excessive automation, exacerbate inequality, depress wages inefficiently, fail to improve labor productivity, and ultimately damage the democratic political process. As Acemoglu (2021) warns:

> *"Although there is no conclusive evidence suggesting that these costs are imminent or substantial, it may be useful to understand them before they are fully realized and become harder or even impossible to reverse, precisely because of AI's promising and wide-reaching potential."*

Meanwhile, scholars like Matthew Gentzkow take a more cautious view about what AI can realistically achieve in the media domain. He emphasizes the inherent duality of AI—namely, that both benevolent and malevolent intentions can be embedded in its applications. Gentzkow (2018) observes:

> *"There is no question that AI will have profound impacts on media markets. ... AI can make it easier for consumers to navigate the bewildering mass of online content through search and personalized recommendations, and to identify cases where third parties are attempting to manipulate them. There is also cause for concern, as AI may tilt content more heavily toward consumer demand in domains where this is at odds with social good, and AI tools may be used to more effectively persuade and deceive."*

These concerns and hopes raise an important question: how exactly is AI reshaping the production and consumption of news today, and what further transformations might it bring about in the years to come?

11.4.1 THE PRODUCTION OF CONTENT

On March 17, 2014, when a 4.7-magnitude earthquake struck California, the first article that appeared on the Los Angeles Times website was written entirely by artificial intelligence and algorithms (Oremus, 2014). By 2016, AI-generated reports on finance, sports, and weather had already been commercialized. Today, in various parts of the world, numerous initiatives are underway to experiment with different ways of applying artificial intelligence in news media. In this climate, many AI experts and scholars predict that in the near future, journalists will rely heavily on AI tools, and that fully autonomous, AI-generated news content will proliferate across the media landscape.

In fact, among frontline journalists and media executives, the level of interest and expectation surrounding AI is already very high. In a December 2020 survey conducted by the Reuters Institute for the Study of Journalism—targeting 234 senior media executives from 43 countries and asking them, "Which technology will be most important for media companies in the next five years?"—69% of the 227 respondents identified artificial intelligence (Newman, 2021). In a later Reuters Institute survey summarized in Fig. 11.2, respondents expected that smarter recommendation

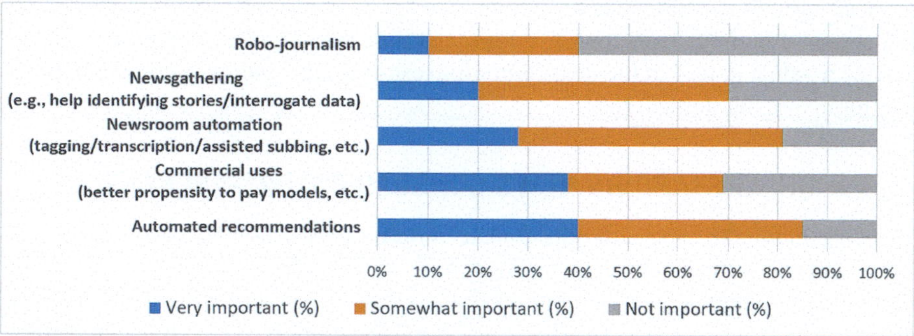

FIGURE 11.2

Which newsroom uses of AI will be most important in 2022?

Source: Newman (2022).

algorithms, improved operational efficiency, and AI-based tools such as automated translation would become increasingly important in journalism as well.

Indeed, the era in which journalists rely on AI in their daily news production has already begun. In areas such as data gathering and cross-verification of past cases, AI has capabilities that far exceed those of humans. It also has the potential to correct factual errors that typically result from human carelessness, and may even help address frequent shortcomings of experienced journalists, such as logical leaps or mistakes rooted in confirmation bias. Artificial intelligence could function not only as a fact checker but also as a constant quality checker for content produced by humans. In this role, AI could assess background knowledge and factual accuracy, identify logical inconsistencies, and measure problematic reporting practices—such as the overuse of anonymous sources or the blending of facts and opinions in a single article. It might also be able to determine, in real time, whether a news report is the first or nth article on a particular issue, and compare it with other articles covering the same topic in terms of length, factual density, and relative bias.

However, many scholars remain skeptical of the prediction that artificial intelligence will not merely assist human journalists but eventually produce original news content independently of humans. They argue that while AI may be effective in reporting simple, structured information—such as sports results, weather updates, or stock market movements—it is far less capable of autonomously reporting on complex societal issues. Unlike traditional manufacturing or service industries, the media and content industry fundamentally depends on human judgment, interpretation, creativity, and communication.

For this reason, even if AI technologies for content production advance significantly, it is difficult to foresee them reaching a level where they can fully substitute for human insight. And even if so-called "AI journalists" do emerge, the algorithms powering them will likely remain under close daily human supervision and control.

In short, even if AI does not take on the role of an autonomous journalist, it still holds substantial promise for dramatically improving the quality of news content, as many newsroom executives and journalists hope. It can clearly help overcome the limitations of human error, cognitive bias, and time constraints. In particular, it may become a valuable tool in the near future for restoring the quality of content that has deteriorated in the digital era.[21]

11.4.2 UNDERSTANDING NEWS CONSUMERS' PREFERENCES

Artificial intelligence can not only transform news production but also create consumption conditions that news consumers have never experienced before. AI can be used to identify and deliver the optimal content that each consumer desires. Already, platform companies such as Facebook and YouTube employ algorithms that display personalized advertisements and content tailored to individual users. If the level of these algorithms were to improve dramatically—particularly in the domain of "personalizing" or "customizing" content—the impact on the news media, the news market, and broader society could be profound.

However, contrary to such expectations, some scholars argue that AI faces structural limitations when it comes to delivering truly personalized content. A careful review of how personalization is currently implemented on web portals, social network services, and e-commerce platforms suggests that the actual performance falls far short of public expectations.

Search services on web portals have indeed seen technological advances aimed at improving the relevance of search results. Yet, progress in the domain of personalization remains limited. According to Hannak et al. (2013), 90% of Google search results were not personalized, and only 10% reflected factors such as users' geographic location. This fundamental pattern has not changed significantly since. Although Facebook's business model revolves around content and advertisement personalization, the level of personalization in ads that users commonly see remains quite rudimentary.

In practice, most Facebook users encounter ads related to products they have already purchased or places they have already visited. Research by Meta executive and scholar Eytan Bakshy and his colleagues found that a significant portion of the Facebook News Feed is not based on finely tuned individual recommendations, but rather on a combination of "items shared by friends" and general "predictions of content popularity" (Bakshy, Messing and Adamic, 2015).

Gentzkow (2018) refers to this reality—where the actual performance of personalization falls short of its promise—as "the personalization paradox." Current levels of search and recommendation quality suggest that personalized content remains limited in scope and mediocre in quality. In fact, Facebook's core algorithm,

[21] In December 2020, the Reuters Institute for Journalism surveyed 234 media executives from 43 countries, asking "Who do you think will benefit most from artificial intelligence?" Among the 226 respondents, 66% answered "large media companies," 16% expected a balanced outcome, and only 3% cited "small media companies." (Newman, 2021). These responses reflect widespread expectations of increasing inequality in AI adoption and benefit distribution.

which brought social media into the mainstream, did not rely on sophisticated AI technologies but on a remarkably simple and intuitive rule: one did not need to analyze a user's specific preferences or their content consumption history—just knowing who their friends were and what those friends consumed was sufficient. It was a powerful insight born of a simple principle: people are likely to enjoy what their friends enjoy.

So why does the personalization paradox, as Gentzkow describes it, arise in the first place? He suggests that advanced technologies like AI tend to be deployed to meet users' common expectations rather than their individual ones. Gentzkow and Shapiro (2011) provide empirical support for this idea, showing that despite their political differences, Republican and Democratic supporters in the United States derived high utility from many of the same news and political websites. That is, while users may have distinct political preferences, their shared human desires for certain types of content may outweigh those differences. Gentzkow and Shapiro explain this further through an analysis of the average utility of news sites among supporters of the two major US parties:

In Fig. 11.3, the x-axis represents the average utility that Democratic supporters derive from various websites, while the y-axis shows the same for Republican supporters. Each point on the chart corresponds to a news or political website. The

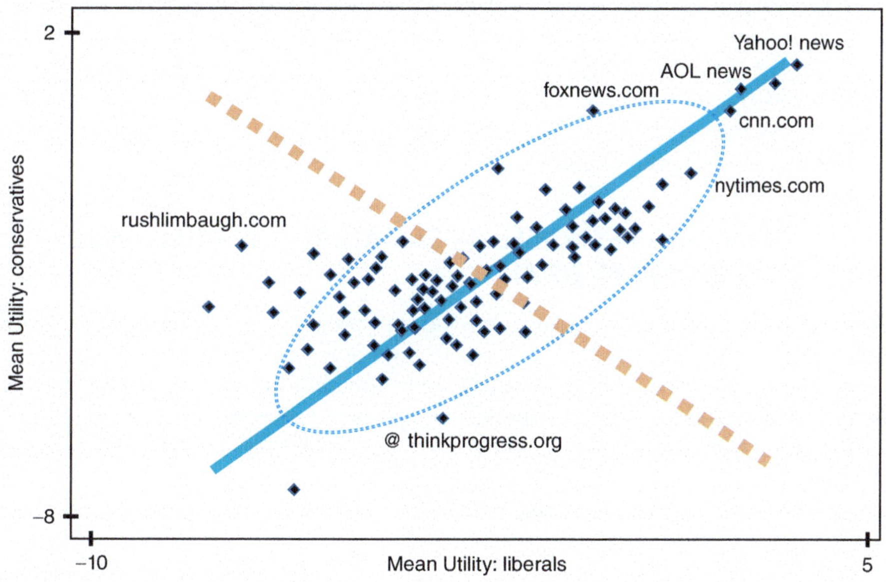

FIGURE 11.3

Average utility of news sites for conservatives and liberals. Note: This figure is a simplified visual reconstruction based on Gentzkow and Shapiro (2011). It preserves the directional pattern (upward-sloping relationship) but omits precise data points and original formatting. Recreated for illustrative and educational purposes only.

location of each point reflects the average utility that supporters of both parties gain from that specific site. For example, the point in the upper-right quadrant labeled "Yahoo! News" suggests that both Republicans and Democrats derive high utility from Yahoo's content.

Now, if political alignment were the most critical factor, the distribution of these points would cluster around a downward-sloping red line from the top-left to the bottom-right. That is, websites offering high utility to Republicans would offer low utility to Democrats, and vice versa—creating a strong inverse relationship between the x- and y-axes. In such a world, identifying individual ideological leanings and tailoring content accordingly would be essential for news and information providers.

Note: This figure is a simplified visual reconstruction based on the study by Gentzkow and Shapiro (2011). It preserves the directional pattern (upward-sloping relationship) but omits precise data points and original formatting. Recreated for illustrative and educational purposes only.

However, as Fig. 11.3 clearly shows, most data points lie along an upward-sloping blue line, indicating a strong positive correlation. While it's true that Republicans tend to prefer sites like foxnews.com and Democrats favor nytimes.com, these ideological differences are overshadowed by the fact that both groups derive higher utility from these two sites than from more ideologically extreme outlets like rushlimbaugh.com or thinkprogress.org.

In this context, Gentzkow writes that "we have tended to overestimate the importance of stable individual differences relative to the other kinds of variation." He concludes that "There is no question that the quality of search and recommendation systems will continue to improve dramatically with advances in AI. It may well be, however, that these gains continue to be more about improved communication with users and overall ranking of content than about personalization."

11.4.3 PROVIDING DESIRABLE INFORMATION: THE CHALLENGES AND PROMISES OF AI

Many observers believe that today's most serious problem in the media is not that it fails to deliver what consumers want, but rather that it provides what they want even when it is socially undesirable. As discussed throughout this book, people tend to prefer sensational soft news to hard news, and partisan reporting to balanced journalism. At times, they even show an enthusiastic appetite for blatantly false information. If artificial intelligence and algorithms further enhance the ability to satisfy such preferences of news consumers, the democratic political process could be seriously undermined—as Acemoglu has pointed out.

Conversely, AI can be used to block socially harmful information or news. For example, one study found that the implementation of Facebook's fake news countermeasures (algorithms) led to a sharp decline in the circulation of fake news on the platform. Allcott, Gentzkow and Yu (2019) tracked the diffusion of content from 569 fake news websites and 9540 fake news items on Facebook and Twitter from January 2015 to July 2018. As shown in Fig. 11.4, engagement with false content increased

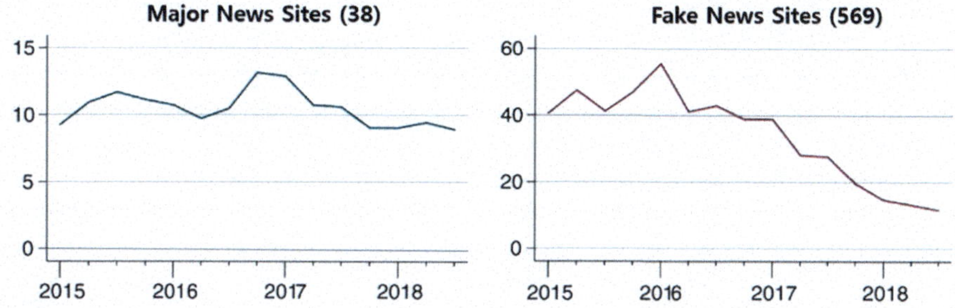

FIGURE 11.4

Trends in Facebook engagement from 38 major news sites and 569 fake news sites, 2015–2018 (Mentions on Facebook/Shares on Twitter).

** Source: Allcott, Gentzkow, & Yu (2019). * Quarterly average of the ratio of Facebook mentions to Twitter shares for content published on websites.*

steadily on both platforms, but dropped sharply on Facebook after the end of 2016. The researchers attribute this decline to Facebook's algorithmic interventions after the 2016 US presidential election.

Search portals can also revise their algorithms to assign greater weight to the "social desirability" of content, thereby excluding antisocial materials from top search results. For instance, Google removed Holocaust-denial websites from the top search results for users who searched the term "Holocaust" (Sullivan, 2016).

More recently, initiatives such as Meta's fact-checking partnership program, Google's News Lab, and AI-based automated fact-checking tools (e.g., Full Fact, ClaimReview) have actively experimented with using AI for information hygiene. In 2024, the European Union formally adopted the AI Act, establishing binding regulatory frameworks for trustworthy AI systems, including content moderation and transparency in algorithmic decision-making. Likewise, Meta and Google updated their content moderation and fact-checking systems in response to growing concerns ahead of global elections in 2024, reflecting continued efforts to institutionalize responsible AI use in media governance. However, providing desirable content and blocking harmful information is technically, economically, and ethically complex. Especially since platform companies optimize algorithms based on clicks and views rather than accurate information, a gap exists between profit motives and the provision of public-interest information. Consequently, there remains a fair degree of skepticism about whether AI can genuinely improve society's information environment.

This raises a critical question: can AI be used to remove extremely biased or socially undesirable content from platforms like social media and portals, and instead deliver content that promotes democracy or is socially beneficial? Most economists remain skeptical. They argue that "fixing bias through AI is far more difficult than improving search results." Social objectives like "truth" or "promotion of sound democratic values" are much harder to define or quantify compared to individual user preferences. In other words, defining what content is "socially desirable" is inherently subjective and difficult to measure. For example, while the training data for delivering optimal search results and recommendations can be automatically generated through user clicks, the training data for detecting misinformation typically must be hand-coded by human fact-checkers (Gentzkow, 2018).

In short, most efforts to combat bias and misinformation have so far relied on human judgment. While the idea of using AI to fight fake news is broadly appealing, the most effective interventions to date have involved filtering out websites distrusted by consumers and labeling content with additional sourcing and fact-checking information. These tasks still rely far more heavily on human decisions than on machine intelligence.

Meanwhile, concerns remain that AI-based content curation—the process of selecting and recommending news and information—could suppress freedom of expression or be exploited as a tool of censorship. Content curation refers to the algorithmic processes by which platforms decide which news or content to display to users. AI systems analyze past click behavior, interests, and social networks to recommend content automatically. But this inevitably raises the question: "Which news is shown to the user, and which is not?"

In particular, when certain content is judged to be false or manipulative and is demoted or excluded, political controversy can arise. If the workings of the algorithm are not disclosed, it becomes difficult to determine who filtered the content and on what basis. Without proper ethical oversight, AI could become a powerful gatekeeper of information, posing a direct threat to the democratic principles of free expression and diversity of viewpoints.

Nonetheless, given that human judgment still plays a central role in today's news filtering landscape, AI can serve as a valuable tool for reducing human error and complementing tasks such as fact-checking, source credibility analysis, and verifying authenticity. In tasks such as excluding websites distrusted by news consumers or offering additional source information, AI can make meaningful contributions. While AI cannot replace all human decisions, it may become increasingly important in domains of information verification where human attention is inconsistent or prone to error.

No one can easily predict the future of AI in the fields of media and communication. But one thing is clear: the human role in the media industry will not disappear, and AI will continue to serve both beneficial and harmful purposes. This is why societal efforts to maximize the positive functions of artificial intelligence and minimize its negative consequences will continue. Furthermore, it must not be forgotten that freedom of expression is not merely a function of technological neutrality but a foundational value of democratic societies, and AI must remain a tool to support that value.

> *"The historical record suggests that dismal prophecies about the economic and social impact of great technological advances rarely come to pass."*
>
> **—Trajtenberg (2018, p. 185)**

References

Abernathy, P.M., 2018. The Expanding News Desert. University of North Carolina Press.

Acemoglu, D., 2021. Harms of AI. NBER Working Paper 29247. https://doi.org/10.3386/w29247.

Agirdas, C., 2015. What drives media bias? New evidence from recent newspaper closures. Journal of Media Economics 28 (3), 123–141. https://doi.org/10.1080/08997764.2015.1063499.

Allcott, H., Braghieri, L., Eichmeyer, S., Gentzkow, M., 2020. The welfare effects of social media. American Economic Review 110 (3), 629–676. https://doi.org/10.1257/aer.20190658.

Allcott, H., Gentzkow, M., Yu, C., 2019. Trends in the diffusion of misinformation on social media. Research & Politics 6 (2), 2053168019848554. https://doi.org/10.1177/2053168019848554.

Allcott, H., Gentzkow, M., Song, L., 2022. Digital addiction. American Economic Review 112 (7), 2424–2463. https://doi.org/10.1257/aer.20210867.

Allcott, H., Gentzkow, M., 2017. Social media and fake news in the 2016 election. Journal of Economic Perspectives 31 (2), 211–236. https://doi.org/10.1257/jep.31.2.211.

Angelucci, C., Cagé, J., 2019. Newspapers in times of low advertising revenues. American Economic Journal: Microeconomics 11 (3), 319–364. https://doi.org/10.1257/mic.20170306.

Aridor, G., Jiménez-Durán, R., Levy, Ro'ee, Song, L., 2024. The economics of social media. Journal of Economic Literature 62 (4), 1422–1474. https://doi.org/10.1257/jel.20241743.

Armona, L., 2025. Online social network effects in labor markets: evidence from Facebook's entry to college campuses. Review of Economics and Statistics 107 (4), 873–888. https://doi.org/10.1162/rest_a_01354.

Bakshy, E., Messing, S., Adamic, L.A., 2015. Exposure to ideologically diverse news and opinion on Facebook. Science 348 (6239), 1130–1132. Available from: http://www.sciencemag.org/content/348/6239/1130.full.pdf. https://doi.org/10.1126/science.aaa1160.

Bergemann, D., Bonatti, A., 2011. Targeting in advertising markets: implications for offline vs online media. RAND Journal of Economics 42 (3), 417–443. https://doi.org/10.1111/j.1756-2171.2011.00143.x.

Berry, S.T., Haile, P.A., 2014. Identification in differentiated products markets using market level data. Econometrica 82 (5), 1749–1797. https://doi.org/10.3982/ECTA9027.

Braghieri, L., Levy, R., Makarin, A., 2022. Social media and mental health. American Economic Review 112 (11), 3660–3693.

Bursztyn, L., Egorov, G., Enikolopov, R., Petrova, M., 2019. Social Media and Xenophobia: Evidence from Russia. National Bureau of Economic Research., (No. w26567).

Cagé, J., Hervé, N., Mazoyer, B., 2020. Social media influence mainstream media: evidence from two billion tweets. Working Paper.

Cagé, J., Hervé, N., Viaud, M.L., 2020. The production of information in an online world. Review of Economic Studies 87 (5), 2126–2164. https://doi.org/10.1093/restud/rdz061.

Choi, J.P., Yang, S., 2021. Investigative journalism and media capture in the digital age. Information Economics and Policy 57, 100942. https://doi.org/10.1016/j.infoecopol.2021.100942.

Enikolopov, R., Makarin, A., Petrova, M., 2020. Social media and protest participation: evidence from Russia. Econometrica 88 (4), 1479–1514. https://doi.org/10.3982/ecta14281.

Enikolopov, R., Petrova, M., Sonin, K., 2018. Social media and corruption. American Economic Journal: Applied Economics 10 (1), 150–174.

Fergusson, L., Molina, C., 2019. Facebook causes protests. Documento CEDE, 41.

Gentzkow, M., 2007. Valuing new goods in a model with complementarity: online newspapers. American Economic Review 97 (3), 713–744. https://doi.org/10.1257/aer.97.3.713.

Gentzkow, M., Shapiro, J.M., 2011. Ideological segregation online and offline. Quarterly Journal of Economics 126 (4), 1799–1839. https://doi.org/10.1093/qje/qjr044.

Gentzkow, M., 2014. Trading Dollars for Dollars: The Price of Attention Online and Offline (unpublished working paper). Stanford University.

Gentzkow, M., 2018. Media and artificial intelligence. Available from: http://web.stanford.edu/~gentzkow/research/ai_and_media.pdf.

Gentzkow, M., Shapiro, J.M., 2008a. Competition and truth in the market for news. Journal of Economic Perspectives 22 (2), 133–154.

González-Bailón, S., Lazer, D., Barberá, P., Zhang, M., Allcott, H., Brown, T., Crespo-Tenorio, A., Freelon, D., Gentzkow, M., Guess, A.M., Iyengar, S., Kim, Y.M., Malhotra, N., Moehler, D., Nyhan, B., Pan, J., Rivera, C.V., Settle, J., Thorson, E., Tromble, R., Wilkins, A., Wojcieszak, M., Kiewiet de Jonge, C., Franco, A., Mason, W., Stroud, N.J., Tucker, J.A., 2023. Asymmetric ideological segregation in exposure to political news on Facebook. Science 381 (6656), 392–398. https://doi.org/10.1126/science.ade7138.

Guess, A.M., Malhotra, N., Pan, J., Barberá, P., Allcott, H., Brown, T., Crespo-Tenorio, A., Dimmery, D., Freelon, D., Gentzkow, M., González-Bailón, S., Kennedy, E., Kim, Y.M., Lazer, D., Moehler, D., Nyhan, B., Rivera, C.V., Settle, J., Thomas, D.R., Thorson, E., Tromble, R., Wilkins, A., Wojcieszak, M., Xiong, B., De Jonge, C.K., Franco, A., Mason, W., Stroud, N.J., Tucker, J.A., 2023a. How do social media feed algorithms affect attitudes and behavior in an election campaign? Science 381 (6656), 398–404. https://doi.org/10.1126/science.abp9364.

Guess, A.M., Malhotra, N., Pan, J., Barberá, P., Allcott, H., Brown, T., Crespo-Tenorio, A., Dimmery, D., Freelon, D., Gentzkow, M., González-Bailón, S., Kennedy, E., Kim, Y.M., Lazer, D., Moehler, D., Nyhan, B., Rivera, C.V., Settle, J., Thomas, D.R., Thorson, E., Tromble, R., Wilkins, A., Wojcieszak, M., Xiong, B., De Jonge, C.K., Franco, A., Mason, W., Stroud, N.J., Tucker, J.A., 2023b. Reshares on social media amplify political news but do not detectably affect beliefs or opinions. Science 381 (6656), 404–408. https://doi.org/10.1126/science.add8424.

Hannak, A., Sapiezynski, P., Kakhki, A.M., Krishnamurthy, B., Lazer, D., Mislove, A., Wilson, C., 2013. Measuring personalization of web search. In: Proceedings of the 22nd International Conference on World Wide Web, 527–538.

Kemp, S. (2025). Digital 2025: Global Overview Report. DataReportal. https://datareportal.com/reports/digital-2025-global-overview-report.

Lazer, D.M.J., et al., 2020. Computational social science: obstacles and opportunities. Science 369, 1060–1062.

Leung, T.C., Strumpf, K.S., 2023. All the headlines that are fit to change. Center for Technology, Innovation & Competition, University of Pennsylvania.

Levy, R., 2021. Social media, news consumption, and polarization: evidence from a field experiment. American Economic Review 111 (3), 831–870. https://doi.org/10.1257/AER.20191777.

Müller, K., Schwarz, C., 2023. From hashtag to hate crime: Twitter and antiminority sentiment. American Economic Journal: Applied Economics 15 (3), 270–312. https://doi.org/10.1257/app.20210211.
Newman, N., 2021. Journalism, Media, and Technology Trends and Predictions 2021. Reuters Institute for the Study of Journalism.
Newman, N., 2022. Journalism, Media, and Technology Trends and Predictions 2022. Reuters Institute for the Study of Journalism.
Nielsen, R.K., 2017. Media capture in the digital age. In: Schiffrin, A. (Ed.), In the Service of Power: Media Capture and the Threat to Democracy. Center for International Media Assistance, pp. 33–42.
Nix, N., Johnson, C.Y., Zakrzewski, C., 2023. Changing Facebook's Algorithm Won't Fix Polarization, New Study Finds. Washington Post., Available from: https://www.washingtonpost.com/technology/2023/07/27/social-media-research-meta-political-views/.
Nyhan, B., Settle, J., Thorson, E., Wojcieszak, M., Barberá, P., Chen, A.Y., Allcott, H., Brown, T., Crespo-Tenorio, A., Dimmery, D., Freelon, D., Gentzkow, M., González-Bailón, S., Guess, A.M., Kennedy, E., Mie Kim, Y., Lazer, D., Malhotra, N., Moehler, D., Pan, J., Thomas, D.R., Tromble, R., Rivera, C.V., Wilkins, A., Xiong, B., Kiewiet de Jonge, C., Franco, A., Mason, W., Stroud, N.J., Tucker, J.A., 2023. Like-minded sources on Facebook are prevalent but not polarizing. Nature 620 (7972), 137–144. https://doi.org/10.1038/s41586-023-06297-w.
Oremus, W., 2014. The First News Report on the L.A. Earthquake Was Written by a Robot. Slate.
Pew Research Center. (2016). State of the news media 2016: digital news audience behavior. https://www.pewresearch.org/journalism/2016/06/15/state-of-the-news-media-2016/.
Pires, A.J.G., 2014. Media diversity, advertising, and adaptation of news to readers' political preferences. Information Economics and Policy 28, 28–38.
Sullivan D., Google's Top Results for 'Did the Holocaust Happen' Now Expunged of Denial Sites. Search Engine Land. (2016). Available from: https://searchengineland.com/google-holocaust-denial-site-gone-266353.
Sunstein C.R., (2001). Republic.com. Princeton, NJ: Princeton University Press. https://doi.org/10.2307/20050172.
Taneja, H., Webster, J.G., Malthouse, E.C., Ksiazek, T.B., 2012. Media consumption across platforms: Identifying user-defined repertoires. New Media & Society 14 (6), 951–968. https://doi.org/10.1177/1461444811436146.
Trajtenberg, M., 2018. Artificial Intelligence as the Next GPT: a political-economy perspective. The Economics of Artificial Intelligence: An Agenda, 175–186.
Vosoughi, S., Roy, D., Aral, S., 2018. The spread of true and false news online. Science 359 (6380), 1146–1151. https://doi.org/10.1126/science.aap9559.
de Vreese, C., Tromble, R., 2023. The data abyss: how lack of data access leaves research and society in the dark. Political Communication 40 (3), 356–360.
Waldman, S., and Working Group on Information Needs of Communities, 2011. The information needs of communities: The changing media landscape in a broadband age. Federal Communications Commission.
Wilson R., Biden Leads Newspaper Endorsements - Just Like Clinton. The Hill. (2020). Available from: https://thehill.com/homenews/campaign/522841-biden-leads-newspaper-endorsements-just-like-clinton.

Yang, S., 2021. Media Capture and Media Bias in the Digital Age. (PhD Dissertation). Graduate School, Yonsei University Department of Economics.

Yang, S., 2020. Media bias with a digital intermediary. International Telecommunications Policy Review 27 (4), 1–23.

Zhuravskaya, E., Petrova, M., Enikolopov, R., 2020. Political effects of the internet and social media. Annual Review of Economics 12 (1), 415–438. https://doi.org/10.1146/annurev-economics-081919-050239.

Index

Note: Page numbers followed by "*f*" indicate figures, "*t*" indicate tables, and "*b*" indicate boxes.

Printed and bound by CPI Group (UK) Ltd, Croydon, CR0 4YY
25/09/2026
02222748-0015